DIPLOMATS IN CRISIS

DIPLOMATS

United States-Chinese-

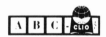

Santa Barbara, California
Oxford, England

Edited by

IN CRISIS

Japanese Relations,   1919-1941

RICHARD DEAN BURNS & EDWARD M. BENNETT

252185

Library of Congress Catalog Card Number 74-76444
ISBN Clothbound Edition 0-87436-135-4
Paperbound Edition 0-87436-136-2

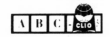

American Bibliographical Center—Clio Press, Inc.
2040 Alameda Padre Serra
Santa Barbara, California

European Bibliographical Center—Clio Press
Woodside House, Hinksey Hill
Oxford OX1 5BE, England

Designed by Barbara Monahan
Composed by Camera-Ready Composition
Printed and bound by Publishers Press
in the United States of America

Contents

Preface

WE HOPE students and scholars will find this transnational study of diplomats and diplomacy useful. These essays provide the reader a glimpse into the personalities and political turmoil which inextricably shaped the great Pacific drama of the 1920s and 1930s. The thirteen vignettes do not, of course, systematically organize all the issues which led to the Pacific War. Rather they explore the perspective and limitations of individual diplomats during a frustrating period.

For readers without extensive knowledge of the issues and events which dominated the various national perspectives, brief introductions are offered. For scholars who wish to pursue further personalities and issues variously introduced, footnotes and an index are provided.

Finally, the editors acknowledge, with appreciation, the contributors who so patiently assisted in the completion of this arduous venture. We are especially indebted to several people for their assistance and advice, particularly Professors Taketsugu Tsuratani and Thomas Kennedy of Washington State University, and Al Coox of San Diego State University. We, of course, are solely responsible for the deficiencies and errors which remain.

RICHARD DEAN BURNS
EDWARD M. BENNETT

Introduction

THIS BOOK is a significant study of failure. It analyzes the search for a Far Eastern settlement through twenty years of sometimes intense diplomatic effort. The thirteen interwar diplomats representing China, Japan, and the United States, who carried much of the burden and on whom these essays focus, were capable men by any standard. Still their diplomacy triumphed only if they favored settlements by force, for their endeavors terminated in war. And the challenges unleashed by their faltering diplomacy transcended the necessity of fighting a major war in the Pacific. The war quickly released new forces for change in the Orient which none of the three governments could control and which resulted in the destruction of one—that of China.

That the Far Eastern diplomacy of the interwar years ended in tragedy does not necessarily condemn the formal and personal diplomatic effort of the pre-Pearl Harbor years. None of the thirteen diplomats favored war, and all labored under the assumption that successful diplomacy would enable them to either stabilize or legitimize the pressures for change in the Far East. Why did they fail? Were their exchanges clouded by limited insight; or did they perform imaginatively amid forces that overwhelmed them or rendered their efforts irrelevant? If the demands of their governments were irreconcilable, did they merely relay the uncompromising and non-negotiable views of their home offices and thereby deny themselves any leadership role, any search for initiative, or any claims to superior knowledge? Did they act as unquestioning bearers of official demands and thus encourage the drift toward war, or did they advocate decisions which might have sustained some measure of peace only to be overridden by the policymakers at home? Such questions suggest that these thirteen well-meaning and competent men failed to prevent war in the Pacific for a variety of reasons, some of which absolve them of personal responsibility. These questions are even more illustrative of the role of the foreign diplomat in the twentieth-century world. For the decisions of all three governments responded far more to pressures and assumptions generated domestically than to the judgments of their embassies abroad.

China, Japan, and the United States attempted to resolve their differences in East Asia for the first time in the twentieth century through direct negotiations at Versailles in 1919. This confrontation was not reassuring, for Japan based its demands not only on industrial and military efficiency, but also on special interests in China that were clear enough for the vast bulk of the Japanese people to accept. The United States and China, however, based their case on China's legal and moral right to possess and govern her own territory. Ambassador V. K. Wellington Koo's rhetorical defense of Chinese integrity at Versailles was legally uncontestable. According to Secretary of State Robert Lansing, Koo "simply overwhelmed the Japanese with his argument." The Japanese retention of Shantung demonstrated, therefore, that moral suasion was ineffective against superior military force in the absence of collective security. The Western powers, including the United States, had clearly displayed a limited interest in China's economic and territorial integrity. Following Versailles the Far West thus emerged as a troubled region with challenges, alternative responses, and costs of diplomatic failure obvious enough for all to see.

At the Washington Conference of 1921-1922 Koo (whose career introduces the Chinese section of this volume) sought to defend his country against the danger of renewed Japanese pressure and to rid China of the unequal treaties. His position was again legally sound and won the support of the Western powers who wrote their preference for the Open Door into the Nine Power Pact. The Western powers, however, would not give up the special privileges they enjoyed in China under the unequal treaties. By accepting the Lytton Report of 1932 the League of Nations upheld China's legal rights in Manchuria, but the relationship between these legal and moral triumphs and the maintenance of Chinese integrity and peace in the Far East remained in question. Japan proceeded to solidify her control over Manchuria.

China's choices were reduced to either the acceptance of a formal *modus vivendi* with an expanding Japan or continued resistance built on promises of collective security. Throughout the decade following the Manchurian crisis of late 1931, the protection of China's integrity against established Japanese purpose seemed to be such an apparent interest that there was absolute unity between Chinese officials at home and those who represented China in Washington and elsewhere. Hu Shih, like Dr. Koo a Wilsonian internationalist, attached his defense of China's interests to the creation of a rational world order based on the principles of non-aggression and self-determination. Hu Shih sought to bind the United States to China throughout the critical years of 1937 to 1941, in the hope that Washington, in the name of the Open Door and the Wilsonian principle of peaceful change, would support China's integrity against Japanese demands. Hu Shih and his government, convinced that United States support would eliminate the need for compromise, warned Washington against coming to terms with Japan or compelling China to do so.

Unfortunately the success of Chinese diplomacy depended upon a credible base of power among the Western states that shared China's interest in the protection of the Far Eastern treaty structure. But Western interests in China were secondary, whereas Japan's were primary. Consequently Chinese efforts to create a deterrent through collective security and to preserve the *status quo* without war were doomed to failure. Still, in pursuing the illusion of collective security, Chinese officials never faced the Japanese challenge forthrightly; they made no effort to come to terms with Japanese power and efficiency. They demanded nothing less than total victory for their cause and pursued that objective with a program of public relations. Hu Shih correctly perceived that the United States would, in the long run, support the anti-Japanese policies of the Chinese government. He worked hard and effectively to prevent a compromise during the crisis of November 1941. The support Hu Shih sought in the United States came easily enough, and if the noncompromisable goals he pursued demanded, after November, a direct United States military involvement in the Pacific, then Pearl Harbor was indeed the final measure of his success. But how well did Hu Shih's diplomacy serve the interests of China or of his government? However brilliant and successful his diplomacy may have been outwardly, it ended in disaster because he failed to recognize the military and political weakness of his government and the limited Western interest in sustaining the purposes and even the existence of that government.

Throughout the decade which separated the Manchuria crisis from the attack on Pearl Harbor, Japanese diplomats sought to avoid war with the United States. As spokesmen for a government which could no longer reconcile its promise to uphold the Far Eastern treaty structure with its East Asian objectives, Japanese diplomats nevertheless advocated policies which eventually drove the United States into a defense of China. The task of Japanese diplomacy after Manchuria was clearly to gain major influence in the Chinese economy without provoking war in the Pacific. Following the Marco Polo Bridge incident of July 1937, the Japanese accepted the cost of limited war in order to impose their will on China. Thereafter they confronted an uncompromising China supported by a generally disinterested but equally uncompromising United States. Thus after 1937 Japan faced the unfortunate choice of fighting an endless and enervating war on the Asian mainland or of terminating that war on Chinese terms. Japanese diplomacy vis-à-vis China and the United States sought to escape this dilemma—while framing policies acceptable to the Japanese military and the Japanese public, who both agreed overwhelmingly that Japan required and merited a new order in East Asia.

Three Japanese diplomats—Hirota Koki, Shigemitsu Mamoru, and Matsuoka Yōsuke—helped propel Japan into the Far Eastern crisis. Hirota, trapped between Japan's military leaders who demanded some encroachment on Chinese integrity and Chiang Kai-shek's refusal to compromise, chose war. In exploiting the Marco Polo Bridge incident Hirota faced no diplomatic resistance which might have compelled him to localize the struggle. Shigemitsu, too, desired peace but also favored the expansion of Japanese power and influence in the Pacific. Matsuoka, faced with the unpleasant prospect of an expensive war on the Chinese mainland and the *status quo* policies of Washington and London, became bitter toward the West. He remarked that "the Western Powers had taught the Japanese the game of poker but . . . after acquiring most of the chips they pronounced the game immoral and took up contract bridge." Matsuoka realized that international law was in fact the law of the Western powers, for it admirably served their interest in the *status quo*. For Matsuoka Japan was the natural leader of East Asia and should have been permitted to reorganize the Pacific world in accordance with the laws of nature. Finding no official support for Japanese purpose in the Western capitals, Matsuoka, backed by the Japanese military, negotiated the troublesome Tripartite Pact with Germany and Italy, promulgated in September 1940.

Nomura Kichisaburō, an admiral little versed in the art of diplomacy, arrived in Washington in February 1941 to conduct Tokyo's final effort to reach an agreement with the government of the United States. Historians, as well as Secretary of State Cordell Hull and Nomura's own Japanese contemporaries, have condemned Nomura's inaccurate and overly-optimistic reporting. Whether this mattered in the ultimate breakdown of United States-Japanese relations that year is doubtful; for under no circumstance could Tokyo have satisfied Hull's principles of peaceful change without capitulation. Although Nomura exaggerated the possibilities of a compromise agreement, he nevertheless attempted to improve, not undermine, the state of United States-Japanese relations. Nomura regarded war between the two Pacific powers as the ultimate tragedy, and he believed with justification that his superiors in Tokyo shared his determination to avoid an open conflict. Until 1941 neither Washington nor Tokyo wanted a war in the Pacific; yet both preferred war to the acceptance of the conditions the other sought to impose. Ironically, neither the United States nor Japan gained in postwar China what it demanded in 1941.

Nomura accepted the mission to Washington only with the assurance that the Japanese government desired a rapprochement with the United States. He had long denounced the Tripartite Pact. True, he never favored Japanese capitulation to Hull's four principles of April 1941, but he challenged Foreign Minister Matsuoka's anti-American attitudes and behavior at every turn, including Matsuoka's 1941 diplomatic mission to Moscow and Berlin. More than once he attempted to explain away Matsuoka's belligerency toward the United States. Nomura supported the Walsh-Drought-Walker treaty draft of January 1941, which included a restatement of the Open Door, a guarantee of Chinese independence, and the withdrawal of Japanese troops following a settlement between Japan and China. This formula promised peace with a Japanese withdrawal from southeast Asia and some limited Japanese gains in China. For Washington the proposal was too vague and compromising to be acceptable. During the critical months of June and July 1941, Nomura pressed his superiors for assurances that Japan's intentions remained peaceful. In the end Nomura's diplomacy had no chance against Tokyo's determined search for *lebensraum* in East Asia and Washington's total rejection of such expansion. Indeed, the historic conflict between Tokyo and Washington over China's future virtually eliminated diplomacy as a means of avoiding war, whether that diplomacy centered in China, Japan, or the United States. Nomura's experience reveals not so much the failure of diplomacy in 1941 as the fact that negotiations had no chance of success.

This volume also concentrates on five United States diplomats concerned with the Sino-Japanese conflict of the thirties. Three of the five—Nelson Trusler Johnson, John Van Antwerp MacMurray, and Stanley K. Hornbeck—defended the basic thrust of United States policy in the Far East; two—W. Cameron Forbes and Joseph C. Grew—opposed it. Undoubtedly Johnson created and sustained a high level of official cordiality in America-Chinese relations during his long tenure as United States Ambassador to China. His pro-Chinese sympathies conformed in large measure to the general tendencies in public and official American attitudes. He believed that America's failure to condemn Japan categorically after Manchuria was tantamount to approval of the aggression. Thus by most standards of diplomacy Johnson's ambassadorship was successful, even triumphant; whether his efforts to strengthen the United States' identification with China in the thirties served either the interests of the United States or the cause of peace in the Far East is less clear. Nor was Johnson's anti-Japanese bias helpful to any resolution of the burgeoning United States-Japanese confrontation over China. His observation of June 1941, that the United States was now "out of the miserable game of appeasing Japan" again conformed to the views of those Washington officials, journalists, and citizens who attributed diplomatic success to uncompromising firmness in behalf of principles. Such assumptions, however, led to war, not to Japanese capitulation and peace.

For all his self-confidence on matters of China and Japan, Ambassador MacMurray no less than Johnson failed to come to grips with the choices confronting the United States in the Pacific—either to accept some new order in East Asia or to prepare for war. War would serve the Far Eastern interests of Russia alone; for MacMurray, therefore, the avoidance of war with Japan was the key to successful American policy. To this end MacMurray recommended a passive attitude. The United States should cling to its principles while rejecting any special responsiblity for their vindication in the Far East. United States policy, he wrote, should minimize America's liabilities, reduce its military presence in the Pacific, and view Japan with an open mind. The United States, in short, should acknowledge its limited interests and avoid trouble in China. Still, it should not abandon American principles; there was no reason, he insisted, to repeal the Decalogue because there was a crime wave. Such notions conformed well to much of the official opinion in Washington favoring peace and the maintenance of principles. Unfortunately the United States could not anchor its diplomacy to principle and simultaneously escape responsibility for what occurred in the Far East. MacMurray's advice, consequently, was less than sound.

Both United States ambassadors in Tokyo during the thirties—Forbes and Grew—engaged in determined, if ultimately futile, efforts to alter United States policies and attitudes toward China and Japan. Forbes' brief tenure as ambassador coincided with the Manchurian crisis. From the beginning he rejected the Hoover and Stimson doctrines for dealing with Japanese aggression. Whether American "get tough" policy, designed to protect the *status quo* in China, was based on moral rhetoric or economic sanctions, Forbes argued that it would neither stop Japan nor serve American interest. Verbal recriminations to arouse world opinion against Japan would merely exacerbate the tensions in the Far East. To Forbes both the multinational declarations emanating from the League and the militant denunciations expressed by Stimson exceeded the bounds of intelligent reaction. Japan was far more important to determining American interests in the Pacific than the Far Eastern treaty structure. Forbes believed, as did Hirota, that the laws of nature still functioned in international affairs—that energy and efficiency were more important than the rights of possession. Persistent condemnation of Japan, never accompanied by the intention to act, would accomplish nothing except to drive that country into the hands of its military extremists. In March 1932, Forbes, backed by the entire embassy staff in Tokyo, warned Washington that Stimson's "constant nagging" would lead to war between the United States and Japan. Even if it limited the American defense of China to moral strictures alone, wrote Forbes, the United States, by challenging Japan's right to expand, would emerge as that country's chief enemy.

Joseph Grew, who reached Tokyo in 1932, urged Washington from the onset to consider Japan's needs and aspirations in delineating its policies in the Far East. It seemed essential to him that the United States recognize Japanese expansion as a program of self-preservation. Japan possessed two alternatives to solve its population problem: territorial or industrial expansion. Any effort to restrain Japanese commerce, Grew warned, would propel that country into a course of territorial expansion. Like Forbes before him, Grew hesitated to condemn Japan for employing her superior efficiency to satisfy internal needs, even at the expense of China. Grew explained to Washington why Japan was becoming increasingly hostile toward the United States: "It is true that the Japanese fighting forces consider the United States as their potential enemy . . . but that is because they think that the United States is standing in the path of the nation's natural expansion and is more apt to interfere with Japan's ambitions than are the European nations." Only a compromising United States posture, he believed, would permit Japanese moderates to maintain an official cordiality toward the United States and permit the Tokyo government to control its military extremists. Throughout the years that followed Roosevelt's Quarantine speech of October 1937, Grew admonished the administration that economic sanctions would prove both ineffective and dangerous. As late as 1940 he warned the President in a series of private letters that a boycott would drive Japan into open aggression, perhaps even into war with the United States. Determined to prevent a general war in the Pacific, Grew argued for modification of the official hard-line approach to Japan as reflected in the views of Stimson, Knox, Morgenthau, Hornbeck, and Hull.

Grew's appeals made no impression on the Roosevelt administration, which became increasingly uncompromising with the passage of time. Eventually Grew, to protect his usefulness to the administration, adopted a more non-compromising tone. But even in 1941 he still distinguished between the short-term American interest in avoiding war and the long-run interest in stabilizing the international politics of the Far East. Grew hoped, moreover, that his tougher stance in Tokyo might encourage some modification in Japanese policy by reminding Japanese officials that the alternative to some agreement with Washington might be war. Unable to penetrate the secretiveness which surrounded Roosevelt and Hull, Grew eventually found himself eliminated from a policy-making role entirely. In a diary notation of October 1940, Grew explained why ambassadorial views, especially on important issues, were often ignored in Washington:

I am inclined to think that the chief stumbling block in perfecting machinery for exchange of information on policy lies in a certain reluctance in the Department to place on the official records matters which are still in flux and which have not yet reached a decision. That reluctance may spring partly from the fact that our foreign affairs are subject to dual control, the President and the Secretary of State, but perhaps even more from the fact that the Administration, more than in other democracies, must have constantly in mind the elements of opposition in Congress, the press and the public, and the premature leakage of official records can cause embarassing repercussions. Officers of the Department might disagree with me about this, but I have a shrewd conviction that the foregoing thought is always, at least subconsciously, present.

Grew complained again in January 1941 that Washington's secrecy rendered his ambassadorship useless. "If ambassadors are something more than messenger boys," he noted, "they must be allowed to see behind the scenes." In the critical months after July 1941, Grew admitted reluctantly that his opinions were no longer welcome in Washington.

Ultimately it was the Chinese diplomatic corps, not the American or the Japanese, that found favor in Washington. Still the blending of United States and Chinese purpose in the Far East came slowly. Until 1940 the course of United States policy was determined not by the desire to defend China but by the desire to defend the post-Versailles treaty structure. Unpunished aggression, however limited its immediate impact on the world balance of power, would encourage other aggressions and thereby undermine the legal foundations of world security and endanger peace everywhere. While this notion of indivisible peace demanded a policy to counter and hopefully terminate Japanese aggression, it did not establish any concern for China that might justify war in her defense. Only in the sense that Japanese expansion violated the treaty structure and thus threatened world stability did it challenge American complacency. Johnson and MacMurray agreed with United States officials in Washington, including Hornbeck, that Japanese aggression in Manchuria touched no vital American interest; therefore the United States should maintain a "hands off" policy. But when Washington comprehended the magnitude and violence of the Japanese assault on China after July 1937, United States officials began to reconsider the Japanese threat to American security and world peace. Haltingly Roosevelt raised the question of collective security in his Quarantine speech of October. Nevertheless, United States policy continued to show little direct regard for China even as it moved toward economic sanctions in 1940. It was only after the outbreak of war in Europe in September 1939, followed by the Japanese thrust into southeast Asia several months later and the Tripartite Pact of September 1940, that the United States began to view China as an ally in a burgeoning struggle against the totalitarian powers. Aid to China replaced trade with Japan as Washington embarked on a program of anti-Japanese sanctions after mid-1940. China would no longer suffer the consequences of American appeasement.

No official in Washington represented the suppositions of United States policy more clearly than Stanley Hornbeck. He is the one spokesman for American Far Eastern policy included in this volume who labored in Washington rather than in East Asia. Hornbeck's response to the Japanese challenge placed United States-Japanese relations in an ambiguous state. Although the United States had not committed itself to the use of force to maintain its principles, he said, it also had "no right to take action in authorization of their impairment." The United States, in short, would not fight; nor would it compromise. For Hornbeck neither course of action was necessary. Economic sanctions would compel a Japanese retreat and allow America to escape the choice between war and acceptance of some forceful infringement of the treaty structure. During the discussions over the decision to freeze Japanese assets in the United States, Hornbeck wrote: "I submit that under existing circumstances it is altogether improbable that Japan would deliberately take action in response to any action which the United States is likely to take in the Pacific, which action, if taken by Japan, would mean war between that country and this country." Hornbeck simply assumed that the Japanese would capitulate under the pressure of United States economic policy. Unfortunately the Japanese had no intention of permitting the United States such a cheap victory in the Far East. In late November, even as Hornbeck assured the administration that the Japanese would avoid war with the United States at all costs, Tokyo dispatched its task force to Pearl Harbor.

Historians can legitimately question the performance of such national leaders. Foreign Service Officer Joseph C. Ballantine once insisted that Hornbeck readily yielded in an argument on policy and practice when "it was shown that he had failed to consider material factors of which he had not been aware or had misjudged." Unless Hornbeck desired war between the United States and Japan his misjudgments were almost universal. He stood in the vanguard of Washington hard-liners who identified the United States' hopes for peace with the absolute rejection of compromise with Japan. With other Washington officials Hornbeck placed the *status quo* of the Far East on the altar of American inflexibility. The assumption that this country could guarantee the peace in direct proportion to its diplomatic inflexibility proved to be tragically wrong. Later in his *Memoirs* Hull admitted that he could have reached an agreement with the Tokyo government at any time by accepting a compromise. He continued, "We should have negated principles on which we had built our foreign policy and without which the world could not live in peace." Somehow Hull could never understand that his policies had not served the cause of peace. Nor had they guaranteed the triumph of his principles.

Diplomats—especially the thirteen included in this impressive volume— gave the three-power relationship of the thirties whatever human quality it had. These essays reveal the individuality, the thoughts, the hopes and fears of men laboring at the task of strengthening ties among nations so that conflicting purposes might terminate in negotiated settlements rather than wars. Ultimately the long-range goals of China, Japan, and the United States eliminated all room for diplomatic maneuvering. This relegated the diplomatic corps to the role of functionary, explaining national positions and carrying out instructions but unable to influence the policies themselves. Some, it is true, did not try to alter established policies, either because they agreed with existing trends or because they were reluctant to question the wisdom of their governments. Yet a significant minority challenged the uncompromising attitudes and aims of the decade in their effort to avoid war. Grew and Nomura lamented their loss of influence. But the diplomats had no chance against the decisions of governments in China, Japan, and the United States to go to war rather than retreat from established goals. And so the Pacific war came.

NORMAN A. GRAEBNER

Chronology

Sino-Japanese War	July 25, 1894-April 17, 1895
Anglo-Japanese Alliance	January 30, 1902
Russo-Japanese War	February 8, 1904- September 5, 1905
Japan's "Twenty-one Demands" on China	January 15, 1915
Chinese "May Fourth Movement"	May 4, 1919
Washington Conference	November 1921- February 1922
Five Power Naval Treaty	February 4, 1922
Nine Power Treaty on China	February 4, 1922
Kellogg-Briand Pact	August 27, 1928
London Naval Conference	January 21-April 22, 1930
"Mukden Incident"	September 18, 1931
League creates Lytton Commission to investigate	December 19, 1931
Stimson's "Nonrecognition Doctrine"	January 7, 1932
"Shanghai Affair"	January 28, 1932
Japan creates "Manchukuo"	February 1932
League endorses Nonrecognition Doctrine	March 11, 1932
Lytton Commission Report to League	September 4, 1932
League votes to censure Japan	February 24, 1933
Japan withdraws from League	March 27, 1933
T'ang-ku Truce	May 1933
Amau "Statement"	April 17, 1934
Second London Naval Conference	December 9, 1935- March 25, 1936

"February 26th Affair"   February 26, 1936
Sian Episode   December 12-24, 1936
Marco Polo Bridge "Incident"   July 7, 1937
Nine Power Conference (Brussels)   November 3-24, 1937
Panay Incident   December 12, 1937
United States "moral embargo" of Japan   July 16, 1938
Japanese occupy Hainan Island   February 10, 1939
United States abrogation of 1911 Commercial
    Treaty (effective January 26, 1940)   July 16, 1939
War breaks out in Europe   September 1939
United States oil "embargo"   July 25, 1940
United States iron and steel "embargo"   September 26, 1940
Triple Alliance (Japan-Germany-Italy)   September 27, 1940
Japan occupies Indo-China   July 24, 1941
United States freezes Japanese credits   July 26, 1941
Pearl Harbor   December 7, 1941

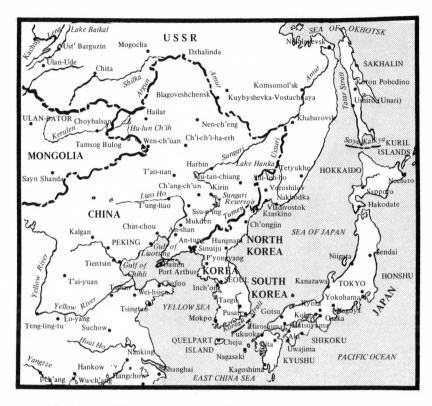

Northeast China, Korea, and Japan

Part I

UNITED STATES

United States Diplomacy and Diplomats, 1919-1941

America's Asian policies during the interwar years were linked to China and enshrined in the long-nurtured Open Door. The Open Door had a simple and logical appeal to Yankee merchants in the eighteenth and nineteenth centuries because they felt all entrepreneurs were entitled to an equality of commercial opportunity in foreign markets. The Treaty of Wanghsia (1844) secured a commercial status in China for them equal to that enjoyed by the British through employment of the "most favored nation" clause—a device thereafter used by all nations to gain the same privileges granted by China to any single nation.

The Open Door policy in China was slowly formulated by the United States. Germany, Russia, France, and Japan challenged the idea of commercial equality late in the nineteenth century by securing new lease-ports and establishing "spheres of influence" along the coast of China to obtain special privileges for their businessmen. These activities resulted in the Boxer uprising—the first indication of Chinese antiforeign sentiment in the twentieth century—which isolated foreign legations in Peking.

Secretary of State John Hay formally elaborated the American concept of the Open Door in a series of diplomatic notes in 1899 and 1900. The so-called "Open Door Notes" cautioned foreign nations against the implementation of preferential commercial practices and warned them not to partition the collapsing Chinese empire. Hay was especially concerned over the impairment of Chinese sovereignty implied by the Boxer uprising and the subsequent occupation of Peking by several thousand foreign troops. That threat ended with the Boxer Protocol of 1901 wherein Chinese authorities

3

agreed to pay cash indemnities to foreign powers* and promised to protect foreign businessmen and their interests in China.

The Open Door principles were formally accepted by Britain, France, the United States, Japan, and China at the Washington Conference of 1922 when they signed the so-called Nine Power Pact. That instrument required the major powers to:

(1) Respect China's sovereignty, independence, and territorial and adminis-trative integrity.
(2) Provide China a full and unembarrassed opportunity to develop and maintain an effective and stable government.
(3) Use their influence to effectively establish and maintain an equal opportunity for all nations to participate in commerce and industry throughout the territory of China.
(4) Refrain from taking advantage of China's internal conditions to seek special rights and privileges which might abridge the rights of subjects or citizens of friendly states or from condoning any action inimical to the security of those states.

American disputes with China during the interwar years resulted mostly from Chinese demands to end "unequal treaties" collateral to the tradition of the Open Door. Those treaties that granted extraterritorial privileges (e.g., the right to trial in their own tribunals for criminal offenses committed against Chinese citizens), those which ensured the presence of foreign military forces in China (e.g., United States naval patrols on the Yangtze River and the presence of Marines in Shanghai), and those which provided for foreign control of the Chinese tariff system were especially galling to Chinese of all political persuasions.

Diplomatic relationships between the United States and Japan were generally amicable during the 1920's. The Five Power Pacific Naval Treaty, another product of the Washington Conference, momentarily achieved significant progress toward the regulation of the naval arms race. The Wash-ington conference proposed a stabilization of capital ship tonnage. Great Britain and the United States were each to be allowed 500,000 tons and Japan 300,000 tons—a 5:5:3 ratio. This ratio was subsequently modified to include other classes of warships by the London Naval Treaty (1930). Later, however, Japan's aggressive military leaders terminated all naval limitations (in December 1936). Japan and the United States were among the several nations to sign the Kellogg-Briand Pact (the Pact of Paris, August 27, 1928) and pledge to outlaw the use of military force as a means of resolving international disputes. Subsequent Japanese military activities soon indicated that the pledge was unrealistic.

*The United States set aside its share of indemnities to finance the education of promising Chinese students in American universities.

The Manchurian Incident (September 18, 1931) created the first major crisis between Washington and Tokyo.* Japanese forces precipitated a serious diversionary incident in January 1932 at Shanghai (the "Shanghai Affair"). The "Amau Doctrine" enunciated by an obscure member of the Japanese Foreign Ministry in 1934 sought to justify the role of Japan as the protector of East Asia but did little to repair the worsening situation. The Marco Polo Bridge Incident (July 7, 1937) then precipitated full-scale hostilities between Japan and China. Already strained American-Japanese relations were brought to the point of acute tension on December 12, 1937, when Japanese bombers attacked and sank the *U.S.S. Panay* near Nanking on the Yangtze River.

These events evoked a series of critical policy responses from Washington. Secretary of State Henry L. Stimson announced that the United States would not recognize the Japanese puppet government of Manchukuo. The "Stimson Doctrine" and its policy of "nonrecognition" was subsequently adopted by the League of Nations Assembly on February 24, 1933. The United States demonstrated its disapproval of Japanese behavior following the outbreak of Sino-Japanese hostilities through more drastic measures. The United States trade agreement with Japan was terminated in 1939 and Washington gradually placed embargoes on American materials and credits sought by Tokyo.

The failure of American diplomacy became painfully evident at Pearl Harbor on December 7, 1941.

*The Japanese Army in Kwantung independently contrived an incident at Mukden which led to the seizure of all Manchuria.

*Herbert J. Wood**

Nelson Trusler Johnson

The Diplomacy of Benevolent Pragmatism

NELSON TRUSLER JOHNSON (1887-1954) spent the whole of his adult life in the diplomatic service of the United States, with thirty-four years devoted primarily to Chinese affairs. As a fledgling Foreign Service officer during the pre-World War I years, Johnson saw the struggle of foreign powers to protect their interests in China, and particularly the rivalry for influence between Japan and Russia. He witnessed stirrings of discontent which led to the overthrow of the Ch'ing dynasty and the establishment of the Republic of China. Appointed as Minister early in 1930, Johnson became the first American ambassador to China after the legation was raised to embassy status in 1935. He continued his assignment to Chiang Kai-shek's government through aerial bombings and Chinese political crises until the spring of 1941.

For a little more than eleven years, then, until seven months before Pearl Harbor, Johnson served in China as the State Department's principal observer and the American government's chief spokesman. During these years he was concerned with Japan's expansion into Manchuria, her activities in North China and Shanghai, and finally with the Japanese attempts to control all of China and to exclude other foreign influences. Unlike his American diplomatic colleagues in Tokyo, Johnson was able to observe directly the actions of the Japanese military, which were often not in accord with official press reports or with public statements of spokesmen for the Japanese

*For their assistance in making manuscripts available for this study the author is grateful to Mrs. Nelson T. Johnson; to Arthur G. Kogan, Chief of the Research Guidance and Review Division, Historical Office, Department of State; and to David G. Mearns, Chief, Manuscript Division, Library of Congress.

7

government. He also had the advantage of personal contacts with prominent Chinese who had been trained in Japanese military schools and who were aware of the concept of Pan-Asianism advocated there, with Japanese leadership in mind.

Johnson recognized that the best guarantee for the peace of the Pacific would be a China strong enough to maintain her territorial integrity. Consequently, he repeated this view to the State Department on several occasions, arguing that the protection of American interests would be best served by a policy that encouraged the establishment and development of a strong Chinese nation.[1]

One of Nelson Johnson's great assets was his fluency in Chinese. He was equally at ease swapping stories with coolies riding with their animals in a baggage car or discussing diplomatic affairs with Chiang Kai-shek. Shortly after he arrived in China as Minister, the officials of Tsingtao entertained him at a formal affair. When the mayor's formal speech had been translated into English, Johnson rose, bowed, and proposed a toast in Chinese. At his first words "an electric tension was perceptible, followed by a rustle of adjustment and a low murmur of appreciation. Surprised and pleased, Chinese hosts and guests nodded to one another, smiled and nodded again and then settled themselves to listen attentively."[2]

Although a *New York Times* dispatch once credited Johnson with knowing more about China than any other American, no doubt because of his language skills and experience in various diplomatic posts, he insisted that no foreigner was really knowledgeable. He therefore made a special effort to learn more of China's history and to become aware of its problems. He told Hallett E. Abend, the *New York Times* correspondent, that he had come to China with an open mind and intended to keep it open, for "nothing gets into nor comes from a closed mind."[3]

When Johnson arrived in China to take up his duties as Minister, he was fully aware of the complexity of his new job. He had no illusions that he could do more than continue the friendly relationship between the two governments or that anyone could clear up the problems in China within a generation. "I feel confident," he wrote, "that when my tour of duty is ended I shall leave to my successor as many problems as I shall find when I reach my desk in Peking."[4]

I

Personable and intelligent, Nelson Johnson possessed many of the human traits that augured well for a successful diplomatic career. His sense of humor and his ability to poke fun at himself and the diplomatic service enhanced his effectiveness, while his ready wit and compassion contributed immeasurably to his building a hard-working, intensely loyal staff.[5]

Descended from old-line New England stock, Nelson could point to an American heritage that began with his ancestors' arrival in Boston during the 1760's. In the century and a half that followed, his branch of the family moved westward to settle in Indiana, where his father, Jeremiah Johnson, was born. A neighbor, acquaintance, and political supporter of Benjamin Harrison, Jeremiah followed the President-elect to Washington, D.C. There, after graduating with a Master of Laws degree from Georgetown University in 1886, Jeremiah met and married Nelson's mother, Salome Trusler, daughter of Colonel Nelson Trusler, who had died shortly after the Civil War.

Not long after the birth of Nelson Trusler Johnson on April 3, 1887, Jeremiah suffered financial reverses in the nation's capital and moved his family to Oklahoma where, after participating in the opening of the Cherokee Strip, he practiced law and published a weekly newspaper. Some of young Nelson's earliest memories were of frontier western America. As a boy he was sent back to Washington to live with his grandmother and to enroll in Mr. Sidwell's Friends School. According to his own testimony, his grandmother played a major role in shaping his values and outlook toward life during his maturing years. "She was," in the words of the author of a recent monograph, "a woman of superb character, determination, humor and, although stern, was deeply loved by her grandson. She read to him, encouraged him in his school work, nursed him when ill, and more important, instilled in him the homespun traits that were her forte."[6]

When he graduated from Friends School in 1906, Johnson entered George Washington University. (Though his ambition had been to attend Yale, the financial resources were not available.) Near the end of his freshman year in 1907 Nelson read a notice of examinations to be given by the Department of State for Foreign Service student interpreterships in China and Japan. Intrigued by the prospects of adventure, but without much hope of qualifying, he signed up. That summer he worked at the Library of Congress, preparing for the general examinations and privately studying German to meet the foreign language requirements. To his surprise and that of his family, Nelson Johnson passed the tests and departed for China just after his twentieth birthday.

When he reached Peking, he found himself "enrolled" in an unorthodox language program with an assigned Chinese tutor who spoke no English. Yet from this slow beginning he gradually learned to speak Chinese well. At the end of his long career, Johnson was said to speak Chinese "like a native," although he admitted that his ability to read and write it never advanced much beyond an elementary level.

After two years of intensive language study in Peking, Johnson was assigned as Vice-Consul, first at Mukden in 1909 and then at Harbin in 1910. In 1911 he was sent to Hankow and later in the year to Shanghai to serve as Deputy Consul-General and Assessor attached to the Mixed Court. Following a short term in 1915 as Consul in Chungking, he served another three years as Consul at Changsha before returning to Washington for four years as a member of the Division of Far Eastern Affairs in the Department of State. Then after two years as Consul-General-at-Large, during which time he visited most of the posts in its jurisdiction, Johnson returned to the Division as its Chief in 1925. He held the office of Assistant Secretary of State from 1927 to the end of 1929, when he was appointed Minister (Ambassador after 1935) to China.

At the height of the Japanese-inspired Manchurian crisis, Johnson married Jane Beck at Tientsin on October 10, 1931. She was the daughter of George Beck, a former state senator from Cody, Wyoming, and a long-time friend of Nelson's family. When the Japanese renewed their military campaign against China in July 1937, Johnson moved with the Nationalist government first from Nanking to Hankow and then later, on August 2, 1938, to Chungking where he remained, separated from his family, until May 1941. At that time, at his own request to be reunited with his wife and two young children, he accepted a lesser post as Minister to Australia and thus ended his direct connections with China.

When Johnson wearily concluded his long career in China, E.F. Drumright, second secretary of the embassy in Chungking, wrote that the retiring Ambassador received

> the most extensive send-off yet accorded a foreign diplomat in the annals of China's modern diplomacy. His long service in China, his knowledge of the Chinese language, culture and customs, his sympathy and considerations of every class of Chinese, his cheerful nature and perennial optimism at a time when China was undergoing great trials and his spirit of democracy, all endeared him to Chinese officialdom and to the Chinese people alike. It may be truly said that his departure is universally regretted.

The success of his mission, Drumright wrote, may be judged by the developing character of Chinese-American relations. "These have ever been cordial during Mr. Johnson's incumbency and they were never better than at present. In this light Mr. Johnson's mission may be regarded as a complete success."[7]

II

Not much given to theoretical construction or abstract analysis, Johnson may perhaps be best described as an enlightened pragmatist. His rare comments about the nature and conduct of international relations are found in connection with specific Asian problems. Acquainted with virtually every significant scholarly work relative to East Asia and American relations with the Far East, he often despaired of the ignorance about China, her people and customs, that he found exhibited in the views of some of his acquaintances, including a few in high positions. For these self-styled experts he used the epithet "Treaty Port Minds" or "Shanghai Minds."

Cognizant as he was of China's problems, Johnson never allowed his sympathy for China to cloud his vision of America's national interests. His faith in the American character and goals that inevitably stemmed from the "frontier experience" gave direction to his pragmatism. This confidence was built around his concept of America's "pioneer spirit," which he found embodied in Abraham Lincoln. He believed America to be a cultural "melting pot" which derived the best of its qualities from its European heritage. An American so created was (as expressed in Professor Buhite's reconstruction of Johnson's scattered observations)

a complex person, a person who was individualistic, resourceful, materialistic, inventive, and sympathetic, and who was willing to help his neighbors, if in so doing, he did not become involved so intimately in his neighbor's affairs that he lost his freedom for individual action.[8]

Americans were inclined to pursue a foreign policy, Johnson believed, based on the dualism resulting from this "frontier experience." Pioneer necessity and deprivation had taught them to cherish materialism while, at the same time, it had evoked a genuine sympathy for peoples less fortunate. This combination of traits had generated the strength through which the United States had developed into a world power. Aware of this strain of "idealism" in American foreign policy, beginning with Woodrow Wilson and continuing during the 1920's, Johnson warned that in a showdown between ideals and interests the latter would probably prevail. "We ourselves must obey and not forget that side of our development," he noted. "The spirit is in our blood and we will forget our altruism and our idealism if and when we become convinced that our interests are at stake."[9]

Johnson was sympathetic to the aspirations of the Chinese for a strong, unified, stable government. Nevertheless, he was not optimistic that the proper steps would be taken toward that end. He often deplored in his despatches and private letters China's paucity of ideas for future goals and the lack of effective leadership, especially among the military men who aspired to rule China. Although Johnson saw a need for the use of armies as police power to open and maintain communications and to protect life and property, he realized that the difficulty in China was the pariah mentality traditional in officers as well as privates. As a result, military leaders "neither inspired nor did they receive the support of the people as a whole." They cooperated with civilian or political leaders only when they considered it "necessary or wise to invite civilians to support them with slogans and other political claptrap."[10]

Johnson at one time explored the idea of promoting some cooperation among military officers with a number of prominent political leaders. He finally concluded, however, that the effort was useless, that personal animosities were too great, and that no leader was willing to sacrifice his own interest for the common good. He retained these views toward both military and political leaders during most of the decade of the thirties. Much as outsiders might wish to help, the problem of attaining unity in China would continue for a long time, until the Chinese themselves were ready to resolve it. The best role for the United States would be to help the Chinese escape from outside interference. Surrounded by advisors, the Nationalist government did not lack for suggestions. Acting on the advice, however, was a Chinese problem alone.

Johnson's long residence in China and his ability to communicate with Chinese in all walks of life made him acutely aware that the lot of the peasantry was indeed a hard one, despite the regard for peasants in traditional Chinese society. Population pressure on available land was so intense that land prices and rents rose increasingly beyond their reach; consequently they saw only the landlords benefitting from their misery. The peasants, with their roots in the soil, had little to lose and everything to gain from revolution. Johnson perceived the struggle of embittered farmers in Kiangsi and Hunan against the conditions of tenancy as a threat to the very survival of the Nationalist government, although Chinese leaders did not seem at all concerned. He suggested to H.H. Kung, a prominent Kuomintang political leader, that neither military suppression of revolt nor support for the landed gentry would save the situation. Instead, he proposed a plan whereby the government would give deeds to the farmers for the land they had seized and thus ensure their loyalty. To reimburse the landlords who had fled to Shanghai he suggested the government give pensions or government bonds. They too would then have an interest in maintaining a government strong enough to make the payments! But his advice was not accepted. In treatment of the peasantry, he reflected, "the government at Nanking will find either its triumph or its Waterloo."[11]

Communist activities in Kiangsi and Hunan after 1911 prompted Johnson to write to E.O. Clubb, the Vice-Consul in Hankow, that the peasants supported the movement "simply because those people fear the return of a government that desires to restore a local regime which they have come to hate." Though not hopeful about Communist leadership, he thought that if indeed the revolution was reaching the people, "the movement is of tremendous importance."[12]

Some years later, after the war with Japan had been renewed in 1937, Johnson criticized the Communists for using the threat of Japan as a rallying cry for national unity. He maintained that under the cloak of resistance to the Japanese, Communists were pursuing their political work among the peasants, with the aim of an eventual takeover of the government. Clashes during the war between the two major groups in China would continue, he predicted, "but some day they will have to fight it out."[13]

After the 1931 Manchurian Incident, Johnson warned that specious or legalistic arguments used to justify non-compliance with treaty obligations might lead to dangerous consequences. Japan's insistence that her actions did not constitute war, but were rather defensive measures, made the Kellogg Pact a "hideous farce." Since no signatory "categorically condemned" Japanese activities, Johnson warned that other Asian countries would assume Western approval. "What, therefore, must be the conclusion in the East as to the motives and intentions behind the League Covenant and the Kellogg Pact?" he asked. In the larger view, he spoke of the "international tragedy of our Asiatic stage which . . . has set the world back a good many years."[14]

Pragmatically, Johnson maintained that the United States would "get nowhere by mixing morals in the international cocktail, especially out here. International relations are the result of conflict and of composition of conflict." Both "produce the facts of international intercourse. The moralities have little to do with either conflict or its composition."[15]

Although he had been a staunch supporter of the League, the Nine Power Pact, and a world community governed by multilateral treaties and international law, Johnson gradually lost confidence in the ability of these international services to quench flames ignited by national passions. Reviewing the Manchurian affair, he wrote in June 1932 to his former chief, ex-Secretary of State Frank Kellogg, that none of the present arrangements for international peace could handle the chaos brought on by fanatical young Japanese militants. "Matters of belief or faith among people," he noted, "are not subject to judicial determination."[16]

A cautious man, Johnson gradually shed his isolationist or neutralist view of the 1920's as the Japanese pressed their ambitions at the expense of American interests. In April 1934 he told Stanley K. Hornbeck, who held his old job as chief of the Department's Far Eastern Division, that American interests required "that we enjoy the right to send our ships upon their legitimate occasions, unhampered in the far highways of the Pacific. These are our interests in the Pacific and in Asia, and for these interests we will be and must be prepared to fight." A year later he declared that war was inevitable, that to Japan it would be a defensive war, "and to us it will also be a defensive war if it comes, but we must be ready for it."[17]

By 1935 Johnson had given up on a policy of neutrality in the war-clouded western Pacific. He was coming around to accepting the view of another former superior, ex-Secretary of State Henry L. Stimson, that in world affairs it was unlikely that the United States could stay out of war by declaring neutrality: "In some ways the quickest way to take sides in an international squabble is to attempt to be neutral."[18]

III

The increasingly insistent nationalism in China during the eventful years from 1923 to 1928 when the Kuomintang was rising to power produced many new problems for Johnson, then Chief of the Division of Far Eastern Affairs and later Assistant Secretary. Secretary of State Frank B. Kellogg seemed to rely heavily on his judgment in formulating Far Eastern policy, and instructions sent to American representatives in China usually bore the initials FBK and NTJ. Since the Division was quite small, Johnson as the most experienced member played a prominent role.[19]

To deal with the turbulence of these years, the United States sought to follow its traditional policy of avoiding military pressure on China. There were times when Americans in China, private citizens and government officials alike, as well as some diplomatic personnel of other foreign legations, pressed the United States to join in military demonstrations to force one faction or another to pursue a particular course of action. When such situations arose, however, the Department, and especially Kellogg and Johnson, insisted on adhering to general policy.

On January 15, 1927, for example, when it appeared that Shanghai might be in the path of the Nationalist forces of the Kuomintang in their northern expedition, J.V.A. MacMurray, at that time Minister in China, recommended that American military forces join others to defend the International Settlement at Shanghai. He believed that defense of the Settlement and protection of American lives and property were inseparable. Johnson, however, disagreed and recommended to Kellogg that the United States refrain from joint action in defense of the Settlement against any Chinese faction, lest they be accused of taking sides in internal Chinese disputes. This policy was adopted with the proviso that American armed forces would be used to protect American lives and property against troublemakers from any faction where the Chinese authorities were unable to provide such protection.

At the same time that the threat to Shanghai arose, insistent demands for treaty revision by Kuomintang authorities again raised the question of the use of force. In a personal letter to Clarence Gauss, Consul-General in Shanghai, who had a few days earlier expressed concurrence with MacMurray's views, Johnson outlined American policy:

> For your private information you should know that there is no sentiment here in the United States in favor of using naval or military force for the purpose of preserving the present treaty situation in China. Sentiment here is very much in favor of treaty revision and Americans in China should accept this as future policy. The administration will be in for difficulties if we allow ourselves to become involved in any effort to preserve by armed force the present status of the International Settlement at Shanghai. I think that

you understand this and that Admiral Williams understands it. The administration will be supported in its efforts to give protection to Americans against attacks.[20]

Later the same year, after the Nanking Incident, MacMurray again urged the use of sanctions to force the Chinese to accept a satisfactory solution. Johnson, though he too was impatient with Chinese delay, recognized that sentiment in the United States would not support the use of force, except to guard American lives. In Nanking force was finally necessary, but he carefully explained that the American barrage was directed against undisciplined Chinese troops who, with the connivance of their officers, were attacking foreigners unjustifiably. In this instance Americans had not interfered in Chinese affairs, nor had they attempted to defend Nanking; force had been employed solely to protect American lives. Johnson observed that "in international relationships that old rule of equity must prevail, namely that if you would have equity you must be prepared to give equity." In this particular situation and elsewhere, if the Nationalists wanted recognition, they had to guarantee protection to Americans peacefully carrying on their business.[21]

In determining United States policy toward China, Johnson was clearly aware of the interrelationship of the foreign powers upon which the whole treaty structure vis-à-vis China rested. The Department always tried to cooperate with the other powers, especially Great Britain, Japan, France, and Italy. At the same time, Johnson recognized that American interests did not always coincide with those of other nations. In the crucial spring of 1927, he saw China as the unwitting pawn of Russia, Great Britain, and Japan. He therefore recommended that the United States remain aloof from their maneuvering. "Indirectly, of course, we are concerned but the time when we can speak effectively does not seem to me yet to have arrived."[22] Later, in reviewing the modifications of the treaty on extraterritoriality, Johnson further defined his position, declaring that he was not opposed to working with the other powers, as long as the United States was "free to make its own terms on the subject, uninfluenced by the [other powers'] special interests."[23]

When the Chinese finally demanded revision of the treaties relating to foreign control over the tariff, as well as those relating to extraterritoriality, the United States continued to follow its cautious policy. In accordance with agreements reached at the Washington Conference of 1921-1922, a special tariff conference representing the various powers and China met in Peking on October 26, 1925. Though the American delegation was empowered to grant tariff autonomy, the conference adjourned in 1926 without tangible results because no government could speak for the whole of China. Johnson recognized early in 1927, however, that the newly declared Nationalist government, which demanded the revision of treaties, was growing stronger, and he therefore began analyzing American rights in China. He realized that growing Chinese pressures would make the conduct of American trade in China increasingly more difficult. Commenting on the objection of American merchants to additional taxes by Chinese factions, he wrote that the United States could not effectively oppose those taxes and that the situation would not stabilize until organized government appeared. Meanwhile, it would take "every bit of finesse, tact, patience, and diplomacy that American business men and our government representatives in China are possessed of to keep going in the face of these obstacles."[24]

During the autumn of 1927 Johnson worked with MacMurray on the details of a proposed treaty recognizing China's right to tariff autonomy. The opportunity to consider such revision did not arise until July 1928, when the Nationalist government seemed firmly in control. Negotiations by the two governments, concluded quickly in China, led to an agreement on tariff autonomy and by implication extended recognition to the new government. Although there was little consultation with other powers, Johnson held that the spade work had been done, most of them having agreed to autonomy at the earlier tariff conference. Public sentiment in the United States, Johnson wrote, was "continuously growing in favor of doing something toward the improvement of our relations with China. The Chinese situation was one that seemed to need someone to give it a push and the best way to do that seemed to be to go ahead on our own as no one was willing to take the risk."[25]

Johnson was also preparing to move ahead on a revision of the extraterritoriality treaty. Kellogg had already indicated in a January 1927 speech that the United States was willing to negotiate with any group that could speak for China. As the Nationalists extended their control over more territory, Johnson realized that the time might be approaching for a step in this direction too. Such action would promote a stable government if the new regime showed any evidence of being acceptable to its own people.[26] When there were indications near the end of 1929 that China might attempt to end extraterritoriality unilaterally, Johnson suggested that the United States "let her go ahead and try it out," but he believed that sooner or later the terms under which it would be achieved must be settled by negotiation.[27]

Discussions on extraterritoriality in Washington proved fruitless, so early in 1930 the talks were transferred to China, where Johnson had recently taken up residence as Minister. The meetings were long and tedious for the Chinese demanded immediate and total abrogation while the United States insisted on gradual relinquishment. The outbreak of trouble in Manchuria on September 18, 1931, forced postponement of Chinese attempts to revise the treaty, just as Johnson was about to proceed from Peking to Nanking for the drafting of what was hoped to be the final agreement.

Discussions resumed early in 1934 when the Chinese government suggested revision of the American commercial treaty of 1903. In a series of four long letters written over a ten-day period in February 1934, Johnson outlined his views to Stanley Hornbeck.[28] Convinced that the Chinese would ask for a treaty based on equality and reciprocity, he urged that the United States be ready with a draft before a formal demand was presented. He predicted that Chinese insistence would increase with the passage of time. From the Chinese point of view extraterritoriality was a sinister thing, "an anachronism in any treaty." The United States had joined other powers at the Versailles Peace Conference in 1919 in forcing the end of extraterritorial rights in China for the Germans; now the Chinese could not understand why the Americans kept those rights for themselves.[29]

Johnson feared that Washington would be reluctant to sign a new treaty when the Chinese government could not guarantee enforcement and when local governments indiscriminately ignored all treaty arrangements. Johnson pointed out, however, that a new treaty would be more enforceable if it granted equality and reciprocity and thus satisfied local authorities. He admitted, however, that this hope was somewhat tenuous. Unless the United States was prepared to follow Japan's example and ram a treaty down the throats of the Chinese and force its own interpretation upon them, "we can only make such concessions and negotiate such treaties as the Chinese will accept, and hope for the best."[30]

No substantial progress was made at the time, but early in January 1937 the Chinese government again pressed for the abolition of extraterritorial jurisdiction. In answer to a query from Washington as to whether reopening negotiations would have a disturbing effect upon the general situation in the Far East, Johnson replied that any disturbance it might cause would be offset by its beneficial effect on the prestige of the Chinese government among its own people at a critical time. He thought it would be compatible with existing American policy and would also enhance American prestige (which had recently received a boost with the plan to grant autonomy to the Philippines). "The question of the efficiency of Chinese law and administration seems less important to me now," he wrote, "than a more satisfactory treaty arrangement" in behalf of privileges and protection for American activities. Let China take the initiative and the United States could then bargain for the removal of the numerous restrictions recently imposed on foreigners. "Advantages thus gained will render the changed situation more palatable to American interests in China."[31]

The resumption of war between China and Japan on July 7, 1937, delayed negotiations again, but finally in 1943 the United States and Great Britain terminated extraterritoriality. When Johnson, by this time Minister to Australia, received the news he wrote:

I remember very well our conversations early in 1928 on the subject of China and the question of extraterritoriality. I remember also, on one occasion in 1930 when we were discussing extraterritoriality with the Chinese that I expressed my considered opinion then that the only way to get rid of extraterritoriality was to get rid of it, and that the quicker we did it the better. I was never enthusiastic about the progressive method which we adopted. It is sad to think that we had to wait until the Chinese had armed themselves and were at war with the Japanese, and were actually fighting our battle for us against the Japanese, before we gave up something which had ceased to have any meaning because the Japanese had occupied the cities where our die-hards were located. However, I am glad that extraterritoriality has gone, and gone forever, and that that chapter of our relations with China has finally closed.[32]

The problem of Manchuria, which had at times delayed the settlement of the extraterritoriality issue, had been brewing for a long time. The Manchurian crisis of 1931 did not come as a complete surprise to Johnson, but the speed and boldness of Japan's action was unexpected. He had long been aware of the complexity of interests and aspirations in Manchuria involving nations other than China, the nominal suzerain. He watched the settlement of Korean farmers in Manchuria and the growing influence of Japan after the Russo-Japanese War of 1904-1905. He observed, as well, a great influx of Chinese farmers after 1908 whose pressure on the alien Koreans led to the demand to reserve the land for Chinese. In addition, no one could deny Russian interest in Manchuria. Looking ahead Johnson foresaw trouble and concluded that the whole area was "marked with red flags of warning for Americans." He hoped that there was "some way in which the United States could stay out of the question of Manchuria."[33]

Johnson consistently believed that there could be no real settlement of the Manchurian question without consideration of Soviet interests. He favored recognition of Russia as early as the period of the Hoover administration, and he established an informal relationship with Russian diplomats in Peking even before the United States extended recognition in 1933. When the Japanese moved into Manchuria with force in 1931, Johnson at first believed that Japan was strengthening herself for eventual conflict with Russia.[34] Only gradually did he come to see Russia as simply another one of the major powers Japan would have to defeat to secure her own dominance in Asia.[35]

At the onset of Japan's expansion on the Asiatic mainland in 1931, Johnson viewed the dispute essentially as a Sino-Japanese problem that the United States should stay out of, even though it might not approve Japan's actions. A strong supporter of the Nine Power Treaty, the League of Nations, and the Paris Peace Pact, he believed that the nations of the world meant what they said when they signed those documents. Since Japan openly flouted the agreements by its move into Manchuria, he agreed that China, also a signatory, was completely justified in appealing to the League. He was pleased when the League decided to send a special commission to examine the causes of the incident.

This commission, headed by Lord Lytton, decided at the conclusion of its investigation to write its final report in Peking. Johnson talked with several individual members and their advisors and was appalled to learn that they planned to make recommendations for action. To his mind, the Lytton Commission should limit itself to a statement of the facts of the situation and leave suggestions for policy to League members. He regarded it as essential to rally public opinion, but he feared that world attention would be diverted by consideration of plans of action, thereby neglecting the main point at issue. If the commission thought that it was required to make recommendations, those should appear in a separate document. To clinch his argument, he made the prediction that the Japanese would not yield under any circumstances and that the Manchurian question was "settled to all intents and purposes."[36] From Johnson's point of view, then, a more basic issue transcended the question of the future of Manchuria. It was no less than the fate of the whole treaty structure's capability to peacefully settle disputes.

In the absence of effective aid from the League and in recognition of China's military weakness in the face of territorial encroachments, some Chinese leaders hoped that America would actively aid in their defense. Johnson reported that Dr. H.H. Kung had become "much interested in the idea of a war between the United States and Japan, in which China would supply the manpower." Johnson noted that the idea of a war in which the United States would figure as "the champion and savior of China" was current "among many other Chinese occupying official positions." He did what he could on all occasions to "discourage this idea among the Chinese."[37]

As a consequence of the events in Manchuria, Johnson feared that Japan might become isolated or even more belligerent, and turn away from the West altogether. Japan's successful use of force, with no Western counterresistance, threatened to increase her prestige to such an extent that the West, and particularly the United States, would no longer have influence. On the other hand, he recognized the possibility that Japan's program might be so costly as to produce internal collapse. Either eventuality, isolation or internal upheaval and bankruptcy, would be disastrous for American interests, which depended upon joint agreement of all the Pacific powers, including Japan, Russia, and China.

Given the seriousness of the situation, Johnson did not believe the United States could afford to let things drift without doing something to alter the course of events. After discussions with his staff in Peking, he suggested to the Department that an opportunity might arise in Geneva, where League discussions on Manchuria were taking place, for the United States to propose a conference on all matters relating to the Far East. Recognizing that Japan had legitimate grievances against both Russia and China and that all Pacific powers had interests in Asia, participants would be invited "to lay their cases on the table in all their truth, in order that we may discover whether it is possible for us to deal honestly and honorably among ourselves with the situation." Johnson thought the Japanese would be pleased and more willing to participate if such a conference were held in Tokyo.

If Japan rejected the whole idea, or if such a conference failed, at least all interested parties would know where they stood and could act accordingly. Failure to do anything, in Johnson's view, would lead to a future fraught with difficulties and dangers. Reflecting on his youthful Oklahoma experiences, he observed that the man who was ready to shoot walked the streets in undisputed control, until the day came when the people were prepared to combine against him. Faced with a Japan ready and willing to use force, the United States "must be either prepared to shoot or yield the street."[38]

Johnson's proposal for an Asian conference found little support in the Department and failed to evoke any enthusiasm from Secretary Stimson. Under Secretary William R. Castle, Jr., an urbane confidant of President Hoover's, vigorously opposed the plan and complacently observed in his reactions set down for Stanley Hornbeck that

The time will come . . . for a conference . . . and if it is not the Japanese themselves who propose it, they will at least be in a receptive mood for it. This will be when the retention of Manchuria and perpetuation of the "Manchukuo" fiction definitely proves inexpedient and unprofitable.

Castle enumerated many factors which ultimately would force Japan to recognize the folly of her policy, among them "sustained Chinese armed and economic resistance, nonrecognition of 'Manchukuo' by the leading powers, the United States particularly, and an uncompromising legal attitude with regard to their substantive rights in Manchuria under treaties with China." Implying that Japan could not hold out against the "inevitable" opposition at home and abroad, he observed: "Other nations have made mistakes of this nature and backed out gracefully . . . so why not Japan?" Hornbeck dourly noted that Japan would scarcely back out voluntarily: "Not on all fours—or even on threes or twos."[39]

The Japanese move into Shanghai late in January 1932 marked a significant change in Johnson's understanding of their aims. He had earlier believed the Sino-Japanese dispute over Manchuria to be a minor, local affair. He could see no reason for this expanded Japanese action, however, unless it formed part of a longer-range plan of the military, who were obviously flouting the regular civilian government as well as the interests of other foreign powers.[40] From this time on he realized that the civilian government mattered little in Japan because the military leaders, particularly the younger ones, formulated and carried out Japanese policy in Asia.

Discussions with Japanese military officers directed toward a settlement of the Shanghai affair in May 1932 convinced Johnson that a new force was shaping Japan's actions. He concluded that the aggressive policy resulted not only from economic pressures and the need to provide for a growing population but also from the fervor of a "purification movement going on among the youth of Japan, characterized by an idealism" in revolt against the old order. The young military officers believed themselves to be above sordid motives and were prepared to risk all to achieve dominance and thus to "save Japan."[41]

Later Johnson wrote that the Japanese position in Asia was not under the direction of "any of the regularly established agencies for controlling such situations." From the very beginning of Japanese expansion in Manchuria, Japan was controlled by the younger group of military officers, "who never approved of the policies of the Japanese Cabinet and particularly the Foreign Office, who were fed up with Japanese politics and political life general- ly . . . and who set about putting into effect their own ideas. . . . " The older officers were forced to follow them, "for they dared not disown their actions." They even isolated themselves from moderating influences, lest they suffer contamination in the eyes of the younger men who dictated policy. This leadership disregarded treaties and was contemptuous of the outside world.[42]

In the spring of 1935 Johnson noted that the Japanese military apparently decided, for the moment, to seek economic advantage in China by negotiation. The talks, however, were conducted by military officers, with whom regular representatives of other foreign governments could not maintain proper contacts.[43] The actions of Japanese military leaders had impressed upon the Chinese, and reluctant Japanese too, that "no one might act" in matters concerning China "without the approval of the military general staff, the real rulers of Japan." As a result they inspired such fear among the Chinese that no one dared to oppose any request they might make. "The Japanese Army," Johnson wrote, "is determined to break China to its will, whatever the consequences may be."[44]

When Japan renewed military hostilities against China after the Marco Polo Bridge Incident of July 7, 1937, captured seacoast towns, and drove the government inland ultimately to Chungking, Johnson found his worst suspicions concerning Japanese militarism confirmed. Events within Japan provided further evidence that the real ruler was the army. The Cabinet then in power, in his view one created by the army, was proposing certain economic reform measures which were opposed in the Diet by "so-called capitalistic and industrial classes." Support for the suggested reforms came not from "any civilian, agrarian, communistic or proletarian elements in the people" but from the army officered by young men of the disaffected agrarian classes, indoctrinated by their leaders and mobilized like fascists to keep Japan from being "destroyed by the 'laissez-faire' methods of modern industrialism."[45]

The only issue of concern to Johnson was how the United States should react to Japan's challenge. He had been a staunch supporter of Stimson's "nonrecognition" policy of January 7, 1931, for it seemed to him the only course of action open since the American people were not willing to impose sanctions. Stimson's policy, he declared, was the "manly, straight-forward, honest thing to do."[46] Nonrecognition kept the record straight, Johnson felt, pending the day when the Washington treaties (1922) were re-negotiated. Before long, however, Johnson began to feel that more forceful measures were necessary. He wrote to Joseph Grew in Tokyo in October 1932 to "keep our powder dry and be watchful," for the future in the Pacific was "full of portents." Since the Japanese had destroyed the new system developed by Western nations in the 1920's, the United States must prepare to use the methods and meet the conditions of "what we had wished to consider a buried past."[47]

Japan, meanwhile, proceeded to justify her actions. On April 17, 1934, Amau Eiji, spokesman for the Japanese Foreign Ministry, informally stated that Japan considered that it had a special responsibility to maintain peace in Asia, and he condemned the activities of other nations in aiding China "to resist" Japan's efforts to accomplish this mission on the mainland. Johnson bristled at this so-called Amau Doctrine: "This statement should not be permitted to pass unchallenged," he told Washington, "as it runs counter to the spirit and the letter of the Nine Power Treaty. . . . " If Japan persisted, he warned, America's national and commercial interests in China would be severely restricted. Johnson continued to insist that China's independence was not the main issue; the rights of Americans in the Pacific were at stake.[48] Secretary Cordell Hull chose to avoid challenging Tokyo at this time, and another of Johnson's suggestions was relegated to the Department's files.

The outbreak of Sino-Japanese hostilities in July 1937 found Johnson firmly committed to an anti-Japanese stance. He scorned initial suggestions (and attempts) by Western powers to mediate the dispute; indeed, he opposed any idea of additional Chinese concessions. In his opinion, "any appearance of urging China to purchase peace with the loss of sovereign rights would appear to be encouragement to a predatory national policy on Japan's part."[49]

The Ambassador was pleased when President Roosevelt's "Quarantine Address," delivered in October 1937 in Chicago, called for isolation of those countries afflicted with the disease of aggression. He felt that the declaration cleared the air as far as the United States was concerned. In the depressing months that followed, Johnson reluctantly approved Washington's cautious Asian policy, but he often expressed the belief that the world was entering a period, perhaps a long period, of lawlessness. Even if he did not aggressively press for greater American aid for China or more stringent sanctions against Japan, Johnson did applaud each step in this direction from 1939 onward. "We must begin now," he wrote, "to show our teeth . . . or we may forever find ourselves stopped from taking action. . . . We cannot afford to wait too long."[50] On August 27, 1940, he predicted to Hornbeck from Chungking that "sooner or later there will have to be a showdown of some sort between us and the Japanese."[51]

Johnson's observations then, based on the events of the 1930's, might be summarized as follows: (1) Japan had ignored the existing treaty structure for peaceful settlement of international disputes, especially that relating to the Far East; (2) a Japanese military clique had substituted naked force to secure its objectives in East Asia; (3) it was useless to negotiate with the regularly constituted Japanese government because it was powerless to control the military forces; (4) the possibility suggested by some observers that Japan would collapse internally because of the cost of military ventures on the mainland was too remote to contemplate; (5) China was incapable of defending her territory and sovereignty, much less of inflicting a military defeat on Japan; (6) the Japanese were determined to drive all Westerners out of East Asia and to treat the areas as their colonies; and (7) the United States had an implied commitment to defend the Philippines even though independence should be granted.

The Ambassador therefore watched with increasing apprehension the younger Japanese officers' grasp upon the army. Referring to a clash in Shanghai in 1940, he noted that after the whole affair had been settled, the younger military officers took control and compelled their seniors "to sign statements and letters that no self-respecting leader would ever have allowed himself to use. This is what we are up against and sooner or later it will devour the Japanese government itself which seems to be leaderless."[52] Not until he had left his post in China and taken up his new position in Australia did the Japanese Army under General Tōjō actually take over the government in Japan. Reacting to this development Johnson commented:

> The Japanese Army has at last been forced by circumstances to take the responsibility for the political future of the country. We have waited for a long time for this to happen. Personally, I think that it is all to the good, because the army can no longer hide behind puppets, like Konoye, of their own creation. For the first time in twelve years we are in a position to deal directly with the power that has been running Japan and Japanese policy.[53]

After his return to the United States in June 1941, Johnson wrote to General William Crozier, whom he had known in China, that he was glad the United States was now "out of the miserable game of appeasing Japan. It was a sleazy sort of business at best, paying tribute to pirates, a thing which we had once refused to do when we were smaller and of much less account in the world."[54]

Johnson foresaw that the conflict would be a long one, and he wondered whether the American people were really aware of "the century or so of strife that is ahead until control of sea and air has once more been decided. We are going to have to fight for our rights in both elements against hostile forces determined to dominate them to their own ends."[55]

Notes

1 Nelson T. Johnson Papers (Library of Congress, Manuscripts Division, Washington, D.C.) contain an example in Johnson's letter to William R. Castle, Jr., March 25, 1931, vol. 13. Unless otherwise indicated, all citations are from the Johnson Papers.

2 *New York Times*, March 16, 1930, 7:1.

3 *Ibid.*, January 29, 1930, 5:2.

4 Johnson to Nicholas Roosevelt, special correspondent and editorial writer for the *New York Times*, November 15, 1929, vol. 10.

5 Russell D. Buhite, *Nelson T. Johnson and American Policy Toward China, 1925-1941* (East Lansing: Michigan State University Press, 1968), pp. 1-3.

6 *Ibid.*, p. 9.

7 May 6, 1941, United States Department of State Files 123/Nelson T. Johnson/634/734 (National Archives, Washington, D.C.). Cited hereafter as DSF.

8 Buhite *Johnson*, p. 14.

9 *Ibid.*, p. 15.

10 Memorandum of conversation with Sir Frederick Whyte, Advisor to Nanking government, June 10, 1930, vol. 33.

11 Johnson to Frederick McCormick, former newspaper correspondent in Asia and author, July 10, 1931, vol. 14; Johnson to Edward C. Carter, Institute of Pacific Relations, New York City, May 27, 1933, vol. 17.

12 Johnson to E.O. Clubb, July 21, 1932, vol. 15.

13 Johnson to Theodore Roosevelt, January 19, 1941. Johnson Papers in unbound collection at the home of Mrs. Nelson T. Johnson. Cited hereafter as Johnson Papers II.

14 Johnson to Mrs. Ann Archbold, c/o Morgan & Company, Paris, January 6, 1932, vol. 15.

15 Johnson to Edwin Neville, Counselor of Embassy, Tokyo, January 24, 1934, vol. 22.

16 Johnson to Frank B. Kellogg, June 11, 1932, vol. 16.

17 Johnson to Stanley K. Hornbeck, April 12, 1934, vol. 21; Johnson to Edwin M. Borchard, Yale University School of Law, March 13, 1935, vol. 23.

18 Johnson to General William Crozier, Peking, August 27, 1935, vol. 23.
19 See for example, the memorandum which provided the basis for the settlement of the Nanking Incident of March 1927. Drafted by Johnson and dated November 3, 1927, it bore also the initials of Kellogg. United States Department of State, *Papers Relating to the Foreign Relations of the United States, 1927* (Washington, D.C.: Government Printing Office, 1942), 2:232-233.
20 Johnson to Gauss, February 15, 1927, vol. 2.
21 Johnson to Paul Monroe, professor of education at Barnard College, May 16, 1927, vol. 4.
22 Johnson to Silas H. Strawn, Chicago, June 6, 1927, vol. 4. Strawn had been a member of the American delegation to the Special Tariff Conference held in Peking in 1925.
23 Johnson to William R. Castle, Jr., September 7, 1930, vol. 11. Castle had just returned to the Department of State to resume his position as Assistant Secretary after a short term as Ambassador to Japan.
24 Johnson to Mr. Theodore Harr, Standard Oil Co., Shanghai, August 24, 1927, vol. 3.
25 Johnson to Ray Atherton, American embassy in London, August 22, 1928, vol. 5.
26 Memorandum of conversation with Mr. Setsuzo Sawada, Japanese Chargé d'Affaires, July 14, 1928, vol. 31.
27 Johnson to Douglas Jenkins, American Consul General, Canton, China, October 2, 1929, vol. 9.
28 Letters dated February 16, 17, 21, and 26, 1934, Johnson Papers II.
29 *Ibid.,* February 26, 1934.
30 *Ibid.,* February 17, 1934.
31 Johnson telegram to Secretary of State, March 22, 1937, DSF 793.003 #855.
32 Johnson to Hornbeck, April 27, 1943, Johnson Papers II. For a fuller discussion of this issue see, John Carter Vincent, *The Extraterritorial System in China: Final Phase* (Harvard East Asian Monograph, No. 30), 1970.
33 Johnson to Robert E. Olds, April 9, 1928, vol. 5.
34 Johnson to Frank B. Kellogg, January 12, 1932, vol. 15.
35 Johnson to Roy Howard, newspaperman, August 15, 1936, vol. 27; Johnson to Roy Howard, October 11, 1937, Johnson Papers II, written three months after the renewal of military conflict between China and Japan on July 7, 1937. Johnson observed that "the Japanese seem to be on the move now to defeat or to the accomplishment of their long entertained and planned design to eliminate British and American influence from the continent of Asia. Their plans also include eliminating the influence of Soviet Russia."
36 Johnson to Hornbeck, June 29, 1932, vol. 15. Hornbeck replied that he had shown the letter to the Secretary of State and that he had authorized Johnson, if it became necessary to state his views, to "discreetly and in confidence make known in appropriate quarters that it is his considered view that the greatest potential usefulness of the report will be achieved in the field of statement and analysis of facts, complete, unbiased, and thoroughly objective." Telegram, August 11, 1932, DSF 793.4 Commission/319A.

37 Memorandum by Johnson containing opinions of Chinese authorities in regard to the political future of the Far East, May 24, 1932, vol. 35.
38 Johnson to Hornbeck, September 13, 1932, vol. 15. This letter was an elaboration of a telegram which Johnson had sent to the Department on September 7. Telegram #1078, Johnson to Secretary Stimson, DSF 894.00/431-2/6. Cover memos by Castle and Stanley K. Hornbeck, September 16, 1932. Under Secretary Castle commented that it was a good suggestion, but the time was inopportune, so it was therefore useless. He was certain that a Japanese "back-to-Asia" movement had no significant following and that there was no "real hostility" in Japan toward the West.
39 *Ibid.*
40 Johnson to Henry Kittredge Norton, newspaper man, June 10, 1932, vol. 16. "There is no doubt in my mind," he wrote, "that the blunder at Shanghai put an entirely different aspect upon Japan's position in Manchuria."
41 Johnson to Robert E. Olds, legal adviser to Chinese delegation at the League of Nations, June 11, 1932, vol. 16.
42 Johnson to B.D. Hulen, Washington Bureau of the *New York Times,* March 10, 1933, vol. 18.
43 Johnson to Secretary of State, March 21, 1935, vol. 25.
44 Johnson to Secretary of State, July 10, 1932, vol. 25. Similar ideas were expressed in another letter to the Secretary dated January 15, 1936, vol. 28.
45 Johnson to Admiral Yarnell, USN, August 12, 1937, Johnson Papers II. In another letter to a friend in Washington, D.C., F.W. Wile, on October 28, 1937, he commented on the machine-gunning of civilians by Japanese airmen and added, "They play dirty ball in all of this business. Some day the world is going to have a very nasty time with them."
46 Johnson to Tyler Dennett, June 8, 1934, vol. 20.
47 Johnson to Grew, American Ambassador to Japan, October 21, 1932, vol. 15.
48 United States Department of State, *Papers Relating to the Foreign Relations of the United States, 1934* (Washington, D.C.: Government Printing Office, 1950), 3:143-144; see also Buhite, *Johnson,* p. 96.
49 United States Department of State, *Papers Relating to the Foreign Relations of the United States, 1937* (Washington, D.C.: Government Printing Office, 1954), 3:385-386.
50 United States Department of State, *Papers Relating to the Foreign Relations of the United States, 1939* (Washington, D.C.: Government Printing Office, 1955), 3:507-512.
51 Johnson to Hornbeck, September 28, 1940, Johnson Papers II.
52 *Ibid.,* Johnson to Hornbeck, August 13, 1940.
53 *Ibid.,* Johnson to McCormick, October 25, 1941, from Canberra.
54 *Ibid.,* July 30, 1941.
55 *Ibid.,* Johnson to Henry Luce, April 21, 1941.

Thomas Buckley

John Van Antwerp MacMurray

The Diplomacy of an American Mandarin

AN "OLD CHINA HAND," John V.A. MacMurray found it increasingly difficult during the 1930's to adapt either to the chaotic nationalism of China or the shifting climate of American opinion. Strongly "realistic" in his approach to policy, he believed that the basic interests of the United States in China were immutable. Thus MacMurray deplored the unilateral, vacillating, idealistic tendencies he detected in many American proposals and preferred cooperative policies with other nations, the use of force when necessary, and deliberate, cautious negotiation. He disapproved of accommodating American principles and interests to the revolutionary Chinese scene and insisted that the Chinese government fulfill its international obligations. Any crack in the wall of treaties surrounding and controlling China, he argued, threatened the entire structure. When China proved itself worthy, then—but only then—should treaty revision occur, and this revision should unfold at a pace determined not by China but by the treaty powers. Meanwhile, if it appeared necessary to compel China to meet her treaty obligations, he did not hestitate to call for the "big stick."

The formulation and execution of American policies toward China proved most perplexing and trying for MacMurray throughout his career, whether in his capacity as Chief of the State Department's Far Eastern Affairs Division (1919-1924), Assistant Secretary of State (1925; he was the first Foreign Service professional to achieve this rank), or Minister to China (1925-1929). Although he approved of a "benevolent attitude" toward China, he questioned its applicability in a revolution-torn society where no group appeared wiser or stronger or more promising than its competitor. Cynically but realistically, he expected the Chinese to pursue their own interests with little or no regard for foreign feelings.

There was considerable merit in MacMurray's analysis of the Chinese situation as well as in his capable reporting, his judgments on human nature, and his often shrewd prophecies. His immediate reaction, however, too often relied on sheer power; this ignored the practical difficulty of applying force in revolutionary situations and did not take into consideration the effect on American public opinion. If his philosophy proved congenial to Secretary of State Charles Evans Hughes, his open disagreements with Secretaries Frank B. Kellogg and Henry L. Stimson impaired his effectiveness as Minister to China and brought about his resignation from the Foreign Service. Yet he was neither the first nor the last American to support traditionalism in diplomacy.

MacMurray's failure as Minister was not for lack of courage or ability; it was for want of perspective. While in Washington he lost sight of the new forces building in Peking, and while in Peking he lost touch with the political barometer in Washington.

I

Born in 1881 into an old upper class family, John V.A. MacMurray was descended from one of the first Dutch settlers in New York. His father, Janius Wilson MacMurray, fought on the Northern side in the Civil War and thereafter remained in the regular army; he later served as a professor of military history at Cornell University and gained some stature as an authority on the history of the American Indian. One can conclude with some justification that the father instilled in his young son a belief in order, organization, and military solutions, but perhaps more importantly, he suggested a paternalistic attitude toward the Indian that was paralleled by the son's approach to the Chinese a generation later.

The future diplomat's upbringing in a military family may also have contributed to the aura of certainty, self-confidence, and even dogmatism that characterized his personality. Young MacMurray clearly grew up in a secure, well-ordered community where stability and certitude were the rule rather than the exception and where deviations were viewed as abnormal and transitory in nature. This respect for traditional values perhaps accounts for MacMurray's later fondness for old traditional China and his disdain for the unstable new China of the 1920's. His early education at Captain Wilson's military school tended to reinforce his upbringing before he entered Lawrenceville in 1896 and Princeton in 1898.

A man of character, given to deliberation, MacMurray prepared carefully for a career in the diplomatic service. He followed a well-known path to appointment: graduation from an Ivy League school (Princeton, '02) where he displayed talent for literary composition and debate, *le grand tour d'Europe* for a year, a law degree from Columbia in 1906. "Jack," as his friends called him, began his campaign by requesting prominent men to write letters in his behalf, designed to influence a Congressman to recommend his appointment to the diplomatic service. One of his references, then president of Princeton, Woodrow Wilson, suggested that a career in the Foreign Service would be a waste of MacMurray's literary abilities. Marking time, he returned to Princeton to study the influence of the Renaissance on Elizabethan drama. He received an offer of a preceptorship in the English department but turned it down, to the benefit of later historians who would read his diplomatic and private correspondence. The polish of his despatches compares favorably with that of a later, more renowned member of the Foreign Service, George F. Kennan.

MacMurray received a Master's degree in English in May 1907 at the age of twenty-six, and President Theodore Roosevelt appointed him Third Secretary of the American legation in Bangkok. Siam was the first of many posts in his thirty-three-year career. He left for Russia in 1907 and served in St. Petersburg as Second Secretary. From 1908 to 1911 he was Assistant-Chief of Information in the Department at Washington; the two following years he was Assistant-Chief and then Chief of the Division of Near Eastern Affairs.

MacMurray nostalgically recalled the golden days of his service as the four years after 1913 when he was Secretary of the legation in Peking under the relaxed supervision of Minister Paul S. Reinsch. Whether he was hoisting his five-foot-nine frame on the back of a small pony, gathering his dog "Ting" in his arms for a ride or romp in the hills outside Peking, or savoring the brilliant spectacle of the ancient Chinese capitol, MacMurray studied and observed, made friends, and sharpened his diplomatic skills. There he came to conclusions about China and American policies that he was to hold tenaciously ever afterward. But it was China of the nineteenth century, dying in the twentieth, that impressed itself upon MacMurray's mind. Government chaos, nationalistic reactions to foreign rights and privileges, threats to American interests—these unattractive results of the Chinese revolution were in the future. MacMurray found time to begin the compilation of a two-volume edition of treaties pertaining to China that became a standard reference work and helped establish his reputation as a Far Eastern expert.[1] He met and married Lois Goodnow, the daughter of Frank Goodnow, American legal adviser to the Chinese government and president of Johns Hopkins University.

The sojourn in Peking ended in 1917 when MacMurray was sent on a two-year tour of Japan as counselor of the embassy in Tokyo. Now an authentic old China hand, he was uncomfortable in Japan, and it was with relief that he returned to Washington in 1919 to become Chief of the Division of Far Eastern Affairs.[2]

By the time he returned to Washington, MacMurray had formed views not only on China but also on the diplomatic service, including the role of a diplomat and his proper behavior. As both Chief of the Division and later Minister to China, MacMurray personified the public image of a diplomat, from his tailored British suits to his Parisian wine cellar in Peking. He quickly developed a fierce loyalty to the diplomatic service. Along with Joseph C. Grew and Nelson T. Johnson he shared an *esprit de corps* rarely appreciated or understood by either the American public or its even more parochial Congressional representatives. Whether dispensing advice to neophyte officers, writing long and careful fitness reports, or extolling the virtues of the service, his pride in the corps was apparent. He admitted that the Department had its faults, for it was a human institution, but he argued that it maintained "traditions of service of which it may well be pretty proud as things go in a wicked world."[3]

As to the diplomat's role, MacMurray wrote from Peking in 1927: "I conceive my functions to be those of the shipmaster and local pilot whose business it is to do the actual navigating under general order from you [the Department of State] who are the shipowners." While in agreement that it was within the purview of the Department to specify the voyage, he assumed the Department would heed his advice "that in a certain reach there is not enough water to float the ship . . . and that nobody except the pilot is in a position to prescribe a speed or course to be followed with reference to water level, currents, winds, or other local conditions." He once complained that the Department had too often ordered him to "put my helm hard aport in a narrow passage, or has made me stop my engines and lose steerage way when fighting against a heavy current." He always believed that time and distance necessarily allowed the diplomat on the spot a certain independence of action; he clearly sought to preserve that freedom in Peking in the later 1920's.[4]

After he became Minister to China, MacMurray did not hesitate to show his hand, even to his putative superiors. In a remarkable letter to Stanley K. Hornbeck, he wrote that he had opposed the latter's appointment as Chief of the Far Eastern Division. He then carefully instructed Hornbeck, his superior, on the proper relation between the Department and the Minister, concluding that "there is nothing to get mad about if each end of the wire plays the game according to the rules . . . which as I have worked them out in my own experience, are not complex or difficult." In this curiously frank letter, MacMurray stated that of course a telegram from Washington would always "make me turn hand-springs," but the "almost limitless power to control my official actions" should be tempered by the fact that "I am closer to the situation." Any facts the Minister communicated to Hornbeck were "authoritative and must be accepted as conclusive." It was, he admitted, a "truism that there is no such thing as a clear-cut fact here in China," since much depended on the judgment and experience of the Minister. All things being equal, the "man on the spot" was the best judge of what means should be adopted to achieve a given result under the existing circumstances. If the Minister was overruled, the Department must explain its position and reasons. This "pull-and-haul" was "a necessary process by which accommodation is made between sets of considerations."[5]

II

MacMurray's general approach to China, first as Chief of the Division of Far Eastern Affairs and then Minister, centered around essentially nineteenth-century ideas: nonintervention in China's domestic affairs, cooperative policies with other powers, and respect for treaty obligations. America's basic interest on the Asian mainland, as he saw it, was the opportunity to compete in safety on an equal basis in the Chinese marketplace. This situation was assured by the commercial, tariff, and most-favored-nation clauses of nineteenth-century treaties; protection of American citizens in China, whether working for profit or soul, came under the extraterritorial and protecting clauses of these agreements. Largely, but not completely devoid of political purposes, the United States' nineteenth-century China policy then represented a realistic appraisal of interests and a coupling of limited means and goals.

American statesmen only began to change policy toward China into public, explicit statements emphasizing political goals at the end of the century, with acquisition of the Philippine Islands and the threatened partition of the Manchu Empire into spheres of influence. While the first Open Door note of 1899 in effect recognized the existence of spheres of influence and insisted on continued equality of opportunity for American commerce, the second Open Door note in 1900 made it the policy of the United States to "bring about permanent safety and peace to China, preserve Chinese territorial and administrative entity, protect all rights guaranteed to friendly powers by treaty and international law, and safeguard for the world the principle of equal and impartial trade with all parts of the Chinese Empire."[6]

MacMurray's concept of nonintervention in China's domestic affairs led him to urge the United States not to choose sides in China's revolutionary struggle; he saw no need to invite the dissident Cantonese government to the Washington Conference of 1921-1922 since such action would amount to interference. In 1922 when a British member of a financial consortium proposed unifying China by financing a combination of *tuchuns*—warlords— who might defeat other contenders and set up a government favorable to the

Western powers, MacMurray registered strong opposition to Secretary of State Charles Evans Hughes. "It contemplates an unwarranted partisanship in the internal factional disturbances of China"; and besides, "this is not a promising horse to back." The United States government, he added, "has no favorites in the present dog-fight in China and they all look alike to us." He characterized Chang Tso-lin as a pirate, Tuan Ch'i-jui as a squarehead, Wu P'ei-fu as a washout, Feng Yu-hsiang as a canting renegade, and Sun Yat-sen as a Chinese William Jennings Bryan.[7]

MacMurray was honest enough, however, to confess to "a certain staleness" since my ideas of what China is remain pretty much determined by what I recollect of my own observation five years or more ago." From that vantage point, seeing "no honest and disinterested leaders," he concluded the United States "should keep out of the mess and merely pray that somebody, whoever it may be, may lick his rivals completely enough to make possible the establishment of some government." He saw no choice but to go on with the fiction that Peking was the legal government, so that the United States could hold someone responsible for China's treaty obligations.[8]

By stressing cooperation with other nations in Chinese affairs, MacMurray hoped to present a united front so that China could not manipulate the powers with her ageless policy of playing one barbarian against the other. It would then be possible to hold China to her treaty obligations. Furthermore, such a front would help prevent the sort of international rivalry that in the past led to spheres of influence that infringed on Chinese sovereignty and raised obstacles to American economic and political interests. He concluded that a constructive policy could be followed only in cooperation with other nations thus preventing "a reversion to the old system of international competition and intrigue."[9] The Washington Conference, in which MacMurray played an important part, emphasized this cooperative political spirit; he referred to it constantly as the ideal pattern, and in later years he bemoaned its failure. His greatest economic hopes rested in a financial consortium, and he was certain that another withdrawal of Western financiers, as had occurred during the Wilson administration, "would retard American trade to China for perhaps a generation—just when our country must be assuring itself of the opportunity for commercial expansion in the remaining undeveloped markets of the world." Because of America's vacillating consortium policy, MacMurray asserted that throughout China "we have become a byword for well-intentioned futility [and] the real confidence and affection which Americans enjoy in China is qualified by the belief that we never really do anything."[10] While approving the cooperative aspects of the consortium in its broad approach to China, he was aware that successful operation would benefit the United States more than any other power.

To MacMurray's mind proper Unites States policy toward China hinged on the insistence that the Chinese government fulfill its obligations and responsibilities. Here, more than anywhere else, MacMurray had his greatest influence on Secretary Hughes. The fine hand of the Chief of the Far Eastern Division is evident in one of the Secretary's private notes in 1923: "Duty compels us . . . to hold the Chinese government as rigorously as we may to the fulfillment of foreign obligations which, no less than the rights of sovereignty, are incident to its enjoyment of a position in the family of nations." MacMurray opposed remitting the Boxer Indemnity at a time when the United States found its treaty rights harder to sustain than ever. When missionaries in China wanted to give up extraterritorial rights, both Hughes and MacMurray argued that the voluntary surrender of rights, no matter what the spirit behind it, would impair the whole system of treaties.[11] As Minister to China, MacMurray returned to this theme with even greater emphasis and persistence.

The very hallmark of MacMurray's China policy was unquestionably the need to back up diplomacy with force. Even as a young Secretary of legation during the Reinsch era, MacMurray displayed a disposition toward strong proposals and the use of force. He sharply protested the withdrawal of Western troops from China in August 1914, arguing that American and Japanese forces were responsible for "protecting general foreign interests"; more American ships and marines would thus fill an important function of cooperative action.[12] To this and other entreaties of a similar nature, President Wilson's Counselor in the Department, Robert Lansing, replied that while the American government had an interest in the welfare of the Chinese people, "it would be quixotic in the extreme to allow the question of China's territorial integrity to entangle the United States in international difficulties."[13]

Although rebuffed, MacMurray urged similar action on future occasions. The Coltman incident of December 1922 is a good example of his propensity for strong stands. Charles Coltman, an American merchant, died as a result of gunshot wounds received from Chinese soldiers who had stopped his car, searched it, and accused him of breaking Chinese financial laws. Moreover, the American Consul was in the same car. The American Minister, Jacob Gould Schurman, protested to the Chinese government and demanded the arrest of the soldiers. MacMurray supported him, calling the incident "a critical case dealing with the protection of our citizens in China." He insisted on "promptness and vigor of action," including removal of the military governor of Kalgan. Hughes took MacMurray's advice, but the Chinese government delayed settlement despite Schurman's demand for action. Clearly influenced by MacMurray, the Secretary implied that the Department of State might refuse to give *de jure* recognition to the Chinese government unless settlement of the Coltman case was concluded forthwith.[14] A Chinese apology materialized, but MacMurray claimed it lacked an "appreciation of the seriousness of the case," and Hughes, using some of MacMurray's words, called for a "genuine acknowledgement of regret." On May 4 an official apology was indeed made, a $25,000 indemnity determined, and the Chinese military officers dismissed. Hughes and MacMurray had taken a tough stand and forced the Chinese to settle. Both men, however, must have read the subsequent report from the Department's solicitor with embarrassment. The solicitor concluded that Coltman "was assisting Chinese to evade and violate Chinese regulations, was abusing his extraterritorial privileges, and was deceiving the American consul, whose assistance he had sought to enable him to pass the Chinese authorities."[15]

For a few short months before his appointment as Minister in 1925, MacMurray served as Third Assistant Secretary of State, replacing the venerable Alvey A. Adee who died after serving in the Department since 1887. It was well known that Hughes used such appointments as a reservoir from which to select future ministers.[16] MacMurray had been giving consideration to resigning and taking up an academic career, but passage of the Rogers Act in 1925, reforming State Department personnel practices, and Hughes' open admiration led him to accept the assistant secretaryship with the clear expectation of appointment as Minister to China when Schurman retired.[17]

III

Almost immediately upon his arrival in China, MacMurray clashed with Secretary Hughes' successor, Frank Kellogg, over principles and conduct of policy. Two major issues incited and sustained this conflict of wills: first, the Coolidge administration, counter to MacMurray's advice, had bowed to domestic pressures for the abolition of the tariff and extraterritorial privileges granted to foreigners in China; and, second, Washington consistently refused to endorse MacMurray's request for a policy of "cooperative firmness" to meet anti-American (or anti-foreign) outbreaks in China. Consequently, the two men engaged in a running battle over China policy throughout Kellogg's four years in office.

MacMurray had often received advice from colleagues in China while he was Assistant Secretary. Undoubtedly aware that he was next in line, they informed him that the situation had changed since his previous tour of duty. One former colleague noted the government's instability and pointed out that a *tuchun* could be President one day and out the next, "without even the cheapest and skinniest of his concubines to while the hours away"; more important, this friend advised that "military force is not applicable to hydra-headed China of today. Military force is no terror, compared with what it was." Another former colleague warned from China that the American government "will not be willing to use force to coerce China" and concluded that "we might better give up gracefully what we cannot keep."[18]

Puzzled by these comments, MacMurray found the situation "almost hopelessly obscure." He visualized the Chinese people, oblivious to the struggle for power, as "steers on a cattle-ship . . . milling about wild; while the ship sails on completely independent of what the cattle in the hold are doing." There was obviously a new psychology between East and West, and Westerners would have to "forego the privilege of kicking a rikisha coolie and otherwise comforting [their] own inferiority complexes."[19]

When finally appointed Minister in April 1925, MacMurray wrote the retired Hughes that he knew the difficulty of the task but hoped he might "maintain the policies that you formulated and put into operation there." Perhaps more to the point, he confessed to his mother that the tide had set in strongly against previously unquestioned foreign rights and "we must accommodate to the new situation." Pessimistically, he concluded that "China is not now a field in which one can hope to achieve any positive results. . . . It is a man's job, which even if done manfully will have all the appearance of failure, but which has to be done."[20]

Suitably forewarned, MacMurray went out to China in the summer of 1925 to begin what proved to be five eventful years. Upon arrival he was quick to convey his impression to Kellogg. He noted that Chinese feelings, primarily racial, secondarily national, were greatly aroused, but he believed them fundamentally Chinese and not Bolshevist-inspired. Chinese leaders, smarting under an "inferiority complex," revolted against the "overbearing attitude of the white man toward the Chinese" and lashed out at the treaties. MacMurray concluded that hostility reflected not so much a dissatisfaction with the treaties as with the feeling that they symbolized inferiority for China. He called for consideration of Chinese proposals "on a psychological basis rather than from the standpoint of strict logic or of systematic political concept," but he advised against concessions.[21]

Strong domestic pressure, however, made Kellogg more sympathetic to Chinese aspirations.[22] He informed President Coolidge that "we shall have to give up those rights sooner or later"; it is now time to "help China . . . to aid her in the accomplishment of her aspirations." Although he was willing to take steps leading to tariff autonomy, Kellogg did question the advisability of giving up extraterritoriality without further study. Senator William E. Borah, who pressed for the United States to voluntarily surrender her treaty rights in China, charged that "there is no place where the blood of helpless children is so coined into dollars and cents as in China." The leader of many popular movements in the 1920's, the "lion of Idaho," found support both in Congress and the public at large to influence the Coolidge administration.[23]

The points at issue between Kellogg and MacMurray were clearly and precisely drawn. One of MacMurray's major tasks in China was to prepare for the often-postponed special tariff and extraterritorial conferences provided by the Washington Conference treaties. MacMurray, however, did not want to discuss tariff autonomy without some *quid pro quo* from the Chinese; he therefore favored holding China to the Washington Conference position and, if she upheld her obligations, allowing further advantages. Kellogg meanwhile announced that the United States government would consider comprehensive revision of the tariff but awaited further investigations and Chinese reforms before similar revision of extraterritorial rights. MacMurray soon was arguing from Peking that concessions to the government would help consolidate its power and discourage more liberal elements.[24] Despite this advice the Minister and his colleague for the forthcoming tariff conference, Silas Strawn (who also served as a delegate to the extraterritorial conference), received instructions to include proposals looking to "ultimate tariff autonomy." Differing openly with MacMurray, Kellogg wrote: "It has been my idea from the beginning that within the near future we would have to release China from its conventional tariffs and give up extraterritoriality."[25]

The Peking government worked assiduously for tariff autonomy at the conference of 1925, but MacMurray insisted, and here he found support from Strawn, that the Chinese abolish an internal tax (*likin*) as a condition. More important, he announced that the United States government could agree to nothing beyond a higher tariff as envisioned by the Washington treaties.[26] The American delegation reported to Kellogg that the abolition of *likin* was essential and that if "China should really be determined upon repudiating treaty obligations we should not acquiesce but should allow the entire responsibility for such action to rest clearly upon China." MacMurray also wrote to his mother: "I do not flatter myself that any of us will reap much glory from the business; it is a tragic comedy."[27] Neither of the conferences in Peking succeeded in its purpose, and both problems—tariff and extraterritoriality—remained to plague relations between China and America, and between MacMurray and Kellogg, in the years that followed.

Shortly after his arrival, MacMurray was struck with the lack of respect shown foreign powers by the new forces in China. He wrote the Assistant Secretary of State Nelson Johnson, that China had changed: "I deceived myself [while Chief of the Division], going on thinking under the illusion that China was the same last May as it was in 1918." It was an "unreal world," as he confessed, "I set no show by my own knowledge or wisdom; my seven months as Minister have been mostly spent in unlearning whatever ideas I had formed as counselor in days gone by." With some bitterness he concluded that China "thanks us for nothing"; the government wants a return to the days of the Manchus who "insisted that foreign envoys should knock their heads on the ground in deference to the celestial kingdom." Later he expressed continued amazement adding that the situation was going "beyond Alice-in-Wonderland into sheer insanity. . . . What is going to come of all of it, I can't guess. I do not pretend to see so much as forty-eight hours into the future."[28]

The first serious confrontation with the Chinese came with the Taku Incident of March 1926. When Chinese forces involved in civil war fired on foreign ships, MacMurray promptly called for a reassertion of treaty rights since both sides had violated the Boxer Protocol of 1901 guaranteeing foreigners free access to Peking from the sea. Acting Secretary Grew approved MacMurray's request to take a strong stand, and as in days gone by, the envoys ordered a joint naval demonstration and ultimatum to both sides. Grew immediately came under fire: first, from American missionary representatives who were against such actions; and second, from Kellogg, who thought Grew had "declared war on China." Both Grew and Kellogg expressed relief when the Chinese met the demands and opened the river channel without hostilities.[29] But in the course of student demonstrations in Peking against capitulation to the Protocol powers, the Chinese police killed forty demonstrators and wounded eighty more, an event not lost upon American critics of traditional policies. Annoyed at Washington's faint-heartedness, MacMurray later wrote, "I have never doubted, at the time or since, that . . . the best means of protecting American (and other foreign) interests was the use of potential force." Shortly thereafter, however, he decided not to make a visit to southern China on an American naval vessel lest the Chinese, like the editors of *The Nation*, call him "America's gunboat minister."[30]

As Minister—without gunboat—MacMurray recognized the weakness of the Peking central government and questioned the advisability of continued recognition unless it fulfilled international obligations and gathered greater internal support.[31] When the competing Canton government attempted to collect taxes from the British and other foreigners, however, MacMurray protested. Such a step, he warned, signalled the destruction of the treaty system; he called for resistance, even "by means of a naval blockade, or of some feasible measure of force similar to that."[32] When Peking unilaterally repudiated the treaty of extraterritoriality with the Belgians, he predicted that China would find some excuse to void the similar American treaty due to expire in 1934, even if the United States made concessions beyond those contemplated at the Washington Conference. Unless the Chinese were pressured, he predicted a "new war in a not very distant future in the Far East."[33]

MacMurray believed that the Canton government, whose actions emboldened the Peking regime, was testing Western powers, thus threatening to provoke the same conditions that had led to the unequal treaties almost a century before. If this happened, he reasoned, "Western pressure will force new conflicts and once more begin the old cycle: hostilities over a long period, subjugation, and special conditions for intercourse imposed."[34] The Minister believed that the United States bore the "responsibility for effort directed toward saving the Chinese from their own folly." Giving in to

Chinese demands would help no one except those persons desiring funds to carry on the civil war. Aware that the Chinese wanted to end the "stigma of racial inferiority," he argued that intelligent Chinese would not abrogate the treaties if only the powers would "save China's face by . . . some apparent renunciation of their special treaty rights."[35]

During these first months back in China, MacMurray learned to his disgust that even the British, the Imperial rulers of the nineteenth century, no longer respected the ancient diplomatic rules toward China. He hoped that the appointment of his old friend Sir Miles Lampson as Ambassador to China would make it possible to "salvage something from the catastrophe," but he was disappointed.[36] The British "Christmas present" of December 1926, written without consulting the British Ambassador, appeared to MacMurray to condone "all but the graver contraventions of treaty rights." He construed the "ill-judged" British proposal as a "somewhat blundering assertion of their leadership" in a situation where no one else appeared willing to act. Still, there was another alternative to renunciation of the treaties by the powers or by China: "Orderly negotiation . . . with insistence upon full respect for existing obligations." Gloomily predicting that British actions "will compel us whether we like it or not to offer the same concessions on our part," he wrote Strawn that American rights would now be "treated with contempt."[37]

The British surrender greatly aggravated the sense of frustration MacMurray derived from his uncertainty as to Kellogg's views (indeed he suspected that Hughes' successor was as soft as the British). In a letter of December 30, 1926, he asked Kellogg about the "lack of mutual understanding as to the purpose which it is my duty to serve under your direction. I do not feel that I have made clear to you the facts of the situation that day by day confronts us here, and I infer from your instructions that you find my various recommendations and suggestions unresponsive to your desires." He asked to come to Washington for consultation and got as far as Japan in January 1927 when events in China forced Kellogg to ask him to return to his post.[38]

Kellogg indeed had a problem and MacMurray had little sympathy with it. Congressman Stephen G. Porter's resolution proposing that the United States give up extraterritoriality reflected growing domestic pressure in early 1927 for improved relations with China. The Secretary cabled MacMurray that he intended to respond. On January 27, 1927, Kellogg announced that the United States government, either in tandem with the powers or alone, would negotiate with China on questions of tariff autonomy and extraterritoriality.[39] MacMurray complained that "carefully handpicked witnesses" had testified "half-truths or bunkum" in behalf of the Porter resolution, and its passage would only "embarrass us" in any dealings with the Chinese. He had it from a direct and authoritive source that Grover Clark, editor of the *Peking Leader*, had written the resolution "practically letter for letter" although the influence behind it was undoubtedly Ambassador Sao-ke Alfred Sze. It would embitter relations that were now "merely unsatisfactory" and expose the "skeleton in our closet in the form of an issue as to the Chinese exclusion laws."[40] The resolution passed the House 262-43 despite MacMurray's fulmination, but to his relief it died in the Senate Foreign Relations Committee.

By early 1927 MacMurray's temper was thoroughly aroused. Denied the opportunity to return home or to preview Kellogg's announcement (although he could not have been too surprised), MacMurray unloaded his frustrations in a fifteen-page letter to Under Secretary Grew. Americans, so his theory ran, were facing a "grave emergency affecting our rights and position in the Far East not only in the present but for an indefinite future." It was a new China, "absolutely incomprehensible to those who have not known it," with strong manifestations of Chinese ethnic superiority. In this difficult situation the "Department has let me down," and MacMurray proceeded to list seven examples, including the Taku Incident and Canton customs dispute, in which he felt that Washington had made a "mug of its Minister" (the words of the British chargé). He realized that different conditions existed but insisted that the principles of American policy remained; what was needed were slight alterations to make those principles applicable to the new situation. He charged that the Department directed its China policy with a "hestitating and unsteady hand." Could not the Department, he asked, take a stand against

sentimentalists who conceive that the responsibilities of our government are towards the Chinese rather than towards our own people, and who would wish to have our Government give away our whole stake in China and play the role of an international St. Francis in the hope that the Wolf of Gubbio would be so moved by our spirit of renunciation that it would shake hands with us and join in praises to the Lord? Alas, it's not that kind of a wolf; and I hope I am not doing an injustice to the American people when I predict that if the wolf really gets ugly we are likely to forget that we are cast for the role of St. Francis and go in for something more in the line of St. George.[41]

MacMurray spoke out against policies of "renunciation, pacifism, and of defeatism" and the independent, isolationistic nature of American policy. He would only bring himself to adopt a pro-Chinese stance when he was convinced that it was in the American interest and would secure a favored position for the United States. "Without meaning to be cynical," he wrote, "I do not think that it is in human nature for an aggregate of people to feel any real or permanent gratitude for favors done them." The Chinese refused to acknowledge that anything but "the genius of the Chinese race" had saved them from partition, rescued them from Japan, or given them back Shantung; again he stressed that the movement was not so much a national as a "racial upheaval." China did not respect the United States since America usually let others "do the dirty work ... [and] invariably played the jackal, feeding where more courageous animals had killed." MacMurray found his position "uncomfortable and sometimes even humiliating." He asked if he should make way for someone else. Grew replied carefully that the administration had confidence in him, but added that assessments "of public opinion ... must be taken into consideration."[42]

In an even more candid letter to Consul Willys Peck, written the same day, MacMurray complained that the "tutelage of the Department" had become "oppressive and stultifying." He pleaded for more backbone in American policy toward the Chinese and for more honesty in gauging American interests and actions in China. Complaining that he had gone sour, he nevertheless suggested that the United States "keep the flag flying," even though the government had "abandoned or actively repudiated" all it stood for. He stated that when he had been Chief of the Division he had "never hauled down the flag. And now our flag is never up." What was the cause and who was responsible? "I am ashamed—almost day by day ashamed—of what I gather my Government wants of me."[43]

IV

At the very time MacMurray and Secretary Kellogg were so much in disagreement, the so-called Nanking Incident of March 1927 precipitated the largest crisis in American-Chinese relations during the 1920's. Nationalist troops entered the city on March 24 and one American and five Europeans were killed in the pillaging and plundering that followed. British and American naval vessels moving up the river shelled the Chinese when they attempted to surround the Standard Oil compound where foreigners had taken refuge.

MacMurray advised strong and immediate action but found that no one agreed. He called for withdrawal of American citizens from China and a blockade of Chinese ports.[44] Coolidge pointed out, however, somewhat inaccurately, that there were already 13,200 American military men in China to protect 14,038 American citizens, implying that the United States need not take stronger actions nor make demands.[45] Kellogg was certainly not receptive to British demands for joint sanctions, envisioning a use of force which "would never be countenanced in this country." The British proposal was one of MacMurray's last attempts to foster a cooperative, forceful policy; it failed, and each nation negotiated separately. MacMurray observed that the Nationalists, despite their disclaimers, were clearly responsible for this "systemized plan to drive us out of Nanking." He had protested but to no avail and concluded that the "time will come when they will either fire me or force me to resign."[46]

MacMurray found himself isolated as rumors of his resignation began to circulate.[47] He crustily pointed out that the Chinese were seeking closer relations with United States "not in order to grasp an outstretched hand but to spit in our faces." He continued to express the belief that force "is, I fear, the only sedative that can calm the hysteria which again and again throughout their history has been produced by a sense of wounded vanity—loss of face—inferiority complex." Washington indicated that it was not only uninterested in pressing the Nationalists but was working on a new treaty that would abolish most American rights.[48]

The Nanking Incident deeply rankled MacMurray. He viewed with discouragement how American public opinion had "satisfied itself that the label 'Nationalist' was an accurate description of what was inside the bottle, and assume it to be a good omen"; a year prior he had concluded it was a "crisis of racial emotionalism, converted by artificial means into a spurious nationalism."[49] That same public opinion seemed to believe that the "four-hundred millions of Chinese would be a different people day after tomorrow if we could only get across to them how much we love them."[50]

On March 30, 1928, MacMurray concluded a settlement of the Nanking Incident with the Nationalists that involved compensation for damages and expression of regret.[51] Perhaps to smooth MacMurray's still-ruffled feelings, Hornbeck sent MacMurray a letter from "a man well up on Far Eastern affairs" (Hughes?) who congratulated Hornbeck and MacMurray on their settlement. He called it "the best piece of diplomatic work since the Boxer treaties, perhaps in all American intercourse with China. It is a genuine triumph of intelligent, sane statesmanship." Unaccustomed to such praise, Hornbeck told MacMurray: "I think he is right. . . . In achieving this agreement you gave a great exhibition of diplomatic skill and scored heavily." The Chief of the Far Eastern Division also later wrote that the Nanking Incident had taken a great deal of public opinion pressure off the Department to do something for China.[52]

Even the negotiations over tariffs which MacMurray conducted and concluded at the behest of Kellogg did not bring about a rapprochement between the two men. The Secretary had written Senator Borah in mid-1928 that "very confidentially my plan is to make a simple tariff treaty renouncing tariff control" and providing for non-discrimination against the United States. He reserved judgment on the abolition of extraterritoriality. Shortly thereafter MacMurray signed a tariff treaty with the Nationalist government allowing tariff autonomy in return for a most-favored-nation status.[53] Done with speed and some secrecy, the treaty, which did not mention *likin,* was the culmination of Kellogg's efforts to revise the tariff in line with Chinese aspirations. In signing the agreement, however, MacMurray had acted independently and had not informed his diplomatic colleagues in Peking; he was, as he put it, "extremely economical with the truth." Thus, even in this negotiation MacMurray found himself in difficulty with Kellogg who expressed displeasure at MacMurray's methods after the signing of the treaty. Hornbeck advised: "I suggest that, whenever possible, you await, where matters of large policy are concerned, a final indication of the Secretary's desires." The irrepressible Minister complained to a fellow officer of "an exceedingly sharp rap on the knuckles" from the Secretary and in a candid letter to Hornbeck said the Chinese were trying to make an "utter fool" of the Secretary. "Again," he wrote, "a case of failure to realize that the man who is doing the fishing will catch more fish and break fewer lines and nets if the owner at home lets him watch the current and does not try from afar to tell him how the fishing ought to be done." The "greatest" Secretary in recent years, Charles Evans Hughes, had depended a great deal on the legation, and Kellogg should do the same.[54]

Such were MacMurray's bouts with the Kellogg administration of the Department of State. There had been, moreover, some close run-ins with Hornbeck as well as arguments with journalists, on and off the scene, such as Thomas Millard, J.B. Powell, and Walter Lippmann. MacMurray wrote the latter that he had a distaste for popular journalism that attempted to make it appear that "we alone are righteous if not indeed goody-goody, and that everything good that foreigners have done in China was done because we shamed others into doing it." He criticized the many Americans who swallowed this line in the belief that if America advertised herself as having a "monopoly of virtue" the Chinese would then feel a special affection for the United States. The Chinese, however, "whatever their other faults and virtues . . . are pretty shrewd judges of human nature and are not all deceived by our readiness to deceive ourselves.[55]

MacMurray hoped the change of administrations in Washington at the end of 1928 (Coolidge-Kellogg to Hoover-Stimson) would bring changes in China policy. He felt that the previous "four years of subservience to the idea of a possible China which is wholly incompatible with the actual China" had failed, but he supposed that "idealism, even of Mr. Kellogg's marked-down-to-39¢ variety, doubtless has its value."[56] He advised the new Secretary early in 1929 that the Chinese intended to force the extraterritorial issue and called for cooperative opposition from the powers; this, of course, would mean a return to the policies of the Hughes era. Meanwhile, Stimson asked for the Minister's opinions in detail.[57] Eager for the chance to place his views before the new Secretary, MacMurray argued that China had "evaded, ignored, or repudiated" her obligations assumed at the Washington Conference; the fault lay with China and not the treaty powers. He believed that a possible Chinese abrogation of extraterritoriality was "so vital an emergency" that the United States, despite domestic opinion, should take a stand. He concluded that it was possible for the United States to stand or give in, "but it would be deceiving ourselves to assume that we would gain any assurance of better treatment for American citizens . . . by giving up any right."[58]

MacMurray's position and tenure in China, however, remained uncertain, and in late 1929 he finally decided to resign, to head the new Page School of International Relations at Johns Hopkins University. He claimed that the tone of Department communications had become "brusque and fault finding . . . to haze me," that someone wanted his job and was attempting to hasten the "funeral." His stand on extraterritoriality, he felt, had not found acceptance in the Department; he could not continue without a "head-on collision" on extraterritoriality. He therefore acted to "get my hand car off the track before the train came by" in order to "relax from the strain of indecision and the feeling of purposelessness."[59]

V

After retirement MacMurray was careful to make few public pronouncements on China since he did not want to embarrass his successor. "I am conscious of sufficient difference between Nelson T. Johnson's and my own reactions to present developments in the matter of extraterritoriality."[60] Johnson's influence on Kellogg had been considerable, and he had taken a different view of the Chinese situation than had MacMurray. As a recent writer has neatly pointed out, while both Johnson and MacMurray respected the Washington Conference agreements, "MacMurray viewed them in terms of obligations on the part of the Chinese while Johnson viewed them in terms of commitments by the powers."[61]

The Japanese invasion of Manchuria upset the equilibrium in the Far East, but even this, MacMurray argued, resulted from "China's reckless and irresponsible attitude toward her treaty obligations."[62] "Anomalous and one-sided" though the treaties were, he could not persuade himself that they were either "harsh or unreasonable." He still held that the capitulation of the powers to China in the late 1920's was a mistake; it was not too late, even in 1932-1933, to fall back and work out a Far Eastern settlement within the "framework" of the Washington treaties. He wrote Hornbeck that he was not as critical of the Japanese measures taken to defend their "nationals and vested interests" as others. The Japanese unfortunately then stepped beyond purely defensive measures.[63]

MacMurray again spoke officially about China policy and general Far Eastern policy in the mid-1930's. He had returned to the Foreign Service as Minister to Estonia, Latvia, and Lithuania in 1933 (he was later to serve as Ambassador to Turkey from 1936-1942). In the summer of 1935 Hornbeck asked his advice on the Far East. The result was MacMurray's important memorandum on "Developments Affecting American Policy in the Far

East."[64] He pointed out that the policy of cooperation had lapsed from 1925 to 1929 and that the United States now had to adapt itself to the new situation created as a result. The United States, he believed, had sought nothing but an equal chance in the China market, "but our claim to it was one of vital principle, justifying abnormal efforts and sacrifices." The Nine Power Treaty of 1922 had not committed the government to a defense of Chinese rights and interests, and the United States had acted out of "enlightened self-interest. . . . Only disillusionment could come out of an assumption of more altruistic motives."

Japan, until 1931, was "scrupulously loyal in its adherence to the letter and spirit of the Washington Conference." But the Nationalists, advised by the Bolshevists, had abandoned attempts to win support from the Western nations by new concessions and embarked on a campaign of anti-imperialism and abolition of unequal treaties; they thus "nullified and proclaimed their disdain" for the Washington settlement and "frustrated the genuinely earnest and loyal efforts of the powers" to bring about peaceful evolution from the unequal treaties. The British also had refused to cooperate and acted "rather *de haut en bas.*"

Public opinion in the United States naively and romantically supported the Nationalists; the Porter resolution of 1927 had "put the government on the defensive for not having done more instead of getting credit for its liberal policies." Both the British Christmas note of 1926 and Kellogg's announcement of 1927 encouraged the Chinese mood of irresponsibility and violence. American handling of the Nanking Incident of 1927 did "more credit to the benevolence of our intention than to the realism of our understanding of the situation and of Chinese psychology."

When the Japanese opposed Chinese demands, MacMurray continued, the State Department became partisan against Japan, as did public opinion. By 1929 Japan "could have carried away no impression but that we Americans were pro-Chinese." Japan had tried for years to preserve the Washington Conference policy of cooperation, but that policy was "wounded in the house of its friends and scorned by the Chinese," so Japan decided "it could depend only on its own strong arm to vindicate its rightful legal position in Eastern Asia." The Chinese in Manchuria, "in effect, had asked for it" by their scorn of obligations and had brought on the catastrophe. China, he advised, could win against Japan only in the long run; she could not help herself and no other nation would undertake the burden. The major danger was that Japan might overreach herself and bring on a serious conflict.

MacMurray prophetically cited the United States' alternatives in 1935: (1) to actively oppose Japan, (2) to acquiesce or even participate with the Japanese, or (3) to take a passive attitude. The first would mean war and "nobody except Russia would gain from our victory in such a war." Indeed the avoidance of a war with Japan must be a "major objective" of American policy. Any large opposition to Japanese policies might "lead them to make even a desperate attack" which could "force us into a war we do not want." MacMurray believed the third alternative was the most feasible—to maintain American principles "even though we do not find it prudent to go crusading in furtherance of them." He found no reason for the United States to make herself a leader of "any forlorn hope for the purpose of vindicating them in the Far East." The United States had no mission to undertake any duties or responsibilities in behalf of China, for China had become an "almost negligible factor" while Japan had become of "paramount importance."

"It is," MacMurray observed, "plain common sense to stop rowing when a falling tide has grounded our boat in the shallows." American policy should "minimize our involvements and liabilities," reduce land and sea forces overseas, and look at Japan with an open mind. There should be no abandonment of American principles, however, for there was no reason "the Decalogue should be repealed because there is a crime wave." Now was the time to husband American strength, to write down American interests in China to their present "depreciated value," to deal with Japan fairly and sympathetically, to be guided by the national interest, and not to wander into false trails whether pro- or anti-Chinese, or pro- or anti-Japanese.

Clearly, MacMurray had not altered his basic diplomatic creed nor his criticism of America's "soft-line" toward China in the 1920's. In outlining a future approach to Far Eastern issues, the dispossessed mandarin deviated probably less than he imagined from the Roosevelt administration's policies.

Notes

1 John V.A. MacMurray. *Treaties and Agreements with and Concerning China, 1894-1919* (New York: Oxford University, 1921), vols. 1 and 2.
2 The foregoing paragraphs are based on the papers of John V.A. MacMurray deposited at Princeton University. Cited hereafter as MacMurray Papers.
3 *Ibid.*, MacMurray to Ernest Price, January 26, 1925.
4 *Ibid.*, MacMurray to Joseph C. Grew, February 12, 1927; MacMurray to Frank J. Goodnow, October 1, 1929.
5 *Ibid.*, MacMurray to Hornbeck, February 2, 1928; Hornbeck's tactful reply made no mention of following MacMurray's rules. Hornbeck to MacMurray, April 4, 1928, Hornbeck Papers (Stanford University, Hoover Institution on War, Revolution, and Peace).
6 United States Department of State, *Papers Relating to the Foreign Relations of the United States, 1900* (Washington, D.C.: Government Printing Office, 1902), p. 299.
7 Memorandum by MacMurray to Hughes, "Self-Constituted Constitutional Government of China at Canton," September 28, 1921, United States Department of State Files 893.00/4080 (National Archives, Washington,

D.C.). Cited hereafter as DSF; MacMurray to Grew, October 9, 1924, DSF 893.458/14; MacMurray to Hughes, April 1, 1922, DSF 893.00/4710; MacMurray to Frederick A. Sterling, November 6, 1924, MacMurray Papers.

8 MacMurray to Nelson T. Johnson, October 19, 1923, Nelson T. Johnson Papers (Library of Congress, Manuscripts Division, Washington, D.C.). Cited hereafter as Johnson Papers. MacMurray to Hughes, November 19, 1923; DSF 893.000/5286; MacMurray to Sterling, November 6, 1924, MacMurray Papers; *Ibid.*, MacMurray to E.T. Williams, February 2, 1924.

9 Telegram from MacMurray to Robert Lansing, August 6, 1918, DSF 893.51/1951; MacMurray to Hughes, November 17, 1922, DSF 893.51/4085/2.

10 MacMurray to Hughes, April 3, 1922, DSF 893.51/3777.

11 MacMurray to Hughes, June 15, 1923, DSF 393.1123 Lincheng/153; Hughes to George B. Lockwood, August 2, 1923, DSF 711.94/457; MacMurray to Roger S. Greene, February 4, 1924, MacMurray Papers; United States Department of State, *Papers Relating to the Foreign Relations of the United States, 1924* (Washington, D.C.: Government Printing Office, 1939), 1:602.

12 United States Department of State, *Papers Relating to the Foreign Relations of the United States, 1914* (Washington, D.C.: Government Printing Office, 1923), supplement, pp. 161-162.

13 *Ibid.*, pp. 186, 190.

14 Schurman to Hughes, December 13, 1922, DSF 393.1123 Coltman, Chas/2; MacMurray to Phillips, December 19, 1922, DSF 393.1123 Coltman, Chas/2; Hughes to Schurman, December 20, 1922, DSF 393.1123 Coltman, Chas/3; Hughes to Schurman, April 17, 1923, DSF 393.1123 Coltman, Chas/76.

15 MacMurray to Hughes April 20, 1923, Hughes to Schurman, April 26, 1923 DSF 393.1123 Coltman, Chas/77; Solicitor Metzer to Hughes, August 28, 1923, DSF 393.1123 Coltman, Chas/91.

16 *New York Times,* November 19, 1924.

17 Hughes to John W. Latané, December 6, 1924, Charles Evans Hughes Papers (Library of Congress, Manuscripts Division, Washington, D.C.).

18 Willys Peck to MacMurray, November 21, 1924, Ferdinand Meyer to MacMurray, December 20, 1924, MacMurray Papers.

19 *Ibid.*, MacMurray to Willys Peck, January 29, 1925; MacMurray to Ray Atherton, March 17, 1925.

20 *Ibid.*, MacMurray to Hughes, April 13, 1925 (William S. Culberson was the other leading candidate for the position); MacMurray to his mother, April 4, 1925.

21 MacMurray to Kellogg, July 28, 1925, DSF 893.00/6453.

22 See Robert H. Ferrell, *Frank B. Kellogg and Henry L. Stimson* (New York: Cooper Square Publisher, 1963).

23 Kellogg to Coolidge, June 26, 1925, Kellogg Papers (Minnesota Historical Society); Borah statement, June 10, 1925, Borah Papers (Library of Congress, Manuscripts Division); Kellogg to Henry P. Fletcher, July 22, 1925, Kellogg Papers.

24 United States Department of State, *Papers Relating to the Foreign Relations of the United States, 1925* (Washington, D.C.: Government Printing Office, 1940), 1:808. Cited hereafter as *FRUS, 1925,* vol. 1; Department of State to MacMurray, September 2, 1925, DSF

793.00/163A, Kellogg's offer was made in a speech to the American Bar Association; *FRUS, 1925*, 1:738.

25 *Ibid.*, 842.

26 *Minutes of the Special Conference on the Chinese Customs Tariff* (Peking, 1928), pp. 94-96, 169.

27 American delegation to Kellogg, November 17, 1925, DSF 500A4e/465; MacMurray to his mother, November 25, 1925, MacMurray Papers.

28 MacMurray to Johnson, November 13, 1925; MacMurray to his mother, February 21, 1926 and April 11, 1926, MacMurray Papers.

29 *Ibid.*, Grew to MacMurray, March 23, 1926.

30 *Ibid.*, MacMurray to Hornbeck, February 2, 1928; MacMurray to Admiral C.S. Williams, July 30, 1926.

31 United States Department of State, *Papers Relating to the Foreign Relations of the United States, 1926* (Washington, D.C.: Government Printing Office, 1941), 1:671. Cited hereafter as *FRUS, 1926*, vol. 1.

32 *Ibid.*, 868.

33 *Ibid.*, 997.

34 *Ibid.*, 899.

35 *Ibid.*, 999.

36 MacMurray to Ray Atherton, November 30, 1926, MacMurray Papers.

37 *FRUS, 1926*, 1:919-921; MacMurray to Silas Strawn, December 23, 1926, MacMurray Papers.

38 *Ibid.*, MacMurray to Kellogg, December 30, 1926.

39 Ferrell, *Kellogg and Stimson*, pp. 73-74.

40 MacMurray to Willys R. Peck, March 11, 1927, MacMurray Papers.

41 *Ibid.*, MacMurray to Grew, February 12, 1927.

42 *Ibid.*, Grew to MacMurray, May 31, 1927.

43 *Ibid.*, MacMurray to Willys R. Peck, February 12, 1927.

44 United States Department of State, *Papers Relating to the Foreign Relations of the United States, 1927* (Washington, D.C.: Government Printing Office, 1942), 2:166-167; see also Dorothy Borg, *American Policy and the Chinese Revolution, 1926-1928* (New York: American Institute of Pacific Relations, 1947). Cited hereafter as Borg, *American Policy*.

45 Ferrell, *Kellogg and Stimson*, p. 70.

46 Kellogg to British Ambassador, May 2, 1927, Kellogg Papers; MacMurray to his mother, April 24, 1927, MacMurray Papers.

47 *New York Times*, May 3, 1927.

48 MacMurray to Russell T. Mount, June 21, 1927; MacMurray to his mother, July 2, 1927; Johnson to MacMurray, September 29, 1927, MacMurray Papers.

49 *Ibid.*, MacMurray to Sir Francis Aglen, January 11, 1928; MacMurray to Robert F. Fitch, January 29, 1927.

50 *Ibid.*, MacMurray to George T. Pettengill, January 27, 1928.

51 Borg, *American Policy*, pp. 382-384.

52 Hornbeck to MacMurray, June 6, 1928; Hornbeck to MacMurray, July 3, 1928, Hornbeck Papers.

53 Kellogg to Borah, July 16, 1928, Borah Papers.

54 MacMurray to Hornbeck, November 15, 1928; Hornbeck to MacMurray, July 31, 1928; MacMurray to Hornbeck, August 8, 1928, Hornbeck Papers.

55 MacMurray to Walter Lippmann, December 18, 1928, MacMurray Papers.

56 *Ibid.*, MacMurray to Ferdinand Mayer, March 20, 1929.
57 United States Department of State, *Papers Relating to the Foreign Relations of the United States, 1929* (Washington, D.C.: Government Printing Office, 1943), 2:578, 582.
58 *Ibid.*, 585-590.
59 MacMurray to Ferdinand L. Mayer, October 21, 1929, MacMurray Papers.
60 *Ibid.*, MacMurray to William Cullen Dennis, March 31, 1930.
61 Russell D. Buhite, *Nelson T. Johnson and American Policy Toward China, 1925-1941* (East Lansing: Michigan State University Press, 1969), p. 24.
62 John V.A. MacMurray, "Manchurian Diplomacy as an Asiatic Problem," *Yale Review*, 23(September, 1933):66-77.
63 Speech by MacMurray, "The Treaty Situation in the Far East," April 27, 1932, MacMurray Papers; MacMurray to Hornbeck, December 1, 1932, Hornbeck Papers.
64 Memorandum by MacMurray, November 1935, MacMurray Papers.

Gary Ross

W. Cameron Forbes

The Diplomacy of a Darwinist

IF THE ANNALS OF American diplomacy rarely mention the name W. Cameron Forbes, it is because the calamitous times during which he served seemed to depersonalize and eclipse the subordinate official. Forbes' tenure as Ambassador to Tokyo, from 1930 to 1932, coincided with the militarists' seizure of control over Japan's foreign policy evidenced by the army's aggressive expansion and consolidation of Nippon's interests in Manchuria and Northern China.[1] Although he found Japan's new direction distasteful, Forbes soon found himself in heated disagreement with his chief, Secretary of State Henry L. Stimson, over America's critical response.

To Forbes, who avowedly ascribed to Darwinist principles, Japanese international behavior might be deplorable and even immoral, but the historical fact remained that dynamic nations grew at the expense of the weaker ones. Stimson, in gravitating toward a "get tough" policy, grew extremely annoyed with his Ambassador's incessant appeals for a "hands off" attitude. The Secretary failed completely, however, to grasp Forbes' point: if you are going to act tough, you must be prepared to back up your threats with military force. United States' indulgence in verbal recriminations and threatening grimaces, Forbes argued, would only exacerbate future political tensions in the western Pacific.

The dramatic thrust of Japan's ultranationalists had caught both Washington and, apparently, Tokyo by surprise. Whatever rationalization these alarmed officials might produce, this aggressive action challenged those instruments of peace which embodied the hopes of internationalists during the 1920's. Japan had forceably laid claim to the economic wealth of Manchuria and Northern China in violation of the Washington treaties of

1922 and the Kellogg-Briand Pact of 1928; by default or otherwise, the principles of the Open Door and the "outlawry of war" became obsolete.

In these circumstances, Forbes tried unsuccessfully to influence the new direction of Japanese-American policy. Not only were the subtlety and realism of his approach unappreciated at that time, but historians have subsequently dismissed his behavior as unimaginative and unimportant. In either instance, Forbes was probably not surprised; he had considered himself inadequately prepared to be a diplomat in the first place.

I

If overriding events obscured Forbes the Ambassador, so did his close identification with the Philippine Islands in the mind of the general public. Indeed, it is no exaggeration to regard the Filipino's welfare as Forbes' lifetime preoccupation. Born in 1870, well educated at Milton and Harvard, Forbes entered the world of business and finance at age 24 and climbed steadily to a position of control over such prestigious enterprises as Stone and Webster, United Fruit, and the American Telephone and Telegraph Company. His search for action not satisfied by football, yachting, and polo, Forbes entered public service at Theodore Roosevelt's invitation in 1905. From that moment, he attached his name indelibly to the history of the Philippines, first as Commissioner of Commerce and Police in the Islands, then as Governor-General under President Taft, and finally as collaborator with Major General Leonard Wood in the investigation of the Filipinos' request for independence. Throughout his long retirement at Naushon Island off Cape Cod, Forbes unremittingly advised a succession of Presidents on the double dangers of statehood and independence for the Philippines.[2]

In 1930, however, just prior to his retirement, Forbes reluctantly accepted the invitation from President Hoover to serve as Ambassador to Japan. To that position he brought a combination of attitudes which largely determined the degree of his success as America's representative.

A strong distaste for the Tokyo assignment—a lack of *esprit*—figured high among Forbes' predispositions. His correspondence in 1930 is replete with misgivings about the new responsibilities. He despaired at the "unwonted and unwanted" duties before him, lamented the "exile at hard labor" to which he was "sentenced," and secretly wished the Senate of the United States would refuse to confirm his nomination. These reservations about the job did not abate even after Forbes took charge at the embassy. He continued to express his discontent, sometimes privately to close friends, sometimes publicly to the Japanese people, as was the case on February 12, 1932, when he said "it is my hope and expectation that when I relinquish this position I shall have permanently left the Government service."[3]

Behind these disclaimers lay considerations of personal health, finances, and qualifications—Forbes insisted that he lacked the training and experience commensurate with ambassadorial duty. As Ambassador, he consistently refused the title of "diplomat," for he conceived of public service in behalf of the government as being incompatible with his self-image as a decision-maker and man of business. Such a designation, he maintained, implied a "more abject form of slavery than that from which our black brethren were freed at the time of the Civil War." He often contrasted his plight with the more favored position of policy-makers in Washington, but Forbes found his relations with officials at the post equally disturbing:

I am out here in Japan very much like a fish out of water. The real work of the Embassy has to be done by trained men. Things are constantly coming up for decision which I should normally feel competent to decide, but [which] I must not decide contrary to precedent; and so I call in the trained counselor and secretaries for consultation and find out how similar problems have been met in the past. I often find that things have to be done differently from what I should have done were I starting off anew.[4]

Fish out of water, perhaps! But what bothered Forbes more, in his own words, was that "I don't even know how to *drink* like a fish." Indeed, the role of social functionary was as foreign to Forbes in inclination as that of diplomat was in training. He lamented he had no wife "to lap up" the pomp and circumstances of his ceremonial position, and he compared himself to a non-smoking governor over tobacco-rich terrains. To his cousin J. Murray Forbes he pined for the day when he could soak his ambassadorial toga in kerosene and ignite it in public view, so repugnant was the life associated with "silk hats, cutaways and spats, frock coats and white gloves."[5]

For ostentation Forbes substituted a strong practical bent, and this attribute influenced his conduct in Japan as surely as his dissatisfaction with the assignment. A carpenter by avocation, Forbes confronted untoward circumstances—like the misplanned embassy in which he resided—with humble skills. He had little respect for esoteric theorems, like those of his maternal grandparent, the transcendentalist Ralph Waldo Emerson. Indeed, when asked about his relationship to Emerson, Forbes denied all resemblance in matters of scholarly power. "I have my line in material affairs," he said on one occasion, and he underscored this character trait by chiding academic institutions in Japan for neglecting the *application* of theoretical science to practical conditions. "A few years of further experience," he predicted, "are apt to give them [the Japanese] the degree of ballast that comes from having tried their theories out in practice and having found that some of them work and some do not."[6]

This innate practicality blocked the inroads of religion as well as secular philosophy. On more than one occasion Forbes belittled the church as irrelevant to his needs. In reply to Senator David I. Walsh, who remarked to him about the lack of religious feeling in the United States, Forbes observed that this trend should be reversed, but he quickly excepted himself from the matter. "As in the case of prohibition," he said, "I believe thoroughly in it for others but do not practice it myself."[7]

No myth of human brotherhood could delude a man of such temperament, and an unpleasant incident in Forbes' memory served only to reinforce his poor opinion of mankind. That incident was his summary removal from the governor-generalship of the Philippines by Woodrow Wilson in 1913, causing Forbes ever after to regard himself the victim of partisan politics. Wilson's failure to give Forbes official notification at the time of his removal—he left this detail to the new appointee—only aggravated personal relations between the two men.

Forgiveness being absent from Forbes' makeup, he refused as long as he lived to overlook this grievance against Wilson. To friends he berated Wilson's "pettinesses and meanness of character" and pointed to "the camouflage of happy verbiage with which Wilson deluded his admirers." With special severity Forbes condemned Wilson's idealism as nebulous, impractical and high-sounding phrase-making. One who knew of this sustained grudge can hardly have doubted that Forbes would extend his dislike for Wilson the man to a disapproval of the latter's approach to diplomacy whenever an occasion presented itself.[8]

Tepid enthusiam for the tasks at hand, a strong sense of the practical—these characteristics stood out in bold relief as Forbes arrived in Japan in 1930. In addition, they combined with another, derived from his collegiate years, which seemed to contradict his usual aversion to the theoretical. Forbes profoundly respected, and incorporated into his own thought, the revolutionary hypothesis of Charles Darwin. Natural history stood first on his list of "most helpful" courses in college, even above William James' pragmatism, and this study never ceased to influence his view of life. But Forbes applied the "survival of the fittest" thesis to the course of nations, not individuals. The following statement, pregnant with implications, illustrates this point well:

I have not the least intention of arguing that because nations have waxed strong that their record in the past has been right or that they can be relied on to do the right thing as they go along. Far from it. On the other hand, as between a nation grown strong and one grown weak I should say the presumptive evidence was very much in favor of the strong nation as having pursued the right course, otherwise it could not have become strong. But I also recognize that the general rule of growth by which the corrupt fall to the ground and decay and fertilize the ground for the strong to absorb is one of the rules of the universe, and that artificial devices put in the way of preventing this happening I imagine in the long run are bound to fail.[9]

II

Other more impersonal factors over which Forbes had little control narrowed his freedom of action as surely as any character trait. The Manchurian Incident was the foremost of these, but its challenge to the new Ambassador was magnified by the immigration problem, the effect of the world depression upon men of wealth such as Forbes, and the civil-military relationship inside Japan.

The problem of immigration into the United States concerned Forbes from the beginning of his tenure in Japan. The Johnson Immigration Act of 1924, which excluded Japanese from the quota system controlling other immigration, seemed to act reciprocally with the Manchurian crisis to aggravate United States-Japanese relations. The exclusion act sustained Japanese hatred of America, provoking suspicion of her policy in the Manchurian episode. That incident, however, in turn disclosed Japanese attitudes and policies that concomitantly hardened America's adherence to the restrictions.

Forbes stood in the cross fire. Hoping to strengthen relations between Tokyo and Washington as directed by his government, he understandably urged modification of the vexatious law; yet he knew that Japan's China policy precluded revision and that, besides, a change in the law could emanate only from the American Congress. These realities, coupled with Forbes' view that an abortive attempt to adjust the law might be worse than no attempt at all, sometimes muted his discussion of the issue.[10]

Nevertheless, Forbes advocated revision in the hope that it would facilitate his tasks. During a visit to the United States, he warned the Seattle Chamber of Commerce that continued discrimination would impede Japanese-American friendship. He cautioned Stimson from the embassy in Tokyo against "thinking that Japanese opinion has become apathetic over the possibility of revision." The subject in his view was one "of grave importance, touching the dignity and honor of Japan."[11]

Financial realities of the early thirties naturally alarmed Forbes, but particularly when they impinged upon his own wealth. Business acumen and familiarity with the economic interdependence of nations had made him a logical choice for diplomatic service where trade considerations figured as prominently as in the Far East. Yet his personal accumulation of holdings, a result of that expertise, also stood vulnerable to the uncertainties of the depression.

These financial threats often preoccupied Forbes and distracted him from tasks at hand. To a friend he confided in late 1931 that "the recent unpleasantness in the market has hit the securities on which I depend very hard." The next year he complained that "it looks like busy and troubled times in store for me, with the market tumbling every which way." Even his first love, the game of polo, could not interest him again, he lamented to the Emperor of Japan, so long as financial affairs went so badly for him at home.[12]

The final influence upon Forbes was the peculiar civil-military disharmony in Japanese politics. Credentialed by his own government and duly received by civilian officials in Tokyo, he nevertheless encountered a political situation inside Japan that rendered him virtually powerless to influence Japanese policy, almost a minister without portfolio. Rapid shifts in the relative favor of the two major political parties—the moderate Minseito and the more radical Seiyukai—told only a fraction of the story. More bewildering was the "historical formalism" by which governmental authorities tendered their resignations whenever one of the frequent assassination attempts was made on the Emperor or Prince Regent.[13] This hindered the Ambassador's communication with the civil government, a problem further complicated by the fact that civilian authorities, in sharp contrast to prominent military chiefs, enjoyed no right of access to the Emperor.

Behind this political reality lay the noble tradition of imperial restoration by the military, an act dating back to 1868. Not by accident had the military secured independence of civilian control and direct contact with the Emperor. As a result, the Emperor thwarted the possibility of shogun influence which in previous times had undermined his position, and members of the warrior class, the instruments of his restoration, freed themselves of civilian control.[14]

III

Forbes found embassy life unexpectedly enjoyable during his first year in Japan. Relatively tranquil times permitted the affairs of state to recede into the background, superseded by the pleasures of horse breeding, duck hunting, trout fishing, and scenic touring. Yet beyond these and other extracurricular activities, Forbes' prolonged absences from Japan revealed a restlessness that squared exactly with his earlier misgivings about the job. In early 1931 he allowed himself the luxury of a two-month journey to the Philippines. The late spring of the same year found him travelling to China. On September 19, 1931, with the prospects of a happy furlough before him, Forbes sailed for the United States.

Disturbing cables reporting the Mukden phase of the Manchurian crisis reached him on the high seas, and the fact that he had been America-bound at this inauspicious time thoroughly embarrassed him. This embarrassment was ironic, however, in the light of Forbes' observations about the Ambassador's job. It is "playing for the strategic spot to be in, and being there with the goods at the psychological moment," he once observed. Twice he compared himself to a fire-extinguisher, "sitting idle on the wall waiting for the conflagration which everybody hopes won't come, and yet potentially very necessary."[15]

For one man, however, the Sino-Japanese conflict could not wait. The explosion along the South Manchurian Railway near Mukden, irrespective of the blame that has long been debated, precipitated the intrusion of Japanese militarists onto the Chinese mainland. In rapid succession, they bombed Chinchow in Southwestern Manchuria, occupied Tsitsihar in Northern Manchuria above the Chinese Eastern Railway, garrisoned Chinchow to follow up the earlier aerial bombardment, and attacked the international city of Shanghai. Consolidating these gains, the expansionists proclaimed the independence of Manchuria on February 18, 1932, and began to penetrate adjacent regions.

Such moves seriously impaired China's territorial integrity and prompted an appeal for redress that did not escape the notice of the United States. Turning from initial caution to tactics of bewildering variety, America dispatched naval protection to nationals residing in Shanghai, cooperated with League efforts to forestall Japan by means short of force, and threatened Tokyo with nonrecognition of her forceful gains.[16]

Even after his return to Japan in November 1931, Forbes did not give his undivided attention to the crisis. The attractions of retirement in America increased as the Far Eastern crisis developed, and the Ambassador restlessly vacillated between idealizing the tranquility of Naushon Island and manfully enduring the duties of his embassy. Yet one of Forbes' attitudes hardened each time the flurry of events demanded response and this opinion embraced all of his subsequent thinking on the Far East. Forbes deprecated verbal protestation of Japan's actions in China whether in the form of multilateral declarations in Geneva or single-handed denunciations signed by Stimson in Washington, so long as the frequency and vigor of those protests exceeded the limits of good sense.

The question of war guilt was one of several factors contributing to Forbes' attitude. Protest seemed entirely valid as long as Japan was to blame for the Manchurian affair—a role in which Forbes occasionally cast her. He wrote in his journal that Original Sin dated from 1915, from Japan's "wicked, insulting, preposterous" Twenty-One Demands for rights of exploitation in Shantung, Manchuria, and Inner Mongolia. Unable to resist militarily, the Chinese resorted to economic boycott of Japan's essential trade with the mainland.[17]

Forbes admitted, however, that this view unduly stigmatized Japan and that a variety of legitimate grievances argued in her favor. China, because of governmental disarray, had deprived resident Japanese of normal protection against economic prejudice, currency manipulation, and general lawlessness. Remedial action was an inevitable reaction to such conditions. "Offensive methods," the Ambassador wrote, "were perhaps necessary, and in my opinion it was a situation that could not be handled except by force."[18] Although Forbes qualified this statement somewhat, its purport was obvious: if the Manchurian crisis stemmed from mutual guilt of the parties, isolating one of them for sedulous protest could not be justified.

Assuming for the sake of argument that Japan bore sole responsibility for the incident, did this fact, in Forbes' view, necessarily justify America's recriminations? Emphatically not—the Ambassador's Darwinian outlook precluded such moral evaluation. Culpable or not, Japan enjoyed preponderate power vis-à-vis China, a fact which Forbes considered more potent than matters of legality.

> I am more or less an 'insurrecto' on the whole idea of trying to protect weak peoples against aggression [sic]. If they are weak because they are small, that is one thing; if they are weak because they are rotten, that is another. It is a rule of Nature that rotten things shall fall and that live things should utilize the decayed substance of the other as fertilizer and material to further its own growth. I do not mean by this that I want to see Japan absorb China, but some change was necessary in the governmental structure in Manchuria, and Japan had the punch to provide it.[19]

Another reality in Forbes' opinion also militated against protest. Like the law of evolution, an immutable law of politics was on Japan's side even if legality was not: namely, extremism flourishes most easily when challenged— particularly as a result of foreign interference. The options according to Forbes' argument were thus clear: abstain from such provocation and expect political moderation to prevail inside Japan; or remonstrate indiscriminately and expect world tensions to soar even beyond their present level with the reaction of political extremists. This theme, the most recurrent in Forbes' correspondence and public statements, warrants further elaboration.

Nothing seemed so calamitous to Forbes in his early tenure as Ambassador as the potential demise of the Minseito and its moderate politicians. Since the radical Seiyukai party advocated policies such as inflation rather than the gold standard, industrial expansion instead of heightened efficiency through regulation of existing industries, and, most ominous, cooperation with the military in contrast to inveterate curtailment of the military, it represented a threat to American political and economic theory.

In choosing sides, Forbes believed himself able to buttress the Minseito. He proposed silence as an incontrovertible safeguard against Seiyukai advances. He would continue to observe and report political vicissitudes, but the State Department would be required to restrain its desire to denounce Japan. Diplomatic protest, he predicted, would "result in discrediting the present conservative government and result in its fall with the likelihood of a more militant one to replace it." He warned Stanley Hornbeck at the State Department that "pressure from without makes it more difficult for the 'saner' element in Japan to make [its] influence effective." To another official he explained that Japan was dominated by a war psychology and that "protests are likely to enhance this feeling and silence any conservative element which might otherwise make itself heard."[20]

From the day it first occurred to Forbes, restraint of protest became an obsession and a panacea. He wrote at length of the consequence of "constant nagging," which was "to convince the public mind here in Japan that the United States was their especial enemy." On his departure in March 1932, Forbes canvassed his staff and found unanimous disdain for outside pressure, apparently on grounds that "the policy of sending vigorously phrased protests would lead straight to war." In retirement eight years later Forbes reminisced that "during the time I was ambassador [the conservatives] acted passively by reason of the rather bellicose tone of our State Department's utterances, which enabled the military group to advertise the United States as a real enemy, possibly ready to go to war, and rather choked off the activities of the conservative group."[21]

Unfortunately, however, subsequent events contradicted Forbes' argument. At the end of 1931 a coterie of Seiyukai seized power at the expense of Baron Shidehara's Minseito Cabinet, marking the first step to a military ascendancy Japan did not relinquish until 1945. Subsequent elections to the Diet undergirded the new Cabinet with a decisive parliamentary majority. But Forbes reacted peculiarly to these changed conditions. He denied, for example, that the external-internal equation had operated in the predicted manner. In his judgment, the Minseito fell from power because of their own organizational difficulties, not because of American protests capitalized upon by the opposition.[22]

Nor did the triumph of the opposition cause Forbes to despair or propose restraining a nation now controlled by extremists. Instead, restraint of protest remained his hopeful and viable principle. Outside protest may not have subverted the Minseito, but its absence might still undermine the Seiyukai, for political extremists retain their power only as they are able to fabricate external enemies of the nation. Let America suppress her tendency to protest, Forbes admonished, and the Seiyukai will fall from power, a process which intraparty discord will accelerate.[23]

For the American Ambassador, then, restraint of protest was amply justified whether one viewed Japan as totally or only partially responsible for the Far Eastern debacle. If Japan were not solely to blame, protest against her was somewhat misguided; if she *were* solely to blame, her status in the Far East and the nature of her politics explained that fact. Such a statement, however, fails to fully capsulize Forbes' diplomacy, for it ignores a dimension—thus far only implied—that was startingly novel among American diplomats. Incessant diplomatic protest against Japan was doubly reprehensible because it masked a reluctance to use force in international relations.

In Forbes' view, the element of force conditioned all effective diplomacy. En route to Japan in 1930 to take up his assignment, he derided Woodrow Wilson's complete inability "to make his *actions* square with his words." In his journal he exhorted that "protests not backed up by the mailed fist only stir up ill-feeling without accomplishing anything." Later Forbes declared that ultimatums always imply substantial commitment:

> The proper course for us to pursue is to make no noise or protest, pass the big navy bill, get the British to move their navy to the Pacific—Singapore and Hong Kong—get the French to move their ships to Saigon and then announce that we are all prepared to move together. An ultimatum then would result in acquiescence and war would be avoided.[24]

Russian behavior during the Sino-Japanese conflict clearly exemplified Forbes' theory. Concerned over the Shanghai aspect of that conflict, Russia simply moved 100,000 troops to the Manchurian border. In the Ambassador's estimate, "this was exactly the language the Japanese understood—the language of force, without any threats, so that it obviated the need of face-saving on their part."[25]

The language of force remained an integral part of Forbes' lexicon long after he departed from Japan. "Pusillanimous administrators putting forth words or threats, behind which there is no preparation for deeds," he wrote in 1939, "not only are likely to defeat their object, but they make us ridiculous in the eyes of the world and are quite likely to bring about the evils they are intended to avoid." In a letter of 1944 to Stanley Hornbeck, Forbes idealized the "soft spoken" and "big-stick" diplomacy of Theodore Roosevelt. Somewhat later he told Joseph C. Grew, his successor in Japan, that America could have prevented the Far Eastern crisis of 1931 only through "a vast army, air force and navy," but he quickly conceded that domestic conditions in America at the time precluded appropriations for such a display of force.[26]

The deemphasis of force characteristic of diplomatic protest, however, placed inordinate confidence in the devices of the New Diplomacy which Forbes found equally untenable. Indeed, he quickly perceived that the ultimate significance of the Manchurian episode lay in the questions it raised about "the efficiency of various new devices for settling disputes by peaceable means." Among these, of course, was the League of Nations, an institution referred to so peculiarly by Forbes that one can easily misjudge his estimate of its value. On several occasions he maligned Japan's refusal to lay her grievances before the League with an earnestness which seemed to denote unequivocal faith in that institution's ability to safeguard world peace.[27]

Actually, Forbes loathed both the League and the assumptions which underlay it. In his opinion, that body lacked the military power, the finances, and the political structure necessary for restoring order in Manchuria; it hypocritically eschewed force while many of its members owed "their existence and present strength to previous use of force" and frequently resorted to force for settlement of their grievances. "All the leagues, pacts, treaties and agreements are pretty valueless," he wrote, "when one runs up against the real thing in the matter of a grievance that has been accumulating against a power that understands only force." Above all, the League and similar devices betrayed a basic naiveté and childlike impetuosity about eliminating the scourge of war from the earth. Rather than resort to "quack nostrums" for the prevention of war such as "calling it names . . . or shaking a finger, or threatening, or slapping its wrist," Forbes would undertake arduous, time-consuming investigation into the fundamental conditions that produce war. He was not surprised then when peace agencies and the "new devices" failed to avert the Far Eastern conflict:

If anyone expected that these peace movements and these international pacts would be an immediate panacea and cure for all wars, he was too optimistic for this world. That condition must come slowly by a process of evolution, not by revolution and a complete and sudden change in the habits of people expressed through centuries of intertribal, national, and inter-national warfare.[28]

Why, then, had Forbes castigated Japan's indifference to the League of Nations? The answer lay not in personal esteem for that organization but in his belief that world opinion would more readily have condoned Japan's unilateral action had that action followed a genuine albeit futile reference to the respected League machinery.

IV

Forceful argument alone does not make ambassadors effectual at their post of duty. More than a mere conveyer of official notes from Washington because of his discriminating outlook, but less than a policymaker because his opinions did not prevail, Forbes fell somewhere between the norms of diplomatic behavior. The *New York Times* missed this fact entirely when it dryly summarized Forbes' contribution as one in which he "transmitted numerous messages of protest from Secretary of State Henry L. Stimson to the Japanese Government."

Initially no differences of opinion obstructed the Forbes-Stimson relationship. The Secretary of State's fear of alienating Japanese moderates by premature interference paralleled his spokesman's attitude in Tokyo. "My problem," Stimson wrote in his diary on September 22, 1931, "is to let the

Japanese know that we are watching them and at the same time to do it in a way which will help Shidehara, who is on the right side, and not play into the hands of any Nationalist agitators on the other." Interference, he concluded, would produce the latter result. This accord between Forbes and Stimson was further strengthened by the Secretary of State's belief that Japan had cooperated meritoriously with world powers in the previous decade and his high regard for Debuchi, the conciliatory Shidehara's Ambassador in Washington.[29]

Their relations wore thin, however, as Stimson grew impatient with the policy of verbal restraint, quickened the tempo of protest and hardened its tone, for Forbes could not be dissuaded, finding no indication that requisite military force buttressed America's word. "Secretary Stimson," Forbes lamented, has "made a practice of speaking roughly and not carrying a big stick." He described Stimson as infected with "the fidgets," which made him "keep coming out with new blasts." He decried the "repeated notes, press releases and the publication of letters," counting no less than fifteen representations he was directed to make to the Japanese government. Clearly, his plea for a "single dignified protest" was to no avail.[30]

Stimson's actions continued to alienate his subordinate, particularly when he supported the Leagues' condemnatory resolutions and denunciations of gains wrought by force. This behavior was only one of the factors, although perhaps the most important, that set the two men apart. Forbes also objected to Stimson's "practice of delivering to the Japanese Ambassador in Washington a copy of the message he was ordering me to deliver," for this allowed him no opportunity to comment on the appropriateness of the despatches. Arriving communications designated "for *immediate* delivery to the Japanese Government" similarly narrowed his latitude. Sometimes Forbes complained that he even lacked information as to the actual view of his own government. Finally, the Ambassador claimed that Stimson mishandled the press during the Manchurian Incident, especially by betraying Forbes' productive, confidential talks with Shidehara.[31]

Conversely, Stimson had reason to criticize his representative in Tokyo. "Reports from other quarters both official and unofficial," he telegraphed to Forbes in late September 1931, "contain much more complete data than those emanating from Japan." Besides fuller information Stimson sought, but seldom received, extensive justification for Forbes' quiescent attitude, illustrated by Forbes' single attempt to modify a peace proposal from Washington in order to save face for the Japanese. Furthermore, Stimson never forgot the aggravating fact that Forbes, who once had compared himself to an every-ready fire extinguisher, was absent from Japan at the height of the Manchurian affair.[32]

Overt hostility seldom disturbed the personal relations between the two men, contentious though they were at the official level. Yet precisely because the conflict remained at the level of disputation over policy, it stifled Forbes as a potential policymaker and intensified his restiveness. When he left Japan for retirement at Naushon in March 1932, some observers understandably hinted at estrangement. Forbes himself, though puzzled over the timing of the State Department's acceptance of his resignation, pointed rather to previous commitments, broken health, and disrupted finances than to a "falling out" with his superiors. He expected the Manchurian affair to "take years to adjust" and presumed that Washington felt that "the sooner the man who was to be Ambassador when the time of settlement came got into the saddle, the better equipped he'd be to deal with it."[33]

Forbes assessed his tour of duty without pretension when finally at ease on Naushon Island. "My principal stunt," he told a close friend, "has been trying to keep the United States from being *too insistent* upon checking Japan." Yet to another person he admitted that "some things I tried to do didn't turn out as well as they might have."[34]

Implicitly separating effort from accomplishment, Forbes came very close to the mark. Clearly, he was not the unimaginative, absent-minded, indolent Brahmin portrayed by one scholar of depression diplomacy.[35] The brevity and obscurity of his tenure notwithstanding, he marshalled his efforts behind a trenchant point of view. Japan, it held, enjoyed preponderant power in the Far East, a fact more pertinent than the legality of her actions. Turning from description to prescription, Forbes argued that Japan's power would prevail in the Far East unless countered with commensurate power, not verbal protestation.

Despite this effort to enunciate a point of view, no accomplishment provided the necessary endorsement; nevertheless, it became a ready option for Forbes' successors in Japan and future officials in Washington. The utility of this option will separate realists, who will hail its insight, from idealists, who will bemoan its puerility. But they will surely agree that it was an exceptional viewpoint for its time.

Notes

1 Essential bibliography of the Manchurian episode includes Hilary Conroy, "Government Versus 'Patriot': The Background of Japan's Asiatic Expansion," *Pacific Historical Review,* 20(1951):31-42; Robert H. Ferrell, *American Diplomacy in the Great Depression* (New Haven: Yale University Press, 1957). Armin Rappaport, *Henry L. Stimson and Japan, 1931-1933* (Chicago: University of Chicago Press, 1963); Henry L. Stimson, *The Far Eastern Crisis* (New York: Harper and Brothers, 1936). Henry L. Stimson and McGeorge Bundy, *On Active Service in Peace and War* (New York: Harper and Brothers, 1947).
2 The full-length biography of Forbes remains to be written, but extensive biographical information appears in the *New York Times,* December 26, 1959, 13:5-6. George A. Lensen describes Forbes' life and official service

for a limited period in "Ambassador Forbes' Appraisal of American Policy Toward Japan in 1931-32," *Monumenta Nipponica* (January, 1968), but this study is analytical only in a superficial sense and relies solely upon Forbes' Journals. Another aspect of Forbes' life is handled incisively by Frederick G. Hoyt, "The Wood-Forbes Mission to the Philippines, 1921," (Unpublished Ph.D. dissertation, Claremont Graduate School and University Center, 1963).

3 The Papers of W. Cameron Forbes (The Houghton Library of Harvard College Library, Cambridge, Massachusetts), bMS Am 1524. Cited hereafter as Forbes Papers; Letter Books (Confidential), 5:360; Letter Books, 56:203. Cited hereafter as LBC and LB respectively. See also Journals (2d Series, from which all subsequent citations come), 4:450. Forbes' speech to the Pan-Pacific Club of Tokyo is enclosed in his no. 493 to Stimson, February 13, 1932, United States Department of State Files 123 Forbes/152 (National Archives, Washington, D. C.). Cited hereafter as DSF. Able service in Haiti during 1930, in which Forbes negotiated the withdrawal of the Marines, highly recommended him to Hoover, who refused Forbes' initial attempt to refuse new official duties. After accepting, Forbes frequently noted, as consolation, the proximity of Japan to the Philippine Islands: "My thoughts are constantly traveling southward to the kindly people, dear friends, and pleasant scenes among which I spent such an important part of my life," LBC, 5:384.

4 LBC, 6:29; LB, 57:264.

5 LB, 55:460-461; Journals, 4:191, 113. A niece of Forbes', interviewed in August 1967, remembered him as "pleasant and correct in behavior" but not given to diplomatic suavity and protocol.

6 Journals, 3:223; Forbes to Stimson, no. 23, October 7, 1930, DSF 123 Forbes/39; LB, 55:338; Forbes to Stimson, no. 225, May 16, 1931, DSF 123 Forbes/104. At Harvard Forbes did not aspire to high intellectual achievement but to average performance: "I [operated] on the general principle while in college that if I got less than 'C' I was showing less than average intelligence, and if I got more it showed I was wasting my time in unessentials," Journals, 4:333.

7 LBC, 6:323.

8 Notes from personal interview cited above; see also LB, 58:350 and 55:116-117; Forbes to M.A. Howe, May 1, 1952, Forbes Papers, bMS Am 1524 (483); Journals, 4:105.

9 Forbes' evaluation of his academic life appears in a handwritten autobiography now in the possession of family members. See also LB, 58:381.

10 LB, 55:243, 56:198-199; LBC, 5:425, Journals, 3:489.

11 The speech is enclosed in Forbes' no. 11 to Stimson, October 24, 1931, DSF 123 Forbes/132. See also his no. 290 to Stimson, July 31, 1931, Confidential Correspondence, American Embassy Tokyo, RG 84, 855-Japanese exclusion. Cited hereafter as Post Files, Confidential.

12 LB, 57:436, Journals, 4:80, 62.

13 Forbes to Stimson, January 16, 1932, DSF 894.001 H 61/59.

14 United States Department of State, *Papers Relating to the Foreign Relations of the United States, 1931* (Washington, D.C.: Government Printing Office, 1946), 3:689-695. Cited hereafter as *FRUS, 1931*, vol. 3.

15 LB, 57:447 and 56:421-423; Speeches and Addresses, Forbes Papers, box 2, January 20, 1933. Cited hereafter as S/A Collection. Forbes lamented in his Journals, 4:176, "I knew as soon as the radio began to reach me on the ship that I should have stayed. . . . I have been feeling very badly about my failure to be at the right place at this juncture." These cables did not, however, break the news of Mukden to Forbes. A local Japanese newspaper of September 19 apprised him of the affair, and he reconsidered his travel plans until an aide insisted that he depart on schedule lest, by changing his plans, he exaggerate the gravity of Mukden and unduly alarm the public. See his Journals, 3:485, and Forbes' no. 150 to Stimson, September 19, 1931, Post Files, Confidential, 800-Manchuria.
16 Japan's military advances and world responses are detailed in United States Department of State, *Papers Relating to the Foreign Relations of the United States, Japan, 1931-1941* (Washington, D.C.: Government Printing Office, 1943), vol. 1 and in these specialized secondary articles: Paul H. Clyde, "The Diplomacy of 'Playing no Favorites': Secretary Stimson and Manchuria, 1931," *The Mississippi Valley Historical Review,* 35(1948): 187-202. Cited hereafter as Clyde, *MVHR*; Richard N. Current, "The Stimson Doctrine and the Hoover Doctrine," *The American Historical Review* 59(1954):513-542; and Robert H. Ferrell, "The Mukden Incident: September 18-19, 1931," *The Journal of Modern History,* 27(1955):66-72.
17 Journals, 3:537-538; LB, 58:149; LBC, 6:15-16.
18 *FRUS, 1931,* 3:375-380; LB, 58:157, 108-109.
19 LB, 58:149.
20 Journals, 3:518; Hornbeck Memorandum, February 28, 1932, DSF 793.94/4479.5; United States Department of State, *Papers Relating to the Foreign Relations of the United States, 1932* (Washington, D.C.: Government Printing Office, 1948), 3:364-365. Cited hereafter as *FRUS, 1932,* vol. 3.
21 Journals, 4:21; Forbes to Stimson, March 9, 1932, DSF 894.00/375; LBC, 7:231-233.
22 Forbes to Stimson, no. 422, December 17, 1931, Post Files, Confidential, 800-Japan.
23 In addition to evidence already given of the continuing affirmation of this principle even after the political change cited see Edwin Neville, Counselor of Embassy, to Stimson, no. 560, April 7, 1932, Post Files, Confidential, 800-Japan.
24 Journals, 4:105, 8, 3-4.
25 *Ibid.,* 4. See also Forbes' speech to Harvard Traveller's Club, S/A Collection, box 2, May 13, 1932.
26 "American Policies in the Far East," S/A Collection, box 1, as later printed in *Proceedings of the American Academy of Arts and Sciences,* 73:(2), 5-28. Cited hereafter as "American Policies in the Far East." LBC, 7:354-355, 404-405.
27 LB, 58:130; *FRUS, 1932,* 3:109-115.
28 Forbes to Stimson, no. 470, January 29, 1932, Post Files, Confidential, 800-Manchuria; speech to Harvard Club of New York, S/A Collection, box 2, December 20, 1932; Journals, 4:7-8; LB, 58:117-120; speech to Bates College commencement, S/A Collection, box 4, June 13, 1932.

29 *New York Times,* Oct. 26, 1959; Stimson, *Far Eastern Crisis,* pp. 36-37; Stimson and Bundy, *On Active Service,* pp. 222, 227; Clyde, *MVHR,* 195. See also the references to Stimson's diary in Ferrell, *Diplomacy,* pp. 132-134.

30 LBC, 7:354-355; Journals, 4:21; "American Policies in the Far East," 5-28; LBC, 7:416-425.

31 Journals, 4:16-17; Forbes to Nelson Johnson, American Minister in Peking, March 16, 1932, Post Files, 800-China/800-Manchuria; Journals, 4:32. For the matter of Stimson's press relations, consult Journals, 3:522, 4:203; LB, 58:3, 144; and LBC, 7:118-120, 234-239, 252, 255.

32 Stimson to Forbes, no. 166, September 24, 1931, Post Files, Confidential, 800-Manchuria; *FRUS, 1932,* 3:346-347; Forbes to Stimson, February 14, 1932, Post Files, 800-China; Journals, 3:492.

33 Forbes' resignation and retirement are discussed in Journals, 3:547, LB, 58:202, and DSF 123 Forbes/6, 130, 161. His pessimism regarding an immediate solution of the Manchurian affairs appears in Journals, 4:55.

34 Journals, 4:250; LB, 58:443. The italics were added in order to clarify the statement. Forbes apparently meant to emphasize his aversion to the frequency of Stimson's notes, not his sometimes pro-Japanese feelings.

35 Such an estimate is drawn by Ferrell, *Diplomacy,* pp. 136-137, 281.

Edward M. Bennett

Joseph C. Grew

The Diplomacy of Pacification

JOSEPH CLARK GREW served his decade-long ambassadorship in Japan (February 19, 1932, to December 7, 1941) with a mission in mind and a vision of his place in history before him. In brief, he dreamed of playing an important, if not dominant, role in restoring peace to Asia. That he failed to accomplish this goal was not due to lack of effort or persistence. His vision of resolving the political tensions in Asia often blurred the shortcomings of that hope as a realistic possibility.

When Grew began his assignment to Japan, he entered the most eventful period of his diplomatic career, if not the most successful.[1] He accepted the position eagerly for he knew that he was the first of his generation of diplomats to become Ambassador in a major capital, and he hoped to set a precedent. Moreover, Grew's experience warranted the post. His first position was a consular assignment in 1904 from whence he went through the whole process from Third Secretary to Counselor of Embassy before achieving the rank of Minister, as Secretary of the United States Commission to the Paris Peace Conference. For a short time he was assigned as Counselor to the Paris embassy and then to Denmark as Minister. After a tour as Minister to Switzerland, Grew was sent to Lausanne to negotiate the Turkish Treaty (his first ambassadorial post was later at Ankara). Partially as a result of his success with the Turks, Grew returned to Washington as Under Secretary of State where he was in charge of the mechanics of reorganizing the Foreign Service.

To the seasoned diplomat, Japan's problems resulted from a universal source of societal evil—irresponsible leadership—and the corrective was obviously to imitate the good example to be provided by the American

Ambassador. Grew's urgent plea for more responsible leadership was predicated not only on the needs of Japan and the United States but on his realization that history had taught this lesson to men everywhere in all eras. Change had to come through educational development and an understanding of the past; tearing up old roots without traditions to cling to meant trouble. Balance and symmetry, Grew asserted, along with patience and considered judgment were the chief qualities necessary in a great leader. If Japan could not instill these qualities in her leaders, she was doomed.[2]

While prescribing for Japan, Grew also urged Washington to take a longer, broader view of its policies toward the Orient. He wanted the United States to assess sympathetically the national needs and objectives of Japan and to search for conciliatory means of mutual adjustment of differences. This appeal found little favor in Washington, and as the years passed and tensions grew, American policy, contrary to Grew's pleadings, took a harder, more uncompromising line.

Grew made several attempts during his long stay in Japan to modify America's Asian policy, but after early rebuffs he was careful not to *appear* to be doing so. He recoiled from departmental rebukes with considerable alacrity, but was disturbed by his inability to find out what his superiors were thinking and planning. Sometimes he thought they did not trust him; other times he complained that they did not understand him. The evasiveness of Secretary of State Cordell Hull and the secretiveness of Franklin Roosevelt left him aghast, wondering what he was supposed to be doing in his dealings with the Japanese and the Great Powers represented in Tokyo.[3]

Grew expressed concern about the succession of Japanese governments that formed and disbanded with confusing rapidity. Scarcely had he overcome his partial deafness enough to understand the inflection of one Minister when a change in government produced another. Although he spoke no Japanese, Grew found most Foreign Ministers could converse in English, and whenever possible he tried to engage them in private conversation in order to establish closer understanding and cooperation. Here he was aided by his wife, Alice Perry Grew, who was a direct descendent of the man who had opened Japan to the West. Alice Grew's own residence there as a youth and her knowledge of the language opened doors in the social and political realm that would otherwise have remained closed to Grew. The personal touch came much easier after he had established a long residence in Japan and a reputation for fair dealing with the men at the *Gaimushō* (Japanese Foreign Office). In short, Grew's background, training, and experience established both his strengths and weaknesses for the assignment to Tokyo at a critical juncture in Japanese-American relations.

War came as a distinct blow to the man who had hoped to go down in history as a peace-maker. In a bitter letter to President Roosevelt, composed as he sailed home a repatriate aboard the *SS Gripsholm* in August 1942, Grew accused the administration of failing to take proper advantage of all its options to avoid the Pacific war. This remarkable document was never forwarded; instead, it was characteristically filed in his papers "for the historical record." Even though he later softened his charges, Grew died still convinced that had his advice been properly understood and followed the history of Asia would have been dramatically altered.

I

Given the nature of the Foreign Service, Grew's career in the corps of diplomats was clearly related to his educational experience and social background. He came from a pre-revolutionary family of wealth and prominence; J.P. Morgan was a cousin, and Boston investors and bankers were among his other relatives. Grew's wife certainly did not detract from this image; she was a descendant of Commodores Oliver and Matthew Perry, as well as of Benjamin Franklin, and her father was the scholar Thomas Sergeant Perry. Grew attended Groton and Harvard (the Fly Club provided many of his social contacts in college), a course paralleled by his future chief, Franklin Delano Roosevelt.

Grew carried a lifelong recollection of his Groton and Harvard days as the period that established his values and concepts of social and moral responsibility. He displayed little in the way of intellectual curiosity, however, due in part to the prevailing concern for social activity and in part to his own proclivities. While Ambassador to Japan when the Harvard baseball team toured there, Grew remarked that the Fly Club now ranked first among campus groups but had been third when he was at Cambridge, "but even in its leaner times I would not for anything have sacrificed the good times and congenial and stimulating fellowships I had there. It may be all wrong but the club life and associations in the Fly were the highlights of my college career, and the athletic field was distinctly next; then came the Advocate and Crimson, with the lecture rooms a poor fourth."[4] Although his academic performance was undistinguished, Grew saw the "gentleman's C" as nothing to be ashamed of (it was difficult enough just to get into Harvard); a "C" represented an absorption level adequate to prepare one for a career.

When Grew left Harvard, he spurned the secure life offered by his father in finance or business on Boston's State Street. Edward Sturgis Grew was a firm believer in the old values and the old way of life and could see no good in leaving Boston for any extended period, except for the educational tour every proper young man should make. Joseph Grew's tour was longer than most and far broader. He took eighteen months to travel around the world culminating with a hunt for the Amoy tiger in China. The young hunter searched out the tiger in its lair, crawled in with his big game rifle and risked encounter with the wounded ten-foot animal. Firmly smitten by the wanderlust, Grew returned home and settled on a Foreign Service career to satisfy his longing for a life of adventure and service.[5]

It took the neophyte diplomat more than a decade to learn something more substantial about diplomacy than clerical work. This was not Grew's fault nearly so much as the system and times in which he served his apprenticeship. Theodore Roosevelt, who approved Grew's appointment after he heard of the tiger hunt, had attempted with minimal success to stabilize the Foreign Service. Thus for a diplomat to act with imagination and efficiency was frowned upon for the power of Congress to cut the Department of State's budget to the bone threatened those who knew their positions depended on the capricious mood of the legislators. Grew observed many times that the Department could only attract good men when reforms made it apparent that taking action would not jeopardize their positions. Failing this, the people who functioned most effectively were those who had some other career or fortune on which to rely.

Grew numbered among those who had something in reserve. His diary is full of communications between himself and his brother Randolph on the status of the family fortune, which was not among the greatest in New England but which provided him with security even after the depression in 1929. It was always a matter of concern, however, when a change of office brought new people to power in Washington, and several times Grew returned home to mend political fences at the propitious moment so that he would not be swept out to make room for some political favorite. His closest call came in 1912 when his confirmation as Secretary of Legation was held up in the Senate until the last possible day. To his great delight several old family, Groton, and Harvard friends crossed over party lines to assist him, proving he thought that Groton training and conscience came before party.

The insurance Grew prepared for his position in Tokyo illustrates that he was quite capable of playing the survival game. He supported the reelection of Hoover, not simply because he was a Republican, but because Grew had a good working relationship with Secretary of State Henry L. Stimson and did not want to see the "team" disrupted. Certainly he was also concerned over how close to home disruption might strike and who would succeed his superiors in the Department of State. Immediately before the election, Grew contacted his Democratic friends, some of whom had aided him in 1912, and soon became less apprehensive about a change.[6] Once FDR was elected, Grew hastened to remind "Frank" of their mutual associations: "Groton, Harvard, and the Fly are immensely proud [of your election] —and they have a good right to be. For my part, whether in official or private life, you can count upon my whole-hearted support and cooperation in the great work which lies ahead."[7]

There was always a tendency in the State Department in this era toward the conservative approach to policy questions. No matter how secure the individual, after a number of years in the service he witnessed at one time or another the dismissal of a colleague for reasons of economy, political belief, or errors of commission. Grew's own efforts at personal initiative were for the most part humbling and frightening lessons in the limits that bound an American diplomat. As Counselor of Embassy in Berlin during World War I, Grew found himself for a brief period Acting Ambassador while James Gerard was absent. In an interview between Chancellor Bethmann-Hollweg and Grew, the Chancellor brought up the subject of peace. Grew interpreted it as a hint that the Germans would welcome an American initiative and so informed Washington, stating clearly that this was only an impression.

Grew immediately recognized his error and realized that his career hung in the balance. The Chancellor could easily have claimed that Grew had impertinently misrepresented or misunderstood him and that he had in no way sought an American initiative. Bethmann-Hollweg, however, chose to keep his options open and thus hedged for the moment.[8] The lesson in caution was not lost on Grew, but his overly optimistic reports about the prospects for peace prefigured a later tendency to view events with similar hope.

In the early phases of World War I Grew made the mistake he would repeat at another critical juncture in Japan. His "judgment of temporary relief from the submarine danger introduced a degree of complacency in the American government, contributing to the postponement of Wilson's peace move until it was too late." Grew had been trying to establish the consensus of opinion at the embassy, but he did this at the expense of "underestimating the weight of military imperatives in the decision-making process." As a result, "Grew failed to provide an entirely accurate representation of the forces determining German policy."[9]

Other experiences which tended to promote caution in Grew's later years include his inappropriate praise of Germany early in World War I to family and friends and an accidental slight to visiting congressmen when he was at Copenhagen. More serious, however, was his authorization, as Acting Secretary of State, to John V.A. MacMurray to clear from the Yangtze River a Chinese faction attempting to blockade the American squadron there. When Secretary Kellogg returned to Washington, he accused his Under Secretary of declaring war on China.[10]

On several later occasions Grew recalled his near disasters as lessons in circumspection regarding relations with Congress, public opinion, and the Department of State. He did not become a sycophant, but he did tend to hedge his recommendations to the Department with contingencies and to avoid situations where he might be blamed for taking too bold a stand. He came to abhor rocking the boat unnecessarily which sometimes meant not rocking the boat at all. The result was that the Department did not always get full measure from its Ambassador—the fault, however, was partially the Department's. American foreign policy in the 1920's and 1930's was based on short term interests and long term principles, many of which were mutually exclusive. There was no policy planning staff in the modern sense and very often no planning at all by the leaders in Washington or in the field.

Policy was reactive to each new crisis or problem. This made it exceedingly difficult for the ambassador to know how to approach the government to which he was accredited. When Franklin D. Roosevelt could confide that he had no idea how to develop a long range foreign policy and Cordell Hull could tell his ambassadors to read his and FDR's speeches to discover what American policy really was, it is small wonder that an ambassador whose position rested on a tenuous political relationship with the chiefs in Washington hesitated to expand upon such nebulous policy. That Grew actually suggested policy guidelines indicated his concern for peace and his role in creating it.

II

Grew arrived in Tokyo after the initial diplomatic uproar over the Manchurian crisis had begun to subside, and he promptly began to stress the need for encouraging the moderate political faction in Japan. He wrote to Secretary of State Henry L. Stimson in October 1932 to assure him that there was growing opposition to chauvinistic leaders in Japan but warning that one could not afford to be too optimistic—there was still insufficient evidence that the military was losing control.[11] The last part of the message concerning the realities of Japanese politics particularly impressed Stimson and he marked Grew's judgment as sound. In a short time the Secretary was accepting the same advice from Grew that he had looked upon with skepticism when it had come from the Ambassador's predecessor, W. Cameron Forbes. Stimson now allowed, for example, that national impera- tives and young hot heads were the source of Japan's troubles, that her problems were not easily solved, that she was not likely to respond to external moral pressure and that it was best to work to effect a change of public opinion and to support the moderate group's effort to turn aside the military. He wrote to Grew on January 9, 1933, expressing the degree to which they were in agreement and acknowledging Grew's influence on policy development.[12] This harmony with the Department, however, was short lived.

Eugene H. Dooman, who served in the Far East Division when Grew first went out to Japan and who was later assigned to Tokyo along with Grew, was another diplomat who anticipated good results from a watchful waiting policy. Dooman, too, was generally optimistic in his estimation of the

Japanese situation; consequently, when he and Grew were put in harness together they reinforced each other's optimism. Yet if they recognized a certain "legitimacy" in Japanese ambitions in Asia, they feared the extent of these ambitions and the methods the Japanese might employ to achieve them. Their insights into the Japanese point of view, however, were not shared at the top echelons of the State Department where Secretary of State Cordell Hull presided after March 1933.

Grew maintained that American policy should rest on two concurrent principles: "National preparedness for the purpose of protecting legitimate American interests in the Far East, and a sympathetic, cooperative, and helpful attitude toward Japan, based on larger considerations reaching into the future." Expanding on this thesis, Grew and Dooman pleaded for recognition that there were only two ways Japan's overpopulation problem could be solved: territorial and industrial expansion. They doubted that Japan's use of force to resolve its differences with China could ever be adjusted to everyone's satisfaction, but they warned that restricting Japan's foreign trade would not provide a solution and, in fact, would prompt Japan to undertake further political and territorial expansion.

Grew attempted to acquaint his superiors with Japan's rationalizations and her resentment at being considered on less than an equal footing with the other great powers in Asia. The Japanese, he wrote, imagined an impelling logic in their view of their economic problems, a view which Grew assessed as a normal striving for a higher standard of living. Japan intended to replace the Western powers in exploiting China, and if this occurred at others' expense that was unfortunate. This attitude Grew ascribed to a feeling akin to "manifest destiny" or to a concept close to "the point of view expressed by Kipling in his poems of the British Empire."[13]

Consequently, Grew wanted policymakers to examine the expansionist position of Japan as the "reasonable and logical operation of well-nigh irrepressible forces based on the underlying principle of self-preservation."[14] (Like Forbes before him there was a strain of social Darwinism in Grew.) He feared that Washington might stress the military aspects of Japan's program without carefully considering the driving impulse of the whole nation. At this point Grew suggested the direction American foreign policy should take in Asia with Japan as the focal point. First, Washington should assess Grew's analysis to determine its accuracy. If Washington subsequently judged that Japan *was* indeed faced with a national problem of the utmost gravity brought on by natural developments and that Japan's military program was a manifestation of this problem requiring safety valve outlets, then policy should deal with these realities.

On the basis of these conclusions, the Ambassador asked his government whether the West preferred to preserve its interests unchanged and face war or more realistically to grant Japan larger markets and greater opportunities in Western-controlled territories. Why not the second choice, Grew asked, for it would mean that the increased standard of living and prosperity would eventually tend to stabilize Japan's population and bring her economic ambitions to a level plateau of development.

This document stands as one of Grew's major efforts to influence the course of America's Asian policy. Hull, however, did not—and probably could not—understand Grew's definition of economic elbowroom for Japan. In forwarding these despatches to FDR the Secretary of State cautioned the President that since 1933 the administration had done everything practicable to be cooperative toward Japan. Hull chose to emphasize to FDR only Grew's warning to be prepared for any eventuality and to build the fleet.[15]

On occasion Grew fed the Department's pessimism. For example, he observed that the "Cabinet of Old Men" in the Saito government was trying to keep the brakes on, but the question was moot whether common sense would prevail. He noted that when this Cabinet departed from the scene, the last government comprised largely of men who had guided Japan's rise to world influence would also pass. After them, if no moderate leadership arose, American and Japanese policy would directly conflict unless "someone puts the helm over hard."[16] This view reflected Grew's personal conception of the diplomatic process and, in fact, his view of life. His dire prediction concerning the succeeding government was repeated with virtually every Cabinet change, and yet he almost always found other "moderate hands" reaching for control after the new government came to power. Perhaps he desired the outcome so much that he wished it into existence, but more likely he followed his own advice to acknowledge the possibility of disaster and look for better results.

A subject of special sensitivity for Grew was leadership of public opinion. He criticized the Japanese government for neglecting this area and hence letting it pass by default to the army and navy.[17] Similarly, he was often rankled by Americans who publicly undercut the image of the United States he had so carefully cultivated in Japan. He charged these people with playing into the hands of the military who tried to convey the impression that the United States was either unconcerned with Asia, too weak to stop Japan, too isolationist, or afraid to act.[18]

Grew's desire for the elder statesmen to predominate in Japan became an obsession that he attempted to pass on to Washington. He urged Hull to bear in mind the peculiar structure of the Japanese constitution by which the supreme command of the army and navy lay outside the competence of the civilian government, and he urged patience in dealing with Japan until time had worked fundamental institutional changes, changes which he predicted were definitely in progress. In this fashion Grew led Hull to expect that the tide had turned, and when this did not prove to be an accurate appraisal, the

Secretary placed less faith in Grew's assessments, believing that the Japanese misled him and were untrustworthy.[19]

The Far East Division wanted for the most part to accept the Ambassador's views but found this difficult. On one occasion Maxwell Hamilton explained the Department's dilemma. He admitted that it was possible that liberal elements *were* growing in strength. The problem was that Prime Minister Hirota would be unable to liberalize his policy by sacrificing the objectives that the reactionaries had in mind. He cited the embassy's own assertion that even with the new rhetoric there had been no abandonment of the objectives of the previous aggressive regimes, no decline of military preeminence in the government, and no development of democratic influences in the American sense.[20]

Not only did this memorandum reveal some wariness on the part of the Department regarding real prospects for liberal development (though it implied a hope that such might evolve), but it also revealed a major failing in the American perspective. There was a strong undercurrent of disappointment that Japan could not be expected to play the diplomatic *and* political game by American rules. This refusal to "see things our way" was one of the strong points in Hull's distrust of both Japan's program and leadership.[21]

Although Grew had a basic antagonism toward the Soviet Union, he saw some possible use in Roosevelt's recognition of Russia once it had occurred: it would give Japan cause to think about the growing combination which could blunt her aggressive course. Recognition, along with building the fleet, Grew noted, could not help but act as a deterrent. Later he went so far as to say that even though he urged the Department to assure Japan that recognition was not a direct threat, "after all it may be just as well to let [the Japanese] think what they want to think."[22] This was the kind of pressure that the United States imagined Japan was responsive to right down to the last moments before actual sanctions were imposed in 1939 and 1940.

III

Although he recorded in his diary and told his friends that matters regarding Japan were being handled correctly in Washington, Grew became less and less convinced that this was really true as the 1930's waned. As tensions between the two nations mounted from mid-1937 on, the Ambassador formed the opinion that while Japan needed the United States, the United States was less sure that she needed or could trust Japan. Grew also frequently and distressingly found himself out-of-step with the Department, a situation caused in part by what officials saw as the Ambassador's inconsistencies.

In May 1937, when Washington thought affairs in the Pacific might be improving, Grew took a hard line against new, formal negotiations with

Tokyo. Plenty of machinery existed, he argued, to prevent aggression in the Pacific, notably the Kellogg Pact, the League Covenant, and the Nine and Four Power treaties, but Japan had disregarded them all. Any new pact was dangerous, therefore, because it invited an unrealistic confidence. "If you can't find a rock to build your house on, but only sand," he wrote, "it's much safer not to build a house at all." He concluded that the only safe course was to follow Teddy Roosevelt's advice to speak softly and carry a big stick.[23]

When the Sino-Japanese Incident erupted in July 1937 the situation became more critical, but the American Ambassador quickly returned to his old optimism. Grew felt that neither China nor Japan wanted war and that there were "merely certain difficulties to be overcome in finding a way out." But he noted that:

> There are plenty of people here who are convinced that the whole crisis in North China was predetermined and carefully engineered by the Japanese; and that they fully intend to take over all of North China now; our Naval Attaché is one of them, and I may have some difficulty in persuading him to square his reports to the Navy Department in Washington with the views of the rest of us. I think the evidence is mounting daily. We shall eventually argue this out in a despatch to the Department. . . . [24]

"Evidence" of the amelioration he sought was not forthcoming.

Sensing a degree of aloofness by the Department toward him, Grew attempted to get back in line. In an effort to offset Department suspicions he wrote in late July, "In connection with a slight possible misunderstanding caused by the phraseology of telegrams . . . I entirely concur and am in sympathy with every step thus far taken by our government in the present Sino-Japanese situation and with the general policy of our government as the Department has outlined it to me."[25]

Grew's spirits were "very much gladdened" on August 4 by a "delightful telegram from Mr. Hull." The telegram thanked Grew for his splendid reporting and commentary. The Ambassador accepted this as deserved commendation for the embassy's handling of the North China Incident. He was also pleased that the Japanese government had seemed genuinely impressed from the outset with the American government's attitude. Adequate protests were delivered concerning the protection of American lives and property, but every step was taken without fanfare, quietly, courteously, and with a minimum of publicity. What was important to Grew was that Japan was made aware of American interests without fulmination. He acknowledged that the achievement of course included Hull's actions in Washington. The Japanese people had expected, Grew thought, some sort of Stimsonian outburst and were steeled to respond in kind. When this was not forthcoming from the Roosevelt administration, he noted that the Japanese took every opportunity to show their appreciation.[26]

Grew was obviously delighted that at last the Department appeared ready to follow his advice. Diplomacy, he thought, was about to triumph over moralizing, and the inevitable result would be to lessen the pressure on Japanese-American relations and to allow the civilian government to begin asserting that long-awaited moderation. His point was that the United States could emerge from the Asia tangle with its prestige intact and its relations with Japan based on a new cordiality. This would, in turn, overcome the animosity engendered by the Stimson notes, the naval issue, and possibly even the Exclusion Act. The Japanese, above all other people, were inclined toward gratitude when gratitude was due. He concluded:

If we in the Embassy, by our advice and recommendations to Washington (which are most considerately listened to by Mr. Hull and Stanley Hornbeck) and by our tactics, methods and manner of procedure here, can contribute to the development of a genuine as contrasted with a merely theoretical friendship between the United States and Japan—a friendship thorough and sound enough to stand without serious injury the periodic knocks which it is bound to experience from time to time—then I shall feel that our work here has been constructive and perhaps a satisfactory climax to a fairly long go of it in the profession of diplomacy. In all of this Dooman concurs and he is a solid rock of support.[27]

This most significant entry among the many volumes of Grew's diaries illustrates the man and his perspective; it explains, too, his subsequent reactions to Washington's policies and actions. To speak in terms of genuine friendship in the international realm was perfectly in keeping with the American approach, and especially Grew's approach, to diplomacy. That particular phraseology had been used broadly in the twentieth century, especially by Woodrow Wilson and later by Roosevelt and Hull in the Good Neighbor Policy. Grew believed that this was precisely what he had provided in the Turkish-American relationship; now in 1937 with his preeminent desire for a place in history, the opportunity had at last presented itself for diplomacy in his style. The prophet, so he hoped, was about to find honor in his own camp.

Emboldened by Hull's praise, Grew analyzed the general situation in Asia on August 27 and recommended three lines of policy. First, the United States should avoid involvement; second, it should protect to the limit the lives, property, and rights of American citizens; third, it should maintain if possible its traditional friendship with both combatants while simultaneously observing complete neutrality. America was well known, said Grew, for her position on idealism, disarmament, and international ethics and principles. While not abandoning those convictions, he suggested to the administration that it could be of greater future service to world peace and keep its own interests on a sounder footing if America retained the friendship of both China and Japan. Grew also recommended, if it were not incompatible with the above objective, that the administration attempt to secure advantages for the future American position and interests in the Far East. He urged a dignified silence in pursuit of these ends as the course of wise statesmanship, save when Americans or American interests were involved. If only he could sit down with Hull and talk the subject out, Grew believed he could convince the Secretary how clearly this policy supported American interests and how important it was to keep calm.[28]

Finally, on September 15 the Ambassador decided to press his views on Hull more directly through an informal letter. Apologizing for the nature of his communication, Grew expressed his conviction that if he and Hull could talk through Asian problems they would find that their views were quite similar if not identical, although each viewed the issues from a different perspective. Because they could not talk it over, however, he reiterated the embassy's viewpoint and requested the Department's, especially Hull's, ideas because it was his fundamental aim to express and carry out that policy. He brought this matter up, he said, because with respect to his suggestions he felt that the Department had accepted the first two and rejected the last. He now wished to explain why the last recommendation was also within the limits of policy the Department had accepted earlier.

Grew praised Hull's speeches putting the United States protest on record but asked that official comment be dropped at that. He reminded Hull how long it had taken him to overcome Japanese antagonism after the Hoover-Stimson rhetoric. Then Grew pleaded with Hull to recognize that any American attempt to thwart Japan's course in China had no chance of success if done with manifestations of disapproval on legal or moral grounds. He did not consider that his policy implied appeasement, which he thought the Department sometimes inferred. Grew explained that he did not recommend acting as friendly broker, for he did believe that conditions could arise when America might desire to change its attitude in order to prevent absolute chaos in China. The current communistic trend, he warned, might create such a necessity; he merely had in mind the constant aim of President Wilson at the beginning of World War I—to place the United States in the most favorable position to exert a moderating influence.[29]

On October 5, 1937, Grew's worst fears concerning American policy became reality. On that day President Roosevelt delivered his famous Quarantine Speech in Chicago, suggesting that Japan as an aggressor should be treated like the carrier of a communicable disease. Grew recorded his sense of doom. Acknowledging that he had not felt much like opening his diary since his entry of September 25, he was now compelled to do so.

I have no right as a representative of the Government to criticize the Government's policy and actions, but that doesn't make me feel any less sorry about the way things have turned. An architect who has spent five years slowly building what he hoped was going to be a solid and permanent edifice and has seen that edifice suddenly crumble about his ears might feel similarly. Or a doctor who has worked hard over a patient and then has lost his case. Our country came to a fork in the road, and, paradoxical as it may seem to a peace-loving nation, chose the road which leads not to peace but potentially to war. Our primary and fundamental concept was to avoid involvement in the Far Eastern mess; we have chosen the road which might lead directly to involvement.[30]

Grew was not just dejected and disappointed; he was bitter and self-righteous. His dream of a career capped by the successful avoidance of American entry into a Far Eastern war and the possible establishment of peace in that area had all but disintegrated. What remained was the task of making it clear, for the historical record, that he had been right and his government wrong when it unjustly robbed him of his historic role. If this sudden "turnabout" achieved anything in the present or future, he would applaud; history and experience, however, proved that such was not possible. Moral suasion was ineffective, he wrote, and economic or financial sanctions were not only ineffective but dangerous.

The "astonishing development" of Japanese sentiment against Great Britain and in favor of America during the few weeks prior to October 5 further substantiated Grew's assessment. His gloom deepened when Count Kabayama stopped by after FDR's speech to tell him that America had now lost her influence and position in Japan.[31] Shortly after this, Grew's depression was completed by Hull's response to a request for closer communication with the Department. Hull told Grew that radio and cable contacts were not secure, and therefore he could not be more intimate in his instructions. The Secretary charged in addition that it was Japan who should wake up to the fact that she had created her own problems.[32]

Grew's spirits revived momentarily in late 1937 and early 1938. He wrote that he had been reluctant to send further recommendations to the Department because he felt they fell on stony ground, but a number of requests for information and several commendations, such as the ones for his mediation in the *Panay* Incident and the settlement of the Alaskan fisheries dispute, lifted his spirits.[33] He even commented favorably on Secretary Hull's defense of administration foreign policy before the National Press Club, referring to it as a powerful and effective presentation. Grew then reflected "that man, in my opinion, grows steadily in stature." He was, however, less willing to praise the whole Department operation. The Ambassador believed that the Department was overly concerned about how the official record looked from a current and historical viewpoint and furthermore that it was secretive regarding the direction of developing policy. (Ironically, Grew faulted the Department for keeping the historical record in mind when that clearly was the purpose of his own daily diary.) He also reiterated one of his most consistent complaints: the lack of information concerning the evolution of policy in Washington and the slow communications between the Department and the embassy.[34]

If during 1938 Grew became less conciliatory toward Japan, this attitude did not extend to economic sanctions. Although he was reluctant to offer new recommendations because of the multitude of factors involved that could be better appraised in Washington, Grew wrote in January 1939 to remind the Department that the effect of sanctions would be abrasive in Japan. He warned the Department that such a course should be taken only if it were to be pursued to the ultimate conclusion which "might mean war." He added that to threaten sanctions or to impose them and then back down would absolutely destroy American influence in Asia.[35]

Before returning home in May for conferences, Grew sought to assess the United States' future position in Asia. He judged that the American record of support for Chinese territorial and administrative integrity was "almost perfect." Then he posed several questions:

Can we and ought we continue permanently to support that principle in the face of hard realism? And what will be the result in the long run if we do? Would we do so if by compromise we could eventually help to bring about peace? And if by refusing to do so, the war would be indefinitely prolonged? These are just a few of the headaches that confront us.[36]

Once in Washington, Grew finally had his chance to talk out Far East policy issues with the Department and the President. Regretfully he noted that face to face meetings did little to enlighten either party. He got only a modicum of information regarding a clearcut definition of policy. Despite this, he was able to discern some answers to the questions he had posed before leaving Japan.

Grew detected "an unmistakable hardening of the Administration's attitude toward Japan and a marked disincliniation to allow American interests to be crowded out of China." In two sessions with FDR, Grew reiterated his opposition to economic sanctions. He forewarned the President that oil sanctions, if imposed, would lead Japan to seize the Dutch East Indies. FDR answered that the United States "could easily intercept her fleet." Grew perceived an unmistakable course as the administration had denounced the 1911 Commerce Treaty with Japan and had stationed extra ships and planes at Pearl Harbor and Manila. "[It] is going to be up to me," he concluded, "to let this American temper discreetly penetrate into Japanese consciousness. Sparks will fly before long."[37]

The mood of the government and the general public at home shocked Grew. If he hoped that another explanation of Japan's problems to the Department and the President might achieve a softer line and a recognition of the "realities" in Asia, he quickly abandoned that prospect and shifted his attention to averting the impending showdown. The best approach now seemed to lie in showing Japan the folly of a course that would inevitably bring down upon her the full force of American economic and military power. Grew decided that there still might be a chance of strengthening Japanese moderates by a forceful, but discreet, illustration of that inevitable fact.

Sometime during the stateside visit, with the concurrence and assistance of Stanley Hornbeck and Maxwell Hamilton, Grew settled upon the idea of a hard hitting public speech in Japan to bring home the American position in a way that could not be ignored. In this fashion Grew's "Straight from the Horse's Mouth" address to the American-Japan Society of October 19, 1939, was conceived. Once back in Japan, however, Grew experienced a change of heart and relapsed to his old argument that relations were improving. Fearing that such a speech might set the wrong tone, he telegraphed the Department on October 16 and tried to back out. The Far East Division was adamant; Japan must be told to respect the American rights and interests in China or bear the consequences.[38]

Grew suggested that "we should now offer Japan a *modus vivendi*, in fact if not in name, that we should commence negotiations for a new treaty, without ratification of such a treaty until favorable developments appear to justify such ratification." Senator Key Pittman had at the time presented a resolution to the Senate promoting an embargo, and Grew argued that if it passed, its implementation should be delayed until Japan had an opportunity to change her treatment of American interests in China. Japan must now recognize that she could not proceed in the reconstruction of China without American aid, he felt, and this had to influence her course. The alternative, he concluded, was to accelerate the move toward a break in relations.[39] Hornbeck and others in the Department construed this as additional evidence that Grew was moving even further towards appeasement.

With some trepidation Grew delivered the address on October 19. The response in the United States was carefully examined by the Department of State, and the press generally approved the speech. In Japan Domei, the official news agency, blustered about Grew's failure to understand Japan any better than the man on the street. Grew pleaded that neither editorial comments nor official public statements reflected the submerged currents of moderate opinion; what really counted, he said, were the reactions he was receiving privately from people of influence. After the message had had time to sink in, he judged that concessions would be forthcoming.[40]

Grew sent the Department a statement from the influential Japanese Institute of the Pacific on November 4, 1939, pointing up the differences between Hull and the Ambassador. The institute's statement argued that peace to the Americans meant preservation of the *status quo* and that all too often Americans envisaged peace in a legalistic sense—the mere absence of warfare. This definition they could not accept.[41] Grew thought the message pointed out the futility of moral posturing, but Hull read the message differently. The Department responded by issuing even more complaints to Japan concerning violations of American rights.[42] The Department moved to a tougher policy and permanently cast aside any hope for moderate forces gaining control in Tokyo; any new conciliatory attitude in Japan therefore would be nothing more than the same old stall.

The growing world crisis apparent at the end of 1939 prompted Grew to outline what may be described as his wishful solution. At many points in his diary he declared that the greatest threat to the world was Russian communism. This concern had provoked his initial opposition to recognition of Russia. As each new Soviet Ambassador to Japan arrived, however, Grew judged him to have far more acceptability than one would expect from a Communist. When the Russo-Finnish War broke out, he quickly condemned the Russians for actions that, when taken by Japan in China, he excused or rationalized. His feelings surfaced when he wrote on December 31, 1939:

If I were to make any political prophecy with regard to the decade we are now entering, it would be that before it is out we shall see Great Britain, France, Germany and Japan fighting together against Soviet Russia, and I do not think that such a prophecy represents too great a stretch of the imagination. My prediction would however add that Mr. Hitler will not be on board at that time.[43]

Once again Grew was not in tune with the tenor in Washington. Henry Morgenthau recorded in December 1939 that FDR desired China to continue to play the game with Russia in order to keep Russia and Japan apart.[44] Grew would have preferred a reverse emphasis, isolating Russia.

IV

Joseph Grew's optimistic hope for peace continued, with some reservations, almost down to the attack on Pearl Harbor. In the last phase of his mission, Grew worked feverishly for accommodation of relations from both directions, but as he did so the chances for impressing his policy on either Japan or the United States diminished significantly. Japan adopted a confidence born of desperation while the men in Washington assumed that Japan would succumb to economic pressure.

In 1940 Grew decided that the best course open to save the situation in Asia lay in direct appeals to the President, and thus he inaugurated a series of "Dear Frank" letters. FDR answered to the first of these that he had always desired to have Grew's estimates of the situation and thoughts regarding the direction American policy should be taking. The President's response said he was giving his consideration to the Far Eastern issue along with other questions.

I believe that you will find that the steps which we take will be characterized by more of patience, and of understanding, along with persistence, than some of our critics expect of us or will give us credit for.

I am delighted with your handling of delicate tasks in a difficult situation. More power to your pen, your voice and your diplomatic personality.[45]

The appeal had been intended for FDR alone, but the President actually sent the letter to the Department of State to answer.

FDR was not impressed by Grew's continued if now restrained optimism. On December 14, 1940, Grew again wrote the President that he would give a great deal to know FDR's views regarding Japan. It seemed increasingly clear, according to Grew, that America and Japan were headed for a showdown; the vital question was whether it should be sooner or later. Everything hinged, he wrote, on whether and when England was likely to win the war and whether war with Japan would so handicap aid to Britain as to make the difference between English victory and defeat. He wondered to what extent American policy in the Far East should be timed to a preparedness program which had not yet altered the relative strengths of the Japanese and American navies. After eight years of trying to build up something permanently constructive in American-Japanese relations, Grew lamented that diplomacy had been defeated by trends and forces utterly beyond its control. His work had been swept away, Grew said, as if by a typhoon. He charged Japan with unashamedly becoming one of the predatory nations of the world, determined to wreck everything the United States represented. If not confronted by insuperable obstacles, Japan would dig in permanently in China and press her advance southward.

Grew tried to accomplish two aims through this letter: to assure the President that he was not blind to Japan's program and its results and to make sure that FDR understood the consequences of whatever course he pursued. Grew still tried to convince the President that direct economic pressure would immediately push Japan to aggression unless she was absolutely convinced that the United States would fight a full-scale war against her; even that might not deter her. If it were made absolutely clear to the Japanese public that their government's course was leading to war, it might discredit the military, revive civilian control, and permit "the resumption of normal relations with us leading to a readjustment of the whole Pacific problem." Grew requested FDR to advise him on the grand strategy, and he offered congratulations on the magnificent way the chief was "piloting the old ship of state."[46]

FDR's response of January 21 argued that the United States needed to recognize that the hostilities in Europe, Africa, and Asia were part of a single world conflict that could not be isolated. This meant that America was defending her "way of life and vital national interests" wherever they were seriously threatened. Strategy in such a contest, he stated, had to be global and centered on total security. In view of this, he concluded that the American problem was "one of defense, [in which] we cannot lay down hard and fast plans. As each new development occurs we must, in the light of the circumstances then existing, decide when and where and how we can most effectively marshal and make use of our resources."[47]

Never had Grew received a more precise answer to his request for guidelines. Obviously his own suggestions had been rejected; his desire for a straightforward announcement to Japan was overruled, and a pragmatic approach was clearly announced. Grew recognized that further entreaties for a conciliatory or cautious course toward Japan were not going to receive a sympathetic hearing in Washington; if he continued to urge such policies, his usefulness was at an end.

That Grew took a harder line with the Japanese thereafter is partially explained by this realization and partially by Japan's refusal to recognize that a change in China policy was necessary if she were to avoid being crushed by the United States, leaving all of Asia open to Russian adventures. Grew had not yet abandoned hope that a contest might be avoided by some miracle, but he became far more circumspect in his briefs to the Department. The desperate nature of Japanese policy, also, contributed to changing Grew's mind. On September 12, 1940, he sent to Washington his "Green Light" despatch which he described as a reluctant necessity.

Until the fall of the Yonai Cabinet in July, Grew noted that his messages to the Department fell into the "Red Light" category, advocating conciliatory methods and avoidance of coercive measures. This changed, according to Grew, when Japan increased her violations of American rights and interests. Yet the Ambassador hestitated to urge sanctions because he wanted to preserve the possibility of Japan swinging back toward the democracies. He faulted the Department and, possibly, the President for this state of affairs. He did not know if Japanese inclinations toward the Axis could be stemmed or if a gesture by the United States could strengthen democratic elements in the country. He still believed, however, and swore he would never change his mind, that a gesture could have been tried without sacrificing basic principles. The absence of such a gesture indicated to Japan that there was no hope of rapprochement with the United States and pushed her into the arms of the Axis powers. Thus the "Green Light" message was based on the failure of what Grew believed had been the best policy and represented his only remaining alternative that might shock Japan into a more reasonable attitude. He felt that Japan ignored American interests partly because she thought that America's pacifism and isolationism would prevent the use of force against Japan. Only by undermining this conviction could effective diplomacy again become a viable alternative to war.[48]

Grew expressed surprise in November at the Department's reaction to his entreaties. Washington opinion concluded that the Ambassador was suggesting that a threat of force by the United States would not be attended by any risk of war and would force Japan to retreat. Wearily he explained once again that a laissez-faire policy, such as that being followed, would lead to war, while a firmer one might not; no one of course could be sure. Despite all this, Grew was still bouyant enough on December 31 to predict that better things would come in 1941.[49]

In January, Grew requested from the Department its perspective regarding actual and hypothetical developments in the Far East. The response was most discouraging, and Grew's frustration was apparent. It seemed simply foolish to act as if hypothetical situations could not be met until they materialized, and he concluded: "If ambassadors are something more than messenger boys, they must be allowed to see behind the scenes."[50] Whether he realized it or not, Grew struck the open nerves of administration policy. First, the Department had taken no more than rudimentary steps for contingency planning and did not usually meet hypothetical situations until they were realities. Second, the ambassadors, unless they had the special confidence of the administration, *were* becoming mere messenger boys. In addition, it was difficult to know what or whom to believe regarding intelligence. Grew noted that there was "a lot of talk around town to the effect that the Japanese, in case of a break with the United States, were planning to go all out in a surprise attack on Pearl Harbor." He guessed, however, "that the boys in Hawaii" weren't "precisely asleep."[51] Yet when Grew got around to reporting this to the Department he described it as a "fantastic rumor."

Unquestionably Grew's last year in Japan was one of frustration and constantly diminishing expectations. He was pleased by a critique of his mission's history done by Hugh Byas of the *New York Times*. Byas agreed with Grew that the Japanese could not understand foreigners because they could not understand themselves and that the Foreign Ministers were not so much duplistic as powerless in the face of the military. He summed up Grew's mission just as Grew was inclined to assess it: it was highly successful given the limits within which the Ambassador was forced to work.[52]

Grew welcomed the Nazi attack on Russia in June 1941 because it accorded with an earlier prediction of his and because it had to benefit the Anglo-American cause. Russia would fight harder than many believed, he thought, and in any case it would give America and England badly needed time to build their military forces. Hopefully Japan would be encouraged to sit on the fence awhile longer.[53]

In attempting to assess Foreign Minister Matsuoka's position, Grew observed that everything he did and said disregarded and discounted a forceful move by the United States, and this might be his undoing. Matsuoka's recklessness upset some high officials, and Grew was told by one of them that in the event of a crisis with the United States the Cabinet would fall in order to get rid of Matsuoka.[54] When the Cabinet was restructured in July leaving Matsuoka out, it did not have the desired result, but Grew remained hopeful despite the danger signs he noted everywhere. During the Japanese move in Indo-China he warned Foreign Minister Toyoda that no one believed his assurances that this was a temporary expedient, for too often such assurances had proved worthless. "The Government proposes," he said, "the Army disposes."

Woefully Grew assessed the situation. The United States and Great Britain were through with "so-called appeasement." Unless something drastic happened, it was "difficult to see how the momentum of this downgrade development in our relations can be arrested, nor how far it will go. The obvious conclusion is war." Still Grew did not believe a break would come for he thought the Washington conversations being carried on between Ambassador Nomura and Hull might create a new chance.[55] That new chance would be a meeting between Roosevelt and Konoye. The details of the exchanges between Washington and Tokyo are too familiar and available to need reiteration; the important point here is Grew's reactions to the situation. The tenseness of the American Ambassador at this juncture is evident in the diary, and each delay in coming to grips with the essential questions at issue made him more frantic as did each incident that made the talks less feasible or dampened their possible effectiveness.

Convinced that Japan desperately wanted a way out, Grew thought the meeting between Konoye and FDR would provide the means. When a Japanese Prime Minister was willing to shatter precedent and come hat in hand to a meeting outside of Japan, Grew judged it an indication of desperation and resolve. No preliminary planning would be effective; only at the meeting itself could Konoye propose concessions that would represent a commitment he could not escape.[56] Grew fretted and wondered at the delay; when he urged action and was ignored, he concluded that the Department once again was side-tracking him.

Grew was aware of the Department's view of his "vacillations." But he became particularly aroused at a letter from Stanley Hornbeck, reminding him that the Department had indeed followed his suggestions on Japanese policy and citing eight pages of excerpts from Grew's earlier despatches in which he had indicated that the time for conciliation was "*then*" past. Obviously irritated, the Ambassador quickly came to his own defense.

I do not quite know just what was in Stanley Hornbeck's mind in sending me those excerpts unless it was in the. belief, and with the purpose of calling attention to that belief, that I am now advocating so-called 'appeasement' in counter-distinction to my former recommendation for a stronger policy. In the first place, 'appeasement,' through association with Munich and umbrellas, has become an unfortunate ill-used and misinterpreted term. It is not appeasement that I now advocate, but 'constructive conciliation'. . . . I can find nothing inconsistent in my recommendations during these past several years, and if we are able to avoid war with Japan it will be largely due to the fact that those recommendations have in the main been followed.[57]

Grew judged that he had made possible the saving of the peace, and the chance had been ignored. When his suggestions were rebuffed in October, Grew was both furious and dejected: "They might at least have consulted me . . . but I have the feeling, whether justified or not, that my opinions are not particularly welcome nowadays."[58] Three days later, with even more apparent gloom, Grew noted that the Konoye Cabinet had fallen.

On November 29, Grew was buoyant again. He had passed through many critical days in Japan; they had been surmounted, he wrote, and could be again. "I haven't packed a thing and do not intend to."[59] On December 1, however, a note of impending disaster reappeared in the diary. A succession of callers warned Grew that the final moment of decision was at hand and requested that the Washington conversations be immediately brought to a successful conclusion. The Ambassador was impressed by the overriding pessimism of all his callers and considered their concern ominous. He was especially disturbed when he saw Count Kabayama at the Tokyo Club looking "grey and worn." The Count told Grew the Cabinet had decided to break off the conversations. Grew responded that in that case he feared that everything was over; he would soon be leaving Japan.[60]

All of Grew's efforts at "salvaging something" from the "mess" in the Far East, of course, came to naught on December 7. The events of that day were meticulously recorded in his diary with a note of finality and, almost, relief. He had called on Foreign Minister Togo to deliver FDR's last appeal, and it was refused as he was informed that the conversations were being abandoned. "On leaving [Togo's] official residence," Grew recalled, "I had not the slightest feeling that a break had occurred except for a break in the conversations."[61] He returned to his residence intending to play golf when the spokesman for the Foreign Office with trembling hands delivered the announcement of the commencement of hostilities. When he heard later that Togo had not known of the attack at the time of their talk, Grew speculated that once again the military had plunged Japan into a disastrous war without the knowledge of the Foreign Office.

V

On February 19, 1942, Grew forwarded his observations on the last weeks before the attack in his "Report of the Final Development in Tokyo leading to the Outbreak of War Between the United States and Japan." This despatch was somewhat defensive regarding the embassy's position in those final days. This was mild in comparison to a letter Grew began composing to FDR on the *SS Gripsholm* en route to the United States on August 14, 1942. He appended to this letter a copy of his final report to the Department. He told the President that he might want to read the report because it would be carefully weighed by future historians as contemporary evidence bearing on the question "as to whether, compatible with our national interests and without sacrificing any point of principle, war with Japan could have been avoided." This was a rhetorical question, for in the letter Grew made it more apparent than he had in the despatch that he was convinced that war was unnecessary. The American government, he charged, had failed to take the last hurried steps to postpone if not eliminate the Pacific war. Now posterity would know that the Ambassador in Japan had not failed his government; it had failed him and the world.[62]

The letter was never sent, and Grew attached a comment to it dated January 10, 1943, explaining his change of heart. On his return to Washington he saw evidence unavailable to him in Japan that affected the administration policy and somewhat altered the situation. Most significant, of course, was the Japanese correspondence secured by breaking their code. Nonetheless, Grew did not give up his effort to prove or at least rationalize his position, and on March 26, 1943, while preparing his book *Ten Years in Japan,* he requested permission to use some of his telegrams to the Department from Tokyo bearing on the proposed meeting between the President and Prince Konoye. Grew pointed out considerations supporting his contention that such a meeting would have succeeded, and he argued that the story was incomplete without the inclusion of the telegrams.

The Department did not object to publishing the telegrams but did remind Grew that in those communications he had called attention to the restricted viewpoint of the embassy in Tokyo and had presented his views with due regard to the "far broader field of view" of the President and the Secretary of State. Hull noted that the facts known in Washington illustrated that, "while [the Japanese] were prepared to give lip service to vague generalities, they were not prepared to give up insistence upon a right to station large bodies of troops in large areas of China for an indeterminate period of time and to give up otherwise their purpose of carrying out the program of general aggression and domination of the whole Pacific area." This all should be included as clarification, Hull said. Grew should remember that FDR and Hull both thought that in view of the stall tactics previously used a meeting without an advance agreement on general principles and provisions regarding some of the basic questions would be futile. Besides, the nation was now at war.[63]

Hull tried to show Grew how he had influenced the final course. He quoted Grew's despatch of March 30, 1941, in which the Ambassador said it was time to get tough with Japan, for it was the last and best hope to convince her that the United Stated meant business. It seemed evident to Hull that the Department had taken Grew's policy recommendations to heart, and he could not understand the Ambassador's peevishness.[64]

Perhaps Grew was correct in arguing that the Roosevelt-Konoye talks at least could have done no harm, but Konoye's own testimony illustrates equally that they would have done no good, a fact which Grew never believed even when the Konoye diaries came into American hands. He believed to the end of his life that Konoye would have given way (as Grew said he would) when he faced the American President across the conference table. Grew never lost his conviction that he had been robbed of his historic role as "the peacemaker."

Notes

1 Waldo Heinrich's excellent volume on Grew's diplomatic career establishes beyond doubt that his greatest success as a diplomat occurred when he conducted negotiations at Lausanne for the peace treaty which would officially terminate hostilities with Turkey in 1923 and set the pattern for amicable U.S.-Turkish relations for several decades. See Waldo Heinrichs, Jr., *American Ambassador: Joseph C. Grew and the Development of the United States Diplomatic Tradition* (Boston: Little, Brown and Co., 1966).

2 The Papers of Joseph C. Grew (The Houghton Library of Harvard College Library, Cambridge, Massachusetts), bMS Am. 1687.5, Diary, vol. 65. Unless otherwise indicated all citations are from the Grew Papers, Diaries; Grew to Stimson, June 30, 1932, United States Department of State Files 894.00/423 (National Archives, Washington, D.C.). Cited hereafter as DSF; Grew to Stimson, February 23, 1923, DSF/G 861/454. The author is indebted to the Harvard College Library for permission to use the vast collection of the Grew Papers.

3 References to these reflections of Grew may be found as follows: 1938, 93:3741 and unnumbered page following page 3939; October 1940 and November 1940, 101:4561, 4613; Grew to Hull, September 15, 1937, 85:3463.

4 August 17, 1934, 72:1150-1151.

5 Heinrichs, *Grew*, pp. 6-10.

6 Grew to Miss Margaret Perry, February 13, 1932, Grew Papers, Letter Books, 1932, vol. 2, K-Z.

7 *Ibid.*, Grew to Franklin Roosevelt, November 12, 1932.

8 Heinrichs, *Grew*, pp. 28-30.

9 *Ibid.*, p. 30.

10 1939, 94:4191.

11 Grew to Henry L. Stimson, October 22, 1932, DSF 894.00/448½.

12 January 9, 1933, 65:413-414.

13 Grew to Cordell Hull, February 6, 1935, with accompanying cover memorandum by Eugene H. Dooman of February 26, 1935, DSF 894.00/541.

14 *Ibid.*

15 *Ibid.*

16 Grew to Prentiss Gilbert, May 17, 1934, with cover memorandum from Hornbeck to William Phillips and Hull, June 6, 1934, DSF 894.00/521.

17 Grew to Hull, December 14, 1933, DSF 894.00/498; See also, for example, Franklin Delano Roosevelt Library, Hyde Park, New York, President's Secretary's File, Japan, May 11, 1934, "National Defense Propaganda and Its Effect," a report prepared by the Military Attaché in Tokyo and accompanying despatch from Grew. Cited hereafter as FDRL.

18 Grew to Hull, April 6, 1933, DSF 123 Grew, Joseph C., 861/537.

19 Grew to Hull, April 6, 1934, DSF F/G 894.00/510.

20 Despatch of May 3, 1935, with cover memorandum of May 23, 1935, by Maxwell Hamilton and commentary of March 5, 1936, by Stanley Hornbeck, DSF 894.00/544.

21 Memorandum of conversation between Cordell Hull and Ambassador Saito Hiroshi, May 29, 1934, The Cordell Hull Papers (Library of Congress, Manuscripts Division, Washington, D.C.), Memorandum of Conversations, Great Britain-Japan, Box 59, Folder 228. Cited hereafter as Hull Papers.

22 November 20, 1933, 71:784.

23 March 1937, 85:3197.

24 July 21, 1937, 85:3278.

25 July 31, 1937, 85:3303.

26 August 13, 1937, 85:3330.

27 *Ibid.*, 3332-3333.

28 August 1937, 85:3405-3409.

29 Grew to Hull, September 15, 1937, Correspondence Section, vol. 85.

30 October 1937, 85:3473.

31 *Ibid.*, 3474-3476; October 5, 1937, 85:3487.

32 Hull to Grew, October 16, 1937, 85:3487.

33 October 30, 1937, 85:3515-3517; Heinrichs, *Grew*, pp. 257-258; January 10, 1938, 93:3670.

34 April 1938, 93:3741-3742.

35 January 1939, 94:3954.

36 May 1939, 94:4080.

37 Leave of Absence, 1939, 94:4083-4084.

38 Grew to Hull, October 16, 1939, with cover memorandum by Maxwell Hamilton of the same date, DSF 123 G 861/814.

39 December 1, 1939, 94:4155-4156.

40 Grew to Hull, October 31, 1939, DSF 123 G 861/831.

41 Grew to Hull, November 4, 1939, DSF 123 G 861/836.
42 Grew Papers, bMS Am. 1687.3, Conversations 1939-1940, p. 72 ff., p. 179 ff.
43 December 1939, 94:4200-4204.
44 FDRL, The Henry Morgenthau, Jr. Papers, The Morgenthau Diaries, Book 230, December 1939, p. 408.
45 FDR to Grew, January 18, 1940, FDRL, Official File 197, Japan— 1933-1945, Box 1.
46 Grew Papers, bMS Am. 1687.8, January 21, 1941, Personal Notes, no. 144, pp. 4792-4793.
47 *Ibid.*
48 September 1940, 101:4506-4520.
49 *Ibid.*, 4613 ff; December 31, 1940, 101:4697.
50 Grew Papers, bMS Am. 1687.8, January 1941, Personal Notes, no. 143, p. 4716. Footnotes 51 through 61 are from Personal Notes.
51 January 1941, no. 143, p. 4735.
52 *Ibid.*, 4763-4765.
53 June 1941, no. 148. There is no page number for this entry; it comes after the cover page for June 1941.
54 May 1941, p. 5100; June 10, 1941, p. 5217.
55 July 1941, p. 5332.
56 September 1941, pp. 5624-5632.
57 *Ibid.*
58 October 13, 1941, p. 5838.
59 November 29, 1941, pp. 5973-5974.
60 December 1, 1941, p. 6097.
61 December 1, 1941, pp. 6102-6110.
62 Grew Papers, bMS Am. 1687.1, Despatch no. 6018; Official Report after returning to the United States with unsent letter to Franklin D. Roosevelt, August 14, 1942.
63 Hull Papers, Subject File, Great Britain-Hull, Cordell, Box no. 66, Folder no. 292, Grew, Joseph C., *Ten Years in Japan.*
64 *Ibid.,* Memorandum of August 25, 1943.

Richard Dean Burns

Stanley K. Hornbeck

The Diplomacy of the Open Door

SCHOLARLY, CONSCIENTIOUS, and tenacious, Stanley Kuhl Hornbeck (1883-1966) left a distinct mark on America's Far Eastern policies during the interwar years. As the State Department's leading expert on Asia during the 1930's, he has been pictured as a man of generous contradictions. In the diplomatic game of "give-and-take," Hornbeck often emerged as an ardent foe of compromise;[1] a self-taught expert on the Far East, he usually seemed to ignore European or "global" issues; and a deliberate man of several hundred carefully honed memoranda, he occasionally indulged in extravagant political speculation.

Yet if Hornbeck appeared dogmatic in his insistence that Japan live up to its treaty obligations, he was equally critical of China on identical grounds. If he seemed to react to every issue "in specific relation to the Far Eastern situation and the Far Eastern situation alone" as one State Department colleague has suggested,[2] this attitude stemmed from his belief that the principles at stake in Asia were truly universal and thus affected America's affairs worldwide. And if his occasional indulgence in prophecy sometimes dramatically misfired—and it should be noted that his colleagues' prognostications were hardly more distinguished—it was usually because he failed to allow for the irrational.

Thus although historians have frequently quoted Hornbeck, they have rarely understood him. In spite of the appearance of contradictory behavior, Hornbeck was—over a lifetime of wrestling with difficult political and economic issues—more consistent than not. During his early schooling, he absorbed a brand of nineteenth-century internationalism that espoused voluntary, cooperative international action which, when successful, would define all nations' common interest in independence, order, and justice.[3] At the same time, his study of history convinced him that, apart from national safety, the United States' major diplomatic achievements lay in the adoption of a noninterventionist attitude and the development of an Open Door policy. To Hornbeck the historic Open Door policy meant simply that American citizens should have equal opportunity with all other foreigners to trade their goods and invest their capital in the less developed countries. He refused to believe that the allied noninterventionist principle constituted such American commercial enterprise as imperialism; only when a nation (such as Japan in the 1930's) employed political advantage and military force to create preferential markets did imperialism take place. When this latter behavior threatened, particularly in Asia, Hornbeck sallied forth as a jealous champion of the Open Door.

I

After nearly twenty years of apprenticeship as author, lecturer, technical adviser on international political and economic affairs, and special expert on Asian matters, Dr. Hornbeck became, in 1928, Chief of the State Department's Division of Far Eastern Affairs. He held this desk under Secretary of State Henry L. Stimson during the Hoover administration and, from 1933, under Cordell Hull during the New Deal era; in 1937 he was promoted to one of the newly created offices of Advisor on Political Relations.* Occupying an important middle-echelon position, his influence on foreign policy decisions depended on his personal reputation for expertise, his confidence in his own policy contentions, his ability to articulate his view convincingly, and, most vital of all, his access to receptive higher officials. In each category he scored well; indeed it is Arthur N. Young's considered opinion that Hornbeck was "influential at the highest level in policy matters relating to the Far East, including policy toward Japan on the eve of Pearl Harbor. In particular, he was close to Secretary Cordell Hull who relied heavily upon his judgment."[4]

An unrepenting Midwestern Republican, Hornbeck found his views better received by Hull, the Tennessee Democrat, than by Stimson, a fellow Republican. A clannish member of the Eastern seaboard establishment, Stimson liked to work through his own special assistant, Allen T. Klots, rather than the regular department staff although he did consult frequently with his specialists. Hornbeck was counterbalanced during these discussions by Assistant Secretary of State William R. Castle, Jr., who tended to be more

*Later Hornbeck served as a member of one of the postwar planning groups (1942-1944), as a Special Assistant to Hull at Dumbarton Oaks (1944), and finally completed his career as Ambassador to the Netherlands (1944-1947).

sympathetic to Japan's views than most members of the Department. Hornbeck later recalled that he was almost handed his "walking papers" by Stimson during the Manchurian crisis when he disputed the Secretary's optimistic hope that the Japanese Army might not press its opportunity for additional conquest; another time he reportedly got Stimson "into one of his rages" by making a word by word review of a document whose tone Hornbeck hoped to soften.[5]

Hornbeck welcomed Hull's arrival at the State Department, for the new Secretary was more in accord with his recommendations on Far Eastern policies. If Hornbeck and Hull did not always agree on policy matters, they developed a firm, candid friendship which extended beyond their official contacts. One of their unsuspected intimacies was croquet, a game to which Hull was addicted and to which he frequently challenged his less enthusiastic subordinate. They thought it best not to advertise their private matches; after all, the American public had decided opinions as to which sports were considered manly, and croquet seldom ranked very high among these.[6]

Lively, dark-eyed, and burdened with a slight paunch, Hornbeck brought to the Far Eastern desk a positive, often assertive, personality. Most of his departmental associates saw him as a man of integrity, sincere, intellectually honest, serious, and dedicated to his work. An extraordinarily prolific writer of memoranda, he kept a careful record of his views and recommendations; he was, therefore, "most conscientious in [departmental] debate." Moreover, he poured over departmental drafts meticulously, pouncing on the slightest error in punctuation or grammar. His concern for what he believed to be correct policies led him at times to be forceful and frank to the point of bluntness. If associates and subordinates found him occasionally difficult to work with, they nonetheless respected his abilities. Joseph W. Ballantine, a close, long-time colleague in the Department, could "speak only in superlatives" about Hornbeck. "We often had arguments on procedure and policy . . . but he readily yielded when [and this was infrequent] it was shown that he had failed to consider material factors of which he had not been aware or had misjudged."[7] All in all, co-worker Herbert Feis remembered Hornbeck, in personality and character, as "basically a school teacher."[8]

Religious training and academic accomplishments established themselves early among the forces which molded Hornbeck's life and career. The combined influence of the two were manifest in his later self-discipline and perfectionism. Perhaps, too, they might help account for his devotion to the immutable "principles" governing American foreign policy, principles which he often pressed with a tenacity bordering on religious conviction.

A seventh-generation American of Dutch, German, and English stock, Stanley was born May 4, 1883, in Franklin, Massachusetts, to Reverend

Marquis and Lydia Kuhl Hornbeck. The senior Hornbeck, a devout Methodist minister, served pastorates in Illinois, Massachusetts, and finally Colorado. The family's frequent moves—young Stanley attended nine different elementary and secondary schools—did not seem to disturb the warm, orderly family of modest financial means; indeed, this family developed an enduring, close relationship. Reminiscing about his early years, Stanley recalled that he had been brought up in a "religiously-minded household and in a religion-based college." We "practiced what my father preached," he later remarked. "In our home there was reading and studying of the Bible and there were prayers every day."[9]

As religious training within the home nourished Stanley Hornbeck's character, his academic aptitudes were similarly encouraged. Unusual for their generation, his mother and father were both college graduates; additionally, Marquis served at one time as president of Chaddock College in Quincy, Illinois. Young Hornbeck graduated Phi Beta Kappa from the University of Denver in 1903 and spent the next year teaching high school before accepting one of the first Rhodes scholarships. The following two years he lived comfortably at Oxford where he studied modern European history under the renowned H.A.L. Fisher, an experience which left him less anti-British than most middle-westerners but far from the Anglophile that Cecil Rhodes had in mind.[10] Continuing his graduate training at the University of Wisconsin, Hornbeck received his Ph.D. in political science *in absentia* (1911) after he had left Madison for a first-hand view of Far Eastern politics.

That Hornbeck became an Asian "expert" was due to an accident of circumstance and curiosity, for neither his schooling at Denver, nor his graduate work at Oxford and Wisconsin, exposed him to that mysterious corner of the world. Responding to an advertisement appearing in the local university (Madison) newspaper, Hornbeck secured a position as instructor (1909-1913) at the Chinese Provincial College in Hangchow, Chekiang Province.[11] When he returned from China, his career intermingled academic pursuits—lecturing at the University of Wisconsin (1913-1917) and Harvard University (1924-1928)—with extensive government service.

Hornbeck's initial scholarly studies appeared while he was in China: in 1910 the University of Wisconsin printed his thesis, *The Most-Favored-Nation Clause in Commercial Treaties;* in 1916 D. Appleton Company issued his *Contemporary Politics in the Far East;* and in 1917 the *Proceedings of the Academy of Political Science* published his essay, "Trade, Concessions, Investments Conflicts and Policy in the Far East." His expertise thus established, he became a consultant to the United States Tariff Commission in 1917 and later in 1918 a member of "The Inquiry," Wilson's postwar planning group, where he supervised research on Far Eastern issues. The thirty-four year old Hornbeck subsequently went to Paris with the Presidential party as "a general assistant" to the Peace Commission; once there he represented the United States on the commission studying the disposition of Tientsin.

A prodigious worker throughout his life, Hornbeck devoted most of his early years to the pursuit of his career. Although he was not to raise a family, he did surrender his bachelorhood in 1938 when he married Viviene Barkalaw Breckenridge, who was Dean of Women at American University in the capital. Hornbeck noted approvingly that his wife worked hard "at being a successful *chatelaine*"; that she could aspire to being the mistress of a manor was due in large measure to her husband's wise investments.[12] Not surprisingly, Hornbeck remained a fervent believer in the American "free enterprise" system and in fundamental Republicanism.

II

Hornbeck evolved the ideas basic to his concept of foreign policy quite early in his career. The foundation of his ideological framework rested on two interrelated, but unevenly weighted, premises. First, he believed that his nation's most fundamental interests and attitudes toward the world community hinged on basic, deterministic principles that he found rooted deep in America's past. These principles he defined, at various times, as security, independence, nonintervention, and equality of opportunity; by the latter he meant, of course, commercial equality as embodied in the American tradition of the "Open Door."[13] Second, Hornbeck argued that the United States, as well as all nations, could best achieve these principles through global respect for international law and arbitral procedures. When this respect faltered, he recommended sanctions to persuade recalcitrant nations to alter illegal behavior.

Thus both the essence and the priorities of Hornbeck's foreign policy ideas were relatively uncomplicated. America's diplomacy must be designed to maintain national security and protect commercial opportunity. In what better environment could these prime objectives be achieved than in a cooperative, orderly, judicial-minded international community?

In one of his more graphic metaphorical flights, Hornbeck described foreign policy as "a living thing" growing "not unlike a tree" which drew its life from "its roots." The growth and development of America's foreign policy was similarly conditioned by the nation's historical experiences. These were the product of the American people collectively, not merely an abstract historical process, and were thus identifiable. To explain the immigration from Europe to the new world, he found two closely related motives: the search for fresh, largely economic opportunities and the flight from traditional political and economic oppression. If these twin aspects of

America's heritage first conditioned domestic affairs, they subsequently found a dominant place in the nation's external policies. "The principal major objectives of American foreign policy since the earliest days of the Republic," he argued, "have been, first, to safeguard this country's position as a free and sovereign state and, second, to obtain for American nationals and American trade assurances of equal opportunity and fair treatment in every place to which American citizens, American ships and American goods may choose to go."[14]

Hornbeck viewed the Open Door policy in its worldwide and, particularly, its Asian application as a logical and natural extension of a maturing America. He found its broad antecedents in Washington's Farewell Address and in the Monroe Doctrine. The former, he believed, enunciated the principle of noninvolvement in the political affairs of other nations and restated the principle of impartial commercial relations, both of which aimed at preserving American sovereignty and independence and at reinforcing equality of opportunity. The Monroe Doctrine was even more basic: it was an affirmation by the American people of the superiority of the political system they had brought to this continent. (On one occasion, Hornbeck declared: "Our political ideas are, I believe, superior, in liberality at least, and in reference to international relations particularly, to those of any other nation.")[15] Moreover, he argued that the doctrine was a defensive, self-denying statement which reinforced the principles of nonintervention and equality of opportunity.[16]

Hornbeck's convictions regarding the origins of America's Open Door policy in China were not only formed early; they were simplistic. He questioned neither the purity of American motives nor the salutary nature of the policy; indeed, he, as many of his generation, had seen and approved Secretary of State John Hay's rush to save defenseless China from the wickednesses of "spheres of influence."[17] In Hornbeck's words, "It was the American Government which at this point [the Hay notes] stepped forward and proposed the formal and general adoption of the 'open door policy,' asking the powers to pledge themselves to observe the principles therein involved—the idea being to establish by mutual consent a rule which should operate as a guarantee of equality of opportunity and as a positive force in securing the peace of the Far East and the best interests of all the countries concerned."[18] In 1922 he rejoiced when Hay's program was made into a contractual arrangement (the Nine Power Pact) legally binding its signatories to the Open Door principles.

Hornbeck was explicit on the relationship between the Monroe Doctrine and the Open Door in Asia. "As we have sought under the Monroe Doctrine to prevent interference which would undermine the political *status quo* in the Western Hemisphere, so, under the doctrine of the open door, we have opposed activities tending toward new alterations of the territorial *status quo* or toward international complications, either political or commercial, in China."[19] Characteristically, he failed to comprehend that other peoples might find aspects of economic coercion or imperialism practical under both doctrines.

As early as 1916 Hornbeck considered Japan to be a major threat to America's Asian interests, as may be seen from a chapter in his *Contemporary Politics in the Far East* entitled "Japan's Monroe Doctrine for Asia." This title did not stem from any *official* governmental declaration, he acknowledged, but rather it grew from Japan's general attitude. The Japanese, he wrote

> have justified each and all of the features of their China policy by one or more of the following contentions:
> (1) that Japan must have room for colonization, and that Manchuria and Eastern Inner Mongolia are legitimate fields for her expansion;
> (2) that Japan must have room for commercial expansion, and all China is a legitimate field for that expansion;
> (3) that in her political activities Japan is merely endeavoring to protect China against her own weakness which is a menace at once to China and to Japan;
> (4) that it is Japan's duty and her purpose to maintain the peace of the Far East.[20]

Hornbeck criticized these Japanese contentions on two counts: first, he argued that it was fallacious to compare Japan's Asian policies to the United States' Monroe Doctrine; and, second, he thought Japanese society too politically immature to understand the true benefits of the Open Door policy.

Hornbeck steadfastly denied any analogy between Japan's and America's Monroe Doctrine. The United States, he insisted, might have established the doctrine "for our own benefit," but it "did not endeavor in any way to restrain or coerce the other American states," nor did it ask for "special privilege for ourselves at the expense either of the smaller nations or of Europe." The United States had "sought to protect the smaller, weaker, less wealthy countries against foreign aggression." America, he acknowledged in 1916, had "asked for and secured the Canal Zone in Panama and we have assumed a quasi-protectorate over Haiti and Santo Domingo and in a sense over Cuba—but consider the circumstances!"[21] Later in 1934 Hornbeck argued in a seven-page memorandum that:

> The American Monroe Doctrine is defensive and claims no special privileges beyond a maintenance of the existing *status quo*: the Japanese 'Monroe Doctrine' is aggressive, and is apparently aimed at strengthening and extending Japan's political influence, military position and economic privileges in Eastern Asia, by the use, if necessary, of the same forceable methods which she has employed in obtaining these ends in Korea and Manchuria. Whether this policy of Japan is or is not justified, it certainly bears little relation to the Doctrine associated with the name of Monroe.[22]

In 1916 at least, Hornbeck was inclined to regard as "sincere" the Japanese who persistently asserted that they had not violated their pledge to honor the Open Door and equal opportunity. He thought that these statesmen, bred in a society lacking at least theoretical liberty and equality, were "not in the best of positions . . . to comprehend the fine points of a policy of 'equality of treatment,' or, comprehending, to play the game according to them." These Japanese apparently believed the Open Door to mean "something like 'unimpeded right of admission,' " while equality of opportunity was interpreted as the "right of any one to compete, as best he may, with and against other competitors." Consequently, Hornbeck argued that neither Japanese government nor public understood that preferential loans or special tariff privileges ran counter to the Western view of equal opportunity. "None of these methods of doing business can be declared to be a *direct* violation of the principles of the open door," he wrote. "They do, however, constitute an indirect interference—on the part of the Japanese government—with the natural course of equality of opportunity."[23]

China was not without fault in Hornbeck's eyes, since it was "China's business to put herself in position to maintain her own integrity and to enforce her own treaty obligations. Self-reliance is one of the most conspicuous of China's needs." He suggested five essential programs that the Chinese government should undertake: (1) enforce all treaty obligations and administer laws in such a manner "as to make for a genuine and universal equality of treatment"; (2) respond "liberally toward all foreigners alike who wish to make *bona fide* investments"; (3) arrange for fair and equal assessment of taxes; (4) organize an efficient police system; and (5) institute a uniform currency system. He never endorsed the notion that the United States was responsible for maintaining the territorial integrity of China; indeed, he insisted that "it lies with China in the first and last instance to say and to determine whether the open door shall prevail."[24]

As a result of these critical estimates of Chinese and Japanese practices and ambitions, Hornbeck entered the State Department committed to a personal attitude of "even-handedness" toward the parties. He thought American foreign policy ought to be politically noninterventionist and ought to rest on the insistence that both Japan and China live up to their treaty obligations.

This latter concern reflected Hornbeck's belief in the necessity of international law and order. "Of all the principles cherished by our people," he wrote in 1939, "the most fundamental is that of democracy. Essential to the existence and continuing success of democracy is peace. Essential to peace is national security. . . . There can be real security only in an environment of comparative justice and fair treatment." Justice and fair treatment, he continued, were dependent upon law and order among nations for America "recognized international law as a part of the law of our land."[25]

Hornbeck found both China and Japan delinquent in their respect for the sanctity of treaties. "Almost no Oriental considers that he is under any obligation, either moral or legal," he wrote in 1931, "in relation to a pledge which he had made under duress—and his definition of duress is widely comprehensive." Moreover, he concluded, "the ideal of 'peace' is an ideal of a few Occidental states"; if other governments had agreed to this ideal their people were "not mentally committed" to it. While Hornbeck credited Americans with being sincere in their respect for treaty obligations, he thought this represented "an idealism . . . considerably in advance of the great majority of the human race." By 1936 despair had begun to replace his idealism and hopes for the rule of law; he warned Hull that "no useful purpose is to be served by pushing the world too fast and too far on lines of idealism without due consideration of realities."[26]

When such realities comprised a serious challenge to his basic foreign policy principles, however, Hornbeck was less certain about what to do. He posed the fundamental question as early as 1916: "But what do we do when evidence of policies which run counter to these principles are laid before us?" At that time, when Japan was pressing its infamous Twenty-One Demands, he acknowledged that the "American government in its official advocacy of the open door policy assumed a position of responsibility" and that "this responsibility makes imperative something more than mere reiterated protestations of friendly interest."[27] Yet he was unable to recommend policies other than vague diplomatic undertakings for he never believed that the United States had pledged its military forces to the maintenance of the Open Door or the integrity of China. "We have made no promise to use force on behalf of those principles," he wrote in 1935, but "we have no right to take action in authorization of their impairment." The United States might have to temporarily "acquiesce" in their impairment, but it need not assent to it. In this light, he stressed that "*authorization, assent, acquiescence, diplomatic opposition by force* are all separate and distinct things."[28]

Hornbeck's rejection of the use of military force to maintain the Open Door reflected his attachment to the principles of nonintervention and international adjudication and his belief that war was uncivilized and unproductive. He nevertheless urged the building of a strong navy, argued to have it stationed in the Pacific, and, from 1938-1941, occasionally implied that employing it would be justified. Apparently he considered American military power to be a deterrent and, if this failed, he intended it to defend American soil; at no time did he recommend the employment of American forces in any other sense. On occasion he did argue, rather obliquely, that any nations's denial or discrimination "against the United States in the field of commercial opportunity" would be resented by its citizens. "Such denial will, therefore, always be a potential factor among those factors which may make up a *causus belli*."[29] Remarks such as these do cause one to wonder whether he might have taken a more aggressive posture had the American people been willing to support a more forceful policy.

If he ruled out the use of military force in his policy recommendations, Hornbeck did gradually come to favor the employment of international *economic* sanctions. His initial development of this idea resulted from a canvas during the Manchurian crisis of "every remaining possible course of action" to make American policy more viable. In two short paragraphs he set forth his views:

> An economic boycott is a weapon. It may or may not be regarded as a weapon of force; it is certainly not a weapon of 'war.' It is a weapon midway between a weapon of 'moral force' and a weapon of 'physical force.'
>
> ... [An economic boycott] is a weapon of defense rather than of offense and it can no more be objected to from point of treaty obligations and peace policies than can tariffs, customs procedure, coast guard and coast fortifications. It is a weapon the use of which involves no projection of the efforts of the user beyond his own shores, involves no bloodshed, and destroys (in the long run) nothing.[30]

Hornbeck's appreciation of economic sanctions grew in the 1930's as Japan became more unmanageable; by the end of 1938 he had become a staunch advocate of the use of sanctions.

It may be questioned whether Hornbeck ever fully appreciated the implications of this "weapon." He never seemed to grasp the ease with which its employment could escalate—when used against a determined foe—or the rapidity with which this escalation could lead to hostilities. Joseph Grew later charged that Hornbeck's "wishful thinking" about Japan's reluctance to fight clouded the State Department's vision of the desperate Far Eastern crisis, and in fact, he warned Hornbeck about this frequently during the period 1938-1941.[31] It is perhaps unfair to single out Hornbeck's assumptions regarding economic sanctions; after all most of the internationalists of the nineteenth and early twentieth centuries lauded it. Indeed, Article 16 of the League's Covenant endorsed this device as a means of applying pressure "short of war."

In 1932 Hornbeck concisely summarized those principles he thought ought to guide American foreign policy:

(1) respect for the legal and moral rights of other states and peoples—with the expectation of respect by them for the legal and moral rights of the United States;

(2) in regard to commerce, equality of opportunity and treatment—on the basis of the most-favored-nation practice;

(3) in regard to political methods, abstention from alliances and from aggression;

(4) in the field of diplomatic approach, persuasion rather than coercion;

(5) in regard to sanction, cooperation with other powers wherever cooperation is found practically possible.[32]

III

Three major diplomatic episodes engaged Hornbeck at the Far Eastern desk from 1928 through 1936. First, he encountered the growing pressure of Chinese nationalism during these baptismal years at the Department as China pressed for an end to extraterritoriality. Second, he helped to formulate America's response to Japan's initial continental expansionism of the 1930's—a role which found him ultimately critical of Stimson's "non-recognition" doctrine. Third, he counselled a hard-line naval policy during the lull in tensions between 1934-1936 in the belief that a powerful American navy would deter Japan's aggressiveness. Yet throughout this entire period he espoused a doctrine of "even-handed" treatment of both China and Japan by the United States.

In grappling with China's growing sense of nationalism, Hornbeck usually displayed a cautious, conservative attitude. One example of his reservations occurred in 1928 when Dr. Sao-ke Alfred Sze, China's Minister to Washington, proposed the mutual advancement of embassies to ambassadorial rank. Hornbeck wrote to Stimson that such a move then would be "precocious" since China had failed to live up to its international obligations sufficiently to merit Great Power status.[33] This response characterized Hornbeck's misgivings about China's ability and willingness to honor her pledge to protect American citizens and property, an attitude which he formed as early as 1914 and held well into the late 1930's.

One major source of friction in Sino-American relations in 1928-1931 sprang from China's insistence upon ending all extraterritorial treaty rights. The idea that foreign citizens were exempt from Chinese law and courts was particularly offensive to the increasingly self-aware Chinese. From their standpoint three primary issues were at stake: the surrender of criminal, civil, and police jurisdiction over American citizens in China; the right of appointment of legal counselors by the Chinese government without restrictions; and the abolition of the extraterritorial rights everywhere in China, including any so-called "reserve areas" currently policed by foreign troops.[34] As discussion of those issues progressed, first in the 1920's and then in the 1930's, Chinese officials clearly saw essential difficulties: "The question of extraterritoriality is regarded from two different points of view by China and the powers. China regards it as a political question; the powers regard it as a judicial matter."[35]

Intermittent discussions with Minister Chao Chu Wu from 1929 to 1932 found Hornbeck ardently defending the Department's policy of providing for the abolition of extraterritoriality "by an agreed upon and gradual process." He also stressed that the United States strongly opposed Chinese unilateral action on this issue. One of the most involved technical aspects of abolition proved to be Washington's insistence that any agreement must provide protection for American citizens on a "most-favored-nation" basis. The task of negotiating the abolition of the American treaty while meeting its demands seemed insurmountable, particularly as China had extraterritorial pacts involving various terms with several nations. Washington's refusal to budge on this principle—the equality of treatment—may not have originated with Hornbeck; however, there can be no doubt but that he was one of its staunchest supporters.[36]

Washington's efforts to abolish extraterritoriality did not appear very imaginative to Dr. Wu and the Chinese government. Indeed, Wu declared on one occasion that the American proposals "sounded reactionary"; at another time he argued that the draft seemed designed to perpetuate extraterritoriality rather than abolish it. Throughout these negotiations Hornbeck appeared embarrassed, apparently believing that discussions were much too premature. Once he attempted to shift the conversations from a bilateral basis to a general conference, and when this failed, he sought to move the talks from Washington to Shanghai but was again disappointed. In yet a third maneuver Hornbeck hinted, delicately, that perhaps the Chinese government should devote its energies to domestic issues at this time and resume the negotiations later, an idea that Wu promptly squelched. When Wu suggested that Washington ought to act before London stole the march on them by being the first to agree to abolition, Hornbeck disappointed the Minister by eagerly counselling the Chinese to concentrate their efforts on the British.[37]

Finally on February 7, 1932, Hornbeck expressed the Department's (and surely his) view that "the desperate conditions which prevailed in several parts of China" would allow negotiations only for "a transitional arrangement" regarding extraterritoriality. Complete abolition, he said, must be postponed until "a later date." In justification of this attitude, he pointed to the extraordinary turmoil resulting from "the recent civil war and political contests; to the prevalence of banditry and 'communism' in almost every part of China; to the kidnapping of a large number of foreigners and the murder of some; and to losses which have been suffered generally by all foreign interests and by millions of Chinese."[38] The discussions over extraterritoriality, however, soon took a back-seat to broader diplomatic maneuverings with Japan's subsequent military incursions into Manchuria and North China. Not until 1943 did the United States and Britain unilaterally waive all claims to extraterritoriality in China.

The Japanese Army's sudden march into Manchuria on September 18, 1931, appalled Hornbeck, but it did not greatly surprise him for his writings some fifteen years previously had dwelt on Japan's ill-concealed desire to dominate this region. Now he saw the confusing Manchurian Incident as two contests: one contest, between China and Japan, stemming from China's "political importance and failure to live up to elementary international obligations"; the other contest, pitting Japan against "the Powers of the world," arising from Japan's failure to observe the League Covenant and the Pact of Paris.[39] Gradually however, as Tokyo became increasingly recalcitrant, Hornbeck blamed the Asian turmoil upon Japan and predicted a lengthy challenge to American interests in China.

From the outset of the Manchurian Incident Hornbeck's advice to his superior was unequivocal on one point: Stimson must "guard against . . . possible attempts to lure the American government 'all by itself' into the jungle of this Chinese-Japanese-Manchurian mix-up—which is full of hidden explosives, dense underbrush, [and] quicksand."[40] Washington should leave the initiation of any policies to the League. Also, he consistently opposed either endorsing Tokyo's plea that China and Japan settle their own differences, for this would mean a complete victory for Japan, or offering Washington's "good offices" for mediation as this would find the United States going-it-alone in "the jungle."

Hornbeck's November 1931 canvas of policy alternatives ruled out military sanctions because "none of the powers have any thought of using armed force" to resolve the Manchurian affair. Furthermore, he disapproved of recalling the Ambassador from Tokyo to emphasize Washington's displeasure because such action would serve "no useful purpose." Hornbeck still believed that Japan's illegal behavior warranted formal protest, but he warned that the only policy acceptable to the American public "that would directly and immediately cause Japan to reconsider or to withdraw from her present position and attitude" was economic sanctions.[41] He thus first suggested augmenting the Kellogg Pact so it would become a more viable instrument, and when disillusioned with that device, he explored the possibilities of an embargo.

Previously Hornbeck had argued for "some type of official denunciation of Japan as a law breaker" since she had disregarded the Kellogg Pact when her army chose to resolve Sino-Japanese grievances by other than "pacific means." He thought "a responsibility corollary" was needed to define the obligations of those nations proscribing the use of force for "if we insist on peace, we must be prepared to insist upon good behavior and just settlement as between disputants."[42] One step in this direction could be a "declaration of protest" which would give the Kellogg treaty "teeth" and would rebut charges that the League and other affected governments were impotent. Notice would thus be served upon Japan that these nations would not recognize any treaty or arrangement that allowed Japan to profit from her Manchurian venture.[43]

The deteriorating situation, however, in both Manchuria and Geneva by early December 1931 alarmed Hornbeck. The Japanese appeared determined not "to be deterred by treaty obligations or moral suasion," and the League could not agree upon methods likely to alter this stance. He noted that "Japan has throughout this matter waged two campaigns: one against China, military; the other against the Powers, diplomatic. She has won in the former every battle; and she has at no point been defeated in the latter." To the weary advisor, it looked as though the time was "fast approaching when the Powers have either to 'put up or shut up.' "[44] He believed that while publicly branding Japan a law-breaker might cause Tokyo some slight discomfort only a world wide embargo of Japan would be persuasive.

Although the idea of an embargo received considerable attention in Geneva, it was virtually ignored in Washington circles. Stimson finally asked Hoover on November 27 to consider its possibilities, but neither man was enthusiastic. Hoover particularly disliked the idea of embargoes, and Stimson's attitude, which varied from day to day, tended to be negative.[45] On December 6 Hornbeck requested a thorough examination of economic sanctions on the grounds that, while the idea was previously "out of the question," the current situation required "that every remaining possible course of action must be given solicitous consideration." He thought that sanctions should emanate from the League since it was "obligated" under Article 16 of the Covenant to consider employing a boycott to curb aggressors. The United States, while not so obligated, should indicate its willingness to join such an effort. Any boycott, "if invoked, should be invoked by the whole world, including the United States and if enforced should be enforced by the whole world." The broad application of such economic sanctions, he prophesied, would bring Tokyo to terms "within six months."[46]

The risks and effectiveness of a boycott received a thorough if heated review within the quiet confines of Stimson's home. Assistant Secretary James G. Rogers and Allen T. Klots sided with Hornbeck, but Castle strenuously opposed economic sanctions. The latter argued that a boycott would greatly distress the already troubled world economy and might involve the United States in a military contest. He noted in his diary that "I was against it, and, although I was pretty hard boiled I think the Secretary was inclined to agree. Certainly, the President would." As it turned out Castle had correctly assessed Stimson's and Hoover's views, and for the time being, Hornbeck laid aside the question of a boycott.[47]

Soon thereafter Stimson returned to an idea he had been considering for some time—a "nonrecognition" declaration based on the Kellogg Pact. He had not been alone, of course, in advancing this proposal; Hoover and Hornbeck, among other individuals, had suggested it in early November. On January 7, 1932, Stimson presented his "nonrecognition" doctrine to the signatories of the Nine Power Treaty, including Japan.[48] This unilateral declaration informed both Tokyo and Peking that Washington would not "admit the legality of any situation *de facto* nor does it intend to recognize any treaty or agreement entered into by either party or its citizens in China, including those which relate to the sovereignty, the independence, or the territorial . . . integrity of the Republic of China, nor to . . . the open door policy." Furthermore, the United States did "not intend to recognize any situation, treaty, or agreement" brought about by means contrary to the Kellogg Pact.[49]

Hornbeck had changed his mind meanwhile about such a declaration as Stimson proposed—a point that seems to have confused historians. Stimson recalled in his diary that Hornbeck fought "tenaciously" against the issuance of a definite statement and then softened his tone. His lack of enthusiasm can be easily traced: Hornbeck opposed issuing a declaration *at this time* because it would accomplish very little (in which case it was better to "shut-up") and because he objected to its purpose of moral condemnation. From the beginning he insisted upon a clear distinction between posting legal notice and charging moral delinquency. "Nations which have broken treaties should unquestionably be treated as law breakers. But the breaking of a law or of a contract, whether by a nation or an individual, does not necessarily imply or establish moral delinquency."[50] In any declaration, Hornbeck wanted to leave the door ajar so when Japanese aggressiveness faded, Tokyo authorities could easily reestablish traditional diplomatic processes. Hornbeck questioned whether the strident tones of Stimson's doctrine allowed for the easy resumption of diplomacy and whether it blurred the distinctions between moral and legal charges.

Thus while Stimson, and particularly Hoover, lauded the moral challenge of the nonrecognition doctrine as a means of stimulating world opinion, Hornbeck gloomily viewed it as "flabby and impotent." Ultimately Stimson came to agree. By the mid-1930's he acknowledged that the doctrine had been a mistake; by 1947 he conceded that it had been a failure.[51]

By 1933 Hornbeck had formulated his views of what America's future policy vis-à-vis Japan should be: the United States must try to avoid war, but it also must prevent "the fact [or] the appearance of weakness either in allegiance to our ideals or in equipment for defense." He saw in delay the one hope of averting war since the passage of time might provide "the opportunity to bring about change in Japan's ideals and aspirations; but to insure delay we should give conclusive evidence of possession by us of physical force sufficient to insure our superiority in any armed conflict . . . between the two nations."[52] At a time when he could still exercise the luxury of the longer view, he also thought Japan's encroachment on China should be "given time" to run its course, for eventually "the flood tide of her invasion will reach its height and the ebb will follow."[53]

Hornbeck's view of the Far Eastern situation between 1932 and 1936 remained moderate, confident, and consistent—consistent at least with his idea of the "even-handed" treatment of all Asian nations. He began with the premise that both China and Japan were responsible for Asian problems: China because it was "unprepared" and "politically disorganized" thereby inviting outside interference; Japan because it was "inclined toward 'imperialism,' was organized politically on the lines of military feudalism, and was propelled by a natural inclination . . . to use force" rather than persuasion to achieve its ends.[54] Given such a situation, he urged the United States not to intervene in their disputes, not even by providing aid to China.

Even though he was cautiously optimistic about the initial moderate policies of the first Hirota government, Hornbeck began campaigning in 1934 for an uncompromising American posture on naval matters. He feared that groups in Washington and London devoted to disarmament might agree to adjust upward Japan's naval ratios—formulated for capital ships in the Washington Pact (1922) and for other warships in the London Treaty (1930)[55]—at the forthcoming naval conference. He reasoned from the premise that Japanese "comparative naval strength" was "of more direct and vital concern to us than to any other of the powers." If the British saw fit to offer concessions, as they indeed did, it was probably because they expected Washington to hold the line by playing "defensive fullback." But whatever the British motives were, he argued that "the maximum of insurance which we can take out against injury to ourselves by and from Japan lies along the line of naval construction" for "the Japanese speak and understand the language of force."[56] Expanding on this line of thought, Hornbeck suggested that the United States "would be better off with a termination of naval limitations than with a new agreement" purchased at "a new and a high price." He feared that a new agreement would hamper, if not prevent, "giving reasonable reinforcement to diplomatic efforts in support of our traditional policy of seeking equality of commercial opportunity and disapproving aggression in the Far East."

Much to Hornbeck's relief the American position on naval limitation remained firm throughout the preliminary talks of 1934 and during the naval conference of December 1935 to March 1936. Indeed, this uncompromising stance amidst the collapse of the naval accords—Tokyo's abrogation of the Washington Treaty and the expiration of the London Pact meant both would terminate on December 31, 1936—led the Japanese delegation to walk out of the conference. Miscalculating Japanese determination, Hornbeck repeatedly argued that the island empire's natural resources and economic strength established "a natural limit upon Japan's capacity to create and maintain naval armament." He also argued that as these limits were nearly reached, continued American building of warships would bring Tokyo begging for a conference on Washington's terms.[57] In his fascination for statistics, Hornbeck grossly misjudged the intensity of the smaller nation's commitment, a shortcoming not limited to American leaders of the 1930's.

IV

As the newly appointed Advisor on Political Relations for the Far East, Hornbeck found himself hard pressed after 1937 to devise policies that would maintain the Open Door. Caught unawares by the outbreak of Sino-Japanese hostilities in 1937, he sought unsuccessfully to translate Roosevelt's "quarantine" idea into a workable policy. As a delegate to the ill-fated Brussels conference, Hornbeck watched dejectedly as his program came to naught, and America experienced its Pacific "Munich." During the months that followed he gradually abandoned his long advocacy of the "even-handed" treatment of *all* Asian nations. Opposed by Hull and Grew, he nonetheless persistently argued for more aid to China and for economic sanctions against Japan hoping that these measures might save America's interests in Asia.

Japan's haphazard decision to exploit the Marco Polo Bridge Incident of July 7, 1937, by launching a full-scale military assault on China caught Western officials, including Hornbeck, by surprise. Only a few weeks earlier he had rejoiced that in Asia the United States was now in "a strong and for the moment 'easy' position" and that there was "no particular reason for any apprehension" regarding "our relations with any country in the Far East or our position in the Pacific Ocean." Optimistically, he attributed the military preparedness of Russia, Britain, America, and China with having "a sobering effect on the chauvinistic elements in Japan."[58]

In the aftermath of the gun-fire at the Marco Polo Bridge, Hornbeck's policy recommendations were at first limited and conciliatory, although he occasionally vented his frustrations against Japan. He advised Hull against American mediation of the dispute for reasons similar to those he had cited in 1931-1932, but above all he counselled against indulging in meaningless moral condemnations *à la* Stimson. Hornbeck also formulated the Department's case for furnishing protection to American citizens in the combat areas, and Hull used his views to persuade Roosevelt that despite isolationist outcries American military forces should remain in China.[59]

The escalation of fighting in July increased Hornbeck's frustration and led him to denounce Japan as a "predatory Power" and to urge that "the powers turn their efforts toward causing Japan to desist from hostilities and to withdraw her armed forces" from China. Yet he cast about for several weeks before hitting upon a plan of action that might redress the Far Eastern political equilibrium and guarantee American interests. He proposed calling another conference on Asian affairs similar to the successful 1921-1922 meeting, only this time the focus would be on Japan. The essence of his idea was stated simply: "On the one hand Japan must be restrained; on the other hand Japan must be given a sense of political and economic security." He urged that such a conference aim at a "constructive" program; it should eschew any condemnation of Japan and "devote its attention first to restrictive measures and then to constructive measures." In keeping with his "even-handed" approach, Hornbeck stressed that stopping Japan was not enough if relative stability were to be returned: "We must remember that, although the world is pointing an accusing finger at Japan, the Chinese are, in reference to the cause of this conflict, by no means without guilt."[60]

While he had formulated his basic idea before reading Roosevelt's Quarantine Speech of October 5, 1937, Hornbeck was heartened by what he (and others) misinterpreted as a renunciation of America's passive Asian policies. Unsure of what the President had in mind, Hornbeck warned that "if we mean business and if we intend to be realistic, we must consider earnestly whether we are willing to do anything beyond and further than express opinions."[61] Moreover, Hornbeck did not agree with the application of the analogy of a "quarantine" to the China problem since war was "not a *disease*"; war might be conducted by diseased "madmen," but one restrained madmen "by force" if necessary in order "to cure them." To his timid colleagues who worried that forceful intervention, such as the use of economic sanctions, might escalate hostilities into a general Pacific war, he declared: "In my opinion, when Japan is . . . thoroughly involved and completely preoccupied . . . with her conflict in China, Japan is in no position to take on or risk a war with either Great Britain or the United States."[62]

As for strategy, Hornbeck believed that the Western powers ought not to move too hastily. If heavy casualties and economic losses must be incurred before Japan and China learned that there was no profit in war, then such must be the price of their education. Intervention should wait, he counselled, "until one or the other or both" China and Japan had "reached a point obviously near to exhaustion." Care must be taken, however, that: "(1) China not be decisively defeated; (2) Japan not reach a point of internal explosion . . . [or] economic collapse; and (3) neither China nor Japan come under a controlling influence of the Soviet Union."[63]

The decision to convene the Nine Powers plus guests at Brussels on November 3, 1937, upset Hornbeck's timetable and spurred discussions on American policy.[64] Maxwell Hamilton, who now held down the Far Eastern desk, developed Hornbeck's ideas in a lengthy document; this in turn prompted extended meetings among the senior Department staff, including Hull and Norman Davis (who would head America's delegation), to hammer out a program to save the Open Door system in Asia. The result of all this was a general endorsement of Hornbeck's idea of a "constructive" policy. Roosevelt subsequently agreed that the "constructive" formula should be explored at Brussels and hinted that military aid to China might be an acceptable sanction; above all, however, the President warned Davis not to get ahead of American domestic opinion. Pondering the President's instructions and the Department's plan as he arrived in Belgium, Hornbeck concluded that: "Two of our own objectives are in conflict . . . on the one hand, we do not wish to take leadership in the Conference, but, on the other hand, we wish that the Conference accomplish something constructive." His own suggestion was that the delegation work "from behind the lines" to supply ideas regarding possible courses of action in the hope that a multilateral approach to solutions would develop.[65] Efforts by the Americans to examine sanctions, which were quickly leaked to the press, prompted Hull and Roosevelt to squelch such initiative. The conference had not even discussed the American program when it self-consciously expired on November 24, 1937.

Hornbeck did not attempt to hide his bitterness about Washington's timidity: "It cannot with any accuracy or with intellectual honesty be affirmed that this Conference has exhausted the possibilities of bringing about peace between Japan and China by processes of conciliation. . . . From the point of view of avoiding really difficult tasks and commitments to concrete effort, the Conference has been a great success."[66]

Hornbeck crossed the political Rubicon in 1938. That autumn he cast aside his "even-handed" doctrine and took on a distinct, uncompromising anti-Japanese stance. Where in the past he had clung to the hope that reason and responsibility would somehow reassert itself in world affairs, he now believed that nations espousing the use of force must be countered with policies that spoke directly and firmly to such law-breakers.

Two factors seem to have been persuasive in this shifting of Hornbeck's attitude and policy. First, Japan was sounding the death knell of the Open Door by its action in North China and in occupied coastal regions of China. In response to the Department's October 6 protest of these violations of American treaty rights, Tokyo coldly replied that "It was . . . impossible for Japan now to give an unqualified undertaking to respect the open door." Prime Minister Konoye formally announced on December 22 that a "new order" had united Japan and occupied China and Manchuria in economic cooperation against communism. This new order also effectively curtailed Western economic activity.[67] Second, the aggressive postures and actions of Japan, Germany, and Italy had gradually revealed their disregard for treaty obligations and their reliance upon force to arbitrate international disputes. When in 1935 Hornbeck encountered the notion that the Italo-Ethiopian incident was "none of our business," he had argued that the United States must awaken to its responsibilities. It was the "duty of all members of the community to endeavor to prevent breaches of peace." Now in 1938 he condemned Congress' neutrality legislation as "a snare and a delusion" that rendered Washington impotent. Worse yet, this legislation threw the United States "on the side of those forces . . . which are making for lawlessness" by taking foreign policy decisions out of the President's hands.[68]

In a series of memoranda written during November and December 1938, Hornbeck argued that the United States and Japan were "moving very rapidly toward a head-on *diplomatic* collision." He believed that Japan was now completely controlled by the "military element" and that this group would use "every method, every agency, and every instrument (especially armed forces)" to appropriate American rights and property in Asia. The time would come, he argued, when the United States would have to stop Japan's encroachments or "back down" and accept the consequences. Should Washington choose the former course, it had to be prepared "to use weapons stronger than words." Hornbeck's own suggestions included aid to China, denunciation of the United States-Japan 1911 commercial treaty, repeal of the neutrality acts, retaliatory tariff measures, embargoes on trade and shipping, and disposal of the American fleet in such a fashion "as to indicate to the Japanese Government . . . that we 'mean business.' "But, he counselled these steps should not be embarked upon unless the American people were prepared to commit themselves whole-heartedly to such a program and were prepared to ultimately employ military force if needed.[69] It should be added, however, that he did not believe that Japan would engage the United States in a shooting war; he was confident that Tokyo would realize the disastrous consequences of such action.

Hornbeck at the same time urged an equally tough policy to avert war in Europe. The extent to which the worsening international climate disturbed him and altered his views is underscored in a strongly worded letter to Hull on January 28, 1939. In this revealing document, he foresaw a war in Europe, instigated by Germany and Italy, that would jeopardize America's desire for peace. Urging Roosevelt to exercise his office to mold public opinion, he called for an immediate presidential declaration that in the event of war breaking out in Europe the Chief Executive would throw the whole weight of his authority and influence toward America's support of the democratic states in Europe in resistance to the dictatorships.[70]

Hornbeck's policy recommendations from 1938 onward brought him into the sanctionist camp, along with Stimson, Harold Ickes, Norman Davis, and others. They took this position (at least initially) with the hope of persuading the President to develop a plan of action. Some individuals, such as Secretary of Treasury Henry Morgenthau, Jr., who were only willing to irritate Japan piecemeal, did not always appreciate Hornbeck's position. At the same time, Hornbeck now found himself frequently at odds with Hull, who never believed that economic sanctions would work, and with Sumner Welles, Hamilton, Grew, and others within the Department who still urged conciliatory policies and verbal warnings as a means of easing Pacific tensions.

Hornbeck found progress slow for his newly adopted "get tough" doctrine during the next several months. He actively supported projects aimed at providing aid to China where previously he had been hesitant. One reason for this new emphasis was, in his words, because "it is easier to give assistance to China than to place obstacles directly in the way of Japan." Another reason was equally apparent: "If China is conquered, we will have no open door." At the same time, he ferociously contested those advisors who wanted to concentrate the American fleet in the Atlantic. Bristling at the argument that American interests were less significant in the Pacific, he challenged Washington's tendency to "lay more emphasis upon our moral and legal interest than upon material interests." Hornbeck claimed that the Far Eastern situation had gotten out of hand because Washington had emphasized "defending . . . principle rather than . . . salvaging investments."[71]

Economic sanctions unfolded slowly, meanwhile, but not at all in the planned fashion Hornbeck urged. Angered by Japan's bombing of Chinese cities, Hull announced a "moral" embargo on American sales of selected items, such as aircraft parts. In July 1939 the Secretary abrogated the 1911 commercial treaty with Japan (effective January 26, 1940); this action did not immediately threaten Japan's imports, but it proved a harbinger of shifting attitudes. An oil licensing plan, established on July 25, 1940, provided another minor annoyance without real sting, but the ban on scrap iron and metals of September 26 did strain Japanese industry. The final blow, the freezing of Japanese credits on July 26, 1941, virtually halted Japanese imports of vital war materials from the United States.[72]

As the primary thrust behind economic sanctions came from the highest administrative echelons, propelled by like-minded, more influential principals, Hornbeck's role became more administrative. He did, however, continue to seek support for strong measures in the not-so-friendly confines of the State Department. "*This country is at war,*" he wrote Hull on September 30, 1940; even though American military forces are not engaged, nonetheless "we are already fighting." In determining America's defensive perimeter, he argued that "we should regard our first line of defense as being located in the British Isles *and* in eastern Asia. We should send weapons, economic and military, to *both* of these fronts." When Grew finally came around to a similar position, Hornbeck gruffly acknowledged this belated endorsement as acceptance of views that he had long held.[73]

The year 1941 proved to be a trying one for Hornbeck. He steadfastly urged Hull and Roosevelt to reject any appeasement of Tokyo; in particular, Hornbeck counselled against Prince Konoye's August proposal of a meeting with the President. This idea, strongly endorsed by Grew and at the outset favorably entertained by Roosevelt, was viewed by Hornbeck "with suspicion and disfavor." On this matter Hornbeck and Hull were in agreement. To the former, Japan's actions during the previous four years of aggression in China and the more recent intervention in Indo-China constituted a menace to the Philippines, disrupted the peace of the Pacific, and prejudiced the security of the United States. "In these circumstances," Hornbeck wrote, "any further effort at this time" to pursue negotiations would be regarded in Tokyo as "evidence of weakness and irresolution" and would only "strengthen Japan's determination to proceed with her program of conquest." His preconditions for opening serious negotiations with Tokyo sounded more like the terms of a field commander than a diplomat. The Japanese must renounce the idea that economic growth and national development may be accomplished by force by relinquishing all political and military gains achieved since mid-1937. More specifically relating to the proposed Konoye-Roosevelt meeting, Hornbeck questioned how "authoritative" their pledges would be and whether either or both could successfully fulfill them. "At best," he later wrote, the provisions of any "agreement would be very general in their terms and would be susceptible of widely differing interpretations by the governments party thereto." Roosevelt and Konoye "could, as I conceived it, commit themselves personally, but could not commit their countries effectively and lastingly."[74] Hornbeck did not participate directly in the Nomura-Hull talks during 1941, although he did constantly analyze the Japanese proposals. Throughout these discussions he argued vehemently against making any concessions and reinforced Hull's ultimate diplomacy.

The most glaring weakness in Hornbeck's "get tough" posture was his consistent assumption of rational response by Japanese leadership to Washington's mounting economic pressure. During the discussions over whether to freeze Japanese assets, he wrote: *"I submit that under existing circumstances it is altogether improbable that Japan would deliberately take action in response to any action which the United States is likely to take in the Pacific which action if taken by Japan would mean war between that country and this country."*[75] Herbert Feis' and Grew's criticism of Hornbeck's easy dismissal of the possibility that economic sanctions might escalate into war seems valid; for if Hornbeck constantly warned about the possibilities of war and counselled preparation for such eventualities, he apparently could not bring himself to believe it would happen. This paradox stemmed from his assessment of Japan's war-making potential versus America's vastly greater resources, an assessment in which he presumed that the Japanese would be inhibited by even the most elementary comparative inventory.

This presumption of rational policy-making in Tokyo led Hornbeck to commit his most embarrassing *faux pas*. A week before the attack on Pearl Harbor, he sent Hull a memorandum to be used in briefing Roosevelt which prophesied that the failure of Nomura-Hull talks held little danger for the United States. Not content with this bold estimate, he stated his willingness to give odds on the probability of war: 5 to 1 that there would be no hostilities with Japan before December 15; 3 to 1 before January 15; and even money that there would be no war by March 1, 1942.[76] This unfortunate prophecy haunted him for the rest of his life.

V

Hornbeck's policy recommendations between 1928 and 1941 clearly remained fixed to the maintenance of the Open Door. Infringements upon this doctrine, whether by Chinese or Japanese antagonists, brought an immediate, strongly worded defense of what he discerned to be America's rights and interests. As Japan's aggressive behavior mounted, Hornbeck found himself in a quandry over how to adjust to this new challenge to America's traditional commercial policy and its principle of nonintervention. He resolved this contradiction by advocating the use of economic sanctions, first by international action and later by America alone, in the belief that rational considerations of the ultimate consequences would persuade Tokyo to compromise and retreat rather than fight.

His role in devising policy during this era is difficult to ascertain with certainty since many individuals were pressing similar recommendations upon the Chief Executive. Hull thought Hornbeck was "important and capable, experienced and dependable." Former colleague Arthur Young was even more emphatic: "Hornbeck had a key position as chiefly responsible for drafting state papers and initiating action in his field. The conduct of Far Eastern affairs during about fifteen years bore his strong imprint."[77]

Notes

1 Herbert Freis, *The Road to Pearl Harbor* (Princeton: Princeton University Press, 1950), p. 173.

2 Nancy H. Hooker (ed.), *The Moffatt Papers: Selections from the Diplomatic Journals of Jay Pierrepont Moffatt, 1919-1943* (Cambridge, Massachusetts: Harvard University Press, 1956), pp. 182-183; on one occasion in 1940 Secretary of Treasury Morgenthau even accused Hornbeck (hereafter referred to as SKH) of being "pro-Japanese," see the *Morgenthau Diaries (China)* (Washington, D.C.: Government Printing Office, 1954), 1:133.

3 For an understanding of this internationalism see Warren F. Kuehl, *Seeking World Order* (Nashville: Vanderbilt University Press, 1969).

4 Arthur N. Young to author, May 28, 1969. Young was the economic advisor to the Department of State (1922-1928), an office in which SKH served before joining Harvard University in 1924, and became financial advisor to Nationalist China in 1929. He wrote several important accounts of Sino-American relations during this period.

5 Robert Ferrell, *American Diplomacy in the Great Depression* (New Haven: Yale University Press, 1957), pp. 38, 153; Elting E. Morison, *Turmoil and Tradition* (Boston: Houghton Mifflin, 1960), pp. 316-317.

6 Young to author, May 28, 1969.

7 Joseph Ballantine to author, April 10, 1969; Mr. Ballantine was a former State Department colleague of SKH.

8 Herbert Feis to author, April 21, 1969.

9 SKH, "Autobiography," in the Hornbeck Papers (Stanford University, Hoover Institution on War, Revolution, and Peace). This transcript autobiography is irregularly prepared and lacks consistent pagination.

10 *Ibid.*

11 Anne Hurd, "Our Far Eastern Pilot," New York *Herald Tribune,* October 21, 1928.

12 Ballantine to author, April 10, 1969; SKH, "Autobiography," Hornbeck Papers.

13 According to notes in his private papers, SKH was asked in 1913 by the Carnegie Endowment to prepare a report on the Open Door policy. The completed study was not published (he believed because the Endowment's officers felt it might embarrass Japan and Russia), but he kept revising and adding to it. Sections of this report appeared in his 1916 *Contemporary Politics in the Far East,* but more significantly, it became a sourcebook for his later writing with ideas and phrases appearing in official memorandums of the 1920's and 1930's.

    The notes and "Open Door Policy" manuscripts are in the Hornbeck Papers at the Hoover Library; however, their various revisions and irregular pagination make precise references impossible.

14 SKH, *Principles of American Policy in Relation to the Far East,* Department of State Far Eastern Series, no. 4 (1934), pp. 4-6.

15 SKH, "On Far Eastern Policy and the Consortium," 1921, Hornbeck Papers.

16 SKH, *Contemporary Politics in the Far East* (New York: D. Appleton and Company, 1916), pp. 252-253.

17 "In stepping forward as the advocate of an open door policy it [the United States] could not reasonably be accused of having ulterior political motives," SKH, "Open Door Policy," Hornbeck Papers.

18 *Ibid.*

19 SKH, *Principles,* pp. 11-12.

20 SKH, *Contemporary Politics,* p. 351.

21 *Ibid.,* p. 354.

22 SKH memo, "Japan's 'Monroe Doctrine for Asia'," February 1, 1934, Hornbeck Papers. This and following memorandums may also be printed in various volumes of the *Foreign Relations of the United States;* however in this essay manuscript copies were used when available.

23 SKH, *Contemporary Politics,* p. 265. In 1938, SKH wrote Hull (of a colleague's report on Japanese economic activities in North China) that "this reminds me vividly of statements which I made in a section of a study of the open door policy which I produced nearly twenty-five years ago. I think you might find it interesting to glance through this section. . . . " SKH memo, untitled, July 11, 1938, Hornbeck Papers.

24 SKH, "Open Door Policy," Hornbeck Papers.

25 SKH memo, "On 'Other People's Wars' and 'Minding Our Own Business'," April 24, 1939, Hornbeck Papers.

26 SKH memos, "Manchurian Situation," November 21, 1931, and "Non-Recognition: Ethiopia," May 12, 1936, Hornbeck Papers.
27 SKH, *Contemporary Politics,* pp. 402-403.
28 SKH memo, April 13, 1935, S.K. Hornbeck, Box 8, R.W. Moore Papers, Franklin D. Roosevelt Library, Hyde Park, New York.
29 SKH memo, "Naval Program," May 3, 1938, and memo, untitled, November 23, 1938, Hornbeck Papers.
30 SKH memo, "Manchurian Situation: Economic Boycott," December 6, 1931, Hornbeck Papers.
31 Walter Millis and E.S. Duffield, (eds.), *The Forrestal Diaries* (New York: Viking Press, 1951), p. 91. Also see Bennett's essay on Grew.
32 SKH, "Some Principles of Considerations Underlying American Policy in Relation to the Current Situation in the Far East," United States Department of State, *Press Releases,* April 30, 1932 (Washington, D.C.: Government Printing Office, 1932), 6:395-396.
33 United States Department of State, *Papers Relating to the Foreign Relations of the United States, 1928* (Washington, D.C.: Government Printing Office, 1943), 2:199. Cited hereafter as *FRUS, 1928,* vol. 2.
34 United States Department of State, *Papers Relating to the Foreign Relations of the United States, 1931* (Washington, D.C.: Government Printing Office, 1946), 3:751. Cited hereafter as *FRUS, 1931,* vol. 3.
35 United States Department of State, *Papers Relating to the Foreign Relations of the United States, 1930* (Washington, D.C.: Government Printing Office, 1945), 2:354, 362. Cited hereafter as *FRUS, 1930,* vol. 2.
36 United States Department of State, *Papers Relating to the Foreign Relations of the United States, 1929* (Washington, D.C.: Government Printing Office, 1943), 2:547; *FRUS, 1930,* 2:354, 377-380.
37 *FRUS, 1930,* 2:392, 471, 483.
38 *FRUS, 1931,* 3:731.
39 SKH memo, "Manchuria and Geneva," October 25, 1931, Hornbeck Papers. He also thought Russia contributed to the general instability of the area "but not in so great a degree," SKH memo, "Manchurian Situation," January 13, 1932, Hornbeck Papers.
40 SKH memo, "Manchurian Situation," October 17, 1931, Hornbeck Papers.
41 SKH memo, "Manchurian Situation," November 21, 1931, Hornbeck Papers; see also Armin Rappaport, *Henry L. Stimson and Japan, 1931-1933* (Chicago: University of Chicago Press, 1963), pp. 86-87.
42 SKH memos, "Manchurian Situation," October 10, 1931, and "Manchuria and Geneva," October 25, 1931, Hornbeck Papers.
43 SKH memo, "Manchurian Situation," November 21, 1931, Hornbeck Papers.
44 SKH memo, "Manchurian Situation," December 5, 1931, Hornbeck Papers.
45 Ferrell, *Diplomacy,* p. 148; Rappaport, *Stimson,* pp. 88-92.
46 SKH memo, "Manchurian Situation," December 6, 1931, Hornbeck Papers.
47 Ferrell, *Diplomacy,* p. 148; Rappaport *Stimson,* p. 90.
48 The Stimson doctrine has been developed and analyzed elsewhere at great length: see particularly, Rappaport, *Stimson,* pp. 99ff and Ferrell, *Diplomacy,* pp. 151ff. Also consult Richard N. Current, "The Stimson

Doctrine and the Hoover Doctrine," *American Historical Review,* 59(April, 1954):513-542.

49 For the complete text see United States Department of State, *Papers Relating to the Foreign Relations of the United States, Japan, 1931-1941* (Washington, D.C.: Government Printing Office, 1943), 1:76. Cited hereafter as *FRUS, Japan,* vol. 1.

50 Rappaport, *Stimson,* p. 94; SKH memo, "Manchurian Situation," November 21, 1931, Hornbeck Papers.

51 SKH memo, "Extending Non-Recognition Doctrine," December 8, 1937, Hornbeck Papers; Henry L. Stimson, *The Far Eastern Crisis* (New York: Harper and Brothers, 1936), p. 92; Henry L. Stimson and McGeorge Bundy, *On Active Service in Peace and War* (New York: Harper and Brothers, 1947), pp. 261-262.

52 Quoted in Rappaport, *Stimson,* p. 146.

53 Quoted in Dorothy Borg, *The United States and the Far Eastern Crisis* (Cambridge, Massachusetts: Harvard University Press, 1964), p. 35; consequently, the Amau "statement" of April 17, 1934, appeared to SKH only to confirm his long-held estimates of Japanese ambitions, see United States Department of State, *Papers Relating to the Foreign Relations of the United States, 1934* (Washington, D.C.: Government Printing Office, 1950), 3:141. Cited hereafter as *FRUS, 1934,* vol. 3.

54 SKH memo, "Manchurian Situation," January 13, 1932, Hornbeck Papers.

55 For a recent analysis of these treaties see Richard Dean Burns and Donald Urquidi, *Disarmament in Perspective,* United States Government Research Reports, AD 696-943 (1968), vol. 3, chaps. 13 and 15.

56 *FRUS 1934,* 3:189-193; also see United States Department of State, *Papers Relating to the Foreign Relations of the United States, 1934* (Washington, D.C.: Government Printing Office, 1951), 1:230-231 and Edgar B. Nixon (ed.), *Franklin D. Roosevelt and Foreign Affairs* (Cambridge, Massachusetts: The Belknap Press of Harvard University Press, 1969), 2:54-71.

57 SKH memo, "Naval Conference," October 6, 1934, Hornbeck Papers; United States Department of State, *Papers Relating to the Foreign Relations of the United States, 1936* (Washington, D.C.: Government Printing Office, 1953), 1:35-36, 44.

58 SKH memo, "Relations of the U.S. with Countries of the Far East," May 20, 1937, Hornbeck Papers. Apparently SKH's reflections were based upon the Japanese election during the spring of 1937 which seemed to rebuff the military.

59 On September 2 the Department relented and began urging Americans to leave China. Hornbeck argued that the government ought to compensate its citizens for their losses. Borg, *Far Eastern Crisis,* pp. 285-287.

60 SKH memos, "China-Japan Situation, I and II," August 27, 1937, "Conference of Nine Power Treaty Powers," October 6, 1937, and "China-Japan Situation, IX," October 10, 1937, Hornbeck Papers. Borg refers to SKH's idea as the "constructive" course subsequently adopted by many in the State Department, *Far Eastern Crisis,* p. 402.

61 SKH memo, untitled, October 7, 1937, Hornbeck Papers. Neither SKH nor his colleagues realized at the time that FDR himself was not clear on how to translate this idea into positive action. See Borg, *Far Eastern Crisis,* chap. 13.

62 SKH memos, "China-Japan Situation, XI," October 13, 1937, and "China-Japan Situation, X," October 12, 1937, Hornbeck Papers.

63 SKH memo, "China-Japan Situation, IX," October 10, 1937, Hornbeck Papers.

64 For details of the Brussels conference see Borg, *Far Eastern Crisis,* 399ff and Julius W. Pratt. *Cordell Hull* (New York: Cooper Square Publishers, 1964), pp. 260ff.

65 Borg, *Far Eastern Crisis,* pp. 402-406; SKH memo, "Estimate of the Situation . . . ," November 2, 1937, Hornbeck Papers.

66 SKH memo, untitled, November 21, 1937, Hornbeck Papers; for an interesting but highly questionable argument suggesting FDR had a plan for firm action toward Japan, see J.M. Haight, Jr., "Franklin D. Roosevelt and a Naval Quarantine of Japan," *Pacific Historical Review* (May, 1971), pp. 203-226.

67 United States Department of State, *Papers Relating to the Foreign Relations of the United States, 1938* (Washington, D.C.: Government Printing Office, 1955), 4:93-95; *FRUS, Japan.* 1:785ff, 801ff.

68 Borg, *Far Eastern Crisis,* p. 401; SKH memo, "Further Reflections on Foreign Relations . . . ," October 19, 1938, Hornbeck Papers.

69 SKH memos, "The Tung Oil Project . . . ," November 14, 1938, "Reflections on Current Procedure . . . ," November 4, 1938, and untitled memo dated November 12, 1938; SKH to Assistant Secretary Sayre, December 22, 1938, Hornbeck Papers.

70 SKH to Hull, January 28, 1939, Hornbeck Papers.

71 SKH memo, "Far Eastern Relations . . . ," March 8, 1939, Hornbeck Papers and United States Department of State, *Papers Relating to the Foreign Relations of the United States, 1939* (Washington, D.C.: Government Printing Office, 1955), 3:211.

72 SKH grew impatient with the "confused, illogical, inconsistent and futile" moral embargo, see memo, untitled, July 11, 1940; Feis, *Road to Pearl Harbor* has a detailed account of these developments. Also see A. N. Young, *China and the Helping Hand* (Cambridge, Massachusetts: Harvard University Press, 1963), pp. 192-205.

73 SKH to Hull, September 30, 1940, Hornbeck Papers and Feis, *Road to Pearl Harbor,* p. 102.

74 SKH memo, untitled, August 16, 1941, and SKH's Autobiography file (1941), Hornbeck Papers.

75 SKH memo, untitled, July 13, 1941, Hornbeck Papers (italics his).

76 SKH memo, "Problems of Far Eastern Relations . . . ," November 27, 1941, Hornbeck Papers; also published in United States Department of State, *Papers Relating to the Foreign Relations of the United States. 1941* (Washington, D.C.: Government Printing Office, 1956), 4:672-675.

77 Cordell Hull, *Memoirs* (New York: Macmillan, 1948), 1:181; Young to author, May 28, 1969.

Part II

CHINA

Chinese Diplomacy and Diplomats, 1919-1941

China's foreign affairs during the interwar years were shaped by a variety of highly volatile forces. Internal political chaos seriously muddled Chinese affairs—China was afflicted with revolts, assassinations and civil wars. In these civil wars, independent warlords first grappled for power and later the Communists and Nationalists battled for domination. An aggressive rising nationalism exposed still another dimension of China's diplomatic turmoil, particularly when students and the middle class demanded an end to "unequal" treaties and foreign concessions. Finally, China resisted Japanese demands for the right of "tutelage" over China. In view of these countervailing forces it is not surprising that Chinese diplomats labored under grave handicaps.

An aroused popular discontent ended the Manchu dynasty in 1911-1912 and a new Republic was established. Yuan Shih-K'ai tried to consolidate the revolution but was opposed by ambitious regional strong men who launched the era of warlords, or *tuchins,* from 1916-1928. Presidents and premiers—sometimes with captive parliaments—rapidly succeeded one another in Peking. Actual power, however, resided in the shifting personal alliances of the *tuchins.* Three principal warlord cliques emerged: the *Anfu* (in Anhui and Fukien provinces), the *Chihli* (in Hopei, surrounding Peking), and the *Fengtien* (in Manchuria). A similar scenario was repeated on a smaller scale in South China which held itself independent of the North after 1917. In Canton, Sun Yat-sen struggled to erect a reform government and to strengthen the Kuomintang.

This political fiasco, however, masked the profound changes which were taking place in China. Several factors—disgust with warlord politics, exposure to Western ideas, growth of an active middle class and an industrial working class during the temporary withdrawal of foreign interests during World War I, and accumulated anger at foreign exploitation—combined to foster an intellectual revolution and to stimulate a virulent modern nationalism in China. The intellectual revolution is often designated the "May Fourth Movement" to commemorate the student demonstrations and economic boycotts which occurred in Peking on May 4, 1919, in protest against the Versailles Peace Conference's decision to confirm Japan's control of ex-German concessions in Shantung. Japan's infamous "Twenty-One Demands" (January 18, 1915) which included control of Manchuria, substantial economic concessions and a tutelary role in China's affairs, had already prompted strong anti-Japanese sentiment. Economic boycotts were a frequently used protest tactic against all foreigners after the May Fourth episode.

Government in China had disintegrated and civil war was endemic by 1922. Following the death of Sun Yat-sen, Chiang Kai-shek gradually emerged as the new nationalist leader. He started as commandant of the Whampoa Military Academy near Canton and, in May 1925, became commander-in-chief of the Kuomintang army. Whampoa graduates provided Chiang the tough, disciplined cadre he needed to launch an armed expedition against the northern warlords in June 1926. After Nanking fell to Chiang's forces on March 27, 1927, there was a general outbreak of violence against all foreigners. A bloodbath was prevented only because American and British warships laid down a barrage between the Nationalist forces and the British concession.

The various factions of the Kuomintang party, minus the Communists, formed a Nationalist government at Nanking in September 1927. Chiang soon thereafter drove the Manchurian warlord, Marshal Chang Tso-lin, from Peking. As Marshal Chang withdrew, his train ran over a Japanese-planted mine and he was killed. His son, Chang Hsueh-liang (the "Young Marshal") inherited his father's army. Despite the Nationalist's military victories they failed to demobilize the warlords and unify China.

The occupation of Manchuria by Japan's autonomous Kwantung Army, following the staged "Mukden Incident" of September 18, 1931, complicated China's already difficult diplomatic and political situation. Chiang Kai-shek favored a temporizing policy toward Japan, but his persistent Nationalist opponents, Eugene Chen, Sun Fo (Sun Yat-sen's son), and Wang Ching-wei, urged immediate military resistance. Following the resignation of his political opponents, Chiang negotiated an uneasy truce with the Japanese Army in Northern China (T'ang-ku Truce, May 31, 1933). The resilient Chinese Communists posed a worse menace to China than the Japanese in Chiang's view—he favored internal pacification before engaging in armed resistance against the Japanese invaders.

Chiang launched a campaign against Mao Tze-tung and the Kiangsi Soviet in South China in 1933 to further the policy of internal pacification. Mao, General Chu Teh and Chou En-lai then led the "Long March"—a 5,000 mile retreat to the northern province of Shensi. From their secure position in Shensi the Chinese Communist party openly advocated the destruction of the Kuomintang to further the war against Japan—declared by the Communists earlier in February 1932.

Chiang reacted by ordering the Young Marshal's refugee Manchurian troops against Mao. The Manchurian troops hated the Japanese far more than they did the Communists so the offensive against Shensi province began reluctantly. The Communists then offered to join the Nationalists to fight the Japanese and Chiang was faced with the defection of his entire Northeastern Army in August 1936. He flew to Sian and ordered the Young Marshal to step-up the Shensi offensive. Chang Hsueh-liang refused, his troops mutinied, Chiang and his staff were taken prisoner, and Chang issued a manifesto calling for an end to the civil war. The details of the Sian Incident (December 12-24) are vague, but possibly Moscow insisted upon Chiang's release. A disappointed Mao sent Chou En-lai to Sian to negotiate with Chiang. The latter's only statement regarding the episode, upon arriving back at the Nanking airport on December 24, was "I want no more civil wars."

During the night of July 7, 1937, Japanese troops on maneuvers near the Marco Polo Bridge and the local Chinese forces exchanged gunfire. The Sian agreement and the apparent Nationalist-Communist reconciliation was seen by Japanese expansionists as a mortal challenge to their plans for China. Thus, late in July the Japanese army's strategy abruptly shifted, the piecemeal seizure of North China ceased and a general assault against China began. By December 13, the Japanese captured Nanking and thus held the capital of China, the coast of China, and most of its major cities and rail lines. Yet, the Japanese waited in vain for China to surrender.

At the beginning of the Pacific War in 1941, a three-cornered war was still raging inside China: the Nationalists against the Japanese, the Communists against the Japanese, and the Nationalists against the Communists.

Pao-chin Chu

V. K. Wellington Koo

The Diplomacy of Nationalism

FEW DIPLOMATS in modern times have had a more brilliant career than Dr. V. K. Wellington Koo (Ku Wei-chün); for a half-century, nearly the entire span of Republican China, his was a powerful and respected voice in China's foreign affairs. He participated in almost every major diplomatic event from 1912 to 1966, including the Paris Peace Conference after World War I and the San Francisco Conference at the end of World War II. Yet perhaps the most significant of all his undertakings were those from 1919 to 1932—from the negotiations over the Versailles Treaty to the League of Nation's debate on the Manchurian Incident—when Dr. Koo used his diplomatic talents to pursue China's independence and equality among nations.

Koo's refusal to sign the Versailles Treaty, leaving the Shantung question unresolved, highlighted the Sino-Japanese controversy that shaped Asian affairs during the interwar decades. His defense of Chinese interests at the Washington Conference and in subsequent Sino-Soviet negotiations emphasized Chinese nationalist demands for equality. Throughout this entire era, Koo and his colleagues in "the Anglo-American group"—a small body of United States-trained professional Chinese diplomats—successfully sustained China's attachment to the West in the belief that Chinese interests could best be enhanced by American support.

All the prominent members of the Anglo-American Group, including Dr. Sao-ke Alfred Sze (Chih Chao-chi), Dr. Chengting T. Wang (Wang Cheng-t'ing), and Dr. W.W.Yen (Yen Hui-ch'ing) possessed similarities in character and background. All of these men were natives of southeastern coastal provinces and were sons of prosperous merchants. They received many years of traditional Chinese education during boyhood, and they all studied in the Christian schools of China. Each man pursued advanced training in the United States. Each started his career as an English specialist either as a secretary or teacher, and each served with both the warlord governments in Peking and the Nationalist government in Nanking. The Anglo-American Group usually held diplomatic posts at the appropriate national capitals—Washington, London, or a post near the world organization, in Paris for the League of Nations or New York for the United Nations—and each selected the Anglo-American territories as his place of retirement.[1]

Dr. Koo and his fellow "Anglo-Americans" were indispensable to any Chinese warlord regime, which usually had little choice but to remain within the Anglo-American orbit in the international arena. Their Chinese tradition and Western training, their international reputation, their devotion to Chinese nationalism and the abolition of Anglo-American unequal treaties made them the guardians of administrative independence and territorial integrity in a warring and divided China. The Anglo-American Group secured loan funds from foreign sources and engineered release of the surplus from the maritime customs and saltgabelle for various Chinese governments hard-pressed for money to maintain huge armies and wage civil wars.[2] Throughout the Republican period, public opinion dominated by professors, college students, and journalists in Peking and Shanghai often influenced the decision-making of Dr. Koo and his fellow "Anglo-Americans." As returned students from abroad, this group shrewdly cultivated good relations with the news media and the intelligentsia, and its members utilized the opinion makers to defend their personal integrity and loyalty.

I

Koo was a man molded by family and Chinese traditions, by Western education and experiences, and by social and nationalist causes. Consequently, Westerners thought of him as Chinese, and the Chinese saw him as Western. Both views had merit, but they only discerned that part of Koo which was different from themselves. The Westerners perceived his character and principles as drawn from traditional China, while the Chinese saw only his Western manners, English eloquence, and Anglo-American style of diplomacy. As a matter of fact, Koo was the model for the mainstream of political philosophy of the late Ch'ing reformers, summed up by Governor-General Chang Chih-tung in the 1890's: "Chinese learning as the essential principles, Western learning for the practical applications."[3]

Traditional Chinese family as well as Confucian principles and virtues built up the fundamental character and thought of Koo. He was born to a traditional gentry-merchant family on January 29, 1888. His given name was Wei-chün, and his courtesy name Shao-ch'uan. He was known, however, in foreign circles by his English name, Vi Kyuin Wellington Koo, or in its abbreviation, V. K. Wellington Koo. His father, Koo Jung (courtesy name Ching-ch'uan), served as an apprentice at a customs brokerage house during the day and attended private school at night to study the Confucian classics. When Koo Jung was sixteen he married Chiang Fu-an. Later Koo Jung became so successful that he opened his own hardward store on Foochow Road in Shanghai and joined the gentry-merchants of that city. Chiang Fu-an was a traditional housewife who, with the tiny bound feet usual to women of quality in her generation, firmly ruled the household.

Young Koo, like his two elder brothers, received a traditional Chinese education. He was sent at the age of five to the school of Master Chu, a scholar with the *hsiu-ts'ai* degree who had failed to pass higher examinations. He began his studies with the Trimetrical Classic and the Book of Family Names and gradually progressed to the Confucian Classics.[4] For seven years, until 1898, young Koo studied the traditional Chinese principles.

Koo's family background and his long cultivation in Confucian literature during his formative years developed in his character such qualities as loyalty, filial piety, and diligence. His strict obedience to his parents and eldest brother was shown in his first marriage, in 1908, to a girl he did not meet until his wedding day.[5] That the standard of Confucian virtue governed his conception of duty toward his country was beyond doubt even to his political foes. This traditional training may be a partial solution to the puzzle of why Wellington Koo survived the dangerous cross-currents of the Peking government, where Cabinets came and went, and why, after having undertaken many years of Western education in China and abroad, he remained a true Confucian. Although he conducted a Bible class, he never became a Christian.

The second factor which influenced Koo's character was his Western training and experiences. When young Koo was twelve, he became a student of the Chung'hsi shu-yüan or the Anglo-Chinese Junior College in Shanghai. There he was first exposed to the various disciplines of Western learning, including English, mathematics, physics, geography and even sports. Shortly thereafter, he attended the Yü-ts'ai hsüeh-hsiao or Talent-Fostering school in 1900 in Shanghai. In 1901, Koo enrolled at St. John's University where many prominent diplomats such as Dr. Sao-Ke Alfred Sze and Dr. W.W. Yen had graduated. He stayed at St. John's until August 1904, at which time he followed Dr. Sze to the United States.[6]

After a year of preparation at the Cook Academy in Ithaca, New York, Koo entered Columbia University. He received his B.A. degree in 1908, his M.A. in 1909, and his Ph.D. in 1912, the latter two degrees in political science. He learned more of America by participating in student activities, including the Blue Pencil, Delta Epsilon, and Rho Societies. He received the Philolescean Literary Prize and the Columbia-Cornell Debating Medal and was elected a member of the "Varsity" debating team for 1906-1907. Koo also served as editor of the *Columbia Daily Spectator* and was manager of *The Columbia Monthly*.[7] He organized the Chinese Student's Alliance in America and the Chinese Student's Association of the Eastern States.

Koo's many years of study and practice in English and various disciplines in China and America made him an outstanding speaker in English and in Chinese. His training in international law and diplomacy under the direction of leading scholars such as John Bassett Moore further equipped him with fundamental theory and practice in modern Western diplomacy. He also mastered the Anglo-American bargaining arts and acquired a realistic approach to international negotiations. It was little wonder that Dr. Koo, the youngest delegate representing a weak and divided China at the Paris Peace Conference, impressed the statesmen of the world immediately.

The third factor influencing Koo's career was nationalism. He was raised in a China where nascent nationalism and patriotism were struggling against the decaying Manchu Dynasty and imperialist powers. Koo was born only a few years after China's crushing defeat in the First Sino-Japanese War and the signing of the Treaty of Shimonoseki in 1895. When he was about ten, China was forced to "lease" Liaotung to Russia, Kiaochow to Germany, Kwang-chow Bay to France, and Weihaiwei to Great Britain. The partition of the "sick man's belongings" seemed only a matter of time. A few years later the bloody ending of the Hundred Days Reform killed the hopes of patriotic intellectuals for mild reform under a constitutional monarchy and drove them into the arms of the violent national revolutionaries. The disaster of the Boxer movement greatly affected the mind of this boy of fourteen years. The intellectuals whose nationalism had been submerged in the lesser loyalties of province, guild, and clan arose in a fury of patriotism. Thousands of young men vowed to dedicate their lives to China's salvation, and many left home to study in Europe, Japan, and America in order to absorb the Occidental ideas and ways they considered necessary for China's modernization. Young Koo was one of them.[8]

Perhaps in no other city in China was the impact of the unequal treaties more obvious and intimate than in Shanghai. The Shanghai Settlement existed as a state within a state. Extraterritoriality made all the foreigners a class of human beings superior to the indigenous population. The right of inland navigation put all the Chinese in Shanghai constantly under the threat of guns from foreign warships flying their colors on the Huang-p'u River. The foreign garrisons put every Shanghainese at the mercy of bayonets of the foreign marines. The domination of foreigners over the Chinese Maritime Customs, Post Office, and most of the huge plants and corporations reduced most Shanghainese to the status of economic serfs. All these conditions were only too clear for thousands of young and awakened students to endure with equanimity.

Personal experiences in childhood contributed greatly to Koo's resentment of the unequal treaties. For example, while he was a student at the Anglo-Chinese College in 1899, Koo chose to try his new bicycle near the Shanghai racecourse on Saturday afternoon. A British boy of his age was riding a bicycle ahead of him; when the boy moved to a cement sidewalk Koo followed. Suddenly an Indian policeman appeared. Although he allowed the English boy to pass, he stopped young Koo who was handed over to a Chinese policeman and taken to the police station of the Concessions. Reacting to this unequal treatment, he protested to the police officer: "I don't know the rule, I only followed that English boy." All explanations and protests were in vain, and he was fined five yuan. Subsequently, with this incident in mind, Koo devoted his Ph.D. dissertation to "The Status of Aliens in China."[9]

When the Nationalist Revolution succeeded in establishing a new republic in 1911, hundreds of students rushed home, eager to employ their newly acquired knowledge in China's revitalization. Koo had hardly finished his dissertation when he received a telegram from T'ang Shai-i, Premier of the new Chinese Republic, summoning him back to serve this government.[10] With the encouragement of Professor Moore, Koo took the first steamer. He arrived in Peking via the Trans-Siberian Railway in April 1912, and Premier T'ang took him immediately to see President Yüan Shih-k'ai. Koo was appointed English secretary to the President and, concurrently, one of the eight secretaries in T'ang's Cabinet. After a short "exile" with Premier T'ang to Tientsin when T'ang broke with Yüan, Koo was appointed English Secretary to Foreign Minister W. W. Yen in August 1912, and thus began his distinguished diplomatic career.[11]

In October 1912, Koo was promoted to Councilor to assist in the negotiations with the British on the Tibetan provisional agreement concluded between 1913 and 1914.[12] In 1915 Foreign Minister Lou Tseng-tsiang (Lu Cheng-hsiang) and Vice-Foreign Minister Ts'ao Ju-lin brought Koo Japan's ultimatum on the infamous Twenty-One Demands while he was a patient at the foreign hospital in Peking. Koo worked all night to draft the English answer.[13] In July 1915, at the age of twenty-seven, he was recommended by Vice-Foreign Minister Ts'ao to be appointed Chinese Minister to Mexico. Three months later while en route to his post, his assignment was changed, and he became Minister to the United States and Cuba.

II

Dr. Koo labored to advance the national interest as defined by the Chinese intelligentsia and bourgeois classes. The major aims of Koo's diplomacy—derived from his traditional family experience and education, his Western training and experiences, and his nationalistic social environment—can be reduced to three: the abolition of the unequal treaties, particularly in major treaty ports in the Chinese provinces along the eastern and southeastern coast; the promotion of the Anglo-American alignment with China; and the creation of a national diplomacy above internal disputes and parties.

The fundamental theme of Koo's diplomacy was equality for the Chinese people in the modern community of nations. Consequently, his primary goal was abrogation of the unequal treaties. For this reason, Dr. Koo went abroad to study international law and politics and dedicated his dissertation, *The Status of Aliens in China*, to the problem. When he returned to serve the Chinese government, he accepted the appointment as Chinese representative to the Paris Peace Conference and the Washington Disarmament Conference. On both occasions Koo and his colleagues presented the problem of abolition of unequal treaties to the Great Powers. While China was weak, disorganized, and rent by civil wars, Dr. Koo accepted the Foreign Minister's post in the various Peking warlord governments in order to strengthen the international position of China.

During the period of warlord China, Koo was instrumental in the recovery of a number of significant sovereign rights and he laid the foundation for the restoration of others, particularly tariff autonomy and extraterritoriality. Besides his role in the achievement of the Sino-British Treaty for the Abolition of Extraterritoriality, Koo, as a member of the World War II Commission of Four, maneuvered between the challenging allies, Great Britain, the United States, and the Soviet Union, to implement the United Nations organization. His activities at the Dumbarton Oaks Conversation in 1944 and the United Nations Conference on International Organization at San Francisco in 1945 improved the image of China as one of the five Great Powers. Even Koo's political foes acknowledged his patriotism and dedication to China's rights and position in the family of nations. He himself said his life's goal was "to put China on the map."[14]

Koo's second ambition was international cooperation with the Anglo-American bloc. His many years of education and experience in the United States convinced him that America was a leading democracy with no ambitions in China; he also felt that she was sympathetic toward China's aspirations and rights during the period between the two world wars. At the end of World War I, Koo recognized that China's only opportunity to throw off the burden of unequal treaties, which curtailed her efforts to develop into a first-rate modern state, lay in the peace conference to be held on the basis of President Woodrow Wilson's Fourteen Points. From the time the United States broke diplomatic relations with Germany over the sinking of United States merchantmen by U-boats, Koo "advocated and recommended to Peking to follow the United States' lead."[15] At the Washington Disarmament Conference his cooperation with the Department of State was so close that

Secretary Hughes was thought, by some Chinese intellectuals at least, to be the Superior Plenipotentiary of the Chinese delegation. The Sino-Soviet Agreements of 1924 were signed against the advice of the Anglo-American bloc but only when public opinion created so much pressure that Koo's political life was endangered by the threatening tone of Marshal Wu P'ei-fu. Nevertheless, Koo's fundamental principle of Anglo-American cooperation prevailed.

Koo's posts abroad were at the centers of the Anglo-American bloc in international diplomacy—Washington, London, or cities nearest to the international organizations under the domination of the Anglo-American powers. He served as Chinese Minister to Washington, after Japan's Twenty-One Demands through the end of the Paris Peace Conference; he was then transferred to the court of St. James until after the Washington Naval Conference. After the Manchurian Incident he was appointed Minister to Paris to accompany the Lytton Commission back to Geneva where the League of Nations was under the aegis of the British and the French. When the United Nations was transferred to New York, Koo again moved from London to Washington in 1946. In 1963 Dr. Koo presented his collection of diplomatic papers to Columbia University and, in 1967, chose to live in New York rather than Taiwan after he retired from the International Court of Justice.

The third goal of Koo's diplomacy was the transcending of internal politics and parties. Koo believed that China should always be presented to foreign powers as one unit, and he insisted that the administrative independence and territorial integrity of China supersede domestic disputes and party interests. Slogans such as "working for China without reference to any political clique" and "abolishing unequal treaties is not confined to any one party" became his maxims. He was never identified closely with any party or faction, and his non-affiliation was acknowledged even by the Communists.[16] As long as a Chinese government was dedicated to Chinese nationalism, strong enough to perpetuate its political life, and accepted by the Anglo-American bloc in the international arena as a legitimate government to represent China, Koo was more than happy to serve.

Thus Koo accepted appointment as English secretary of Premier T'ang Shao-i in 1912 and later served in President Yüan's Ministry of Foreign Affairs after T'ang split with Yüan. He became Foreign Minister of the Peking government under the joint operation of the victorious Chihli and Fengtien Parties between May and November 1922, after the defeat of the Anhwei Party under Tuan Ch'i-jui. He was Foreign Minister, and for several months Acting Premier and Premier, between February 1923 and September 1924, under the victorious Chihli Party after the first Chihli-Fengtien War. After the second Chihli-Fengtien War, between October 1926 and June 1927, he was again appointed Foreign Minister, acting Premier, and later Premier of the

Peking government under the domination of the Fengtien Party. After the Mukden Incident in September 1931, the Nationalist government appointed Koo Acting Foreign Minister, and on November 23, 1931, he became the Foreign Minister.[17] He left this post in 1932 to present China's case at the League of Nations and stayed to serve at various Western diplomatic posts until his retirement in 1967.

By emphasizing national diplomacy above factions and parties, Koo was able to act independently at home or abroad to soften the hostility of his political foes. At Paris he employed the principle of Chinese solidarity toward foreigners to quiet the angry demonstrators who surrounded his residence and blocked the Chinese delegates from signing the Treaty of Versailles. In Washington he again employed this tactic to quiet Chinese students and other representatives of the Chinese people so that Dr. C.T. Wang and he could attend the Sino-Japanese negotiations on the problem of Shantung. Time and again, after his return to China in 1922, Dr. Koo advocated the solidarity of all factions and parties in a united China struggling for political independence and territorial integrity. Near the end of World War II, Dr. Koo and President Franklin D. Roosevelt strongly recommended to the Nationalist government the inclusion of a Chinese Communist representative in the Chinese delegation to San Francisco, resulting in the presence of Tung Pi-wu among the Chinese delegates attending the founding of the United Nations in 1945.[18]

III

During the formulation of the Versailles treaty in 1919, Koo dramatically focused Western attention upon China and its problems vis-à-vis Japan. Journeying to Paris in January of that year, he joined a distinguished company of Chinese delegates: Lou Tseng-tsiang, Foreign Minister and head of the Chinese delegation, Chengting T. Wang, Sao-Ke Alfred Sze, and Suntchou Wei (Wei Ch'en-tsu). The Chinese delegation determined to focus on the restoration of Shantung, despite the decisions made at the preparatory conference and the position held by President Hsü Shih-Ch'ang that they should deal with the restoration of the German and Austrian concessions, the removal of foreign troops stationed in China, and the restoration of tariff autonomy rather than the problem of Shantung.[19] On three occasions the Chinese delegation presented its views on the problem of Shantung at the insistence of President Wilson and against the opposition of the Japanese delegation.[20]

Before the Council of Ten, on January 27, Baron Makino presented Japan's claims in China:

The Japanese Government feels justified in claiming from the German Government the unconditional cession of (a) the leased territory of Kiaochow together with the railways, and other rights possessed by Germany in respect of Shantung province; (b) German Pacific Islands north of the Equator . . . in view of the extent of their effort and achievements in destroying German bases in the Extreme Orient and South Seas, and in safeguarding the important route on the Pacific and Indian Oceans and the Mediterranean waters . . . the Japanese Government feels confident that the claim above advanced would be regarded as only just and fair.[21]

Awakening late, Japan was alarmed at European aggression in China. Under her own "Monroe Doctrine," Japan considered that she had the best case for claiming China as her natural sphere of influence. Her position was very strong after the war—economically, militarily, and legally. She had been hurt less and had profited more by the war than most. With Russia and Germany removed from the stage in North China, Japan became the supreme power in the Far East, and this position was strengthened by the renewed Anglo-Japanese Alliance. She improved her legal position by secret agreements in 1917 with Great Britain and France who approved her claims. Japan's secret treaty with China in 1915, as a result of the Twenty-One Demands, and the second secret treaty in 1918 granted her all rights and interests possessed by Germany in Shantung.[22]

On the morning of January 28, 1919, at the Villa Majestic, Dr. Koo asked the Council of Ten for the restoration to China of the leased territories of Kiaochow, the railway in Shantung, and all the rights Germany possessed in that province before the war. He said:

The territories in question were an integral part of China. They were a part of a Province containing 36 million inhabitants, Chinese in race, language, and religion. . . . On the principles of nationality and of territorial integrity, principles accepted by the Conference, China had a right to the restoration of those territories. . . .

The Shantung Province, in which Kiaochow and the railway to Tsinanfu were situated, was the cradle of Chinese civilization, the birthplace of Confucius and Mencius and a Holy Land for the Chinese. . . . Economically, it was a densely populated country, with 36 million people in an area only 35,000 square miles. The density of the population produced an intense competition and rendered the country quite unsuitable for colonization. . . . Strategically, Kiaochow commanded one of the shortest approaches from the sea to Peking, namely the railway to Tsinanfu led straight to the capital.[23]

Baron Makino reminded the council that Japan was in actual possession of the territory under consideration by conquest from Germany and that agreement had already been reached regarding the railways. He held that before Japan could dispose of these concessions to a third party, it would be necessary for Japan to obtain the right of free disposal from Germany. Dr. Koo argued that the treaties and notes made in consequence of the negotiations on the Twenty-One Demands in 1915 had been agreed upon by the Chinese government only after an ultimatum from Japan. Since these were questions arising from the war, they were at best only provisional and temporary arrangements subject to the final review of the conference. Furthermore, "even if the treaties and notes had been entirely valid, the fact of China's declaration of war on Germany had altered the situation in such a way that on the principle of *rebus sic stantibus* they could not be enforced today." In declaring war against Germany, China expressly stated that "all treaties and conventions concluded between China and Germany should be considered as nullified by the state of war between them." Thus Koo argued that "even if the lease had not been terminated by China's declaration of war, Germany would not be competent to transfer it to any other power than China because of an express provision therein against transfer to another Power." He asked for direct restitution, for "it was always easier to take one step than two if it led to the same place."[24]

Koo "simply overwhelmed the Japanese with his argument," Secretary of State Robert Lansing noted. "In fact," Lansing continued, "it made such an impression on the Japanese themselves, that one of the delegates called me the following day and attempted to offset the effect by declaring that the United States would be blamed if Kiaochow was returned to China." Wunsz King, Koo's secretary at the Paris Peace Conference, also recorded that "Koo was dignified and agreeable in manner, skillful in the choice of words, cogent and forceful in argument, firm in tone, though at the beginning a bit trembling in voice."[25] For China it was the beginning of a new diplomatic era with the first Chinese plenipotentiary, in modern times, speaking for his country at a major international conference.

A few days later, on April 2, Koo informed Wilson's intimate advisor Colonel Edward House that the Chinese had from the beginning "favored direct negotiations with Japan on the ground that the Occidental could not be relied upon for effective support. . . ." If China should not receive satisfaction from the Western Powers, he expressed the fear that "the reaction from such an outcome should make the Chinese people feel that their hope lay in the direction of close co-operation with Japan."[26] Koo believed that if the United States would firmly support China the three other principal powers would fall in line. He also contended that Wilson's Fourteen Points nullified in spirit those secret engagements the Powers had made with Japan. Pursuing his point, Koo informed Lansing that "to leave Japan in Shantung would mean to allow her to build up an influence capable of dominating North China," an eventuality which would prejudice the future of China while jeopardizing foreign interests.[27]

Failing to gain Japanese acceptance of Wilson's proposal that the Five Powers act as trustees of the former German rights in Shantung in the afternoon of the same day, April 22, the Big Three requested the Chinese delegation to give up China's claims on Shantung. Despite all Koo's eloquence and background preparations, China seemed on the losing side when Lloyd George pressed Koo: "Which would China prefer—to allow Japan to succeed to the German rights in Shantung as stated in the treaty between China and Germany, or to recognize Japan's position in Shantung as stipulated in treaties between China and Japan?"[28] At this point President Wilson had probably already made up his mind, for the Japanese told Wilson they were explicitly instructed not to sign the treaty if the Shantung question was settled in China's favor. With Italy's absence and Belgium's defection, the President subordinated every other consideration in order to save the League and adopted the Japanese draft of the clauses (which ultimately became Articles 156, 157, and 158 of the treaty) on condition that Japan make a separate declaration reaffirming her promise to return Shantung to China.[29]

Koo and his colleagues were bitterly disappointed when the American decision reached them on the night of April 30. Koo sent the President two protesting memoranda, on April 24 and May 3, without answer. Consequently, at the plenary session on May 6, the Chinese delgation formally registered its disapproval of the resolution on the Shantung question, and Koo subsequently informed House and Lansing of China's intent to sign the treaty with reservation. The Chinese request was refused, however, on the grounds that "it was impossible for China to sign the treaty with a reservation: that China must either sign it in full, or not at all." The Allies did not want to establish a precedent because both Germany and Romania had also asked to sign with reservation.[30]

Dr. Koo and his colleagues suggested that the reservation could be made as an annex to the treaty of peace, but the request was again refused. Eventually Koo made a final compromise effort with "a further modification of the wording, so that the signing of the treaty by China might not be understood as precluding her from asking at a suitable moment for reconsideration of the Shantung question."[31] Even this was not acceptable to the conference. Under the increasing pressure of Chinese public opinion and nation-wide demonstrations, especially the famous May Fourth Movement, the Chinese delegation refused to go to the Hall of Mirrors to sign the treaty on June 28, 1919, despite contrary instructions from the Peking government.[32] Instead, Koo and his colleagues announced to the press that "the Peace Conference having denied China justice in the settlement of the Shantung question and having today in effect prevented them from signing the treaty without sacrificing their sense of right, justice, and patriotic duty, the Chinese delegates submit their case to the impartial judgement of the world."[33]

The Paris Peace Conference profoundly altered Chinese foreign policy, which shifted fundamentally from the pro-Japanese policies instituted by the students returned from Japan to a pro-Anglo-American course sponsored by the English-speaking and American-trained diplomats.

IV

Between 1921 and 1924 Koo participated in two significant series of negotiations designed to reaffirm China's independence and sovereignty. First, the Washington Conference (1921-1922), which saw the governments of the United States, Great Britain, Japan, France, and Italy initiate a naval limitation program, spent much of its time trying to resolve Far Eastern questions. Out of these deliberations came the Nine Power Pact of 1922 which, for the first time, codified in treaty form the basic American principles of the Open Door toward China. The conference also provided the opportunity ·for China and Japan to negotiate a settlement of their long-festering discords over Shantung and Chinese tariffs and revenues. Second, Koo took part in the restoration of Sino-Russian relations during 1923-1924. At long last, he piloted through a treaty which, if it did not fulfill all Chinese hopes, at least recognized the principle of Chinese equality.

At Washington Koo assumed responsibility for the activities of the Subcommittee on Chinese Revenue and the Sino-Japanese conversations on Shantung. When the Root Resolution to respect the territorial integrity and political independence of China was adopted on December 10, 1921, Senator Elihu Root informed Koo that, due to Japan's special rights and interests in Manchuria, the resolution should be applied only to China proper.[34] To this, Koo replied:

> The confirmation of the principles of territorial integrity should not be confined to China proper. . . . The territories of the Chinese Republic were defined in its Constitution. The Chinese Delegation could not discuss any question which might give the impression of attempting to modify the territorial boundaries of China. . . . As regards the point of administrative independence, there was some difference in the existing status of administration in the different parts of the Chinese Republic. . . . But this was an internal arrangement within the Republic and, so far as the outside world was concerned, it would appear clear that the principle of administrative integrity should be confirmed for the Chinese Republic as one unit.[35]

Koo's rebuff silenced the "What Is China" issue.

The Nine Power Treaty, as adopted, consisted of the essential features of the Ten Points submitted by the Chinese delegation on November 16, 1921, and the Root Resolution: (1) to respect the sovereignty, the independence, and the territorial and administrative integrity of China; (2) to provide the fullest and most unembarrassed opportunity for China to develop and maintain for herself an effective and stable government; (3) to use their influence for the purpose of effectually establishing and maintaining the principle of equal opportunity for the commerce and industry of all nations throughout the territory of China; (4) to refrain from taking advantage of conditions in China in order to seek special rights or privileges that would abridge the rights of subjects of citizens of friendly states and to abstain from countenancing action inimical to the security of such states.[36]

Next Koo turned to the question of tariff autonomy and revenue. He declared that the existing International Customs regime in China infringed on China's sovereign right to fix the tariff rate at her own discretion and that since it deprived China of her power to make reciprocity arrangements with the powers, it ran counter to the principles of equality and mutuality. He charged that a uniform rate for all kinds of commodities, without latitude to differentiate rates between luxuries and necessities, failed to take into consideration the economic, social, and the fiscal needs of the Chinese people. Furthermore the current tariff caused a serious loss of revenue to the Chinese Exchequer, and under the existing custom regime it was exceedingly difficult to revise the tariff to an effective five percent. Based on these arguments Koo proposed that: (1) tariff autonomy be restored to China at the end of a certain period to be agreed upon the Powers; (2) the Chinese import tariff duty be immediately increased to 12 percent; (3) and as soon as practicable a new tariff arrangement be agreed upon between China and the Powers, whereby China would be free to levy any rate of duty she might choose on any article imported, up to a certain maximum rate to be agreed upon, thus permitting differentiation.

Koo's proposal failed in the Subcommittee on Chinese Revenues mainly because of Japanese opposition. Odagiri Masunosuke, Director of the Yokohama Specie Bank, stated that trade with China comprised the bulk of Japan's overseas trade. Such a sudden increase in tariff would entail serious consequences for Japanese industry. He therefore proposed to levy a surtax of 30 percent upon export, import, and coastwide trade. Consequently, a British compromise draft agreement on the Chinese tariff, with Dr. Koo's concurrence, was used as the basis for discussion and was adopted by the subcommittee with revisions.

At its seventeenth meeting the Committee on Pacific and Far Eastern Questions reported the completion of the two phases of tariff readjustment for China. A revision commission was scheduled to meet in Shanghai to revise the current tariff in accordance with existing treaties. This revision would become effective two months after publication of the agreement without awaiting ratification. It would provide additional revenue amounting to about $17,000,000 silver. Long-range revision would involve a special conference representing China and the Powers charged with the duty of preparing a way for the speedy abolition of *likin*.* It would likewise put into effect a uniform

*A local transit tax

surtax of 2 percent that would generate additional revenue amounting to approximately $27,000,000. In his final speech to the conference, Koo regretted that the agreements did not include the restoration of tariff autonomy to China, but both of the agreements were adopted by the conference on February 4, 1922, in the Treaty Relating to the Chinese Customs Tariff.[37]

Regarding tariff revision then, the concrete achievements of Dr. Koo were limited. He did achieve an effective duty rate of 5 percent ad valorem without any delay. But Odagiri deemed his major proposal to raise the import duty from 5 percent to 12½ percent effective "out of the question". Nevertheless, Koo laid the foundation for the Special Conference on Chinese Tariff held October 26, 1925, in Peking, at which the thirteen powers agreed on the restoration of China's tariff autonomy as of January 1, 1929.[38]

Chinese diplomacy next addressed itself to the question of Shantung. China had refused to sign the Treaty of Versailles at the Paris Peace Conference and had denied Japanese succession to German interests in Shantung. While Koo was the first representative of China on the League Council, the Peking government cabled him an eight-point resolution presenting its view of the Shantung case. He refrained from submitting it to the council, however, due to the absence of the United States. As the Washington Conference was approaching, Japan became "extremely anxious" to settle this troublesome matter with China before the commencement of the conference in order to avoid another "trial" by the assembled powers. Through the effort of Secretary of State Charles Evans Hughes, Baron Shidehara Kijūrō, Japanese Ambassador to Washington, presented a "proposed Terms of Settlement Respective of the Shantung Question." Foreign Minister Yen rejected this Japanese proposal to return one-half of its interests in Shantung to China.[39]

The Chinese delegation postponed bringing up the issue of Shantung for the first two weeks of the conference, but its patience was growing thin. Reluctant to allow the Shantung question to affect Japan's attitude toward other issues, Secretary Hughes and Arthur J. Balfour, head of the British delegation, pressed both the Chinese and Japanese delegations in Washington and their home governments in Peking and Tokyo to settle this problem. It was decided finally that Hughes and Balfour would introduce the negotiators, offer their good offices, and then withdraw. Subsequent meetings would be attended by two American observers, J.V.A. MacMurray and Edward Bell, plus two British observers.[40] The opening session of the Sino-Japanese negotiations on December 1, 1921, was delayed one and a half hours because Koo was detained by dissident Chinese students and journalists under the banner of "Oppose the direct negotiations" and "Return Shantung to us."[41]

If the heart of China's concern at the conference was the Shantung question, the essence of the Shantung question was the Tsingtao-Tsinanfu

Railway. This subject occupied most of the thirty-six meetings of the Sino-Japanese negotiators, consumed more time than all the other items combined, and brought discussions to a halt at least three times within the short span of two months. The Sino-Japanese arguments were centered on the management, valuation, and the mode of reimbursement for the railway.

Koo rejected the Japanese proposal to make the Shantung Railway a joint Sino-Japanese enterprise, but he suggested that China "would be prepared to redeem or purchase half of the total amount of the valuation of the railway and its appurtenances."[42] He argued that if the railway was a prize of war, it should have gone to China, within whose territory it was situated. Baron Shidehara responded that a total figure of 30 million yen had been tentatively set by the reparation commission in Paris. If China would have to pay to Japan half of the value, or 15 million yen, in order to acquire the whole railway, while Japan by arrangement with Germany was to credit the railway's whole value to German reparation accounts because the Shantung Railway was a private undertaking, Japan would lose 15 million yen. Finally, Koo conceded to pay not only the whole value of the line—the sum of 53,406,141 gold marks—but also the amount that Japan had actually expended during the period of her administration of the railway for permanent improvements on and additions to the railway properties, less a suitable allowance for depreciation.[43] Joint Anglo-American pressure, including President Harding's warning to Foreign Minister Yen, eventually resulted in a compromise formula for payment:

> Deferred payment by Chinese treasury notes running for fifteen years, but redeemable at any time after five years; appointment of a Japanese chief accountant, and of a Chinese chief accountant, of equal powers, both of them subject to the control of the Chinese director-general of the railway; and appointment of a Japanese traffic manager subject to the control of the Chinese director-general. . . .[44]

Koo, Sze, and Shidehara also agreed upon other settlements on Shantung, including the restitution of the leased territory of Kiaochow and the fifty kilometer zone around Kiaochow Bay, transfer of public properties used for administrative purposes within the leased territory of Kiaochow, withdrawal of all Japanese troops from Shantung within six months, and restoration of the Maritime Customs at Tsingtao while permitting the use there of the Japanese language.[45] Moreover, the Tsinan-Shunteh and the Kaomi-Hsuchow lines were to be turned over to the international financial body. In addition the Chinese government was to purchase the salt interests of Japanese companies and nationals along the coast of Kiaochow Bay at a fair price and with a guaranteed quota of salt to be reserved for exportation to Japan.[46]

Another test of Koo's diplomacy concerned the restoration of relations between China and Russia. The essential issues here were the claims of both powers to the ownership of the Chinese Eastern Railway (CER) and the domination of Mongolia. The roots of both problems went back a number of years. After her disastrous defeat at the hands of Japan in 1894, China found Russia pressing the enfeebled Peking government for special rights in the CER and in Mongolia. Further complications came with the outbreak of the Chinese Revolution in 1911 when the Living Buddha (Cheptsun Damba Hut'ukht'u) declared the independence of Outer Mongolia. The pressure of war and domestic politics finally forced the three governments—Tzarist Russia, China, and Outer Mongolia—to sign the Tripartite Agreement of June 7, 1915, in which Outer Mongolia accepted China's suzerainty and China recognized Outer Mongolia's autonomy. Subsequent Mongolian collaboration with White Russian forces to restore its independence, which had been abolished during the 1917 Russian Revolution, offered a pretext for the victorious Soviets to seize Outer Mongolia.[47] At the same time, however, China took advantage of the Russian Revolution to reverse its earlier strategy of granting the Russians special rights on the CER in order to gain Russian protection against Japanese pressure in North Asia. In 1920 Peking recovered both administrative and police power over the CER.

Russia made the first move toward a rapprochment between the two nations. Seeking allies in the East against the foreign troops in Siberia and viewing China as the "most reliable rear base for world revolution," Lev Mikhailovich Karakhan, Acting People's Commissar of Foreign Affairs, and Iakov Davidovich Ianson, Representative of People's Commissariat of Foreign Affairs of the Far Eastern Republic in Irkutsk, dispatched their first declaration to the Chinese Governments at Peking and Canton on June 25, 1919. Its purpose was to initiate negotiations concerning the abolition of all the unequal treaties and agreements between China and Imperial Russia:

> In short, all and everything, either plundered by Tzarist Government alone or in collaboration with Japan and other Allied Powers, would be returned to the Chinese people. . . . The Soviet Government is willing to return to China, without demanding any kind of compensation, the Chinese Eastern Railway. . . . The Soviet Government abandons the indemnity of Boxer Uprising in 1900. . . . In case they [the Russians] commit any crimes they should be subject to the Chinese Law and the local jurisdiction.[48]

Dr. Koo responded enthusiastically to the idea of a restoration of Sino-Russian relations and the abolition of unequal treaties China had signed with Imperial Russia. He immediately began communications with the Soviet representative in London (where Koo had been assigned after the Paris Peace Conference). The Chinese Ministry of Foreign Affairs telegraphed Koo the conditions for opening formal negotiations: (1) the Soviet delegates were to be informal representatives for commercial affairs, not inheriting the title and function of the former Russian Minister; (2) the Soviet delegation would refrain from publishing Communist propaganda; (3) Chinese merchants in Russia would be exempted from all forced services, their goods would not be subject to any confiscation, and no force or limitation would be laid on Chinese workers; and (4) all damages suffered by Chinese residing in Russia would be compensated by the Soviet government according to the results of investigation jointly conducted by China and the Soviet Union.[49] Uncertainty as to the Soviet government's survival prevented the Chinese government from following up this initial offer.

As White Russian resistance in Siberia collapsed, Karakhan presented a second declaration to the Chinese government on September 27, 1920, but it carried a less conciliatory tone. The return of the Boxer Indemnity was now qualified, and Soviet use of the CER was taken for granted, subject only to negotiation procedures. Neither declaration mentioned the vexing problem of Outer Mongolia. Unfortunately these initial exchanges and the subsequent Soviet missions to Peking of M.L. Yurin in 1920, A.K. Paikes in 1922, and A.A. Joffe later in 1922 failed to uncover grounds for mutual agreement.[50]

Meanwhile after the Washington Conference the Koo family returned to Peking and moved into a former palace, provided by the father-in-law, on Iron-lion Lane. Soon Dr. Koo found himself again involved in Sino-Soviet affairs. Due to his distinguished service abroad, Koo overcame the factionalism of current Chinese politics to serve as Foreign Minister in rapidly changing governments.* The victory of the Chihli Party over the pro-Japan Anfu clique so improved the political climate in Peking that Karakhan, who succeeded Joffe as the Soviet representative to China, came to Peking on September 2, 1923. After being officially received by Foreign Minister Koo and Director General C.T. Wang,[51] he issued a third declaration on September 3, 1923, reiterating the Soviet stand. Exchanges of opinion between Wang and Karakhan did not start, however, until Karakhan threatened to leave Peking for the south to establish relations with the Kuomintang regime.[52]

After several revisions dictated by Koo, on March 14, 1924, Wang and Karakhan signed a revised draft Agreement on General Principles for the Settlement of the Questions between China and the USSR and a draft Agreement for the Provisional Management of the Chinese Eastern Railway.[53] Both agreements conceded that within one month a Sino-Russian conference would be held to carry out detailed arrangements. The documents agreed to annul all treaties and contracts between China and the Tzarist government and to replace them with new treaties on the basis of equality. They also

---

*Koo served as Foreign Minister of Tang Shai-i's Cabinet (August 5-November 25, 1922), resumed this office on April 2, 1923, and retained it in the Chihli government of Marshal Ts'ao K'un (which deposed President Li Yuan-hung) during 1924.

stipulated that the USSR recognize Outer Mongolia as an integral part of China and withdraw all Soviet troops as soon as a mutually acceptable timetable was established. The CER was now to be a purely commercial enterprise under the joint operation of China and the Soviets, with all other civil, military, judicial, municipal, tax, and local matters to be administered by China. The USSR also agreed to Chinese redemption of the CER. Finally, the USSR relinquished all special rights concerning concessions, the Boxer Indemnity, the right of extraterritoriality, and the right to impose tariff rates.

The Wang-Karakhan draft agreements met strong opposition in the State Council of March 15 from Koo, Lu Chin, Minister of War, and Wang K'e-min, Minister of Finance. Their objections centered on three issues: (1) that the Soviet-Mongolian Treaty of Friendship concluded in Moscow on November 5, 1921, should also be declared null and void; (2) that Soviet troops should be unconditionally withdrawn from Outer Mongolia; and (3) that the transfer of all the buildings and landed properties of the Russian Orthodox mission to the Soviet government would establish an undesirable precedent.[54]

This refusal to ratify the draft agreements so irritated Karakhan that he sent an ultimatum to Wang on March 16 warning that if the Chinese government did not recognize the draft agreement within three days, the Soviet representative would consider himself released from the agreements. Karakhan also accused the Chinese Cabinet of an anti-Soviet foreign policy. Through the efforts of Koo, the State Council on March 20 abolished Wang's office and transferred Sino-Soviet negotiations to Dr. Koo's Ministry of Foreign Affairs.[55] Sino-Soviet negotiations seemed to have reached an impasse.

No other foreign policy issue since the May Fourth Movement in 1919 caused so much concern in China as the breakdown of the Sino-Soviet negotiations. Within the short period from March 18 to March 26, Marshal Wu P'ei-fu, the powerful general of the Chihli Party, sent six telegrams to the Cabinet urging its ratification. Many military governors from various provinces echoed Wu. Public bodies, university professors, and students in Peking charged that the Peking government was "a running dog of imperialist powers," urged it to recognize the Soviet Union immediately and unconditionally, and condemned Koo and the Cabinet.[56]

To everyone's surprise a Presidential mandate of May 30, 1924, declared that the Sino-Soviet Agreement on General Principles and the Agreement for the Provisional Management of the CER was acceptable and that Koo had been appointed plenipotentiary with full powers to sign the instruments. They were signed the following day, and two days later the office for a Sino-Russian Conference was established.[57] Koo formally introduced Karakhan to President Ts'ao K'un as the first Ambassador to China, and his full credentials were received on July 31, 1924.

A careful examination of the Sino-Soviet agreements reveals their onesidedness, particularly in the cases of the CER and Outer Mongolia. The agreements guaranteed Russian dominance over the line since only Russia could practically provide candidates with technical and educational qualifications to fill its high-salaried posts.[58] China's unilateral refusal to recognize the Soviet-Mongolian Treaty of Friendship did not affect the validity of the treaty or Soviet-Mongolian relations in any way. The withdrawal of Soviet forces from Outer Mongolia and questions such as the time limit of the withdrawal and measures to be adopted for safety along the border were still matters for discussion rathar than conditions of the agreements. In other words, the Koo-Karakhan agreements were identical with the draft Wang-Karakhan agreements with the exception of a few insignificant points, most of which were literary adjustments rather than factual changes.

Nevertheless, the Sino-Soviet agreement was the only treaty based on equality that China signed in modern times with a leading power. Furthermore China achieved the agreement through diplomacy without risking her destiny on the outcome of war. The result was the recovery of many rights, including extraterritoriality and the Boxer Indemnity. Also there was an element of "modern" diplomacy introduced here: the new diplomats of warlord China, including Dr. Koo, kept the public informed by constant publication of all diplomatic notes, including disputes. China's suzerainty and rights were protected at any price, and no territory in Outer Mongolia or elsewhere was to be secretly bartered away merely for party interest or personal power.[59]

V

It took the Mukden Incident on September 18, 1931, to bring Koo back into the international limelight.[60] The explosion at Mukden, which slightly damaged a section of the South Manchurian Railway, signalled the beginning of the Japanese Army's incursions into Manchuria and Northern China, and rallied most Chinese under the banner of nationalism. Wellington Koo was one of many who would respond to this call.

Following his negotiations with the Russians, Koo was for a brief period Acting Premier in Peking after Sun Pao'ch'i's resignation. General Feng Yü-hsiang's "Capital Revolution" in October 1924 forced Koo out of the government and he retired with his wife to the British Concession in Tientsin.[61] He did not return to Peking until after Marshal Chang Tso-lin drove out General Feng's Nationalist Army in May 1926. Under the Manchurian warlord Chang, Dr. Koo served first as Finance Minister, then as Foreign Minister, and finally as Acting Prime Minister. Chang's raid on the Soviet embassy in April 1927, however, provided Koo with the opportunity to resign and he retired to the scenic Western Hills of suburban Peking.

"Aware of political clouds gathering in the south [the Nationalist Canton government] and predicting the destruction of the warlords," his wife has written, "Dr. Koo's shrewd intuition enabled him to make far-sighted prophecies to keep him on the right road."[62] With General Chiang Kai-shek's consolidation of China, Koo, who had been too prominent in previous rival governments, left for a "fishing trip" in Canada and France to avoid arrest. The order for Koo's arrest was cancelled through Marshal Chang Hsueh-liang's efforts after the Young Marshal led Manchuria back into the Nanking central government in late December 1928, and Koo returned to China.

The Koos had just returned to Peking from vacationing at the sea shore resort of Pei-tai-ho when the Young Marshal telephoned, early on the morning of September 19, 1931, requesting an urgent conference about the Mukden Incident. Shocked at the audacity of the Japanese Kwantung Army, Koo went at once to the Young Marshal's headquarters. Koo recommended two steps to Marshal Chang and his officers:

(1) to report the incident to Nanking by telegraph at once and to ask the government to make an urgent appeal to the League of Nations in Geneva in accordance with the covenant of the League; and
(2) to at once dispatch a suitable emissary, who spoke Japanese and knew Japanese military leaders, to see the Military Governor of Port Arthur and Commanding General of the Japanese Kwantung Army to find out what was his real intention and how far he was inclined to push his aggressive plan.[63]

The Mukden Incident changed the attitude of the Nationalist government toward Koo. Koo flew to Nanking where on November 28 he was appointed Minister of Foreign Affairs to succeed C.T. Wang. A few weeks later, however, Koo was designated Chinese assessor to Lord Lytton's Commission of Enquiry, appointed by the League of Nations "to study on the spot to report to the Council on any circumstances affecting international relations, which threatens to disturb peace between China and Japan or the good understanding between them." Koo accompanied the commission from battle-ridden Shanghai to occupied Manchuria at the risk of his life. He was so fully occupied in Manchuria that "he never had time to unpack [the] bullet-proof vest" Mrs. Koo bought for him. Between April and August he and his staff compiled not less than twenty-five lengthy memoranda pertaining to the Japanese aggression in China, and in behalf of the Chinese government they submitted them to the Commission of Enquiry. When the Lytton Commission completed its report in early September 1932, Koo was appointed Chinese Minister to France to accompany the commission back to Geneva to argue China's case at the League of Nations.

The Sino-Japanese controversy had been under consideration by the League since September 19, 1931, when Yoshizawa Kenkichi, the Japanese representative, and Dr. Sao-ke Alfred Sze, the Chinese representative, first brought the issue to the council. The United States, though not a member of the League, was so involved in the question that she was invited to send a representative. Following the occupation of Chinchow by the Kwantung Army, Secretary of State Henry L. Stimson sent his famous note on the Doctrine of Non-Recognition on January 7, 1932. The League appealed to Japan on February 16 to stop its aggression and subsequently declared, on March 11, that "it is incumbent upon the members of the League of Nations not to recognize any situation, treaty or agreement which may be brought about by means contrary to the covenant of the League of Nations or to the Pact of Paris." Four days later Japan replied by formally extending her recognition of an independent "Manchukuo."[64]

The League Council waited six weeks to allow the Japanese time to study the Lytton Report and then reconvened on November 21 to discuss the report. Matsuoka Yosuke, who replaced Yoshizawa as Japan's representative, condemned the report as incomplete and unfounded. He insisted that China was not an organized state, which fact therefore prevented application of the usual methods of solution. He argued that Manchuria was not naturally or necessarily a part of China, that the Kwantung Army had acted in Manchuria in the past due to legitimate self-defense, and that the movement for Manchurian independence was not manufactured by the Kwantung Army.

Koo answered skillfully by quoting the findings of the report: "On the night of September 18, the Japanese military operations could not be regarded as measures of legitimate defense and a carefully prepared plan was put into operation with swiftness and precision." Koo further pointed out that it was the commission's view that "Japan had not exhausted the peaceful methods for settling the many claims against China, and she had forcibly occupied and declared independent of the rest of China a large area that was indisputably Chinese against the Covenant of the League, the Kellogg Pact and the Nine Power Treaty." He asserted that the nationwide sentiment and boycott against Japan was in response to Japan's traditional policy of attempting to control China and prevent China's unification. The Chinese delegation further charged that Japan, a country plagued by financial stress, military domination, and political assassinations, hardly qualified as a good example of an organized state.[65]

On November 28, 1932 at its tenth meeting, the council unanimously resolved (with Japan abstaining) to transmit the Lytton Report to the Assembly. Matsuoka denied the charge that Japan had violated the covenant, the Nine Power Treaty, or the Paris Pact, and his argument that Japan had regarded Manchuria's fate as a question of life and death did not change the attitude of any of the Powers. The Assembly adopted a report which embodied the Lytton Report in its entirety on February 24, 1933; the vote was unanimous except for the single dissenting vote of Japan. The council's report stated that "sovereignty over Manchuria belonged to China" and that "the Assembly cannot regard as measures of self-defense the military operations carried out that night by the Japanese troops at Mukden and other places in Manchuria." It also charged that "a group of Japanese civil and military officials conceived, organized and carried through the Manchurian independence movement and it could only be carried out owing to the presence of the Japanese troops" and that "the vast majority of the population regarded it as an instrument of the Japanese."[66] Following the report, the entire Japanese delegation withdrew.

In behalf of China, Koo concluded after the adoption of the report that "although the requirements of justice could be considered to have been met by the Report, the principal object of the League's existence—the maintenance of peace—remained yet to be fulfilled," for the Japanese Army was now moving to occupy China's Jehol province. He urged the members of the League to stand together and take effective and united action, including the use of various sanctions against the Japanese aggressor.[67] Shortly after his speech, Jehol was placed under Japanese military control and declared a part of the "State of Manchukuo."

The second Sino-Japanese war started on July 7, 1937, with a Japanese attack against the Chinese 29th Army at Wan-p'ing near Peking. China immediately called the attention of the signatories of the Nine Power Treaty to this fresh Japanese aggression. Chiefly because of Koo's appeal, the League's Advisory Committee urged that "the League should invite its members who were parties to the Nine Power Treaty to initiate the consultation and the full and frank communication." The Nine Power Conference finally opened four months later in Brussels on November 3, 1937. Dr. Koo, the head of the Chinese delegation, addressed the conference charging that Japan's perpetual "dual diplomacy," diffused through diplomats and Army leaders, made direct negotiations futile. He said China only desired peace based upon the principles of the Nine Power Treaty and was determined to fight the aggressor to the end. Koo concluded with an appeal for material help to continue effective resistance and asked the Powers to refrain from contributing arms and raw materials to the aggressor.[68]

Japan repeatedly refused to discuss a settlement with any power. This meant no settlement, because the Germans and Italians were reluctant to offend their ally under the tripartite anti-Comintern agreement of November 25, 1936, and because the opposition of the Congress prevented the United States from providing leadership. The passiveness of the Soviet Union after her exclusion from the subcommittee further diminished prospects for accommodation. The conference "suspended its sittings" permanently on November 24 without concrete accomplishment except a declaration that "there existed no warrant in law for the use of armed force by any country for the purpose of intervening in the internal regime of another country." [69]

Throughout 1938 and 1939, Koo continued to urge the Powers to assist China and to refrain from providing raw materials and arms, particularly airplanes and gasoline, to Japan. His success was signalled when the Council of the League of Nations eventually passed a resolution on September 30, 1938, stipulating that Article 16 of the League Covenant concerning economic, financial, diplomatic, and military sanctions was applicable to Japan.[70] After the Vichy government acceded to the Japanese demands in Indo-China, there was little for Koo to do in France. He was again appointed Ambassador to the Court of St. James, where he persuaded the British to sign the "Sino-British Treaty for the Abolition of Extraterritoriality and Related Rights in China" in January 1943 and the "Financial Aid Agreement Between the Republic of China and Great Britain" in May 1944.[71]

Dr. Koo led the Chinese delegation to the Dumbarton Oaks Conference in late 1944 to prepare for the creation of the United Nations. He was the senior member and the designated head of the Chinese delegation at the United Nations Conference on International Organization in San Francisco in early 1945. One year later Koo was transferred again to Washington to join the Nationalist government's representatives at the Security Council where he worked in close collaboration with Chiang T'ing-fu, chief delegate of Nationalist China from 1947 to 1956.[72] He was also instrumental in soliciting American aid of over three billion dollars for Chiang Kai-shek's government to fight the civil war in 1948, and he promoted the "Exchange of Notes between the Republic of China [Formosa] and the U.S.A. for Mutual Security Assistance" in January 1952.[73]

In January 1957, Dr. Koo was elected to the International Court of Justice at The Hague to complete the term resulting from the death of Hsü Mo; shortly thereafter he won reelection for a full term of ten years. When he retired from his seat in February 1967, he was vice-president of the World Court. Koo's career ended as it had begun, in a search for legal solutions to international problems.

Notes

1 Except Dr. W.W. Yen whose father was a missionary and who was taken back from Hong Kong to Shanghai by the Japanese military authorities during World War II.
2 On February 9, 1924, Koo signed the Sino-German Agreement which netted the Peking government $43 million silver. *Wai-chiao wen-tu* (Diplomatic Documents), *Chung-Te hsieh-yüeh chi fu-chien* (The Sino-German Agreement and Annex).

3 According to my interviews with Koo and the autobiography of Koo Hui-lan, he was born in 1888; however, other sources indicate that he might have been born in 1887.

4 Personal data was obtained during an interview with Dr. Koo, August 11, 1967, New York.

5 Koo Hui-lan (Madame Wellington Koo), *An Autobiography as Told to Mary Van Rensselaer Thayer* (New York: Dial Press, 1943), p. 118. Dr. Koo married four times. Koo's first marriage was in 1908 to a daughter of a physician named Chang in Shanghai, under the management of Koo's father. This marriage ended in divorce in 1910 in Philadelphia. Koo's second marriage was with T'ang Pao-yüeh, the eldest daughter of T'ang Shao-i, first Premier of the Chinese Republic, in Shanghai in 1913. She died of a Spanish fever in Washington, D.C. in late 1918. His third wife was Huang Hui-lan (Oei Hui-lan), daughter of sugar king Huang Tsung-han of Indonesia and Malay. They were married on November 11, 1920, in Brussels, the day before Koo headed the Chinese delegation at the opening ceremony of the Assembly of the League of Nations. Koo and Huang were divorced in 1956 in Mexico. Koo's present wife is Yen Yu-yung, widow of Dr. Yang Kuang-sheng who was buried alive by the Japanese in Manila during World War II. They were married in 1959 in Mexico.

6 Interview with Dr. Koo, August 11, 1967, New York; Koo Hui-lan, *Autobiography*, p. 118; Sao-Ke Alfred Sze, *Shih Chao-chi tsao-nien hui-i lu* (Reminiscences of His Early Years as Told to Anming Fu) (Taipei: Chuan-chi Wen-hsüeh She, 1967), pp. 38-39.

7 A.R. Burt *et al.*, *Biographies of Prominent Chinese* (Shanghai, n.d.).

8 Koo Hui-lan, *Autobiography*, p. 117.

9 Interview with Dr. Koo, November 26, 1966, New York; V.K. Wellington Koo, *The Status of Aliens in China* (New York: Columbia University Press, 1912).

10 Koo was President of the Chinese Students Association when he first met T'ang on the latter's visit to Washington, D.C. in 1908.

11 Koo, *The Status of Aliens in China*, pp. 7-8; Koo Hui-lan, *Autobiography*, p. 106.

12 The agreement was not ratified by the Peking government. John V.A. MacMurray, *Treaties and Agreements with and Concerning China, 1894-1919* (New York: Oxford University Press, 1921), 1:581-582.

13 Ts'ao Ju-lin, *I-sheng chih hui-i* (Memoir of Ts'ao Ju-lin) (Hong Kong: Ch'un-ch'iu Tsa-chih She, 1966), pp. 129, 147-148.

14 Interview with Dr. Koo, November 26, 1966, New York.

15 V.K. Wellington Koo to Chu Pao-chin, July 1, 1969.

16 "A List of the Various Cliques among Members of the Central Committee Elected by the Sixth Congress of the Kuomintang" [Confidential, for reference only]. The original biographies of Kuomintang leaders were prepared by the Communist intelligence for confidential purposes in August 1945, translated into English by the Committee on International and Regional Studies of Harvard University, and circulated in February 1948.

17 *Chung-kuo wai-chiao chi-kuan li-jen shou-chang hsien-ming nien-piao* (Table of Names and Titles of the Successive Heads of the Organ of Foreign Affairs of China) (Taipei: Commercial Press, 1967), pp. 53-64.

18 Wu Chün-ts'ai (ed.), *Chung-Kung jen-ming-lu* (A Name List of the Chinese Communists) (Taipei: Kuo-chi Kuan-hsi Yen-chiu She, 1967), pp.

567-568. Tung Pi-wu (born in 1884) studied in Japan in 1910, organized the first Communist cell in Hupei, and attended the First Congress of the Chinese Communists in 1921. He attended the Sun Yat-sen University in Moscow in 1928, became the Chairman of the Supreme Court of the Chinese Soviet Central Government in 1932, attended the San Francisco Conference in 1945, became Chairman of the North China People's Government in 1948, President of the Supreme People's Court in 1954, and has been a Vice-Chairman of the People's Republic of China since 1959.

19 At the preparatory conference held on October 10, 1918, Tuan Ch'i-jui, head of the An-Fu Party and the Commissioner of the War Participation Army, proposed as such, and his proposal was unanimously passed. Ts'ao Ju-lin, *I-sheng chih hui-i*, p. 188.

20 Koo's Memorandum of an Interview with Secretary Lansing, at Hotel Crillon, January 27, 1919. *Wunsz King Collection of V.K. Wellington Koo Papers*, no. 6, p. 15.

21 Secretary's Note (British) of a Convention held in M. Pichon's room at Quai d'Orsay, Paris, on Monday, January 27, 1919, *Wunsz King Collection*, no. 7, pp. 16-18.

22 Memorandums of the Chinese Delegation Submitted at the Paris Peace Conference, no. 1, annex no. 12 and 17. *Wai-chiao kung-pao* (Foreign Affairs Gazette), no. 5 and 6.

23 Koo's Memorandum of an Interview with President Wilson, January 27, 1919, *Wunsz King Collection*, no. 8, p. 20; and Secretary's Notes (British), January 28, 1919, *Wunsz King Collection*, no. 9, pp. 21-22, 24.

24 Ray Stannard Baker, *Woodrow Wilson and World Settlement* (New York: Doubleday, Page and Co., 1923), 2:231.

25 Robert Lansing, *The Peace Negotiations: A Personal Narrative* (Boston and New York: Houghton Mifflin Co., 1921), p. 253; Wunsz King, *China at the Paris Peace Conference in 1919* (New York: St. John's University Press, 1961), pp. 10-11. Cited hereafter as King, *China at the Paris Peace Conference.*

26 Koo meant the pro-Japanese faction in Peking, including Ts'ao Ju-lin, Lu Tsung-yü, and Chang Tsung-hsiang, negotiators of the Nishihara Loans and the Sino-Japanese Agreements on Kaomi-Hsüchow Railway and the Tsinan-Shunteh Railway. Ts'ao Ju-lin, *I-sheng chih hui-i*, p. 194.

27 Koo's Interview with Colonel House, April 2, 1919, *Wunsz King Collection*, no. 11, p. 28; Interview with Mr. Lansing, April 4, 1919, *Wunsz King Collection*, no. 12, pp. 31-32.

28 United States Department of State, *Papers Relating to the Foreign Relations of the United States: The Paris Peace Conference, 1919* (Washington, D.C.: Government Printing Office, 1946), 5:142-143. Cited hereafter as *FRUS, Paris Peace Conference, 1919*, vol. 5.

29 Baker, *Woodrow Wilson and World Settlement*, 2:241, 260-261; *FRUS, Paris Peace Conference, 1919*, 5:363-367.

30 *Wunsz King Collection*, no. 17, pp. 55-57; no. 20, p. 62; no. 22, pp. 66-67; no. 23, pp. 68-69.

31 Wunsz King, *Ts'ung Pa-li ho-hui tao Kuo-lien* (From Paris Peace Conference to the League of Nations) (Taipei: Chuan-chi Wen-hsüeh She, 1967), p. 25. Cited hereafter as King, *Ts'ung Pa-li ho-hui tao Kuo-lien.*

32 American Consul-General Thomas Sammons to the Secretary of State, June 14, 1919, Shanghai, *National Archives Microfilm Publications Microcopy No. 329, Records of the Department of State Relating to*

Internal Affairs of China, 1910-1929, Reel 21, 893.00/3119. Even the representatives of the rival governments from Peking and Canton sent a joint cablegram to Paris warning the Chinese delegation not to sign; Lo Kuang, *Lu Cheng-hsiang chuan* (Biography of Lo Tseng-tsiang) (Taipei: The Commercial Press, 1967), pp. 113-114.

33 King, *China at the Paris Peace Conference*, p. 30.

34 King, *Ts'ung Pa-li ho-hui tao Kuo-lien*, p. 39.

35 *Conference on the Limitation of Armament, Washington, November 12, 1921-February 6, 1922* (Washington, D.C.: Government Printing Office, 1922), pp. 882-884.

36 *Ibid.*, pp. 1621-1629.

37 *Ibid.*, pp. 558-564, 920-928, 1162-1164, 1630-1639.

38 *Kuan-shui t'e pieh hui-i i-shih-lu* (Proceedings of the Special Conference on Chinese Customs Tariff), *Chin-tai Chung-kuo shih-liao ts'ung-k'an*, edited by Shen Yün-lung (Taipei: Wen-hai Press, 1968), no. 160, 1:136-137.

39 United States Department of State, *Papers Relating to the Foreign Relations of the United States, 1921* (Washington, D.C.: Government Printing Office, 1936), 1:617-630.

40 United States Department of State, *Papers Relating to the Foreign Relations of the United States, 1922* (Washington, D.C.: Government Printing Office, 1938), 1:934-936. Cited hereafter as *FRUS, 1922*, vol. 1.

41 Ho Szu-yüan, "Hua-sheng-tun hui-i chung Shantung wen-t'i chih ching-kuo," *Tung-fang tsa-chih*, 19:2, 54-65.

42 *Conversations between Chinese and Japanese Representatives in Regard to the Shantung Question, Treaty for Settlement of Outstanding Questions Relative to Shantung, Agreed Terms of Understanding Recorded in the Minutes of the Japanese and Chinese Delegations Concerning the Conclusion of the Treaty for the Settlement of Outstanding Questions Relative to Shantung; Minutes Prepared by the Japanese Delegation* (Washington, D.C.: Government Printing Office, 1922), pp. 1-2. Cited hereafter as *Conversations*.

43 *Ibid.*, pp. 65-69, 78-81, 105, 136.

44 The Secretary of State to the Minister in China Schurman, Washington, January 22, 1922, and January 25, 1922. *FRUS, 1922*, 1:942-945.

45 *Conversations*, pp. 16-37, 210-229, 263, 266, 275-276, 366, 377-378.

46 *Conversations*, pp. 59-61, 73-75, 230-236, 277-282, 294, 305-313.

47 MacMurray, *Treaties*, 2:1066-1067; Ch'en Lu, Deputy Envoy of the tripartite negotiation at Kiakhta and the first Resident General at Urga, kept a reliable diary under the title *Chih-shih pi-chi* (Taipei: Wen-hai Press, no date).

48 *Chung-O hui-i ts'an-k'ao wen-chien* (Documents Prepared for the Sino-Russian Conference), vol. 2; *Chung-O wen-t'i lai-wang wen-chien* (Documents on the Sino-Russian Problems), pp. 1a-3a.

49 *Ibid.*, Ministry of Foreign Affairs to Koo, February 14 and June 30, 1921, pp. 13a-13b, 14a, 16a.

50 *Ibid.*, pp. 4a-4b; Wang Yü-chün, *Chung-Su wai-chiao ti hsu-mu: Ts'ung Yu-lin tao Yüeh-fei* (The Beginning of Sino-Soviet Diplomacy: From Yurin to Joffe) (Taipei: Institute of Modern History, Academia Sinica, 1963).

51 Chengting T. Wang was designated Director General for Sino-Soviet negotiations on March 27, 1923 when the Sun-Joffe Declaration

concerning cooperation between the Kuomintang and the Communists became known; Chang Kuo-t'ao, "O-te hui-i" (Memoir of Chang Kuo-t'ao). *Ming-pao yüeh-k'an* (Ming-pao Monthly) (Hong Kong: Ming-pao Yu-hsien Kung-szu, 1966-), 2:8, 89.

52 There were several reasons for the delay: (1) the diplomatic corps in Peking opposed China's acceptance of Soviet credentials; (2) the Cabinet refused Karakhan's demand of recognition preceding negotiation; and (3) the underhanded dealings of Karakhan with Japan showed his lack of integrity. *Hua-kuo yüeh-k'an* (Hua-kuo Monthly), no. 3, September 16, 1923, p. 9.

53 *Wai-chiao kung-pao*, no. 36, June 1924, Special Documents, pp. 1-9, 13-22.

54 *Ibid.*, pp. 36-39.

55 *Ibid.*, pp. 22-23; *Tung-fang tsa-chih*, 21(6):2-3.

56 *Tung-fang tsa-chih*, 21(9):135-139 and (13):41.

57 Presidential Directive, no. 882 to Foreign Minister Koo, May 30, 1924. *Cheng-fu kung-pao* (Government Gazette, 115(2944 [June 1, 1924]) and (2945 [June 2, 1924]).

58 *Tung-fang tsa-chih*, 21(13):42.

59 *Wai-chiao kung-pao*, no. 36, pp. 12-13, 28-29.

60 Morishima Morito, *Imbō, ansatsu, guntō: ichi gaikōkan no kaiso* (Conspiracies, Assassinations, Sabers: Reminiscences of a Diplomat) (Tokyo: Iwanami Shoten, 1957), p. 52.

61 Liu Ju-ming, *Liu Ju-ming hui-i lu* (Memoir of Liu Ju-ming) (Taipei: Chuan-chi Wen-hsüeh Press, 1966), pp. 49-53.

62 Koo Hui-lan, *Autobiography*, pp. 232-241.

63 V.K. Wellington Koo to Chu Pao-chin, May 19, 1969.

64 Koo Hui-lan, *Autobiography*, p. 270; *Ko-ming wen-hsien* (Documents on National Revolution) (Taipei: Tang-shih Shih-liao Pien-chuan Wei-yüan-hui, 1958-), no. 7936, 35:1270-1271; V.K. Wellington Koo, *Memoranda Presented to the Lytton Commission* (New York: Chinese Cultural Society, 1932-1933).

65 Westel W. Willoughby, *The Sino-Japanese Controversy and the League of Nations* (Baltimore: The Johns Hopkins Press, 1935), pp. 29-30, 89-97, 371-373.

66 *Ibid.*, pp. 408-413.

67 Assembly Report of February 24, 1933, on the Sino-Japanese Dispute, *Ko-min wen-hsien*, no. 9536, 40:2870-2882.

68 *Ibid.*, no. 9569, 40:2902-2907.

69 Tsien Tai (Ch'ien T'ai), *China and the Nine Power Conference at Brussels in 1937* (New York: St. John's University Press, 1964), pp. 16-17. Tsien Tai was then the Chinese Ambassador to Belgium and a member of the Chinese delegation.

70 King, *Ts'ung Pa-li ho-hui tao Kuo-lien*, pp. 151-158.

71 Ministry of Foreign Affairs (ed.), *Treaties between the Republic of China and Foreign States (1927-1961)* (Taipei: The Commercial Press, 1963), pp. 589-605.

72 Ch'en Chih-mai, *Chiang T'ing-fu ti chih-shih yu sheng-p'ing* (The Life of H.E. Chiang T'ing-fu) (Taipei: Chuan-chi Wen-hsüeh Tsa-chih She, 1966), pp. 128-131.

73 Ministry of Foreign Affairs, *Treaties*, pp. 794-802.

Paul Hyer

Hu Shih

the Diplomacy of Gentle Persuasion

AT A TIME when the Chinese nation desperately needed the material assistance and political support of the United States, Hu Shih (1891-1962) acted as Ambassador to the American people as well as to their government. He reached even the most isolationist-minded Americans by appealing to their sympathy for the underdog and the victimized, as he pleaded for China's future with the gentle, refined arguments of an honest, passionately committed intellectual. His approach proved an excellent one for he understood, as many of his colleagues did not, that China's cause could be successfully promoted only by convincing the American public to endorse a more dynamic role in Asia. But Hu's efforts (1938-1942) to mobilize American popular support to assist China did not prevent him from attending to the more traditional functions of diplomacy. In the swirling, often confusing, negotiations between Tokyo and Washington in 1941, he constantly and firmly reminded the Roosevelt administration of China's determination to fight for its independence.

Better known as a scholar than a diplomat, Hu Shih had already established himself as one of the most illustrious intellectuals of modern China before he joined the Washington embassy. To the critic C.T. Hsai, Hu was the "father of China's Literary Revolution"; however if his vocation was literature and philosophy, his avocation—out of necessity and duty—became diplomacy. Hu's diplomacy encompassed the advocacy of pacifism during World War I as well as the use of force against Japanese expansion in the 1930's. Throughout his career, moreover, he was steadfast in his personal allegiance to Wilsonian internationalism—the world rationally and justly organized. Not surprisingly, Hu eventually represented China in formulating and unveiling the United Nations.

Hu Shih's contemporary diplomatic reputation never equalled his intellectual stature in the United States. A letter he received during his ambassadorship in Washington illustrated that fact: "We would like to have your Excellency give the commencement address at our university. If the affairs of state make this impossible, would you kindly tell us how to get in touch with that celebrated Chinese savant, Dr. Hu Shih, whom we would, in this case, like to ask instead."[1] If Americans confused his identity, the amused Hu never misconstrued his role. He declined nomination as President of the Republic of China in 1948 to continue his life in academia as chancellor of Peking University (1945-1948) and head of China's most prestigious research center, the Academia Sinica, where he remained from 1958 until his death in 1962.

I

Hu Shih was born outside Shanghai on December 17, 1891, the youngest son of Hu Ch'uan, a minor government official. His twin step-brothers and three step-sisters were much older because his twice-widowed father married Hu's mother, an illiterate peasant girl named Feng Shun-ti, late in life. Hu's mother was eighteen when he was born, his father fifty, and he was the only child of this affectionate union. His father died when he was only four, and Hu was raised by his self-sacrificing mother in a domestic situation frequently marred by family tensions and declining financial resources. The example set by his mother during these anxious years profoundly influenced his life. As Hu wrote in his autobiography: "If I have learned a little evenness of temper, if I have learned in some slight degree an amiability that makes me helpful to others, if I am able to forgive others and to sympathize with them I owe all my gratitude to my gentle mother."[2]

Hu owed his mother much. She supervised his schooling and insisted that he obtain a "modern" education, even though she did not realize how much it would challenge traditional beliefs. His acceptance of Western ideas and his mother's allegiance to the traditional social standards created an emotional crisis between them, for she expected him to follow her beliefs. This gulf became exceedingly personal when his mother arranged, in the customary fashion, for his betrothal at the age of twelve to an unknown local girl. Hu, after much soul-searching, honored this commitment, indicating that he had learned his mother's lesson of toleration and compromise. Hu's marriage to Chiang Tung-hsiu in 1917 endured and was apparently affectionate, despite their great disparity in education and experience.

Hu received a traditional Chinese primary education in the classics and began six years of modern education in 1904. That year marked an upsurge of reformist sentiment for it was the year Japan attacked Russia. During part of this time Hu studied at a radical institution established by revolutionary students returned from Japan, yet he did not become actively involved in the 1911 revolution. Still he participated in student politics and edited a Shanghai student newspaper, *Ching-yeh hsun-pao* [The Struggle]. Financed by a Boxer Idemnity Scholarship, Hu continued his studies in the United States at Cornell University. He first studied in the College of Agriculture, but soon changed to a major in philosophy. He graduated with a B.A. degree and a Phi Beta Kappa key in 1914 and completed a Ph.D. in 1917 under John Dewey at Columbia University. Hu has since been recognized as Dewey's most illustrious Chinese disciple. Hu's American education marked him for condemnation (or praise) as the archetype of a westernized Chinese. His independence and his detached, rational approach set him apart from the dogmatic tendencies of most contemporary Chinese intellectuals. He had gained a certain rationalism and skepticism in his childhood from reading his father's poetry and he was particularly influenced by the neo-Confucianist writings of Chu Hsi. His attitudes were strengthened by a translation of T.H. Huxley's *Evolution and Ethics* and his political views and western values were predisposed, in part, by Mill's *On Liberty* and Montesquieu's *L'Esprit des lois*, in Chinese translation, before he ever studied in America.

Politically Hu Shih was a pacifist during World War I when he was at Columbia, but he changed in the 1930's to a position advocating the constructive use of force to deter Japan's expansion on the Asian mainland. At Cornell University Hu was active in the International Federation of Students and other pacifist organizations which flourished during World War I. He also was deeply influenced by Woodrow Wilson's idealistic internationalism, which led him to advocate the establishment of the United Nations in the 1940's. Hu remained firm in his pacifist convictions in spite of Japan's pressure on China to accept the infamous Twenty-One Demands in 1915; even in the face of subsequent militant Chinese nationalism he urged "patriotic sanity." His pacifism changed only when the existence of the Chinese Republic was threatened by Japanese aggression.

Hu Shih returned to China in the autumn of 1917 to become a professor of philosophy at Peking University. He played a major role in the ferment which culminated in the intellectual revolution known as the May Fourth Movement (1919). He soon gained a reputation as an intellectual rebel and as the prime mover in a literary revolution designed to replace the classical written language with *pai-hua* (the vernacular).[3]

Hu's innovations in literature were the most significant contribution of his lengthy and diverse career. He created a new style in popular literature and was able to reach the common people with themes closely related to their lives. Although he was not a prolific writer, he was a master of lucid and straightforward prose. Hu's publications on literary analysis, his re-evaluation of Chinese tradition, and his writings on philosophical subjects were, moreover, his most enduring works and demonstrated his independence of thought. Philosophically, Hu was a moderate iconoclast; he associated with a small group of avant-garde intellectuals in Peking, including such notables as Li Ta-chao, Ch'en Tu-siu, Lu Hsun, and Ch'ien Hsuan-t'ung.

The decade from 1917 to 1927 was one of great intellectual ferment in China. Hu was fresh from the United states in 1917 and his experience there was reflected in his view of the Russian Revolution that had such a profound impact on China. In 1927 the establishment of the Nanking government marked a watershed in China's political development. During these years most progressive Chinese leaders found themselves intellectually alienated from Chinese traditions and attracted to the several western political and social models which competed for their attention. China was emerging from a period of warlord domination almost as traumatic as the Japanese invasion in 1937; both developments had a decisive effect on Hu's career. After 1917 many people advocated divergent solutions to China's problems and the vast majority of advocates were extremists from the right or the left. Hu Shih resisted both extremes and found himself in an uncomfortable no-man's-land—the moderate middle. Hu's experimentalist approach was the result of the influence of his mentor John Dewey. Experimentalism to Hu was the touchstone not only of philosophy and scholarship, for the concept also influenced his approach to social problems and politics. It entailed initial skepticism, a clear definition of specific concrete problems, logical analysis in formulating a conclusion, and careful observation of the results.

II

Hu was an iconoclast with respect to China's traditional culture and he soon came into conflict with his radical contemporaries because he opposed political revolution as a solution to China's problems. He rejected Marxism, which attracted many of his colleagues, because he found it intellectually dogmatic, and he attacked his fellow intellectuals, both Marxist and militant nationalists, for their uncritical acceptance of ready-made panaceas for China's economic, social, and political problems. An example of one of Hu's critiques, published in the summer of 1919, is entitled "Wen-ti yu chu-i" [Problems and -Isms]. Hu argues that revolution is blind, unreasoning, and too easily diverted. Evolution, in contrast, is more easily directed and can avert unnecessary chaos, though it might be slower. These views are also apparent in Hu Shih's other writings, such as "Wo-men tso na-i t'iao-lu?" [Which Road Shall We Follow] (1929) and "Chieh-shao wo tzu-chi ti ssu-hsiang" [Introducing My Own Political Thought] (1930).

If in the philosophical sparrings of the 1920's, Hu was repelled by Marxist circles, neither could he make common cause with neo-conservatives, such as Liang Ch'i-ch'ao, Carsun Chang, and Liang Shu-ming, for they criticized his system of values. Consequently, Hu and a group of his friends began to publish the magazine *Nu-li chou-pao* [Endeavor] in May 1922, the second issue of which included a manifesto written by Hu Shih and signed by sixteen leading intellectuals entitled "Wo-men ti cheng-chih chu-chang" [Our Political Proposals]. This document outlined the basic aspects of good government and sought to enlist public opinion to press for political reforms.

Hu Shih was swept up in the important science-philosophy controversies of 1923 in China and energetically attacked the neo-conservatives. He later opposed the Kuomintang leaders in a similar contest when they claimed that the materialistic West had gained the world but lost its soul. The Kuomintang's pessimistic comparison of East and West relied upon the old *t'i-yung* dichotomy, which viewed Chinese civilization as spiritual and humanistic and western culture as materialistic and legalistic. Hu argued that these premises were false; he urged the conservatives to cease concocting rationalizations that emphasized China's superiority and encouraged obscurantism and resistance to modernization. This tough-minded attitude characterized Hu's lifelong untraditional attitudes and values; unsurprisingly, he was regarded by his contemporaries as the epitome of a westernized Chinese.[4]

The late 1920's brought tension and struggle to China as the Kuomintang-Communist coalition moved northward to crush the warlords and unify China. Hu returned from a trip abroad just after the Nanking government was established and following the Kuomintang's bloody purge of the Communists in 1927. During this critical period (and until his death), Hu prided himself that he belonged to the "no party, no faction" group of independent intellectuals who stood apart while the majority of educated Chinese gravitated to extreme political positions. Hu never became a member of the Kuomintang; indeed his contact with the party, particularly as it came to power, was limited. His inability to admire Sun Yat-sen as a revolutionary leader was prompted, in part at least, by the lack of consistency and precision in Sun's ideology. Hu attacked the Kuomintang on the crucial issue of constitutionalism and "political tutelage," a rationalization, he charged, which perpetuated one-party rule based on Sun Yat-sen's philosophy.[5] Additionally, he challenged the "reactionary" attitude of the Kuomintang toward cultural reform and innovation. He directed his criticism toward the New Life Movement launched by the Nationalist government as a strategy to counter Communism. He saw this movement as a throwback to Chinese culturalism that perpetuated the out-moded thought of Confucianism and other traditional elements rejected by most progressive Chinese.[6]

Hu Shih was critical of the Nationalist government's position on many issues, but he was also unsympathetic to the radical, emotional nationalism of the students who reacted to the Communist demand for a strong stand against Japan. The Chinese Communists declared war against Japan in 1931 following the Mukden Incident; later, however, they undertook their Long March to Yenan in North China to escape annihilation by the Kuomintang. Hu advocated strategic reconciliation with the Japanese and thus supported the Nationalists' temporizing policies during the 1931 crisis. His main anxiety was that the advances already made in the reform of Chinese institutions would certainly be destroyed if all-out war with Japan occurred. But since he could not advocate peace at any price, Hu's pragmatic position toward Japan changed when a general Sino-Japanese war became inevitable. Hostilities broke out in July 1937, following the Sian Incident of December 1936, and Hu then supported a united front between the Nationalists and the Communists.

Six months before Japan's all-out invasion of China, Hu perceived a new set of forces taking shape that gave some "possibilities for stabilization of peace in the Orient." The forces that Hu hoped would counter Japanese expansion were (1) the revival of Soviet Russia as a Pacific power, (2) the rearming of non-Asian nations with vested interests in Asia, and (3) the rise of a stronger China. As conditions in Europe worsened, however, his optimism rapidly disappeared. During the rising crisis, Hu suspended his reform program and declared, "We can't afford to dilute the issue of nationalism with a social revolution."[7] In Hu Shih's view Japan's objectives were to prevent the unification and reconstruction of China and to hinder her receiving assistance from the West.[8] The basic conflict was between Japanese imperialism and Chinese nationalism on one hand and between Japanese militarism and the international order on the other.[9] In the early 1930's Hu commended Chiang Kai-shek's ability to buy time to keep China out of war in the years following Japan's invasion of Manchuria. Yet he still criticized the Kuomintang for duplicity when secret agreements were negotiated with Japan which made concessions behind the backs of the Chinese people.[10] As the public demand for Chiang Kai-shek to confront the Japanese became more intense, Hu Shih cautioned against a conciliatory policy toward the Japanese lest it lead to a sellout. Hu warned that "those few statesmen in Chinese history who negotiated a humiliating peace with an enemy are remembered as traitors."[11]

Hu Shih was officially appointed Ambassador in September 1938. Although he presented his credentials to President Roosevelt on October 8, 1938, he had actually arrived in the United States in the fall of 1937 on a semi-official good will tour to solicit support for China's war effort. When the appointment came, he had been in Geneva for ten months as a Chinese delegate to the League of Nations laboring to invoke Article 16 and thus place an embargo on war material moving to Japan.

III

With the deepening crisis in Japanese-American relations, Hu was an ideal representative for the Republic of China in the United States because of the relatively short "cultural distance" between him and the American people. Americans knew and respected him as a distinguished scholar and man of letters. Hu Shih not only spoke English well but also respected the American way of life; he had championed modern American values among educated Chinese for years.

The government of China badly needed support from abroad. Torn by decades of warlordism, forced to acquiesce in a "united front" with the Communists, and ravaged by the Japanese military aggression in the North, Chiang Kai-shek's regime was on the verge of total exhaustion. Although sympathetic to China's plight, the United States took refuge in the "moral sanctions" of the Stimson Doctrine. If the public and Congress were inclined to favor China over Japan, the majority of Americans opposed sanctions against Japan that might involve the United States in a Pacific war. The recently-passed Neutrality Acts illustrated this ambivalence; but they had not yet been applied in Asia. Such sanctions, the Chinese recognized, would hurt China more than Japan.

The Chinese government thus faced the problem of selling China's cause to both the American government and people. Hu Shih was selected to accomplish that task, and his Ambassadorship was devoted to actively promoting support for China. Hu Shih understandably had some personal limitations. Since he was an ex-pacifist intellectual turned Ambassador through necessity and not a professional diplomat with a political background, he took the typical Chinese intellectual's attitude toward involvement in politics. Hu often remarked that he had "degenerated into an ambassador," that he was a "deserter to books and learning," and that he was "a pawn who could only go forward." He lacked a profound philosophy concerning politics and international relations, but he did believe in the superiority of Western political values; he tended toward moderation, with a willingness to compromise in order to resolve differences.[12]

The university environment which conditioned Hu Shih during his adult years partially determined his approach to diplomacy. He had been eminently successful in lecturing and writing. Through his articles and public lectures, and those of his colleagues at the University of Peking and Shanghai, Hu had launched significant political movements and confronted important international problems. His role in the literary revolution bore an important impact in the field of journalism and mass communications. It should not be surprising that as Ambassador Hu concentrated his efforts and achieved his best results with lectures and writings designed to influence the largest possible number of people.

Consequently, Hu frequently participated in broadcasts on current, controversial subjects. For example, on the Town Meeting of The Air, November 29, 1940, he exchanged ideas with H.G. Wells and Ray L. Wilbur on the question: "What Kind of World Order Do We Want?" While Wells went off on the tangent of "cosmopolitan world socialism" and Wilbur talked vaguely of "world fellowship and citizenship," Hu Shih anticipated the United Nations by five years. He used the identical term and stressed provisions for "peace enforcement." Although Hu was scathingly criticized for his "warmed-over League idea," the discussion gives some idea of the broad gauge and progressiveness of Hu Shih's view of the international system of nations.

Hu believed that public opinion ultimately determined American foreign policy by setting the limits within which Congress or the White House could operate; thus he tirelessly sought contact with the people to gain their understanding. If, in some ways, Hu Shih was ineffectual, the explanation may lie in his conscious abdication of responsibility in certain important areas. He did not want to be responsible for negotiating war loans or armaments, so even before December 1941 much of the burden of such diplomatic negotiations for China's war effort fell to financial experts like T.V. Soong. Even in the area of public relations, where Hu operated best, he reportedly returned to his government $60,000 given to him for the purpose of "propaganda" because he would not "beg for money or carry on propaganda." "My speeches are sufficient propaganda and they cost you nothing!"[13] He insisted that "propaganda is unnecessary for a diplomat who is accredited to a friendly government and people. His duty is to understand and appreciate the country to which he is accredited . . . the rest is easy."[14] Hu saw himself as a universalist and he wanted broad authority from the Chinese government with little responsibility.[15]

Ambassador Hu did not seek to influence the American power structure through political manipulation or to apply the diplomatic "hard sell" to the State Department or the White House. He undertook the herculean task of predisposing American public opinion to accept a more dynamic role for the United States in Asia. He confronted, however, a Europe-first policy determined by Nazi expansion, the fall of France, and the desperate plight of England and Russia. Hu Shih's grasp of the international situation left him less frustrated by American preoccupation with the European crisis than the average Chinese leader. He had a clear concept of China's national interest and felt that the best way to gain support was a direct approach to the elite which formed public opinion. It seems in retrospect that Hu Shih may have overestimated the power of the American people and the nature of the decision-making process in the American political system. He had seen popular movements overcome warlords in China, unify the Chinese through nationalism, bring to power the Nationalist government, and mobilize the country's resources against the Japanese invaders. Devoting his attention to the American public, Hu underestimated the role of Congressmen and the power of the Presidency in setting a course of action for the nation.

Generalissimo Chiang Kai-shek concentrated his diplomatic efforts on trying to convince the Allies that his fight was also theirs. In spite of America's Europe-first policy, he felt that the United States depended on China to protect her Asian interests; he was confident that America would, of necessity, finally yield to his demands and accept Chungking's war strategy and policies.[16] Hu knew this view was short-sighted; yet in promoting sympathy for China's cause at the grass-roots level, he travelled all over the United States making hundreds of speeches at banquets, clubs, rallies, and commencements, stating China's case in simple straightforward terms. He wrote to newspapers, went to conferences, entertained reporters, and published magazine articles. A tribute to his energy and scholarship, if not success, were the twenty-six honorary degrees he received from American universities. By the time he left office, he had generated a sympathy for China's struggle, an awareness of her material needs, and support for lend-lease to China all over America.

During his first year as Ambassador, Hu frequently embarrassed his government by refusing to accept or to propagate a rosy picture of the war. Hu had always been independent in his thought and his intellectual honesty was rigorous. He deliberately refused to give a biased, distorted, or propagandistic view of the China problem in his discussions with Americans. He told Americans that China was literally bleeding to death; for this he was almost recalled by the Chinese government. In December 1938, however, he collapsed of a heart attack, was hospitalized, given six months to live, and by the time he recovered the furor had died down.

Hu generally presented his own view in speeches to Americans rather than the official government line, but the difference between Hu Shih and Chiang Kai-shek in the matter of obtaining American help was more over approach than basic policy. Hu continued to use his own approach whether Chungking objected or not, and finally Chiang learned to go around Hu's office when he felt it necessary. This latter was the function of T.V. Soong—brother-in-law of Chiang Kai-shek, and a very able financier—who was dispatched to Washington in the fall of 1940 and took up residence at the embassy in Washington. Soong's jealousy of Hu Shih hampered their personal relationship, and Hu, feeling he could do more good elsewhere, was frequently absent from the embassy. Chiang Kai-shek *was* the government in Chungking which Hu represented, and the contrast between the two men was great. Chiang was a conservative militarist, a narrow nationalist, and a strong traditionalist. Hu was an intellectual, a progressive scholar, and very much an internationalist.

After he came to the United States there is no indication that Hu Shih attempted to influence policy or developments within China or to encourage Kuomintang reforms in order to broaden the government's base. Nor is there any indication that Hu Shih attempted to dispose Chiang Kai-shek and other conservative Chinese leaders to be more receptive to American advice or to avoid problems such as the Stillwell controversy. More at home in the role of a scholar, he openly acknowledged his desire to return to the academic life.

IV

Hu Shih found hope for his cause in American pronouncements condemning international anarchy and aggression. In the summer of 1939 he pressed Washington officials for abrogation of the United States-Japan Commercial Treaty (1911), and his efforts no doubt contributed to America's discontinuation of the treaty in the fall of that year. American public opinion was rapidly changing in favor of China. Where previous public opinion polls had registered indifference to China's plight, by the summer of 1938 the majority of Americans expressed more concern over Japanese aggression in China than over German aggression in Austria or Spain. The State Department was also revising its attitude toward the China conflict, but it still avoided positive sanctions against Japan which might lead to war and called instead for a "moral embargo" on strategic commodities and technical information. The fact that licenses for exporting arms and munitions to Japan dropped from $8,799,219 in 1938 to $761,684 in 1939 demonstrates the effectiveness of this measure.

American sentiment for China continued to grow from the time of Hu Shih's appointment as Ambassador in the fall of 1938 until Japan's attack on Pearl Harbor late in 1941. Besides Hu's personal influence, however, many other factors contributed to his success in influencing American opinion. Tokyo's announcement in December 1938 of its Greater East Asia Co-prosperity Sphere and Washington's abrogation of the American-Japanese Commercial Treaty in the fall of 1939 buttressed Hu's campaign. The announcement of the Tripartite Treaty between Japan and her European Axis partners in September 1940 stiffened the attitude of United States officials toward Japan. Furthermore, Japanese atrocities and aerial bombing of civilian populations shocked many American isolationists into active concern. Japan's move into Indo-China in 1940 and increased expansion in the area in 1941 brought Japan closer to the point of a diplomatic deadlock with the United States and brought China closer to the fruition of Hu Shih's mission.

The Chinese were disheartened by Washington's decision in 1940, made after months of discussion, to give Britain priority in all aircraft production. This handicap was only partially offset in 1941 by dramatic increases in lend-lease materials to the Chinese—China still received a far smaller portion of aid than either Britain or Russia. The irony of American lip service to China's life and death struggle while virtually all attention was centered on Europe was not lost on the Chinese following the war. Chinese bitterness because of this lack of support for what they regarded as a common cause persists even today. Hu Shih, however, had a broader perspective of the world conflict, and he never seemed to lose hope. His speeches were widely read and warmly received, and the American press was full of praise for the Chinese allies. China's public relations were never better, and the United States even renounced the humiliating unequal treaties which had long outraged China. Moreover, there was talk of China as the fourth "great power."

Hu Shih's most important official discussions occurred on the eve of the Pacific war; circumstances as well as his efforts, however, must be given credit for the phenomenal change in American public opinion. Press coverage of Japanese atrocities, Pearl Buck's sympathetic portrayal of China in *The Good Earth*, anti-Japanese sentiment within the State Department, and a host of other intangibles were influential in the American swing away from isolationism and toward involvement in China's struggle. While such events as Japan's non-aggression pact with Russia were setbacks in the campaign Hu Shih was waging to save China, they were offset by the United States' announcement freezing all Japanese assets in July of 1941 and by two significant events in August: the United States sent a military mission to China and President Roosevelt rejected a personal meeting with Konoye in the Pacific.

Strong countervailing forces were coming to bear on the State Department and the White House in September 1941. Ambassador Grew in Tokyo urged his government to exercise restraint and moderation in order to strengthen the peace faction in Japan. Hu nonetheless spoke optimistically about the United States strengthening its policy, ending the impasse, and coming to China's assistance. He said, "I have always had complete confidence in America's sympathy and helpfulness, and I still have." The fall of the Konoye government in October did not give Hu Shih any indication of a change in Japan's basic policy unless it was for the worse.

Chiang Kai-shek sent a series of worried messages to Roosevelt transmitted by Hu Shih between October 28 and November 5, 1941. His major concern was a Japanese attack through Yunnan to close the Burma Road. Chiang requested a strict American warning against the move, but the State Department delayed an answer to China. Finally Hu Shih was called to Roosevelt's office, and a belated note was sent on November 14. The answer was a vain effort to reassure Chiang, for it completely avoided the question of the Burma Road warning. The United States clearly did not intend to provoke Japan.

Certainly the most critical and dramatic time for Ambassador Hu Shih in Washington was the eve of the Pearl Harbor attack when it appeared that the Americans were on the point of making a deal with the Japanese in order to buy time for military preparations. Chinese anxiety increased on November 16 with the arrival of Japan's special envoy for discussions in Washington. Hu Shih learned on the morning of November 19 from Secretary of State Hull that by Kurusu's initiative the previous day, the prospect existed for a relaxation of tension between the United States and Japan. The *modus vivendi* would re-establish the *status quo ante* July—before Japan's move into Indo-China and before the American embargo. Hull showed a certain eagerness for this attempt by the Japanese diplomats to prevent a final breakdown. Hu Shih's worries were dispelled, however, when operation "Magic," America's cracking of Japan's secret code, revealed that Tokyo had no intention of ratifying an accord on the conditions suggested by her representatives in Washington.

Tokyo's last bargain was the notorious Proposal B, presented by Ambassador Nomura on November 20. The proposal's tone and demands were ominous, but while war was implicit in the secret messages and on the minds of the negotiators, both sides wished to avoid it. At this point the United States could (1) make no reply, (2) reject Japan's final proposal, or (3) make a counter-proposal. Washington chose the last course.

Hull immediately began with a task force to draft a counter proposal, a *modus vivendi* that would be acceptable to Japan as well as to America's allies. Tentative drafts were ready on November 22. Secretary Hull called in Hu to inform him of high points of the discussions with the Japanese, and he invited him to read and take notes on the *modus vivendi*. Hu Shih arose from a sick-bed to keep the appointment and visited the State Department almost every day during the next week, in spite of his illness, to voice China's strong opposition to the proposed United States-Japanese rapprochement. Temporization, he felt, would be paid for with Chinese blood. Hull also briefed the ministers of the allied powers, who were all vitally concerned with any Asian settlement; they all concurred with his approach to the negotiations. National interest clearly dictated the response of each country, including that of the United States. Hu Shih asked whether the proposal would block further Japanese penetration of China to destroy the Burma Road. Hull's negative reply greatly disturbed Hu, but Hull explained that time was the all-important factor.[17] Although China had been under Japan's sword for a decade, Chinese and American intelligence were now reduced to calculating the months before an impending Japanese drive through Yunnan would strike at Chungking, China's last-ditch capital.

Unbeknown to Hu Shih that same day, November 22, Tokyo informed Nomura that there were deadlines "for reasons beyond your ability to guess." He was told, "If you can bring about the signing of the pertinent notes, we will wait until November 29." After that, the "Magic" cable noted ominously, "things are automatically going to happen."[18]

These days were tense for Hu, but he still maintained his basic humanist perspective. One afternoon he barged out of the Far Eastern Division of the State Department and bumped into a Japanese who recognized him and recalled an earlier meeting in Peking in 1935. The two "honorable enemies" chatted peacefully for a few minutes.

The State Department called Hu Shih again for consultation on Monday, November 24, and he was given a final copy of the proposed *modus vivendi*. He objected to a provision allowing the Japanese to maintain 25,000 troops in Indo-China. He suggested that they be limited to 5,000, but Hull explained that General Marshall considered the higher number no menace. Hull reiterated that the military needed time to prepare for the impending Japanese attack and that the duration of the agreement would be only three months.[19]

The War Council, including President Roosevelt, Secretary of State Hull, Secretary of War Stimson, Secretary of the Navy Knox, Chief of Naval Operations Admiral Stark, and Chief of Staff General Marshall, met at the White House at noon on Tuesday, November 25, in an atmosphere of deep concern to discuss the stalemate in the talks with the Japanese. The United States now knew, having broken Japan's secret code and through intercepted messages, that the Japanese had decided to terminate negotiations on November 29. Japan had in effect submitted an ultimatum. Hull returned to his office in the State Department for his afternoon schedule of appointments. Britain's Ambassador Lord Halifax came first with a message that England would support an American counter-proposal to the Japanese *modus vivendi* in order to resolve the crisis, but he urged strong bargaining. The Dutch Minister met Hull next and, concerned about the vulnerability of the Indies, reported that his government favored a truce proposal—the *modus vivendi*. The afternoon was largely spent before Ambassador Hu was able to talk with Hull; his burden was to report China's opposition to the *modus vivendi* proposal. He voiced disapproval tactfully and softened the forcefulness of Generalissimo Chiang Kai-shek's communiqué by explaining that China's Foreign Minister understood the international aspects of the Japanese problem as it affected the United States but that Chiang did not. Hu transmitted the telegram of Foreign Minister Kuo Tai-chi noting Chiang's "strong reaction" to the *modus vivendi*[20] and showing appreciation for being consulted on the proposed accord with the Japanese. This message registered firm opposition "to any measure which may have the effect of increasing China's difficulty in her war of resistance" and hinted at American appeasement of Japan.[21]

Chiang Kai-shek never attained Hu Shih's broad grasp and rational view of the mounting crisis. The Generalissimo and Madame Chiang, in typical China Lobby fashion, sent a flurry of cables to American key leaders. The message of November 25 sent through T.V. Soong to Secretary of War Stimson gravely noted that even unfounded reports of American relaxation would "shake Chinese morale," that "the Japanese had come to a slight understanding with doubtful elements of China and that there was danger that the morale of the entire people will collapse and every Asiatic nation will . . . suffer such a shock in their faith in democracy that a most tragic epoch in the world will be opened."[22] As another example of Chinese pressure, more on the informal side, Owen Lattimore, adviser to Chiang Kai-shek, cabled President Roosevelt's secretary Lauchlin Currie the same day, urging that the President be personally informed of Chiang's feelings. Lattimore said,

> I have never seen him [Chiang] really agitated before. . . . Any *modus vivendi* arrived at now . . . would be disastrous to Chinese belief in America and analogous to the closing of the Burma Road, which permanently destroyed British prestige. . . . It is doubtful whether either past assistance or increasing aid would compensate for the feelings of being deserted at this hour.

Chiang was bitter lest Japan "escape military defeat by diplomatic victory."[23]

The outlook in late November still did not favor any dramatic shift of American policy that would meet Hu Shih's hopes of more active participation to counter Japan's surge of expansion in Asia. President Roosevelt had left the Japanese-American negotiations essentially to the management of Secretary of State Hull. Although the discussions were not progressing well, the situation did not yet seem critical to the man in the street nor to most analysts. Japan was reluctant to give up the new *status quo* established by arms in China, Manchuria, and Southeast Asia. Moreover, she was demanding the relaxation of the United States embargo on oil and scrap iron and an end to United States support of China in return for very small Japanese concessions. Foreign Minister Togo informed Ambassador Grew that major concessions on their part to gain a compromise would mean a loss of face and political suicide for Japan's military leadership. Compromise by Japan was thus impossible.

Since the United States' European allies opposed a strong stand and Roosevelt was unwilling to take a divided America into an Asian conflict, America temporized. The President considered a truce but even set that aside temporarily at the request of Secretary of War Stimson. In addition, "the War and Navy Departments had actually asked the President to avoid any ultimatum to Japan, and to try for some agreement that would 'tide the situation over' for 'several months.' "[24] Ambassador Grew in Tokyo strongly urged moderation in the hope of strengthening the peace faction in Japan. Leading American newspapers felt the key to at least a temporary settlement lay in China's capitulation, and the prevailing tone in Washington was that China should make temporary sacrifices until Hitler was stopped.[25]

Circumstantial evidence seems to confirm this view that the situation was moving in Japan's favor until November 26, 1941. For five days the United States had made great efforts to draw up an agreement to resolve the problem with Japan, even temporarily, while still meeting with the approval of America's allies. Suddenly when the outlook seemed darkest for China, the picture changed. United States officials determined on November 26 to abandon the *modus vivendi,* and at 5 P.M. that same day, Secretary of State Hull gave Japan's envoys the alternate "comprehensive basic proposal."

The role of the Chinese in influencing the turn of events at this juncture was crucial. This was a case when a subjective decision by men in high places would impinge on the historical process, selecting one alternative among several to determine the course of history. Certainly reasons for a change in policy existed. But Hu Shih's little publicized meeting with President Roosevelt on November 26 was paramount. For perhaps the first time in his diplomatic career the soft-spoken scholar Hu Shih lost his temper with top American leadership and objected heatedly to any concessions which would play into the hands of Japan. He reportedly reminded Roosevelt of his many, freely given pledges to China.[26] It should be noted that Roosevelt and Hull had a high regard for Hu Shih and his views. He had ready access to them—a close friend, Professor Ch'en Shou-yi, commented that Hu could get an appointment on a half hour notice.[27]

This strong Chinese pressure against conciliatory moves by the United States in the negotiations with Japan was verified by Hull in later congressional investigations. "The Chinese made a terrific attack on the situation," he stated. State Department memoranda provide further confirmation. On the morning of November 27, Britain's Ambassador Lord Halifax made an urgent visit to Under Secretary Welles and explained that the previous night Secretary Hull had told him by telephone of the last minute decision to drop the *modus vivendi.* He inquired about the reasons for the "sudden change," and as he learned of the role of the Chinese in the matter, he expressed surprise at the vigor of Chinese objections. He explained that he had personally explained to Ambassador Hu that the American proposal would not jeopardize China but on the contrary would relieve the pressure. He asserted that the attitude of the Chungking government was based on false information as well as hysteria. Welles, in reply, informed Halifax of ominous Japanese troop movements reported just that morning which pointed up the gravity of the situation.

The Australian Minister Richard Casey requested a conference with Hull that same day. He expressed concern about the movements of Chiang Kai-shek and others in torpedoing the *modus vivendi* and asked if the proposal had been permanently abandoned. Hull replied that he "so considered it" and explained that one reason this was so was that to do otherwise would be to touch off a bitter fight with Chiang Kai-shek and the hawkish "malcontents" in the United States.[28] Two days later in discussion with Britain's Halifax on November 29, Hull displayed an even greater degree of disappointment in the Chinese government for its role in the failure of the proposed accord. He did not cast a single aspersion on Hu Shih, but he did note that besides sending "numerous hysterical cable messages" to Cabinet officers and high officials, Chiang had ignored President Roosevelt, "intruded into a delicate situation with no real idea of the facts," and disseminated damaging reports to the press.[29]

As the negotiations in Washington went sour, Japan's contingency plans were automatically activated; the situation had reached a point of no return. The United States alerted its forces in the Philippines and the Netherlands mobilized its forces in the East Indies. On December 3 the British Fleet moved into Singapore, and Roosevelt demanded that the Japanese explain their troop movements in Indo-China. By December 4 Secretary of State Hull despaired of any reconciliation, feeling that the gap was too wide. On December 5 the Japanese rejected American terms. Two days later, they bombed Pearl Harbor.

V

It is most difficult to follow Hu Shih's activities from the outbreak of war until his replacement as Ambassador by Wei Tao-ming in September 1942. The news of his dismissal fell like a bombshell. The *New York Times* editorialized on the event, expressing shock and calling the action a mistake unless some higher post was reserved for Hu Shih in China.[30] Gossip was rampant regarding the decision, and the truth of what happened may never be known. Chinese, who tend to interpret history in terms of a network of human relations, emphasize such considerations as the animosity or jealousy between T.V. Soong and Hu Shih or the fact that Wei Tao-ming's wife, who was a close friend of Madame Chiang, coveted the Washington assignment and plotted to arrange it. Some speculate that a factor was the disagreement between China and the United States on the conduct of the war and Chiang Kai-shek's increased dissatisfaction with Hu Shih's approach to his work. Another possible explanation lies in the decline of Hu's usefulness once his speeches and articles were no longer necessary to bring America to China's side.

Hu Shih, on retiring from public life, returned to scholarly work. He remained in the United States and did not take another official position until March 1945 when he went to San Francisco as a delegate to the World Security Conference. He declined the position of Director General of UNESCO although he greatly admired the program and saw it as a potential means of promoting the "intellectual solidarity of mankind."

In retrospect Hu represented China's continued progress in the modern world of international diplomacy. If he was more comfortable in the role of the scholar, he nevertheless undertook his duties seriously and wisely. Hu Shih earned the respect of his diplomatic colleagues as one of the finest Ambassadors in China's history. Secretary of State Cordell Hull came to regard him "as one of the ablest and most effective public servants this government has had in the foreign diplomatic corps in Washington."[31]

Notes

1 E.O. Hauser, "Ambassador Hu Shih," *Life,* 21(December 15, 1941):123. This essay has drawn, in part, from the following: Howard L. Boorman (ed.), *Biographical Dictionary of Republican China,* (New York: Columbia University Press, 1968), 2:67-74; Irene Eber, "Hu Shih (1891-1962): A Sketch of His Life and His Role in the Intellectual and Political Dialogue of Modern China" (unpublished dissertation, Claremont Graduate School, 1965); Jerome B. Grieder, "Hu Shih: An Appreciation," *China Quarterly,* no. 12 (October-December, 1962), pp. 92-101; Kao-yüan Hsü, "Hu Shih hsien-sheng Chung-wen i-kao mu-lu" (Bibliography of Dr. Hu Shih's Unpublished Manuscripts in Chinese), *Academia Sinica, Bulletin of the Institute of History and Philology,* vol. 34, part 2 (1963), pp. 786-812; Hu Shih, *Hu Shih yen-lun chi* (Collected Speeches of Hu Shih) (Taipei: Tzu-yu Chung-kuo She, 1953), 2 vols.; Li Ao, *Hu Shih p'ing chuan* (Hu Shih: A Critical Biography) (Taiwan: The Book World Co., 1964); Li Ta *et al., Hu Shih ssu-hsiang p'i-p'an* (Criticism of Hu Shih's Thought) (Peking: Hsin Hua Shu Tien, 1955); "Selected Bibliography of Dr. Hu Shih's Writings," *Free China Review,* 12(3[March 1962]):65-84; Tiao Chun-min *et al., Hu Shih yü kuo-yün, lun chi* (Hu Shih and the Fortunes of State, a Collection of Essays) (Kowloon: Ming Ta Shu Chü, 1958).

2 Quoted in Jerome B. Grieder, *Hu Shih and the Chinese Renaissance: Liberalism in the Chinese Revolution, 1917-1937* (Cambridge, Massachusetts: Harvard University Press, 1970), p. 11. Materials in this and the succeeding paragraph are taken from this excellent volume which also contains a bibliography of Hu Shih's writings.

3 In January 1917, Hu published his "Wen-hsueh kai-liang chou-i" (Tentative Proposals for Literary Reform) in the influential review *Hsin*

ch'ing-nien edited by Ch'en Tu-hsiu, who four years later became the first Secretary of the Chinese Communist Party.

4 See Hu's preface to *K'o-hsüeh yü jen-sheng-kuan* (Science and the Philosophy of Life) (1923).

5 Some of Hu's most perceptive political commentaries may be found in the literary review *Hsin-yüeh* (The Crescent Moon) established in 1928.

6 His views on cultural reform are set forth in *Tu-li p'ing-lun* (Independent Critic) edited by Hu in Peking from 1932 to 1937. See also *Shih-p'ing so-wei Chung-kuo pen-wei ti wen-hua chien-she* (A Critique of Cultural Reconstruction on a Chinese Basis), Peking, 1935.

7 *New York Times*, August 22, 1936, 3:1.

8 Hu Shih, *Asia*, 36(November, 1936):737-740.

9 Hu Shih, "Fundamental Issues of the Far Eastern Conflict," *China Quarterly* (October 30, 1939), p. 65.

10 "Hu Shih's Demand for Open Diplomacy and Some Recent Developments," *China's Weekly Review*, 72(January 11, 1936):185.

11 Hu Shih, *Asia*, 36(June, 1936):379.

12 Y.C. Wang, *Chinese Intellectuals and the West 1872-1949* (Chapel Hill: University of North Carolina Press, 1966), pp. 410, 413-416.

13 *Ibid.*, p. 123.

14 *Christian Science Monitor Weekly Magazine* (August 1, 1942), p. 9.

15 *Life*, 21(December 15, 1941):132.

16 Tang Tsou, *America's Failure in China, 1941-1950* (Chicago: University of Chicago Press, 1963), p. 123.

17 Memorandum of Secretary Cordell Hull, November 24, 1941. See Joint Committee—Congressional Investigation, *Pearl Harbor Attack* (Washington, D.C.: Government Printing Office, 1946), part 14, pp. 1122-1133. Cited hereafter as *PHA*.

18 Telegram no. 812, Togo to Nomura, November 22, 1941. See exhibits *PHA*.

19 State Department Memorandum, November 24, 1941, "Proposed *Modus Vivendi* for Submission to Japanese Ambassador," *PHA*, part 14, p. 1143.

20 State Department Memorandum, November 25, 1941, "Opposition of Generalissimo Chiang Kai-shek to Modus Vivendi." Exhibits to Joint Committee in *PHA*, p. 1167.

21 *Ibid.*, p. 1171. Telegram from Minister Kuo T'ai-ch'i (Quo Tai-chi) to Ambassador Hu Shih, Chungking, November 24, 1941.

22 *Ibid.*, p. 1161. Telegram from General Chiang Kai-shek to Dr. T. V. Soong, Chungking, November 25, 1941.

23 *Ibid.*, p. 1160. Telegram from Owen Lattimore to Lauchlin Currie.

24 T.R. Fehrenback, *FDR's Undeclared War* (New York: D. McKay Co., 1967), p. 301. See also Herbert Feis, *The Road to Pearl Harbor* (New York: Atheneum Press, 1964), p. 302.

25 *New York Times*, November 27, 1941, 6:4.

26 *Life*, 21(December 15, 1941):123-124.

27 Eber, "Hu Shih," footnote p. 269.

28 State Department Memorandum, November 27, 1941, in exhibits of *PHA*, pp. 1179-1183.

29 *Ibid.*, pp. 1194-1195.

30 *New York Times*, September 3, 1942, p. 18.

31 *New York Times*, June 15, 1942, 4:4.

Han-sheng Lin

Chou Fo-hai

The Diplomacy of Survival

A DIPLOMAT without portfolio, Chou Fo-hai's political maneuverings during the late 1930's and 1940's were unmatched for their audacity. During these years he served as an influential member of Chiang Kai-shek's regime and subsequently as a leader in the "puppet" government of Wang Ching-wei. In this latter role he was a "double-agent" in direct contact with influential persons at the highest levels in both Tokyo and Chungking. His success in influencing policy and affairs in both governments explains why, despite their hatred of Chou, neither Chiang's nor Tokyo's agents dared to assassinate him. He was truly a political "fox."

On trial for treason after the Pacific war for serving in Wang Ching-wei's government, Chou defended his conduct by arguing that he had worked to promote a general peace between China and Japan and, that failing, to better the lot of the Chinese people living in Japanese-occupied areas. He proudly testified at his trial on October 21, 1946, that:

> In the first half of the period when I participated in the Nanking government, I attempted, by keeping in touch with the enemy, to turn things to the advantage of my country; in the latter half, I tried to turn them against the enemy by maintaining contact with my country [the Chungking government].[1]

His testimony often won warm response from the courtroom spectators. When he asked the people in the court whether "the Nanking government under the 'puppet organization' at that time ruled better [than] that of today after victory," the audience replied with hearty applause.[2] Chou also proudly pointed out to the court that the Nanking government returned the southeastern provinces to Chungking without losing ground to the Communists. Thus although he was convicted and sentenced to death for treason, Chou received a special commutation on March 26, 1947, from Chiang Kai-shek. Chou nevertheless succumbed to a heart attack a few months later while still in jail.[3]

Most wartime appraisals of the Wang government were understandably hostile. Secretary of State Cordell Hull declared that "the Axis powers found no difficulty in recognizing Wang Ching-wei but [his] puppet regime was still an effigy of straw and Japanese bayonets."[4] Lawrence K. Rossinger wrote in 1944 that: "The characteristic elements entering into Wang's actions were his inordinate ambition, and his lack of any means of satisfying this lust for power."[5] Since the war this view has been purposely fostered by the "Taiwan historians" and uncritically accepted by many American students of diplomacy.[6]

After the war more sympathetic critics gradually reviewed Wang's and, to a lesser extent, Chou's peace efforts and eventual collaboration with the Japanese. Most of these scholars were disappointed by the capitulation of Wang's group after peace efforts failed, but few have been completely negative in their evaluation.[7]

Wang Ching-wei and Chou Fo-hai are interesting yet puzzling collaborators, especially to Western observers. While the fascinating career of Wang must be a study of its own, the diplomacy of Chou is more suitable to illustrate the pattern of Chinese response to foreign oppression and aggression. Why did Chou, a close associate of Chiang Kai-shek, follow Wang's peace efforts? Why did he persuade Wang to establish a new government against Chiang when these efforts failed?

I

Chou Fo-hai was born to a relatively poor family in 1904 in Yuan-ling, Hunan province. His father died when he was just a boy, and his widowed mother raised him and his younger brother and sister. Chou's school work, particularly his Chinese composition, was excellent, and although his personal behavior was not always prudent, his family and friends encouraged him to continue his studies. Chou, who would not be called handsome, was especially fond of pretty girls. Despite his early marriage to a peasant girl who bore him a boy and a girl, Chou continued to pursue his romantic impulses.[8] He was not an ambitious boy; yet he did hope to become a school teacher.[9]

In 1917, to his surprise, his junior high school principal and a few friends collected more than 130 yüan to send him to study in Japan. Shortly after his arrival in Tokyo, however, Chou learned that Chinese students there were returning to China to protest the military agreement between the

Japanese government and the Tuan Ch'i-jui Cabinet in Peking. Patriotically, Chou followed the crowd. No sooner had he returned to China than he realized that he had made a terrible mistake; his meager funds exhausted, he could not return to his home without a better excuse. Fortunately a fellow Hunanese understood his difficulty and loaned him twenty yüan to return to Japan.

Chou studied diligently in Japan and was admitted to the first high school in Tokyo with a full scholarship covering all of his expenses. After graduation, he enrolled in Kyoto Imperial University where he studied economics. Under the influence of Professor Kawakami Hajime, a prominent Marxian scholar, Chou joined the Communist Party and became chairman of the Japanese branch of the Chinese Communist Party.

Chou went to Shanghai in 1921 as a representative to the First National Congress of the Chinese Communist Party, where he was elected vice-chairman of the Party under Ch'en Tu-hsiu. In this Congress, he worked together with a future friend, Ch'en Kung-po, and an enemy, Mao Tse-tung. Meanwhile, Chou met Yang Shu-hui, a high school girl in Shanghai, and married her despite strong opposition from the girl's father (a returned student from the United States) because of Chou's poor family background and his previous marriage.[10] Yang bore him another boy and girl, and she was recognized as his legal wife (although no record indicates that Chou ever divorced his first wife).

Chou was not a typical Chinese scholar. In appearance he remained simple and unsophisticated; he dressed in plain clothes and seldom combed his hair. Chou was straightforward, sincere, and intelligent, and he always treated people with humility. He enjoyed discussing national issues or love stories with friends, and he was always cheerful. His private life lacked discipline—he was disorderly, emotional and romantic. Even in his later busy political career, Chou continued to pursue the pleasures of wine and women. He drank heavily, which may have caused his heart trouble, and in his numerous wartime romances he fathered two illegitimate children, one by a Shanghai actress and another by a Japanese girl in Tokyo.[11] Chou enjoyed writing traditional poems, although he certainly was not the equal of his two contemporaries Wang Ching-wei and Mao Tse-tung.

Chou's private life, nevertheless, appeared to have little effect upon his active political career. In 1924 he went to Canton to participate in the Nationalist revolution. At the Ministry of Propaganda of the Kuomintang, Mao Tse-tung introduced Chou to Wang Ching-wei. In Canton Chou made numerous acquaintances with the revolutionaries, and he became a professor of economics in both Kwangtung University and the Whampoa Military Academy, a foundation under Chiang Kai-shek's power.

Subsequently, Chou left the Chinese Communist Party and participated in the Nationalist Northern Expedition in 1926. He served as executive secretary to General Teng Yen-ta, Chief of Political Affairs of the Headquarters of the Generalissimo. Teng was a left-wing Nationalist, and when the split of the Chinese Communist Party and the Kuomintang occurred in Wuhan, Chou fled to Shanghai where he was captured by the rightists. The Shanghai garrison commander would have executed him but for his wife's timely appeal to Chiang Kai-shek. Chiang then appointed him Director of Political Affairs of the Military Academy in Nanking. From 1927 to 1938 Chou was Chiang's political confidant and principal writer.

Chou's political activities increased in scope in the 1930's. In 1931 he was elected to the Central Executive Committee by a large margin, a fact which marks his importance in Kuomintang politics. Upon Chiang's temporary retirement in December 1931 because of the Manchurian crisis, Chiang appointed General Ku Chu-tung as Governor of Kiangsu province to prepare his political comeback. General Ku requested Chiang to send Chou Fo-hai as his chief of education and political adviser; General Ku and Chou formed a warm friendship at this time which influenced Chou's later career. In 1932 when Chiang Kai-shek and Wang Ching-wei jointly ruled the government and the party during a period of national crisis, Chou became Minister of the Central People's Training Department of the Kuomintang, a position which he held until 1938. Because of his background in the Whampoa Academy and his close relationship with Chiang, Chou became one of the ten highest ranking members of the "C.C. clique," a political faction within the Kuomintang, and an important official in the Blue Shirts, an intelligence organization sponsored by the Whampoa clique.[12]

Although Chou was a deft politician, he claimed that he was emotionally unfit to be a diplomat because he did not care about formalities and protocol. During the last stage of his career, however, he spent most of his time and energy in diplomatic affairs. From the outbreak of the Marco Polo Bridge Incident in July 1937, Chou was practically in charge of the peace negotiations with Japan. He conducted them unofficially, indirectly and secretly through his personal friends, some of whom were officials in the Ministry of Foreign Affairs. Chou's activities apparently resulted from his belief that: (1) China was too weak to fight against the Japanese, and thus China and Japan must be friends in order to safeguard the interests of East Asia against Communist aggression and Western imperialism; and (2) Chiang Kai-shek could not openly negotiate peace with the Japanese because of his position as the Commander-in-Chief. Chou therefore was negotiating for China in behalf of Chiang himself, even though Chiang did not formally authorize him to do so. In Chinese politics, however, "formal" authorization was not always necessary. Furthermore, as an adept politician, Chou may have seen an opportunity here to advance his personal political career.

Long before the outbreak of fighting in July 1937, a group of prominent politicians and educators including Hu Shih, T'ao Hsi-sheng, Kao

Tsung-wu, and Mei Ssu-p'ing began to meet regularly at Chou Fo-hai's residence in Nanking to discuss the deteriorating relationship between China and Japan and means to counteract this trend. The people in Nanking often called this group the "Low Tune Club." Chiang Kai-shek was not a member of the club, but his position on peaceful relations with Japan was clearly compatible with the club's until the Sian Incident in December 1936 when Marshal Chang Hsüeh-liang and Yang Hu-sh'eng kidnapped Chiang and forced him to commit himself against Japanese aggression.

Chiang had advocated a peace policy with the Japanese since his ascendancy to power in 1928. His political lieutenant Huang Fu, former Minister of Foreign Affairs, signed the infamous "T'ang-ku Agreement" with Japan in 1933, and Chiang published his famous article "Enemy or Friend?" in 1934 under the name of his secretary Hsü Tao-lin. In 1935 Ho Ying-chin, Chiang's chief military lieutenant, signed the infamous "Ho-Umezu Agreement." Following Wang Ching-wei's retirement from politics in November 1935 as a result of wounds inflicted by a would-be assassin, Chiang became President of the Executive Yuan or Premier. He appointed Chang Ch'ün as Minister of Foreign Affairs, and Chang initiated a series of peace negotiations with the Japanese Ambassador Kawagoe Shigeru which, at the point of success, were halted by the Sian Incident.

After this incident and his March 1937 agreement with the Chinese Communist Party to prepare for a war of resistance against Japanese aggression, Chiang was no longer in a position to talk openly of peace.[13] Consequently Chou Fo-hai, as a member of Chiang's inner Cabinet, took over the burdensome peace diplomacy.

The most powerful "peace faction" in China at this time was led by Wang Ching-wei. (Ultimately, it was to Wang and his group that Chou turned for assistance.) Wang is perhaps the most controversial figure in the history of modern China. He was feared and admired, loved and hated. Yet his significance has generally been overlooked by most scholars because of the commanding position of Chiang Kai-shek during the war and the rise of Mao Tse-tung to power thereafter. Without understanding Wang's position in modern Chinese politics, however, it is difficult, if not impossible, to comprehend the importance of the struggle over the issue of peace in the Republican era. Wang was the principal creator of the Kuomintang ideology. He was the composer of the Manifesto of the First National Congress of the Kuomintang, the author of Sun Yat-sen's Will, the architect of the anti-imperialistic foreign policy in his famous draft *China and the Nations,* and the sponsor of the proposals of the Enlarged Conference of 1930, most of which had been adopted by the Nanking government.[14]

As a politician Wang was not only one of the original founders of the Republic but also the first Chairman of the Nationalist government. He was the leading actor in almost all the famous political incidents of the time—the

March 20, 1926, incident, the split of the Kuomintang and the Communist Party in July 1927, the Great Civil War of the Northern Plain in 1929-1930, and the creation of the Canton government in 1931. In the critical years 1932-1935 he served as Premier and his power in the Nationalist government at that time equalled Chiang Kai-shek's.[15] Wang's public appeal was exceptional, no doubt because of his seniority in the party, his reputation as a fearless revolutionary, his powerful oratory, and his accomplishments in traditional scholarship, particularly as an essayist and poet. It is true that he was no soldier, but he had control of certain sections of the Nationalist Army. Even after being wounded by a bungling assassin and retiring from politics in November 1935 to recuperate, he still held the chairmanship of the Central Political Council of the Kuomintang, the highest decision-making body of the Nanking government. Chiang did not become Director-General of the Nationalist Party or emerge as the sole dictator until April 1938, and then only as a result of the war.

Wang's domestic and foreign policies guided most Kuomintang members in the early 1930's. Chiang Kai-shek, Chang Ch'ün, Ho Ying-chin, Huang Fu, and Chou Fo-hai openly supported his policy of "negotiation and resistance" abroad. Wang and Chiang together resisted by word and by deed the numerous pressures from Communists, warlords, patriotic intellectuals, and students for a united front against Japanese aggression. Wang returned from his recuperation abroad in January 1937 and began again to stress his themes of suppression of the Communists, unification of the country through reconstruction, and preparation for democratic rule. He was supported by some liberal leaders and many important lieutenants of Chiang Kai-shek.

At the time of the Marco Polo Bridge Incident in July 1937, Wang and Chiang had convened a political conference at Lu-shan attended by more than one hundred and fifty scholars, among them Hu Shih, Chang Po-ling, Tso Shung-sheng, and Chang Chi-luan, to discuss ways and means to promote national reconstruction and improved international relations.[16] When he learned the news of the incident, Wang urged caution and conciliation in dealing with Japan. Hu Shih and other liberals also appealed to Chiang to use diplomatic means to settle the conflict. Hu Shih recorded in his diary at some length his conversation with Wang Ching-wei at Lu-shan and their peace efforts. Secret negotiations, however, between the Chiang Kai-shek faction and the Communist leaders, in the persons of Chou Fo-hai and Ch'in Pang-hsien, undermined the peace efforts of Wang and Hu.[17]

Back in Nanking, Hu continued to work for peace with some of Chiang's young lieutenants. On July 30, 1937, Hu wrote:

> I went to Mr. Kai Tsung'wu's home for lunch, and those people present, such as Hsiao T'ung-tzu, Ch'eng Ts'ang-po, Fei Fu-heng, were mostly young braintrusters of the Nanking government. We talked deeply about national

affairs, and decided two things. (1) The diplomatic channel should not be severed, and the responsibility of positively opening up this channel should be entrusted to Tsung-wu (Kao). (2) The time is very late, and we must have a great statesman who is willing to take this great responsibility. I called Pu-lei (Ch'en) by phone and advised him to be a good minister for the country, and also asked him to work hard to remedy past mistakes.[18]

Because of these pressures for peace from Wang, Hu, Chou, and many others, Chiang vacillated between the peace and war factions.

In turning to Wang, Chou Fo-hai had initially sought support for a peaceful settlement with Japan. Unknowingly, however, he had ventured onto a path leading to "treason."

II

After the outbreak of fighting at the Marco Polo Bridge area in 1937, Chou's first peace maneuver was to ask Kao Tsung-wu, Chief of the Asian Bureau in the Ministry of Foreign Affairs and a regular member of the "Low Tune Club," to open private negotiations with the Japanese. On July 31 Kao asked Nishi Yoshiakira, Matsuoka Yosuke's protegé in Nanking, to go to Dairen to persuade Matsuoka to use his influence in convincing Prince Konoye of the need for peace negotiations.[19] But it was too late; by then the conflict had spread to Shanghai, and a full scale war had begun.

Diplomats from several major countries offered to mediate the conflict, the most interesting attempt being that of German Ambassador Trautmann. Wang Ching-wei as Chairman of the Fifty-Fourth Session of the Supreme National Defense Council disclosed the basis of the proposed settlement on April 4, 1939, in his famous article "Take an Example." Wang pointed out that the suggested conditions were then acceptable to Chiang Kai-shek, most other generals, and members of the council as a basis for peace negotiations.[20] Trautmann's mediation failed mainly because Japanese armies occupied Nanking on December 12, 1937, and in so doing not only brutally assaulted the citizens of Nanking but also raised their price for peace. On January 16, 1938, Konoye announced that he no longer intended "to negotiate with the Nationalist government" because it had become a local regime.[21]

Chou Fo-hai believed that if the Japanese Army had continued to pursue the defeated Kuomintang Army, instead of robbing and killing in Nanking, the Nationalist government might have collapsed. Moreover, he thought that Konoye's January 16 announcement was premature because China's acceptance of the Trautmann mediation and moderate peace terms had not yet reached Tokyo.[22] Consequently, despite the increasingly hostile attitude of the Konoye Cabinet, Chou continued his pursuit of peace.

Chou and Kao Tsung-wu sent Tung Tao-ning, Chief of the Japanese Division of China's Foreign Ministry, to Shanghai to ask Ambassador

Kawagoe for more reasonable terms. Tung did not obtain a decisive answer from Kawagoe, but he met Nishi who persuaded him to journey to Tokyo. Although he lacked authorization from his superiors for an extension of his trip, Tung went. Pointing out the ill effects of the Konoye declaration "not to negotiate with the Nationalist government," Tung and Nishi worked through certain members of the General Staff to overturn the decision of the Konoye Cabinet. The key figure among these men was Colonel Kagesa Sadaaki, a protegé of Lieutenant General Ishiwara Kanji. Kagesa wrote to Chang Ch'ün and Ho Ying-chin, Kagesa's classmates at the Japanese military academy, appealing for peace negotiations.

In Hankow, Tung did not deliver Kagesa's letter to Ho or Chang but gave it to Chou Fo-hai instead.[23] Chou in turn submitted it to Chiang Kai-shek. Chiang was pleased with the result of the missions of Tung Tao-ning and Kao Tsung-wu, and he personally offered his terms for peace negotiations to Kao and asked him to transmit them to Nishi in Hong Kong. The terms were:

(I) to guarantee security in relation to the Soviet Union, and (II) to protect and maintain the economic development of Japan in China. "In principle, these could be accepted. However, item I should be subdivided as follows: (1) Manchuria, (2) Inner Mongolia, (3) Hopei and Chahar. (1) and (2) could be negotiated sometime later, but (3) must be returned to China. Japan has to respect the territorial integrity and administrative independence of China south of the Great Wall." If the Japanese can understand the above principles, a cease-fire can first be worked out. Then based on these principles, we can proceed to discuss the details of peace.[24]

When Nishi arrived in Tokyo on April 27, 1938, however, he found that circumstances no longer favored peace negotiations. Japan had suffered military setbacks in the battles of Lin-i and Tai-erh-chuang; thus no military leader dared to speak up for peace. Chiang became greatly irritated, and he ordered Kao to stop negotiations with the Japanese military leaders.[25]

After the Hsuchow campaign, however, the situation in Japan changed again. Ugaki Kazushige, who obviously hoped to end the Sino-Japanese conflict, was appointed Minister of Foreign Affairs. Consequently Chiang's confidant Chang Ch'ün sent Ugaki a telegram asking him to open negotiations with Wang Ching-wei or himself. Ugaki in reply suggested Chiang's brother-in-law, Kung Hsiang-hsi, President of the Executive Yüan, as negotiator, because he was afraid Wang and Chang would not be accepted by the war faction in China. The Kung-Ugaki negotiations, however, were interrupted by Ugaki's resignation.[26]

Meanwhile Chou Fo-hai persisted in his peace efforts by attempting to ally himself with Wang Ching-wei. Through his old friend T'ao Hsi-sheng, a member of Wang's Reorganization Group, Chou approached the Wang faction and sought support for his peace venture. He convinced Kao Tsung-wu to continue negotiations with the Japanese despite Chiang Kai-shek's order. On June 14, meeting in the Kwangtung Hotel in Hong Kong, Kao told Nishi that Chou Fo-Hai had a "secret plan." Chou had decided to send him to Japan to negotiate peace on his own initiative, reasoning that if Chiang should reject Kao's efforts, Wang Ching-wei might accept them, and Chiang could then be persuaded. Nishi agreed wholeheartedly with Kao and stressed the importance of Wang in ending the war.[27] Kao and Nishi left immediately for Tokyo.

When Kao returned to Hong Kong he brought "conciliatory" messages from the Konoye Cabinet and the General Staff. Kao then sent them to Chou Fo-hai who immediately reported to Wang Ching-wei in Hankow. Wang was surprised that the Japanese General Staff wanted him to take charge of the peace negotiations, and he informed Chiang Kai-shek at once.[28]

During these discussions, however, in October 1938 the Japanese army occupied Canton and Hankow, encountering little resistance from Chiang's armies.[29] On November 3 after these military victories, Konoye issued another declaration in which he set forth his idea for a "new Order in East Asia." He claimed that Japan wanted no indemnity or territory from China and that she would not only respect China's sovereignty but would also consider returning all Japanese concessions to China and abolishing extraterritoriality in China.[30] The Japanese considered this declaration a major concession, given their successful occupation of Canton and Hankow. On the other side, Chiang Kai-shek, who had just lost two important cities, found the morale of his armies at its lowest point. Had he accepted Konoye's conditions at this time, his political future would have been bleak. Chiang made clear his determination to continue resisting Japanese aggression regardless of cost; on November 12, just nine days after Konoye's peace proposal, he ordered the city of Changsa burned.[31]

Since Chiang was too weak to negotiate terms, Chou Fo-hai, with the support of Wang Ching-wei, pushed the peace negotiations. Chou dispatched Mei Ssu-p'ing, a principal aide of Chiang and a regular member of the "Low Tune Club," to Shanghai as the chief delegate and Kao Tsung-wu as his deputy to conduct the negotiations. The Japanese government sent Colonel Imai Takeo as its chief negotiator and Itō-Yoshio as his deputy. Their meetings ended in the middle of November, and although Imai and Mei argued bitterly, they reached a preliminary agreement. Inukai Takeru, an adviser to Konoye, recorded the Shanghai Agreement of November 1938 as follows:

(1) China to recognize Manchukuo.
(2) Japan to withdraw her armies from China (depending on the restoration of order within a period of two years).

(3) Japanese armed forces to be stationed in North China for anti-Communist defense. (The time limit to be concurrent with an Anti-Comintern Pact to be made between China and Japan).
(4) Japanese concessions to be returned to China.
(5) Extraterritoriality to be abolished in China.
(6) Whether or not Japan should demand an indemnity was left undecided.[32]

The most important points in this preliminary agreement were the recognition of Manchukuo by the Chinese and the promised withdrawal of Japanese armies from China within two years. These terms, which did not differ much from those of the Trautmann mediation and the Ugaki-Kung talks, were actually most favorable to the Chinese.

Mei Ssu-p'ing brought back the agreement to Chungking where Chou, Mei, Wang and his wife, Ch'en Pi-chun, Ta'o Hsi-sheng, and Ch'en Kung-po examined it. When Chiang rejected the offer, Wang decided to leave Chungking and campaign for peace. Later Wang said: "On December 9, last year [1938], after a great and violent debate in the meeting, I realized that it was impossible for Chiang to adopt Konoye's peace proposals. I then decided to leave Chungking on December 18."[33]

When Konoye learned of Wang's successful departure from Chungking for Hanoi, he issued another declaration including the principles of good neighborliness and amicability, anti-Comintern collaboration, and economic cooperation, but he failed to mention the most important clause of the November Shanghai Agreement, namely that Japan would voluntarily withdraw her armies from China within two years. Konoye also mentioned the issue of Manchukuo, despite Kagesa's promise to Kao Tsung-wu in Shanghai that Manchukuo would not be included in the Konoye declaration. Why did Konoye reverse his position so quickly after the Shanghai Agreement? The change of personnel in the General Staff was perhaps one factor, for newly appointed Major General Tominaga refused to be bound by his predecessor's agreement to withdraw Japanese troops from China. Also, Konoye may have dismissed the Shanghai Agreement because Wang had departed Chungking and splintered the Kuomintang.[34] A more realistic supposition, however, might be Konoye's inability to resist the demands of victorious generals who had recently won Canton and Hankow.

Wang responded to Konoye's December 22 declaration with his famous "Yen-tien" (telegram of December 29) appealing for fair terms. He insisted that the Japanese withdraw their armies from China promptly. Furthermore, he maintained that with respect to the principle of "good neighborliness and amicability," Japan should demand neither territory nor indemnity from China and should return her concessions to China and consent to the abolition of extraterritoriality. Wang stated that the principle of anti-Comintern collaboration should be in the same "equal" spirit as similar pacts binding Japan, Germany, and Italy. Finally, he concluded that the principle of economic cooperation should prevent Japan's monopolistic control over China and promote China's relations with third powers. Under these specific terms, Wang was willing to start peace negotiations.[35]

Wang's telegram merely confirmed publicly the Shanghai Agreement. His position was virtually identical with Chiang's as evidenced in the message sent to Kagesa through Kao Tsung-wu and to Ugaki through Kung Hsiang-hsi and the Trautmann mediation—but now the Chungking government condemned Wang as a traitor and expelled him from the Kuomintang. This action, Chou Fo-hai claimed, was totally unexpected.[36] Moreover, the Konoye Cabinet resigned several days after Wang's public response. However significant this resignation was in stalling peace negotiations, the expulsion of Wang in the long run proved most fatal to a compromise peace settlement. On March 21 Chiang's agents in Hanoi attempted to assassinate Wang but mistakenly killed Ts'eng Chung-ming, then Chairman of the Secretariat of the Supreme Council of National Defense. This brutal action forced Wang, Chou, and their followers to leave Hanoi for Shanghai and later, with Japanese encouragement, to go to Tokyo.

III

Under these circumstances Chou Fo-hai's policies began to emerge. He argued that the threat of Chiang's special agents made it impossible to promote the peace movement among the people as Wang had planned; in addition there was no financial support for the peace faction. Only with the establishment of a new, "reformed" government, Chou argued, could the peace faction effectively negotiate a settlement with Japan. He also pointed out that a new government would be in a better position to protect people in occupied areas.[37] After a serious debate among Wang's followers, Chou eventually won his point against the strong opposition of Ch'en Kung-po, Wang's right-hand man.

Wang and Chou proceeded from Shanghai on June 4, 1939, to Japan to discuss with Baron Hiranuma, Japan's new Prime Minister, a peaceful settlement of the conflict and the establishment of a new government in Nanking. In Tokyo, Wang and Chou outlined their programs: (1) the central government was to rule the whole area of China; (2) the government was to be the Nationalist government, its capital was to be in Nanking, the flag was to be the original flag, and the three principles of Dr. Sun Yat-sen would be the basis of the nation; (3) the withdrawal of Japanese armies as originally agreed was to be set up precisely; and (4) within the areas occupied by the Japanese armies, Chinese personal or cooperative enterprises would be returned to their owners. The Japanese military leaders who had so relentlessly castigated the Kuomintang swallowed much of their pride in accepting all of these demands (except for the question of the flag, which ended in a compromise).[38]

As soon as Wang and Chou returned to Shanghai they began preparations for establishing the new government. Chou undertook the responsibility for all administrative matters. His private secretary and political confidant Lo Chun-ch'iang became Director-General of the Preparation Committee while his personal friend Chin Hsiung-pai served as Secretary-General. This committee was responsible for recruiting talent to serve the new, "reformed" Nanking government, scheduled to be established on October 10, 1938.

The establishment of the new government, however, depended on formalization of the Sino-Japanese basic treaty. Chou Fo-hai acted as the chief negotiator in this diplomatic endeavor, with the assistance of Mei Ssu-p'ing, T'ao Hsi-sheng, and Kao Tsung-wu. The Japanese military, in an effort to obtain better terms, dispatched Colonel Kagesa Sadaaki as their chief delegate, with Colonel Yaogi of the army, Admiral Suga of the navy, and Yano Seiki and Shimizu Juzo of the Foreign Ministry. Inukai Takeru served as Kagesa's special advisor. The army's China Board presented a harsh first draft that upset the Chinese delegation. Kao Tsung-wu attacked the terms declaring that "the north does not belong to China, the south does not belong with China; the sea is not China's, nor is the mountain; where then should the Chinese people go?"[39] Mei Ssu-p'ing and T'ao Hsi-sheng also reacted fiercely. Negotiations thus came to a deadlock, and the establishment of the "reformed" Nanking government was indefinitely postponed.

Because of the heated debate in the opening session and in order to insure secrecy, Chou Fo-hai and Inukai Takeru began meeting privately in Chou's residence at night to negotiate an acceptable treaty. Chou sought to force enough Japanese concessions to make the agreement acceptable to Wang while avoiding the accusation of betraying the interests of the Chinese people. Upon learning of Chou's secret negotiations with Inukai and Chou's optimism for conclusion of negotiations, Kao warned Inukai that:

I have learned from Chou Fo-hai that you have negotiated with him every night, that with your efforts you have raised the original thirty points to fifty-eight points, and need merely two more points to enable us not to be traitorous to the country. Chou is more optimistic now. However, the public critics are very severe, and I hope you will ask Chou Fo-hai to take good care of himself.

Inukai replied: "I [have] often told Chou that he took the matter too lightly." Kao believed that Chou was too "anxious to organize the [new] government" and had not been as prudent as he should in protecting Chinese interests.[40]

T'ao Hsi-sheng had already complained to Ch'en Pi-chün (Wang Ching-wei's wife) about the harshness of the draft. He pointed out that Japan intended to divide China into five zones, Manchuria, North China, Central China, South China, and Hainan Island.[41] When Kao and T'ao both appealed to Wang to terminate all negotiations, he finally summoned Kagesa to his residence, formally announcing his decision to end negotiations and move out of Shanghai.

After careful study of the [Japanese] draft, which is far from the Konoye declaration, the present negotiations have led the peace camp to split. Some of us have withdrawn out of pessimism, and the difficulty is bound to increase thereafter. However, I could not overlook your heavy responsibility, and the efforts of you and the members of the Ume organization to ask the Japanese government to make concessions for us. The situation has come to the point that I have decided to abandon the plan of organizing a government and go back to the people to promote the peace movement as we originally attempted. Please forgive us.[42]

Alarmed by this development, Kagesa immediately returned to Tokyo for further instructions. Meanwhile, Wang called together his followers and reported his conversation with Kagesa, asking for possible alternatives. Chou Fo-hai prevailed upon Wang to postpone the final decision to terminate the negotiations until Kagesa's return.[43]

Kagesa returned from Tokyo with instructions to make further concessions to Wang in order to successfully conclude the negotiations. Consequently, Wang, Ch'en Kung-po, Chou, Kagesa, and Inukai concluded the final stage of the negotiations. Wang instructed Chou to draft minimum terms for Kagesa and the Japanese government to consider. Chou returned with the following items for discussion:

(1) withdrawal of the Japanese armies;
(2) economic problems;
(3) Japanese demands for a naval base in Hainan Island;
(4) the railroads in Central China;
(5) qualifications of administrative personnel in the local government (mainly the temporary and reformed governments).[44]

After some deliberation Kagesa and Inukai reached agreement on all issues, except the Hainan Island matter. Here the Japanese Ministry of Navy had given specific instructions to its own delegate. Chou declined to negotiate with Admiral Suga about this matter, perhaps because be believed that the Japanese Navy would not yield any ground. Wang then instructed Ch'en Kung-po to meet with Admiral Suga; however, neither Ch'en nor Suga would yield, and Wang eventually intervened to ask Ch'en to compromise.[45]

Wang's capitulation on several Japanese demands disappointed all Chinese nationalists. Not only was Hainan Island to become a Japanese naval base, but Manchukuo was to be recognized as an independent state. Furthermore, Wang and Chou accepted terms similar to those of the infamous 1915 Twenty-One Demands, granting Japan the right to station armies in Mongolia and Chinese Turkistan, to create Shanghai and Amoy as special cities, to jointly develop Chinese resources in North and Central China, to employ Japanese advisers and technicians, and to stop "anti-Japanese thinking." Wang and Chou made these concessions, however, in the wake of military defeats and enemy occupation. In return they did gain concessions from the Japanese, namely the transformation, in name at least, of the "puppet" government into a new "reformed" government, the return of most seized property in occupied areas, the gradual abolition of Japanese concessions and extraterritoriality, and, above all, the withdrawal of Japanese armies from China proper as soon as possible. [46]

Kao Tsung-wu and T'ao Hsi-sheng were totally dissatisfied with the result of the peace negotiations and they termed the basic treaty traitorous. Both feigned illness and refused to sign the treaty. On January 4, 1940, Kao and T'ao left for Shanghai with a copy of the text. They then published the treaty in the *Ta-kung-pao* (Chungking) on January 23. The defection of Kao and T'ao and the publication of the draft shocked Wang and Chou, as well as Japanese leaders.[47] Chou, however, quickly turned this setback to his advantage. He appealed to the Japanese for further concessions to counter Chungking propaganda.[48] With the subsequent Japanese concessions, Chou consolidated his power in the new government. Finally, on March 30, 1940, Wang and Chou formally signed the Sino-Japanese Basic Treaty and established the "reformed" Nanking government.

Even prior to this success, Chou had intensified his efforts to bring about peace. He was convinced that Japan was tired of war and willing to compromise; now the main obstacle to peace, he believed, was Chiang's stubbornness. Consequently Chou sought to use the threat of establishing a new government to force Chiang to agree to new peace proposals. Chou reasoned that only a display of power, such as the creation of a rival government, would bring Chiang to accept reality and, thus, peace.[49]

In addition to sending numerous messengers to sound out Chungking's conditions for peace, Chou formally endorsed three peace missions: the first by John Leighton Stuart; the second by General Itagaki and Colonel Imai; and the third by Matsuoka Yosukē, then Japanese Foreign Minister, and Ch'ien Hsin-chih, Chiang's old friend.

Stuart was president of Yenning University and a personal friend of the Chiang family. He had good connections with the State Department, and in fact, Stuart became the American Ambassador to China after the Pacific war. With the encouragement of Wang Ching-wei and Chou Fo-hai, Stuart went to Chungking personally to mediate between Chungking and Tokyo. Chiang seems to have been interested in Stuart's peace efforts, perhaps because of the threat of a "reformed" Nanking government, but the deteriorating relationship between the United States and Japan ruined the effectiveness of Stuart's mediation.[50]

The overtures of General Itagaki Seishirō, Commander-in-Chief of the China Expeditionary Army, indicated the military's interest in ending the conflict. Since the failure of the Kao Tsung-wu mission in 1938, however, Chiang was suspicious of the Japanese military; consequently he only ordered his agents to seize the opportunity to collect military intelligence. The peace overtures of General Itagaki and Colonel Imai were therefore never seriously considered by the Chungking government.[51]

The last peace effort, undertaken by Matsuoka and Ch'ien, however, almost succeeded. Chiang was serious in negotiating peace at this time not only because the Tokyo government threatened to recognize the "reformed" Nanking government but also because Chiang was about to split with the Chinese Communist Party. Chiang actually dispatched his friend and political confidant Chang Chi-luan, Editor-in-Chief of the *Ta-kung-pao,* to make contacts with Ch'ien in Hong Kong. Unfortunately, the Japanese response to Chiang's demands came several hours too late and Chang returned to Chungking without learning of them.[52]

Chiang gave up all hope for a negotiated peace after Japanese recognition of the "reformed" Nanking government on November 30, 1940. The activities of Chou Fo-hai therefore also entered a new phase. Chiang Kai-shek had once before urged Chou, through a brother of Ch'en Li-fu, to prepare for the overthrow of Wang Ching-wei from within, but Chou refused to betray Wang, who had always treated him as a scholar and a statesman.[53] Nevertheless, Chou did accept other orders from Chungking. He secretly set up two radio stations to maintain contact with Tai Li, Chief of Chiang's special agents, and Ku Chu-tung, Commander-in-Chief of the Third Area Corps, both of whom were old friends of Chou's.

In Nanking, Chou was appointed Vice President of the Executive Yüan and Finance Minister in the new government, but his major function was to conduct negotiations with the Japanese. As he outlined his responsibilities, he was to (1) negotiate with the Japanese in order to recover as many lost rights as possible; (2) develop a sound financial system and eliminate Japanese currency in order to protect the people in occupied areas from being exploited by the Japanese Army; and (3) organize a security force sufficient not only to maintain law and order but to meet any future contingency.[54]

Relations with Japan were still problematic. As Ch'en Kung-po put it, there was no "Sino-Japanese Basic Treaty," because Ch'en and Chou fought continuously to revise it once it had been signed. While Ch'en dedicated himself to the promotion of nationalism through education, Chou employed every possible means to protect the people in occupied areas from Japanese exploitation. He took advantage of antagonisms between junior and senior Japanese officers, between their civil and military authorities, and between the Japanese Foreign Minister and the China Board. He frequently exploited their conflicts to his benefit. He even threatened to resign to achieve certain objectives. Other times he appealed to the idealism of the Japanese top-ranking officers. Chou also realized that Japanese leaders sought to employ him as a bridge to the Chungking government for peace negotiations; he more than once played on this desire in order to demand favorable terms as a demonstration of Japanese sincerity. Finally, Chou never hesitated to exploit the prestige of Wang Ching-wei among the Japanese people to control the arrogance of young Japanese officers. (Wang frequently wrote open letters appealing to Japanese intellectuals or sent memorials to high Japanese authorities, even the Emperor, for redress of grievances.) Chou's methods for promoting Chinese interests were indeed cunning.

Chou continued to work slowly but steadily to improve conditions in occupied areas prior to the coming of war in December 1941. The most important achievement under Chou's guidance was stabilization of the currency. At first Japanese armies and their puppet governments had issued paper money without deposit, thus robbing the resources of the people in occupied areas. After a year of bitter discussions with Japanese authorities, Chou secured the establishment of the Central Reserve Bank, a national bank with the power to issue legal tender to replace other currencies. This Central Reserve Bank received a substantial deposit in gold, silver, and foreign currencies to back up its money. Consequently, the Nanking government enjoyed relative economic stability despite various Japanese attempts to plunder its resources.[55]

In June 1941 Wang's Japanese supporters, including Konoye and General Tōjō Hideki, sought to strengthen the Nanking government as a means of achieving peace in China. Wang and Chou paid a formal visit to the Japanese Emperor and other top officials, and on June 23 the two governments issued a joint communiqué expressing their mutual cooperation. In this spirit, Japan agreed to support the Nanking government in preserving its sovereignty and extended a 300 million yen loan to Nanking for armaments and economic improvements. Japan also promised to return the houses and factories that had been confiscated by the Japanese Army.[56] While Wang returned to Nanking, Chou remained in Tokyo to iron out the details. Ultimately, Japan did not live up to its promises because of the outbreak of war, but at the time the Japanese government did press its allies to recognize the Nanking government and did provide funds for Nanking's armaments.[57]

In any event, Wang and Chou continued to struggle for China's freedom and independence. As soon as the Pacific war began, Chou contemplated the possibility of joining with Japan to improve the status of the Nanking government. In July 1942 Chou informed Premier Tōjō of his government's desire to participate in the Pacific war.[58] Although the Japanese government was not yet ready to accept Chou's proposal, Chou obtained a 100 million yen loan for currency stabilization.[59]

Wang continued to urge a Japanese-Chinese war effort, and to this purpose he delivered a memorandum to the Japanese government analyzing the reasons for failure of the peace movement and explaining why the Nanking government should be strengthened in order to contribute effectively to the Pacific war.[60] Finally as a result of this pressure and the necessities of the war, on December 21 the Japanese Imperial Conference detailed a new China policy indicating its readiness to: (1) grant the Nanking government autonomy in local administrative affairs; (2) abrogate or revise extraterritorial rights respecting China's sovereignty and territorial integrity; and (3) restrain Japanese economic monopoly in China.[61] Wang therefore met briefly with Tōjō, and on January 9, 1943, the Nanking government declared war on Great Britain and the United States. The Sino-Japanese treaty of alliance of 1943 now replaced the unequal Sino-Japanese Basic Treaty of 1940. Wang and Chou had been able to recover most national rights except for the dependent status of Manchuria.[62] After the downfall of Tōjō in 1944, the Koiso Cabinet even considered the possibility of returning Manchuria to China provided Nanking would mediate between Chungking and Tokyo to end that war.[63] After the death of Wang Ching-wei, the Imperial Conference of December 1944 continued to entrust the peace negotiations to the Nanking government in spite of distrust of Nanking among some top-ranking officials, including General Hata, Commander-in-Chief of the China Expeditionary Army.[64]

Nanking was in name then an ally of Japan against the Allies, but in fact, Wang and Chou successfully resisted Japanese pressure to send any forces to fight against the Allies or to dispatch any laborers to help the Japanese war effort. They also devised many methods for preventing the Japanese from employing Chinese resources in the Pacific war. They argued, for example, that the Chinese people must have sufficient food to eat and clothes to wear before they could sell any of these goods to the Japanese. Furthermore, if the Japanese wanted to prevent the Chinese people from joining the Chinese Communist Party or the Chungking government, they should purchase Chinese goods with gold. Even after the Japanese had complied, however, Wang and Chou secretly ordered their subordinates to use every bureaucratic means to stall shipments to the Japanese. In instances of conflict between local authorities and the Japanese, Nanking always protested that Japan had no right to interfere with Chinese domestic affairs according to explicit terms of the new treaty.[65]

Consequently at the end of the war the Japanese were still prevented from exploiting the Chinese resources they so desperately needed, such as iron and copper. Indeed the Japanese spent a huge amount of gold for the goods they were unable to use; in the end, this gold was turned over to the Chiang Kai-shek government after the war. Finally, the Nanking government organized an army of over 600,000 men, which toward the end of the war became a major threat to the Japanese themselves.[66]

Chou had continued all the while to receive instructions from Chungking through Tai Li and Ku Chu-tung. His orders were three-fold: first, when the Allies counter-attacked on the east coast, he was to respond with Nanking's new armed forces; second, he was to pacify the Nanking-Shanghai area in order to prevent Communist expansion of their political base; and third, when the war came to an end he was to facilitate transfer of the Nanking-Shanghai area to the Chungking government. Chou accomplished the last two assignments easily. Because of Japan's surrender after the bombing of Hiroshima and Nagasaki, however, he did not have the opportunity to send Nanking's new army into action. Even Chiang Kai-shek admitted Chou's achievement in his executive order pardoning him.[67] Chou risked his life and fortune undertaking one of the most difficult diplomatic and political tasks in modern Chinese history.

IV

Ironically, regardless of the delicate task the "collaborators" so skillfully performed and the peace efforts they had so nobly promoted, Chinese writers have never fully appreciated their effort or sacrifice. The most condemned names in modern Chinese history are Wang Ching-wei and Chou Fo-hai.[68] The activities of Wang and Chou may have obstructed the defense of Chinese territory in the first place; however, the probability of damaging the Chungking government by their peace efforts and eventually by their collaboration with the Japanese was minimal. There was never a serious battle between Chiang's troops and Japan after the fall of Canton and Hankow in October 1938. Furthermore, the final goal of the war of resistance was to achieve peace and to rescue China from Japanese military and economic domination. Wang and Chou largely achieved these objectives by peaceful, if admittedly unorthodox, means.

The diplomacy of Chou Fo-hai was not only strange to historians' minds but also so complicated as to discourage investigation. Why then, if Chou was so dedicated to peace in China, has history treated him so poorly? Perhaps this is because of the "praise and blame" school of thought which has overemphasized legitimacy and orthodoxy; or perhaps popular emotion, during the war, overwhelmed reason.

In this study of Chou Fo-hai, which clearly suggests the irony of historical interpretations, current presentations of Chinese history seem to be inadequate. It is imperative, therefore, to reevaluate the political development of China in a proper historical perspective. Such a reevaluation will reveal certain consistent historical patterns in Chinese foreign policy exemplified by Chou Fo-hai's colorful career. First, whether or not China was strong and powerful or weak and helpless, Chinese leaders have traditionally pursued difficult paths in achieving peace and have in large part ignored personal glory or humiliation. Second, Chinese philosophical teachings overwhelmingly stress peace and harmony, an emphasis which has markedly influenced the activities of generations of Chinese statesmen. Third, most Chinese leaders have realized that without dedicated leadership neither peace nor harmony can be achieved. Fourth, the continued growth of Chinese culture has resulted from the flexibility of Chinese politics which tolerates humiliation and compromise in exchange for the survival of its civilization. Chou Fo-hai's diplomacy was indeed in keeping with a great tradition.

Notes

1 Chin Hsiung-pai, *Wang Cheng-ch'üan ti k'ai-ch'ang yü shou-ch'ang* (The Beginning and End of the Wang Regime) (Hong Kong: Ch'un-ch'iu tsa-chih she, 1959-1964), 4:106. Chin was an old friend of Chou Fo-hai and a close associate of Chou in the Wang regime.

2 *Ibid.,* 4:121.

3 *Ibid.,* 4:110-111, 123.

4 Cordell Hull, *The Memoirs of Cordell Hull* (New York: Macmillan, 1948), 1:725.

5 Lawrence K. Rossinger, *China's Wartime Politics 1937-1944* (Princeton: Princeton University Press, 1944), pp. 33-34.

6 Kung Te-po, *Wang Chao-ming hsiang-ti mai-kuo mi-shih* (The Secret History of Wang Ching-wei, His Surrender to the Enemy and Sell-out of the Country) (Taipei: n.p., 1963); C. Martin Wilbur, "The Variegated Career of Ch'en Kung-po," *The Chinese Communist Movement* by Ch'en Kung-po (New York: East Asian Institute, Columbia University, 1960), p. 13; David J. Liu, *From the Marco Polo Bridge to Pearl Harbor* (Washington D. C.: Public Affairs Press, 1963), p. 128.

7 F. Hilary Conroy, "Japan's War in China: An Ideological Somersault," *Pacific Historical Review,* 21(November, 1952):367-379; John K. Fairbank, *The United States and China* (Cambridge, Massachusetts: Harvard University Press, 1958), p. 72; Kimitada Miwa, "The Wang Ching-wei Regime and Japanese Efforts to Terminate the China Conflict," *Studies in Japanese Culture,* ed. Joseph Roggendorff (Tokyo: Sophia University, 1963), pp. 123-141; Howard L. Boorman, "Wang Ching-wei: A Political Profile," *Revolutionary Leaders of Modern China,* ed. Chun-tu Hsueh (New York: Oxford University Press, 1971), pp. 295-319. See also John Hunter Boyle, *China and Japan at War, 1937-1945* (Stanford: Stanford University Press, 1972), Gerald E. Bunker, *The Peace Conspiracy: Wang*

Ching-wei and the China War, 1937-1941 (Cambridge, Massachusetts: Harvard University Press, 1972), and my article, "Wang Ching-wei and Chinese Collaboration, 1940-1945," *Peace and Change* 1(Fall, 1972):18-35.

8 Chin, *Wang*, 2:112; Kung, *Wang*, p. 2.

9 Chou Fo-hai, *Wang-i chi* (A Collection of Past Events) (Hong Kong: Ho-chung ch'u-pan she, 1955), pp. 7-12; Chin, *Wang*, 2:112-113.

10 Chou, *Wang-i chi*, pp. 13-24; Chin, *Wang*, 2:117-118.

11 Chin, *Wang*, 2:128-129.

12 *Ibid.*, pp. 113-114.

13 Lyman P. Van Slyke has made a good study of the Sian Incident in his book, *Enemies and Friends: The United Front in Chinese Communist History* (Stanford: Stanford University Press, 1967), pp. 75-91, but unfortunately he has failed to analyze the complication of other political and literary leaders, particularly Wang Ching-wei. See my review of this book in *Journal of Canadian History*, 3(September, 1968):131-132. I further propose that the early release of Chiang without a formal agreement was mainly because of the return of Wang Ching-wei urged by Ho Ying-ch'in and Tai Chi-t'ao. Wang was on his way back to China when Chiang was released. Chiang Kai-shek summarily denied any agreement with Chang Hsüeh-liang for his release, in his pamphlet "Hsi-an pan-yüeh chi" (Records of Half-month in Sian), but his official biographer, Tung Hsien-kuang, acknowledges the agreements between the Communists and the Nationalists in March 1937, which agreements are essentially similar to the demands of Chang Hsüeh-liang. Tung Hsien-kuang, *Chiang Tsung-t'ung chuan* (A Biography of President Chiang Kai-shek) (Taipei: Chung-hua wen-hua ch'u-pan shih-yeh wei-yüan hui, 1954), p. 269. Apparently, the release of Chiang was in the best interest of Chang Hsüeh-liang and the Communists; otherwise they had to face the army of Ho Ying-ch'in and the leadership of Wang Ching-wei allied with Tai Chi-t'ao who had been their bitter foes for a long period. Both Japanese sources, *Taiheiyō senso e no michi* (The Road to the Pacific War) (Tokyo: Asahi Shinbunsha, 1963), 3:332-333, and *Gendai-shi Shiryō* (Source Materials of Modern History) (Tokyo: Misuzu Shobō, 1965), 12:254-255, have paid attention to Wang Ching-wei's return from Europe during the Sian Incident and his subsequent political activities.

14 Ch'en, Jerome, "The Left Wing Kuomintang—A Definition," *Bulletin of School of Oriental and African Studies,* London University (October, 1962), pp. 561-562; Wang Ching-wei *China and the Nations,* trans. and ed. I-sen Teng and John N. Smith (New York: Frederick A. Stokes Co., 1927); Wang Ching-wei and others, *The Chinese National Revolution: Essays and Documents,* ed. T'ang Liang-li (Peking: China United Press, 1931).

15 Li Yün-han, *Ts'ung jung-kung tao ch'ing tang* (From Collaboration with the Communists to the Purification of the Kuomintang), 2 vols., (Taipei: Chung-kuo hsüeh-shu chu-tso chiang-chu wei-yüan-hui, 1966). Li has collected many good documents from the Chinese archives, but his interpretations are generally one-sided with a strong Taiwan flavor. Lei Hsiao-ch'en, *San-shih nien-lai tung-luan Chung-kuo* (Chaotic China in the Past Thirty Years) (Hong Kong: Ya-chou ch'u-pan she, 1955). Lei once was Secretary of the Nationalist government, and his book certainly is one of the most detailed descriptions of Chinese politics from 1927-1931.

Furthermore, it contains many valuable documents. Lei's interpretations are also hostile to the Wang faction. T'ang Leung-li (Liang-li), *The Inner History of the Chinese Revolution* (London: G. Routledge & Sons Ltd., 1930). T'ang was Wang Ching-wei's English secretary and an official biographer of Wang. Despite its favorable description of Wang and his ideas, this book remains one of the most accurate works on the Chinese revolution.

16 Hu Shih, "Hu Shih jih-chi chai-lu," (Selected Records of Hu Shih's Diary), *Chin-tai-shih tzu-liao* (Sources of Contemporary History) (Peking: K'o-hsüeh ch'u-pan she, 1955), pp. 209-211.

17 Tso Shun-sheng, *Chin san-shih nien chien-wen tsa-chi* (A Record of Miscellaneous News in the Past Thirty Years) (Kowloon: Tzu-yu ch'u-pan she, 1952), p. 56. Tso was a leader of the Young China Party and also attended the Lu-shan Conference.

18 Hu Shih, *Hu Shih*, p. 211.

19 Nishi Yoshiakira, *Higeki no shōnin* (The Witness of a Tragedy) (Tokyo: Bunken-sha, 1962), pp. 77-78; Kung, *Wang*, pp. 20-21.

20 Wang Ching-wei, *The Peace Movement in China* (n.p., China Institute of International Affairs, 1939), pp. 6-8. The contents of the Trautmann mediation disclosed by Wang have subsequently been verified by both German and Japanese sources. See *Documents on German Foreign Policy* (Washington, D.C.: United States Government Printing Office, 1949), 1:778-779; and *Taiheiyō sensō e no michi*, 4:125-126.

21 Nishi, *Higeki*, pp. 99-101; Horiba Kazuo, *Shina jihen sensō shidōshi* (History of the War Guidance of the China Incident) (Tokyo: Jiji Tsushin-sha, 1962), 1:131. This is the famous *aite to sezu* statement.

22 Chin, *Wang*, 1:9-10.

23 Kung, *Wang*, p. 41. It indicates here not only Chou's power and influence but also his intimate relationship with Chiang Kai-shek and the peace mission.

24 Nishi, *Higeki*, p. 136.

25 Kung, *Wang*, p. 49. Kung considers Chiang's determination not to negotiate with the Japanese, equivalent to Konoye's *aite to sezu* statement, although Chiang did not overtly declare his determination.

26 Ugaki Kazushige, *Ugaki nikki* (The Diary of Ugaki) (Tokyo: Asahi Shinbunsha, 1954), pp. 327-334.

27 Nishi, *Higeki*, pp. 186-187.

28 T'ao Hsi-sheng, "Luan-liu, I," (Flowing in Chaos), *Chuan-chi wen-hsüeh* (Biographic Literature), 2(April, 1963):6.

29 Imai Takeo, *Shina jihen no kaisō* (Reminiscences of the China Incident) (Tokyo: Misuzu Shobō, 1964), pp. 284-286. According to the recollection of Colonel Imai, the Japanese agents had made close contacts with General Yü Han-mou, Commander of the Kwangtung Army, before the Japanese occupation of Canton, but Imai does not record the responses of General Yü. At any rate, Yü lost Canton virtually without resistance. Kuo Mo-jo, *Kuo Mo-jo wen-chi* (Collected Writings of Kuo Mo-jo) (Peking: Jen-min wen-hsüeh ch'u pan she, 1959), 9:81. Kuo wrote the last official editorial in Wu-han, and he confessed his consistent exaggeration of the war efforts.

30 Kazami Akira, *Konoye naikaku* (The Konoye Cabinet) (Tokyo: Nihon Shuppan Kyōdō Kabushiki Kaisha, 1951), p. 168; Nishi, *Higeki*, pp. 208-209.

31 Despite Chiang's denial that he ordered the burning of this capital city, most contemporary writers who either were then in Changsha or had intimate knowledge of this event blamed Chiang for this senseless destruction because the Japanese armies were still hundreds of miles away and also because thousands of innocent people were burned to death. See Kuo Mo-jo, *Kuo Mo-jo,* 9:218; Feng Yü-hsiang, *Wo so jen-shih ti Chiang Chieh-shih* (The Chiang Kai-shek I Knew) (Hong Kong: Wen-hua ch'u-pan she, 1949), p. 87. Incidentally, both Kuo and Feng were top ranking members of the government who wholeheartedly supported the war efforts.

32 Inukai Takeru, *Yōsukō wa ima mo nagereta iru* (The Yangtze River Is Still Flowing) (Tokyo: Shunju Shinsha, 1960), p. 33. At the request of Kagesa, the Japanese government dropped the indemnity clause.

33 Wang Ching-wei, *Ho-p'ing yün-tung yen-lun chi* (Collected Speeches and Essays on the Peace Movement) (Canton: Chung-shan jih-pao she, 1939), p. 17. Wang's statement is confirmed by the publication of the memoirs of Ch'en Pu-lei, Chiang's private secretary and political confidant. Ch'en Pu-lei, *Hui-i lu* (Memoirs) (Hong Kong: T'ien-hsing ch'u-pan she, 1962), p. 108. Most Japanese records have been generally in error in indicating that Wang's delayed departure from Chungking was because of the unexpected return of Chiang to Chungking, which prevented him from leaving. In fact, Wang and Chiang and other important leaders had scheduled a meeting on December 9 to discuss Konoye's proposals for peace. Chiang was fully aware of the activities of Chou Fo-hai and Kao Tsung-wu. Nishi, *Higeki,* p. 216; Inukai, *Yōsukō,* p. 99; Imai, *Shina,* p. 86.

34 Kung, *Wang,* p. 78.

35 Wang Ching-wei, *The Peace Movement in China,* pp. 3-4. This is Wang's famous *yen-tien* (telegram of December 29).

36 Chin, *Wang,* 1:21.

37 *Ibid.,* 5:96; Inukai, *Yōsukō,* pp. 208-209.

38 Conroy, "Japan's War," p. 377; Kung, *Wang,* p. 110; Inukai, *Yōsukō,* p. 191.

39 Kung, *Wang,* p. 115.

40 *Ibid.,* pp. 117-118.

41 T'ao Hsi-sheng, "Luan-liu II," *Chuan-chi wen-hsüeh* 2(May, 1963):6. Cited hereafter as "Luan-liu II."

42 Inukai, *Yōsukō,* p. 378; Kung, *Wang,* p. 118.

43 "Luan-liu II," 2:7.

44 Kung, *Wang,* pp. 120-121.

45 Inukai, *Yōsukō,* pp. 302-315. Inukai provides a detailed record of the Ch'en-Suga negotiations.

46 *Ibid.,* pp. 217-222; Kung, *Wang,* pp. 127-135. Kung's document was the original draft which was published by Kao Tsung-wu and T'ao Hsi-sheng on January 23, 1940, in Chungking *Ta-kung-pao.*

47 Chou Fo-hai, *Chou Fo-hai jih-chi* (The Diary of Chou Fo-hai) (Hong Kong: Wu-hsing chi shu-pao she, n.d.), pp. 3-19; Inukai, *Yōsukō,* pp. 222-223.

48 Chou Fo-hai, *Chou Fo-hai,* pp. 14-21; Inukai, *Yōsukō,* p. 223; Chin, *Wang,* pp. 84-86.

49 Chin, *Wang,* 5:135.

50 Chou Fo-hai, *Chou Fo-hai*, p. 77; John Leighton Stuart, *Fifty Years in China* (New York: Random House, 1954), p. 133.

51 Chou Fo-hai, *Chou Fo-hai*, pp. 100-105. Chou kept a detailed record of the peace activities of General Itagaki and Colonel Imai.

52 Nishi, *Higeki*, pp. 334-392; Kung, *Wang*, pp. 144-150; Chin, *Wang*, 1:113-114.

53 Chou Fo-hai, *Chou Fo-hai*, p. 156.

54 *Ibid.*, pp. 60-71; Chin, *Wang*, 1:115-125; 2:11-41.

55 Chin, *Wang*, 1:117-121.

56 Horiba, *Shina*, 1:593.

57 *Documents on German Policy*, 13:17-80; Horiba, *Shina*, 1:671-676.

58 Sambō Hombu (ed.), *Sugiyama Memo* (Tokyo: Hara Shobō, 1967), 2:136.

59 Horiba, *Shina*, 1:671.

60 This memorandum was given to the Hoover Institute of War, Revolution, and Peace at Stanford by the Japanese section of the Department of State. The authenticity of this document can be verified by the facts mentioned in the contents and by Wang's "Final Political Testament" published in Hong Kong twenty years after Wang's death, as requested by him. Chin, *Wang*, 5:154-164.

61 Imai, *Shina*, p. 216; Nishi, *Higeki*, p. 400; Higashikuni Naruhiko, *Ichi kōzoku no sensō nikki* (The War Diary of an Imperial Prince) (Tokyo: Nihon Shūhōsha, 1957), p. 157.

62 Hattori Takushirō, *Daitōa sensō zenshi* (A Complete History of the Greater East Asian War) (Tokyo: Hara Shobō, 1968), pp. 367-371; Chin, *Wang*, 1:174-178.

63 Inaba Masao, *Haisen no kiroku* (The Record of a Lost War) (Tokyo: Hara Shobō, 1967), 5:162-163.

64 Kido Kōichi, *Kido Kōichi nikki* (The Diary of Kido) (Tokyo: Tokyo Daigaku Shuppankai, 1966), 2:1185.

65 Chin, *Wang*, 1:175-178; 5:162.

66 Warren I. Cohen, "Who Fought the Japanese in Hunan? Some Views of China's War Effort," *Journal of Asian Studies*, 27(November, 1967):111-115.

67 Chin, *Wang*, 4:110-111.

68 *Ibid.*, 4:114-115. Wang's intimate followers Ch'en Kung-po, Ch'u Min-i, Lin Pai-sheng, Mei Ssu-p'ing and 2,720 others were executed, and 2,300, including Chou Fo-hai and Ch'en Pi-chün, Wang's wife, were sentenced to life in prison. Thousands received jail sentences of a few years. Because most of these people were moderate elements in the Kuomintang, their elimination was indeed a fatal blow to the Nationalist government.

Part III

JAPAN

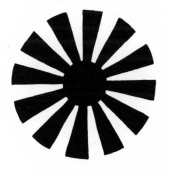

Japanese Diplomacy and Diplomats, 1919-1941

Japan's foreign policies in the twentieth century were concerned with erecting and consolidating the empire which had bloomed with the addition of the Bonin and Kurile Islands (1875), the Ryukyu Islands including Okinawa (1879), Formosa (1895), and Korea (1910). As the empire grew, Japan became increasingly interested in extending its influence onto the Asian mainland. Japanese diplomacy thus became more involved with that of the United States, Great Britain, Russia and, particularly, China. Japanese officials took advantage of the West's preoccupation with the war in Europe to demand (the infamous Twenty-One Demands of January 21, 1915) and receive preferential treatment and special privileges in China. At the Washington Conference (1922), Japanese diplomats yielded to a Western version of the Open Door for China (the Nine Power Pact) and retreated temporarily from their aggressive unilateral China policy.

Virtually all Japanese leaders, however, espoused some form of expansionism. Political and commercial leaders, including most of the diplomatic corps, favored the cultivation of friendly relations with competing nations and friendly persuasion to build a trading empire. Military activists and civilian zealots argued that Western nations would not willingly resign their markets and that force would be required to win and hold a commercial monopoly for Japan in Asia. Japan's foreign policies in the 1920's and 1930's reflected the struggle between these points of view as to which methods should be employed to secure Japan's international objectives.

Japanese diplomats were, as a consequence, forced to consider a bewildering array of political aspirations, illusions and contradictions pressed upon them by competing domestic institutions—grasping family cartels,

197

ambitious government bureaucrats, and zealous military officers. The *zaibatsu* (family trusts such as Mitsui, Mitsubishi, Sumitomo and Yasuda) dominated Japan's economy through their control of banking, commerce and industry. The new Constitution of 1889 imperfectly grafted Western political institutions and ideas on the traditional Japanese society and established a parliamentary form of government. During the interwar years the conservative Seiyukai and Kenseikai-Minseito parties struggled for control of the Diet. The Seiyukai had extensive rural support and both parties were heavily financed by the *zaibatsu*—the Seiyukai by Mitsui, Sumitomo and Yasuda; the Minseito by Mitsubishi. The economic overlords were powerful but they and their political agents ultimately lost control of the government to the military.

The military was politicized by the younger officers loyal to the Emperor and the empire rather than to the traditional military clans. These young officers felt abandoned by their government following the Army's abrupt and abortive withdrawal from Siberia and the "inferior" limitations imposed on the Imperial Navy. When Chinese nationalists challenged Japanese "guidance" in the 1920's, the military zealots accused the government of failing to defend the Emperor's honor and the empire's interests.

The military's rise to power in the 1930's was spurred by political terrorism at home and independent military operations abroad. The young officers supplemented and gradually expanded the activities of nonparliamentary forces. These illegal forces, steeped in ultranationalism and the general desperation brought on by the great Depression, took to the streets in protest and resorted to assassination to inhibit the diplomats and undermine popular government. The oriental Exclusion Law passed by the U.S. Congress in 1924 prohibited emigration and resulted in bitter anti-American demonstrations throughout Japan. For two decades, Japanese extremists pointed to this law to prove the American attitude was one of disdain based on racial superiority. The sporadic right-wing political terrorism was, however, more intimidating to civilian authorities. The political violence employed by the rightists was exemplified in the shooting of Prime Minister Hamaguchi, shortly after his endorsement of the London naval treaty, and the assassination of Prime Minister Inukai in May 1932. The most serious outburst was the "February 26th Affair" in 1936. Troops of the First Division led by junior officers seized the War Ministry and executed four senior government officials.

The rash behavior of the Kwantung army, located in the Liaotung Peninsula, also influenced Tokyo's foreign policy. The Mukden Incident of September 18, 1931, was plotted by its young officers as an excuse for the occupation of Manchuria and encroachment on Northern China. Other aggressive actions followed, notably the Shanghai Affair late in January 1932, which ostensibly resulted when the Mayor of Shanghai refused to end local boycotts of Japanese goods. The Imperial Navy bombarded the city, landed troops, and fighting continued for five weeks.

In the years that followed Japan used diplomatic and military means to extend the "Greater East Asia Co-prosperity Sphere" over East Asia. The militants gradually became more influential. By 1935 the Kwantung army and the South Manchurian Railway Company consolidated Japanese gains in North Asia and were the advocates of aggressive expansionism.

As the extremists' demands grew more strident, particularly the demand for Japanese "tutelage" over China, diplomacy became almost impossible. The United States and Great Britain, despite their own imperialistic pasts, staunchly defended an independent China and a territorial *status quo*. The challenge of this frustrating situation resulted in a seizure of power by Japan's militarists and, ultimately, in war.

*Sidney DeVere Brown**

Shidehara Kijūrō

The Diplomacy of the Yen

SHIDEHARA KIJŪRŌ devised the basic framework of Japan's foreign policy during the 1920's, and more than any other Japanese statesman, he shaped his country's response to Asian problems. Between the dawn of his career in 1896 and its twilight in 1931, Shidehara earned such pre-eminence in his nation's foreign affairs that his name became associated with an entire era of Japanese diplomacy. That diplomacy, formulated while Shidehara directed the Foreign Ministry (*Gaimushō*) during six of the seven Cabinets from June 1924 to December 1931, was essentially an economic diplomacy giving the highest priority to the search for markets.[1] Appropriate to an era in which Japanese capitalism came of age, Shidehara diplomacy largely replaced the older "force" diplomacy which stressed Japan's territorial control over strategic spots in China. While the prospect of profit prevailed, Shidehara's friendship policy toward China made him popular in his homeland. But when the waves of the great world-wide depression rolled in, they undermined the foundations of Shidehara diplomacy both in China and Japan.

It is an historical irony that Japanese policy regarding Manchuria figured so dramatically in Shidehara's career. The future Foreign Minister traced his choice of a diplomatic career to the triple intervention against Japan in April 1895. Like his fellow students at Tokyo Imperial University that spring, Shidehara expressed indignation at the humiliation of Japan by Russia, Germany, and France. Unlike most other critics, however, he believed that forced retrocession of the Manchurian Liaotung peninsula to China

*The author wishes to acknowledge with gratitude assistance extended by the Oklahoma State University Research Foundation.

called not so much for a military remedy as for better mastery of the same
diplomatic rules and tactics that the European powers employed to thwart
Japan. Guided by a sense of personal destiny to promote the national
interests, Shidehara overcame a serious illness after graduation to take and
pass the recently inaugurated foreign service examinations. In 1896 he
entered on a career that made him one of Japan's first professional
diplomats.[2] If the problem of Manchuria initially stirred his desire to be a
diplomat, a later manifestation of the same problem—the 1931 Mukden
Incident—prematurely terminated his professional career.

Internal forces beyond the control of any Japanese diplomat gathered
to destroy Shidehara's work. To the end the Foreign Minister remained the
master negotiator with foreign adversaries, but in the difficult year of 1931
he lacked the means, or perhaps the desire, to win support from domestic
antagonists for his policy. Part of the trouble lay in his elitist disposition.
Although the newly formed political parties provided him with his Cabinet
seat, the aloof Shidehara regarded diplomacy as an Imperial prerogative above
the tempest of party battles. Since he would not join in political partisanship,
he had no base of power from which to rally support when he and his policies
met their greatest challenge at Mukden on the night of September 18, 1931.
Moreover, at this point Shidehara seemed to lack the will to seek such
support. Thus, in those last months he often appeared before the world as an
apologist for the men responsible for undermining his ten years of laborious
diplomacy.

I

The internationalist emphasis in foreign policy was predominant in June 1924
when Shidehara (1872-1951) moved into the aging brick building at
Kasumigaseki to take charge of the Foreign Ministry's 300 employees. He
brought to his Tokyo office greater knowledge and feeling for the
international law of the Western society of nations than did any of his
predecessors. As Japan neared the long-sought goal of respectability in the
community of the Great Powers, late Taishō Japan turned towards the West.
Shidehara in the role of Foreign Minister was eager to adjust policy to this
new orientation.

In his near-foreign dress, Shidehara looked the part of the Westernized
diplomat. A slightly prognathic smile beneath his large, closely clipped black
mustache and rimless glasses suggested a quiet confidence and unruffled
approach to negotiations. His witty repartee, so different from the taciturnity
of traditional Japanese diplomats, delighted Westerners and facilitated talks.
Shidehara was the perfect representative of Taishō Japan's dominant elites.

How had he achieved such a position? What forces shaped his
development? Japan's new public education system, for one thing, provided

this son of peasants with a ticket of admission to the establishment, the prestigious civil bureaucracy. If diplomatic service abroad made him something of an Anglophile, an advantageous marriage allied him with the *zaibatsu,* Japan's plutocracy. To the country at large then, Baron Shidehara symbolized privilege, wealth and the West—assets in 1924 which proved to be handicaps by 1931.

Shidehara was not to the manner born; rather he possessed the assurance of the self-made man who has known humble origins. He was a man of talent who took advantage of the greater social mobility provided by the Meiji leaders' ideology of merit. Their new public school system put a government primary school in the somnolent hamlet near Osaka where Shidehara was born on August 11, 1872, and the school smoothed the path of escape from the hamlet confines.[3] An unusual and ambitious father also contributed to the children's success. Theirs was the ranking family in the hamlet, and the elder Shidehara shut the family gate to children of cruder speech while enforcing a rigid study discipline on his own progeny. Indeed, the father took the extreme step of selling half the family's land to educate his sons properly, not an easy thing to arrange in view of his status as a *yōshi,* an adopted-in husband. Funds thus acquired allowed Kijūrō, the second son, to join his elder brother in the select student body of the Osaka Middle School which ultimately fed students to Tokyo Imperial University.[4]

Along these prestigious rungs of the educational ladder, Shidehara consolidated friendships with future members of Japan's ruling caste. One early schoolmate became manager of Sumitomo Trust Company, one of the Big Four *zaibatsu* combines; another became Prime Minister. The future Prime Minister was Hamaguchi Osachi, Shidehara's chief rival for first class rank at the Third Higher School in Kyoto. Shidehara won the honor, but principally because the intellectually abler Hamaguchi was frail in body and inept in physical education. Together Shidehara and Hamaguchi graduated from Tokyo Imperial University in 1895 (the twenty-eighth year of the Meiji era); they both entered the civil bureaucracy—the former at the Foreign Office, the latter at the Finance Ministry—and they frequented the monthly dinners of the Twenty-Eight Club with their former classmates. Unsurprisingly, Prime Minister Hamaguchi called on his lifelong friend to take the Foreign Minister's portfolio in 1929.

School provided connections, but in addition it allowed Shidehara to cultivate English and to study law—all of which he parlayed into a successful foreign service career. Knowledge of English dictated that the foreign diplomats he knew well were Britons and Americans; it also determined that he should have overseas assignments primarily with the Anglo-Saxon powers (1897-1899, 1911-1913 in London; 1913-1914, 1919-1922 in Washington). This sympathy with England and the English, in particular, made Shidehara a central figure in the powerful Anglo-American clique at the *Gaimushō.*

It was partly by chance that Shidehara learned English. The American teacher at the Osaka Middle School made Shidehara his protegé at the very first class meeting when the eager youth advanced the irrelevant reply, "See ze moon!" as the rest of the baffled class kept silence. An assignment to England in 1897 permitted Shidehara to polish his spoken English, and on his return home, daily association with the American adviser at the Foreign Office, Henry W. Denison, provided the opportunity for perfecting these skills. Shidehara took long, early morning walks around the palace moat with Denison to practice English. He also acquired from Denison a sharper understanding of the intricacies of international law and a firm idea of the meticulous attention to fine shades of meaning required in diplomatic correspondence. Shidehara noted admiringly that Denison had made as many as ten drafts of each of the notes Foreign Minister Komura Jutarō employed to win sympathy for Japan on the eve of the Russo-Japanese War. Shidehara followed Denisons's example, not only in his official Japanese correspondence but also in the diplomatic papers which he drafted in English with a well-thumbed Webster close at hand. By chance he had first studied English; by preseverance he learned it well—surprisingly well—for one who never formally studied abroad. Pride in accomplishment begot overconfidence only once: Shidehara confessed authorship of the "grave consequences" note that so angered senators when submitted by Ambassador Hanihara Masanao just before passage of the 1924 Japanese exclusion legislation.[5]

England, rather than America, commanded Shidehara's greatest admiration. He liked England for her excellent newspapers, suave diplomats, and vigorous life-style. The accurate, restrained reporting of the London *Times* seemed to him to prevent diplomatic crises; Japan, he believed, needed such a paper. The cool professionalism of his personal friends among English diplomats, Lord Bryce and Sir Edward Grey, also attracted Shidehara, and he envied them the secure position that English tradition created in Parliament and public opinion. Foreign Secretary Grey, when asked in Parliament what he planned to do about the murder of an English oil company superintendent in Mexico, replied calmly, "Nothing!", for intervention might provoke conflict with the United States. "If I had made such a reply," wrote Shidehara, "I would have been killed thrice over. How I envy him!"[6] The composure of England's Ambassador to the United States, Lord Bryce, likewise impressed the young Counselor at the Japanese embassy in Washington in 1913. Bryce admonished Shidehara never to press minor claims so zealously as to threaten major conflict, as in the dispute over California's anti-Japanese land ownership laws. In his own case Bryce told the young Japanese official that England would do no more than register formal protest at the treaty-violating Panama Canal tolls. One did not protest excessively unless war was planned, and fighting the United States over such a trivial issue was unthinkable. Furthermore, continued the elderly Ambassador, American history taught that Americans invariably righted the wrongs they inflicted on foreign powers.[7]

Perhaps it was the political maturity of England that allowed these diplomats to act with such detachment and assurance. Shidehara knew this English lifestyle intimately. England was the land where ordinary working-men had the wit and knowledge to challenge learned lecturers, as Shidehara observed at Toynbee Hall. It was the country where parents disciplined their sons to self-reliance—Shidehara's landlord sent his sixteen-year-old son off to South Africa with only enough money to advertise for a position in the Capetown papers.

The American model was less attractive to Shidehara than the English one. California exclusionists were forever making trouble. Moreover, America's shirt-sleeved diplomats did not measure up to their English counterparts. The handwritten notes that Secretary of State William Jennings Bryan dropped off at the Japanese embassy on the way home from work stirred wry amusement in the Japanese legation, especially when harried State Department officials turned up at the Japanese embassy the next day to find out what their own chief had said. The young Japanese Counselor laughed at Bryan's casual business procedures, his confusion of titles in the Japanese peerage, and his uncertainty in face-to-face negotiations—no matter how great his reputation was as an orator. This was not the only instance of Shidehara's criticism of American politicians as diplomats; but for all that, Shidehara got on well with Americans, and Americans liked him. "His attitude toward the United States is particularly friendly," advised Ambassador George W. Guthrie on Shidehara's appointment as Vice Foreign Minister in 1915.[8]

Long service abroad did not denationalize Shidehara, however, and he often repeated Denison's analogy of the Nile, warning against excessive fondness for the West. Only when the Blue Nile bearing decomposed animal bodies joined the White Nile filled with decaying plants and trees did the alluvial soil deposited by the annual flood become fertile, Denison explained. Neither was a complete fertilizer by itself. So with Japan and the West. The revival of national traditions by Tani Kanjō and others in the 1890's had produced a cultural stream which combined with the Rokumeikan group's stream of Westernization to give harmony and strength to the country.[9]

Though the Western orientation predominated over the national in his world-view, Shidehara had not failed to absorb the spirit of Emperor-centered nationalism that accompanied Japan's march to great power status. Nor is this surprising, for Shidehara grew up in country sacred to the patriot. From the study in his childhood home he could see the shrine of Kusunoki Masashige which marked the spot where Japan's premier patriot died in 1336 in defense of the legitimate Southern line of Japanese sovereigns. At the university,

Shidehara's mentor, Professor Hozumi Nobushige (Yatsuka), "the grand old man of the Law Faculty," was the chief proponent of the theory of Imperial absolutism and national integrity. Shidehara was too rational a man to adopt such a mystical theory of the state, but his sponsor's identification nevertheless influenced his own views. He did, at least, take pride in serving as a member of the Emperor's entourage for the traditional Shinto coronation ceremonies at Kyoto in 1915.

Shidehara's reverence for the Throne partially explains the paradox in Shidehara diplomacy. The Foreign Minister resisted that aspect of the People's Diplomacy Movement of the 1920's which sought to democratize the diplomatic service even while he accepted the movement's call for a change in the content of diplomacy (e.g., ending the "force" diplomacy exemplified by the Siberian intervention). Shidehara always maintained that diplomacy was an Imperial prerogative. Someone had to advise the Throne, and Shidehara insisted that professionals, not generals or party politicians, should do the advising. This attitude reflected the confidence and *esprit de corps* of the whole Foreign Ministry bureaucracy.[10]

Although Shidehara advocated "diplomacy transcending parties and factions," as Foreign Minister he practiced an economic diplomacy roughly shaped to fit the big business pressure group interest in Kenseikai and later in the Minseitō. The Mitsubishi combine was considered the principal financial angel to the Kenseikai-Minseitō, and the Katō Takaakira Cabinets (1924-1926) were referred to, not inaccurately, as Mitsubishi Cabinets. Both the Prime Minister and the Foreign Minister were brothers-in-law to Iwasaki Hisaya, Mitsubishi president since his father's death in 1893. Katō married the eldest daughter of the Mitsubishi founder, Iwasaki Yatarō, and Shidehara later wed the youngest daughter, Masako. The one marriage led directly to the other. It was Katō's wife who introduced her sister to the rising young Foreign Service officer in London where the girl was a student and Shidehara was a minor functionary under Ambassador Katō. Young Shidehara had been courting an English girl at the time, but he readily forsook her for an alliance of such position and wealth. The salary of Foreign Minister in 1924 was only 8000 yen (less than $4000), but by reason of his marriage Shidehara enjoyed life in an elaborate mansion and garden that had once belonged to a famous shogun's adviser. This is not to say that Shidehara used his position improperly to further Mitsubishi's purposes; indeed, no taint of financial scandal ever touched him. But he lived and breathed the purpose of the Mitsubishi combine as family ties reinforced party interest.[11]

II

Several themes ran through Shidehara diplomacy, but fundamental to them all was the advancement of Japan's national interest as defined by the bourgeois groups. As a result of this broad commitment to economic development, Shidehara diplomacy came to be identified with three major concerns: disarmament, international cooperation, and non-interference in China.

Disarmament, to Shidehara's mind, implied not mere limitation but "substantial reduction of armaments," as the 1929 Minseitō platform phrased it.[12] This befitted the retrenchment philosophy of Japanese political parties in that era. Arms reduction, in the form it took at the naval disarmament conference in Washington and in London, also promised to diminish tensions with Japan's major trading partners. Shidehara therefore belittled talk of a naval war with the United States. "America is Japan's best customer," he once observed. "One does not fight with his best customer."[13]

A second, closely-related theme was Shidehara's concept of international cooperation with the great powers of the West; this posture, however, was intended to support rather than surrender Japan's vital interests. The Foreign Minister ended a famous 1927 address to the Diet with a ringing endorsement of this principle, urging "that the wisest course for us to follow is to extend honest friendship to all nations."[14] "Honest friendship" in practice meant adherence to the multilateral international agreements of the era—e.g., the Washington Conference treaties. It involved Japan in international organizations such as the League of Nations. It involved prominent Japanese individuals in organized efforts to adjust international disputes by law. (In 1928 Shidehara was chief judge of a five-man panel convened under the German-American arbitration-conciliation treaty.) Basic to this diplomatic philosophy was the concept of an international morality binding all nations and promoting settlement of difficulties at the diplomatic conference table (where Shidehara was so adroit). Specifically, Shidehara ruled out Japan's isolationist tradition of seeking national solutions to foreign policy issues. Morality, however, also coincided with interest, for internationalism brought Japan closer to the West, which promised the greatest trading profits.

The third theme, non-interference in China, likewise had an economic thrust, for China represented an underdeveloped market of awesome potential. Japan's difficult relations with that troubled nation, struggling for political integrity, preoccupied Shidehara. His friendship policy in this sphere was designed to avert the anti-Japanese focus of Chinese nationalism. Based on the assumption that he had found in Chiang Kai-shek a moderate nationalist who would allow Japan to retain her most important economic rights, Shidehara sought to conciliate these authentic nationalists who respected Japanese property and trade with a policy of "live-and-let-live." Outrages against Japanese who were caught in the path of advancing revolutionary armies called not for gunboats but rather for patience and understanding to facilitate the coming of national unity. "We in Japan are industrial producers," Shidehara explained, "and we cannot live unless we have outlets. A China pacified and on the road to progress would be for us a market of priceless value. Far from wanting to see it feeble and divided, we want to see it strong, united, and prosperous."[15]

The focus then of Shidehara diplomacy was primarily economic. Money fairly jingled in the background. Flexible on political issues, Shidehara and his agents were sharp bargainers on economic issues. They proposed, for example, to allow China tariff autonomy under some formula that would leave Japan's trade pattern largely undisturbed. The memory of these negotiations, however, may have deterred the Chinese from believing another favorite Shidehara concept—that political co-existence led to mutual prosperity. The idea that Japanese capital and technical expertise could combine with Chinese resources and education to the benefit of both nations died for want of Chinese interest. Although there was talk of a joint automobile company sponsored by Datsun, such private ventures supported by Shidehara came to naught.

These failures reveal another characteristic of Shidehara diplomacy, one that recent revisionist historians have found ironic. Despite a professed, idealistic concern for China's self-determination, Japan set aside a hard core of territorial rights and interests, particularly in Manchuria, which even Shidehara did not intend to relinquish.[16] Shidehara diplomacy was in this respect the ultimate heir to the legacy of Japanese imperialism and fated to bear its imprint.[17] Shidehara himself felt obliged to defend "Japan's legitimate and essential interests" vigorously as the Minseitō party government came increasingly under domestic fire in 1931.

III

The Washington Conference in 1921-22 unveiled Shidehara diplomacy in embryo. Ambassador Shidehara's aim of moderating Japanese policies spoke neither for party, nor for Mitsubishi or the Iwasaki family, but for the professional diplomatic corps. That this was not a personal policy so much as the consensus of the mainstream *Gaimushō* is suggested by the fact that Shidehara was a negotiator but not a formulator of policy. Still, the main outlines of the Shidehara diplomacy were becoming clear: support for naval disarmament, the Open Door, and conciliation of China. His contribution at Washington was in the deft execution of policy rather than the personal shaping of policy content.

Washington projected Shidehara onto the world stage.[18] The bumbling Prince Tokugawa Iesato served as titular head of the Japanese delegation, but Shidehara, the senior professional Japanese diplomat present, quickly became the best-known Japanese. His speeches and his interviews were in English;

moreover, he revealed a gifted sense of public relations.[19] Unlike the Japanese Ambassador in London who announced that Japan was an "unwilling guest" at the conference, Shidehara—whatever he thought privately—told the press that Japan entered "wholeheartedly and with confidence."[20] Moreover, Shidehara softened American hostility toward the militaristic Japanese by a clever ploy in image projection. It was on Shidehara's advice that the grim, medal-bedecked Admiral Katō Tomosaburō somewhat reluctantly donned civilian clothes to stand in his open auto smiling and waving at welcoming multitudes along the streets in Washington. Ever after Katō was remembered by Americans as the "charming admiral," though in Japan his reputation was quite the opposite.

Tokugawa, Katō, and Shidehara worked conjointly on the several problems on the conference agenda dealing with naval limitation, the Pacific islands, and Japanese rights in China. When division of labor was indicated, Shidehara became Japan's advocate. He knew the diplomatic maneuver of the conference table, and he sensed how to please Westerners with arguments firmly grounded in international law. He presented the lawyer's case to preserve as much as possible while Japan beat a strategic retreat from its overextended World War I position.

Lacking technical expertise, Shidehara played a peripheral role in the important naval disarmament negotiations in Washington. Admiral Katō presented Japan's case on this crucial issue, and the Navy Minister regarded the compromise as a Japanese victory in that Japan was assured of nonfortification of the Pacific Islands in return for acquiesence in the inferior part of the 5:5:3 ratio for capital ships. The admiral had feared that Guam was destined to be another Heligoland.* Typically, Shidehara then successfully pressed the lawyer's case that the seven islands of Izu should be exempted from the nonfortification clause on the grounds that administratively these scraps of territory belonged to Tokyo's metropolitan district. Such minor victories did little to allay the smoldering discontent of several naval officers in the Japanese entourage over 5:5:3. The fierce glare that Vice Admiral Katō Kanji gave his naval superior at the ceremony for affixing signatures on December 15, 1921, did not suggest future harmony. Later, during the London Naval Disarmament Conference of 1930, Shidehara would hear from the unreconciled Admiral Katō Kanji, by then Chief of the Naval General Staff.[21]

Shidehara played a central role in Washington in forging the Four-Power Treaty on Pacific problems. He served as Japan's chief spokesman at the secret talks held by delegation heads for transmutation of the

*Heligoland housed an impregnable naval base for the Imperial German battle fleet prior to and during World War I.

Anglo-Japanese Alliance into the Four-Power Treaty. The agreement stipulated mutual consultation over threats to the peace in the "insular possessions and insular dominions" of the powers in the Pacific area (but not in the continental Far East). The treaty, a reduction to the least common denominator, was "amiable politeness," but it did avert Japan's full isolation and preserved in small measure the prestigious tie with England.

In working toward this treaty, Ambassador Shidehara displayed a sensitivity keenly tuned to the requirements of American domestic politics. He knew how Americans felt about alliances. He had sought unsuccessfully to assure Secretary of State Charles Evans Hughes of the innocence of the Anglo-Japanese Alliance. "By no stretch of the imagination," wrote Ambassador Shidehara, "can it be honestly stated that the Alliance was ever designed or remotely intended as an instrument of hostility or even defense against the United States."[22] Failing to convince Hughes, Shidehara prepared some of the drafts that reshaped the alliance into a consultative pact with United States membership. Furthermore, when it was evident that French inclusion would win Senate votes, Shidehara agreed, for he recognized that in the aura of Marshal Foch's recent triumphant tour of the United States anything French added strength, however minor France's Pacific interests.

One Senate dispute Shidehara was able to turn to his own advantage. Despite his objections Hughes had included the Japanese home islands in the area covered by the treaty. The powerful and conservative Foreign Affairs Council in Japan immediately complained of the "national dishonor" implicit in Japan's position as the only one of the four powers to have its homeland included. Fortunately, the Senate professed to see in this an undue, favored position for the Japanese. One nationalism cancelled the other, and Shidehara was spared a home-front controversy with United States agreement to the exclusion of Japan proper from the treaty.[23]

As the conference turned from Pacific islands to continental China, Shidehara had the opportunity to present an early version of his China conciliation policy. He subscribed readily to the Nine-Power Open Door Treaty, for Japan's purpose in 1922 lay in ending Chinese boycotts, not in securing a protected market in some sphere of influence. Equality of commercial opportunity seemed to favor Japan. "We had no fear about our commerce and industry competing with foreign enterprise," he said. "Japan, in fact, occupied an advantageous position."[24]

No aspect of the conference foreshadowed the shape of later Shidehara diplomacy so much as the Ambassador's handling of the Shantung controversy. Shidehara's forte lay in resolving specific disputes. He realized that for emotional issues such as Shantung, private bilateral talks would be more fruitful than open sessions of the whole conference. For one thing he aimed to muffle the English-language eloquence of Wellington Koo and others who stirred strong support for the Chinese cause among reporters and the public. Shidehara expected his legalistic arguments to have more appeal in the small, two-way sessions with only official observers present, and those mostly Anglo-Saxons conscious of property rights. Although he made obeisance to the principle of China's territorial integrity, the Ambassador was careful to protect Japanese property holdings. The Japanese, who kept the Shantung Railway after World War I, did however consent to return the Kiaochow Leased Territory, including the valuable Tsingtao naval anchorage, and to withdraw their troops from Shantung "as soon as possible."[25] Thus Shidehara traded the political shadow for economic substance while resolving an issue that had threatened to break up the conference.

Shantung was a microcosm of the China problem Shidehara faced during his first term as Foreign Minister (June 1924-April 1927), and the Shantung solution foreshadowed his response to the more intense anti-imperialism of the Kuomintang during its Northern Expedition. Shidehara's term coincided with the period of Comintern aid to the Kuomintang government in Canton and the beginning of the northward military movement which ultimately unified China. The problem, as Shidehara saw it, was how to preserve some remnant of Japanese rights and interests in China while avoiding the full fury of the Chinese rights recovery movement. Largely he succeeded.

Japan's World War I policy of meddling in China's domestic politics had failed disastrously. After 1924, therefore, Shidehara categorically rejected the wartime policy of determining China's political leadership with the use or threat of force. The experience convinced Shidehara that China's disunity was not necessarily Japan's opportunity; he recognized that it lay beyond the power of any outside nation to select China's political leadership even in a time of turmoil. He proposed neither to prop up Japanese puppets nor destroy anti-Japanese regimes for such a policy was impracticable in so large and diverse a country as China. Crushing a single government with anti-Japanese proclivities would not make China safe for Japanese interests, particularly since China was not a nation with a single center like Japan with Tokyo or the United States and New York. "China is a nation of many hearts," he asserted, "and no matter how many you kill, there will always be one beating."[26]

Foreign Minister Shidehara proclaimed his principle of non-interference in China in his very first policy address to the Diet in 1924. "We have no intention whatever of interfering in questions of internal politics," he announced. That this was not mere rhetoric is witnessed by Japan's two early refusals to aid a client warlord, Chang Tso-lin, in Manchuria. Once when the Katō Cabinet was disposed to intervene on the Old Marshal's behalf, Shidehara thwarted the attempt by threatening to resign.

A corollary of the non-intervention principle was minimal use of force for protection of Japanese nationals and their property in China. Shidehara relied mostly on local Chinese powerholders to provide a modicum of security for the vulnerable Japanese. In 1925 Shidehara refused to commit troops to protect Japanese-owned textile mills in Shanghai and Tsinan against destructive strikes on the grounds that interference only provoked more agitation. In a typical maneuver, he compromised with the Chinese provincial governor who suppressed "outside agitators" at the mills in return for the Foreign Minister's promise to encourage Japanese mill owners to improve terms of employment for Chinese laborers.[27]

The Nanking Incident of March 24, 1927, provided the most severe test of the Shidehara policy of restraint in that it jeopardized Japanese lives as well as property. Ill-disciplined units of the advancing Chinese Kuomintang Army deliberately killed several foreigners at Nanking including some Japanese residents. Despite the provocation, nearby Japanese gunboats held their fire although the warships of Great Britain and the United States commenced bombardment to screen the escape of their nationals. Shidehara always disclaimed personal responsibility for Japan's failure to retaliate on the spot. Rather, it was the nervous Japanese residents of Nanking, with the Nikolaevsk massacre of their fellow-countrymen fresh in memory, who had requested the senior Japanese naval officer not to open fire, lest a similar fate befall them. The episode nonetheless reflected the spirit of Shidehara diplomacy.

Shidehara subsequently refused to endorse an ultimatum by the three powers for prompt payment of damages sustained during the outrage. His rationale was pragmatic. Japan had more to lose through the inevitable reaction than the other powers. Whatever might happen to the few Englishmen and Americans present, the 100,000 Japanese in China could not all flee the country at once, and they were bound to suffer more than the other foreigners. Privately, the Japanese may have hoped to turn the anti-English movement to their advantage by standing apart.[28]

Shidehara's moderation had another objective. While he refused to intervene in any positive or forceful way in China's troubles, he was not adverse to interfering in a negative manner if, by inaction, he would help "sound elements" win the upper hand in the Kuomintang. Saburi Sadao, who made a confidential reconnaissance of South China for Shidehara in late 1926, concluded that Chiang Kai-shek might be less difficult to deal with than the Kuomintang with its howling anti-imperialist slogans. Thereafter, Chiang enhanced his image as a responsible nationalist by ordering his troops to respect the safety of foreign nationals and by assuring the Japanese privately that their loans and enterprises would be protected. As for Nanking, Shidehara subscribed to the unproved charge that Communist-controlled troops had assassinated the foreigners in order to embarrass Chiang. He therefore argued that the British proposals for active military measures to obtain recompense would simply "discredit Chiang Kai-shek while the more radical elements of the Nationalist party might gain the ascendency."[29]

This conciliation policy as it had evolved by 1927 passed the decisive tests of Chinese acceptance and general public support within Japan. It was essentially a policy of dealing firmly, but in a friendly manner, with local powerholders (of whom Chiang was one) to protect Japanese economic interests in China. Home newspapers gave Shidehara high marks, before Nanking at least. A *New York Times* reporter wrote, "Scarcely any newspaper has a good word for the Administration as a whole, yet all endorse Baron Shidehara's methods of handling the China situation and virtually all comment published throughout the country is aimed at encouraging his policy of independent friendship with the South."[30] In China, Chiang was shortly to greet the Japanese Minister as "dear friend," and Nanking crowds gave the visitor a rousing reception as they sang the Japanese national anthem.[31]

There were early warnings, however, that the conciliation policy which pleased Nanking might not sustain a domestic clientele in Japan for long. A harbinger of things to come was the savage attack on the Shidehara policy in the Privy Council on April 17, 1927, the eve of the fall of the Kenseikai government. The Privy Council was ostensibly debating the constitutionality of the government's controversial proposals to save the Bank of Taiwan from collapse. But Count Itō Miyoji, an angry nationalist, used this forum in the Emperor's presence to deride Shidehara for allegedly suppressing publication of stories about Chinese atrocities inflicted on Japanese nationals in Nanking. Shidehara denied the charge, but Itō's attack reflected the tenor of rising Privy Council displeasure at Shidehara's "weak and irresolute" posture—even as the Kenseikai Cabinet fell for other reasons.

IV

By 1930 Privy Council ultranationalists were more in tune with the mood of the country in expressing discontent over ratification of the London Naval Disarmament Treaty. The naval limitation treaty won approval, but the domestic political upheaval precipitated by the debate caused the death of Prime Minister Hamaguchi and ultimately destroyed the viability of Shidehara diplomacy.

The more rigorous policy of Prime Minister Tanaka Giichi, who doubled as Foreign Minister, separated the happy first phase of Shidehara diplomacy from its tragic conclusion. The aims of Shidehara and Tanaka may not have differed markedly, but the means of execution were widely divergent. In diplomacy, where symbolism is often as important as substance, Tanaka's "rough approach" to "protection of our nationals on the spot" in China contributed a symbolic element that exacerbated national hostilities in both Japan and China. If Tanaka's ill-fated Shantung intervention angered the Chinese because it took place, it incensed Japanese patriots because it failed. The legacy of this positive policy proved a heavy burden for Shidehara, once again returned to Kasumigaseki, as he tried to revive the friendship policy toward China and international cooperation with the West.[32]

With restricted room to maneuver, Shidehara devised a priority system to maximize opportunities for success. He proposed starting with the most tractable problem, the question of China's tariff autonomy, before dealing with naval limitation and finally Manchuria, where economic warfare had broken out between the Chinese and Japanese railways.

The Sino-Japanese Tariff Convention of January 13, 1930, presented substantial Japanese concessions to Chinese demands. That China would have tariff autonomy was a foregone conclusion; Shidehara, however, held out for some protection of Japanese textiles and finally settled for a three-year Chinese tariff schedule instead of the ten-year schedule he had first sought. China made a few concessions regarding debt consolidation and internal taxes, but press reports from China cast a pall over Sino-Japanese relations. Chinese rumor had it that Minister Saburi Sadao had been so distraught over his country's inflexible attitude at one point that he committed suicide. (Shidehara, who hurried to the scene at Hakone, contended that his protege, a "champion sculler," had been murdered while on a "rowing holiday.") Moreover, the Chinese government, contrary to protocol, refused to accept as Saburi's successor Obata Yūkichi, legation Counselor at the time of the Twenty-One Demands in 1915. Such reactions led the Japanese Privy Council to condemn the government's recent conciliatory China policy even as the council ratified the tariff treaty.

Certainly the Privy Council's tone did not augur well for the London Naval Limitation Treaty then in the process of negotiation and destined to be signed on April 22, 1930. The growing right wing capitalized on the naval treaty issue to build influence, and the bruising five-and-a-half month struggle for ratification provided a classic confrontation between the political right or hard-line militarists on the one hand and the supporters of Shidehara diplomacy, Prime Minister Hamaguchi Osachi, the surviving *Genrō,* and the *zaibatsu,* on the other.[33]

Shidehara made the London treaty cause his own, and his position was a powerful one since he controlled the preparation of instructions for the Japanese delegation. Prime Minister Hamaguchi, the courageous "lion" of Japanese politics, also elected to press personally for the treaty. He regarded agreement with the great Western financial powers on the naval issue as indispensable to the success of his own serious efforts to return Japan to the gold standard (i.e., lifting the gold embargo). The good relations resulting from extension of naval limitation to auxiliary vessels, Hamaguchi thought, would allow Japan to obtain credit in London and New York when the gold embargo terminated. Furthermore, reduction of naval expenditures would enable Japan to become price competitive in the ensuing struggle for markets. Foreign Minister Shidehara, for his part, concluded that he had "no alternative but to endure all criticism" in pressing for compromise on naval ratios with the United States and Great Britain.[34]

Compromise would not be easy, however, if the Japanese Naval General Staff had its way. As the conference neared, the Navy mounted an intensive public relations campaign to win domestic approval for its "three fundamental principles"—70 percent of United States tonnage for heavy cruisers (10,000 tons with 8-inch guns), 70 percent for auxiliary vessels, and 78,500 tons for submarines. The Navy based this demand on the 1923 Imperial Defense Policy which, it contended, required that in fixing building quotas for smaller ships Japan disregard the 5:5:3 ratio imposed at Washington for battleships and aircraft carriers. The Cabinet agreed to these principles, but conflict arose over whether 70 percent was to be an absolute standard or merely a rough estimate, subject to modification. Just eight days before the delegation sailed for London on December 4, 1929, the more flexible Foreign Ministry view prevailed that Japan should negotiate at the conference in accordance with the principle of "no threats—real reduction." Some elements in the navy, indeed, were unprepared to respond to any policy reducing limitations, since the capacity of Japanese shipyards was inferior to that of England or America and financial strength was considerably less.

The Japanese delegation bargained successfully at London to break through the 60 percent ceiling imposed in Washington.[35] As a practical matter it won many but not all of the demands of the Naval General Staff. The compromise pegged auxiliary vessels at 69.75 percent, barely below the 70 percent figure stipulated by the United States. Heavy cruisers remained in the 60 percent category, but the United States promised not to build up to treaty limits, thus giving Japan an effective 70 percent. Submarines were at parity but at 52,700 tons, not the 78,500 tons requested. When the Naval Chief of Staff, Admiral Katō Kanji, objected to signing "on the basis of our requirements for military tactics and strategy," Prime Minister Hamaguchi ordered the delegates to affix their signatures. In justification, the Prime Minister voiced Shidehara's fear that Japan could not afford isolation from the West with the crisis building in China. Hamaguchi also explained his course in terms of domestic social policy. "Today, when there is a critical need for tax reduction, for a social policy, and for unemployment relief," he asserted, "I do not—for the sake of the country—choose to sacrifice everything for a naval race." Accordingly, the Japanese delegates, including Admiral Takarabe Takeshi, the Naval Minister, joined in signing the treaty on April 22, 1930.

Those signatures precipitated a ratification dispute that the Hamaguchi Cabinet barely won, even by mobilizing all its resources. Hamaguchi had to fight on the enemy's ground, on the Supreme Command issue, rather than on the sufficiency or insufficiency of Japan's naval protection. The radical nationalist Kita Ikki had coined the very effective slogan, "non-interference with the Supreme Command." This provided firm ground for the Naval Chief of Staff's protest resignation. Admiral Katō contended that it was the role of the military forces, not the civilian Cabinet, to advise the Emperor on the size and composition of the armed forces. Article XI of the Constitution entrusted the Emperor with the Supreme Command, and Katō argued that the Naval Chief of Staff should advise the ruler directly, not through the Cabinet. The Cabinet, which had arbitrarily signed the London Treaty against Admiral Katō's professional judgment, had thus interfered with the Supreme Command. Moreover, the Grand Chamberlain at the Palace had committed a second offense against the Supreme Command. Retired Admiral Suzuki Kantarō had refused to permit Katō to see the Emperor on this matter ahead of Prime Minister Hamaguchi. The Cabinet, however, rested its case on the contention (based on Professor Minobe Ryōkichi's interpretation of Article XII of the Constitution) that the size of the navy was a political problem that concerned only the Cabinet, not the Naval General Staff.

Hamaguchi pressed for ratification with the knowledge that the navy was internally divided. Navy Minister Takarabe had reluctantly signed in London, but when hard-policy emissaries met him in Harbin, he refused to join their fight against the treaty. Indeed, he secretly passed word to Shidehara from Korea that he would stand firm. With that assurance the Prime Minister obtained the endorsement of the Supreme War Council, *Gunji sangikan kaigi.* There he had convinced the venerable Admiral Tōgō Heihachiro, victor at Tsushima Straits in 1905, to support the minority position by promising to speed up the replacement program in naval building (thereby sacrificing part of the tax reduction). Securing the approval of this military body, Hamaguchi moved against the nationalistic Privy Council clique,[36] which was seeking to extend its control over foreign policy formation. Standing firm on the need for good relations with the West in face of a menacing China problem, Hamaguchi won Supreme Council approval on October 1, 1930. As Shidehara observed, the Council initially "sniffed like a hare" at the treaty but gave in "like a maiden" at the end.

The government paid a large price for this victory. Though it had come to power promising a "social policy" for poorer, newly-enfranchised voters, it had done little to keep the promise, preoccupied as it was with the London treaty question. Now the effects of world depression struck Japan, finding Hamaguchi unprepared. Moreover, strong emotions that had surfaced during the long treaty fight culminated in an ultranationalist assassination attempt on the Prime Minister at Tokyo station on December 14, 1930. The would-be assassin, a member of the Society of Patriots, blamed Shidehara equally with Hamaguchi for Japan's disgrace at London, claiming in his apologia that he would also have shot the Foreign Minister had not Shidehara been elsewhere in the station seeing off Ambassador Hirota Kōki to Moscow.

Acting as Prime Minister during the wounded Hamaguchi's convalescence, Shidehara could barely control the Diet. Opposition Seiyūkai party leaders heckled him unmercifully for each slip of the tongue, and ultranationalists such as Diet member Nakajima Chikuhei (of the aircraft firm family) continued to bait him on the Supreme Command question. Shidehara only saved himself from a crouching, partially hidden assailant at a crowded budget committee hearing by kicking the man (a lobbyist) in the forehead. Even members of the majority Minseitō were restive under the leadership of an elitist diplomat who refused formal membership in their party.

Lacking firm support Shidehara was ill-prepared to grapple with the Manchurian problem in 1931. As the focus of China's rights recovery movement shifted toward Manchuria, Shidehara stiffened his position slightly. But this moderate adjustment in the friendship policy for the major Diet address of January 21, 1931, satisfied neither his critics at home nor the Chinese. He extended "good wishes" to the Chinese government which he observed was "actually following the trail once blazed by Japan in her struggle to emerge from the position of international inequality"; he coupled sympathy with warning, however, cautioning China against bringing the South Manchurian Railway to "ruin"—a project in any case "hardly capable of ultimate realization."

Shidehara was less zealous about Manchuria than the late Prime Minister Tanaka and his successors, for the Foreign Minister regarded Manchuria as part of China, not as territory which might form a special Japanese-dominated political unit. Shidehara was a China-first man who believed that Japan must use her competitive advantage to develop the enormous potential market in intra-mural China rather than jeopardize it with a force policy designed to separate Manchuria. Tanaka had placed Manchuria first. If Japan could exploit the Manchurian investment field to the full, Tanaka believed, she would have the economic advantage plus control of an important strategic area.[37]

Shidehara's more moderate policy of merely preserving the economic *status quo* in Manchuria—the railway and other vested interests—while permitting Chinese political advance no longer seemed acceptable to the Chinese Foreign Minister. In 1931 Wang Cheng-ting called for extending the rights recovery movement into Manchuria, not excluding the South Manchurian Railway or the Kwangtung Leased Territory.

Shidehara's conciliation, therefore, seemed to domestic critics to be feeding the monster of Chinese demands. The Japanese government, consequently, lacked the political strength to make further concessions in China proper when Chargé Shigemitsu Mamoru pressed for more, not less, Shidehara diplomacy. "The Privy Council will use it [further concessions] as ammunition to bring the government down," explained the Foreign Minister.[38] Nationalists on the Privy Council found an increasing number of allies willing to attack Shidehara. Once friendly newspapers such as *Asahi Shimbun* now took Shidehara to task for his January Diet address which revealed "a mistaken understanding of the times." Thousands of small capitalists with investments in the private portion of stock in the South Manchurian Railway attributed a precipitous drop in earnings to illegal Chinese competition countenanced by Shidehara diplomacy. Japanese settlers in Manchuria added to the voices of criticism.[39] The ultimate source of the dissatisfaction, however, was the group of middle-rank officers of the Army General Staff and the Kwantung Army, already plotting to separate Manchuria from China, whether Shidehara agreed or not.[40]

What the leading army conspirator, Colonel Ishiwara Kanji, wanted was a Manchurian base to promote Japanese self-sufficiency for the "inevitable" war with the United States. Inevitable, thought Shidehara later, because envious and frustrated young officers made it so. Government retrenchment in the 1920's had not brought peace through lessened military expenditures, asserted the Foreign Minister, but only a demand from angry, impoverished, non-promoted officers for war and its attendant opportunities. In 1931 Shidehara diplomacy received the blame for that plight as well as the nation's. When it appeared that the Foreign Minister might negotiate settlements with China on the competing rail question, the Captain Nakamura affairs, and other matters in the summer of 1931, the conspirators acted. They struck at Mukden, even as the Chinese were becoming more flexible.[41]

The explosion that marked the Mukden Incident on the night of September 18, 1931, sounded "the funeral march for Shidehara diplomacy."[42] Shidehara continued in office three more months (Elder Statesman Saionji would not allow the Wakatsuki Cabinet to resign), but his effective control over foreign policy ended that night. He was at first optimistic that he might undo the *fait accompli,* but gradually he began to apologize for that which he could not prevent.

First, Shidehara looked to the men at the top of the army command structure for help. Shidehara remarked to War Minister Minami Jirō in a Cabinet meeting, "What has happened could not be helped, but what about the future? Is there any guarantee against escalation?" Minami retired from the room to confer; when he returned he pledged in writing, "It is guaranteed."[43] Minami made his promise in September, but on several subsequent occasions troops advanced in spite of Shidehara's assurances to the powers to the contrary. Apparently, neither Minami nor the Army Chief of Staff could restrain the rank and file.[44]

Next, Shidehara turned to the Emperor's closest advisers, to men such as Elder Statesman Saionji Kimmochi who praised Shidehara extravagantly and counted the veteran diplomat an "elder statesman for foreign policy." Early in October, indeed, there was talk that the court atmosphere was "suddenly unfavorable" to the Japanese Army, but Saionji did not invoke the Emperor's name for any dramatic moves. The Prince drifted with the current, and by November the moment for acting had passed. He told one general on November 18 that "though he had upheld the Shidehara diplomacy as the standard formula which was without danger . . . he had to reconsider it from the point of view of living diplomacy when the entire national opinion called it mistaken and wrong."[45]

Meanwhile, Shidehara had appealed to the Chinese for direct negotiations and to the outside powers for restraint. The Japanese Foreign Minister saw little need for an independent commission of the Great Powers "as he thought that Japan and China could settle amicably matters between them." But the Chinese Minister in Tokyo, an old friend, quickly disabused him of that notion. Their informal conversation during the Chrysanthemum Viewing Festival at Akasaka Detached Palace turned from the substantive matter of Manchuria to an innocuous discussion about Chinese calligraphy when other Chinese crowded in to spy on their own Minister engaged in private conversation with an important Japanese official. Formal bilateral talks were out of the question.[46]

Shidehara's call for restraint in the West won a better reception. Secretary of State Henry L. Stimson had received word from his listening posts of "a conflict between Shidehara and the military clique in Japan." When Shidehara passed along the message that his policy of "peace and friendship" toward China was "not . . . influenced by incidents brought about by military officers under the stress of excitement" in Chinchow, Stimson believed him. "My problem," wrote Stimson in his diary, "is to let the Japanese know that we are watching them and at the same time to do it in a way which will help Shidehara who is on the right side." Stimson wanted to give Shidehara a chance.

Given that chance, Shidehara unexpectedly changed his tone. His September philosophy urging conciliation of the West with promises that troops were "already returning to the railway zone" altered just a few weeks later to a position imposing strong terms on China as the prerequisite to troop withdrawal. Shidehara was now exploiting the leverage effect of the army's presence and position in Manchuria. On October 15, for example, he demanded China's agreement to five joint principles, among them a promise to recognize China's territorial rights in return for "discontinuance of government sanction of boycotts, discrimination against Japanese merchants, or other economic action injurious to the interests of Japan."[47] Withdrawal would take place after Chinese agreement, not prior to discussions. Shidehara now appeared before the world as apologist for the very militarists he despised.

V

There was an air of sadness about Shidehara as he shuffled off the stage of history. He procrastinated, he was vague, and he allowed "discrepancies" to come between promises and performance. Why so? Fear of assassination or the threat of a military coup may have stayed his hand. "If we had carried out a policy of strong suppression, Japan might have had a militarist revolution very quickly," he later asserted.[48] The abortive October plot of the young officers obviously had alarmed him. Shidehara's name stood high on the death list. He no doubt agreed with the subordinate who described these as "the most critical times internally in Japan's history." Personal fear, then, may partially explain the diplomat's erratic behavior.

It is more likely, however, that Shidehara, like Saionji, was responding to the hostile tide of public opinion which had smiled on the friendship diplomacy a few years before. Early in November 1931, there was "much public excitement and opposition to the conciliatory policies of Baron Shidehara,"[49] even as the Foreign Minister had begun to back-pedal. A month later, he was "still being criticized quite sharply by the military and . . . undergoing attacks by the press."[50] Even in Japan the Foreign Minister could not move too far ahead of public opinion, or lag too far behind. Public opinion was one of the external factors prescribing the limits of choice in foreign policy making.

More specifically, the collapse of public support destroyed the underpinnings of Shidehara diplomacy. Economic diplomacy had been the hallmark of the Shidehara approach; in part, this was the philosophy that China and Japan could be mutually prosperous with peaceful, economic cooperation. China had never openly favored such a policy which made Japan the senior partner, but an important business constituency in Japan did back the policy. In 1931, as the world depression spread, Japan seemed to have derived little benefit from a decade of conciliating China. The militarist solution appeared to the public to be more and more expedient.

Moreover, the military conspirators in Manchuria advanced a more glamorous solution than Shidehara. The talk of conciliation and peace had a certain blandness about it that contrasted with a nationalistic fervor favoring spirited defense of Japanese interests. To be sure, Shidehara sought to preserve the *status quo* in Manchuria, but his static policy could hardly compete for public favor with the more dynamic approach of his aggressive rivals.

Nor was the nature of the Foreign Minister's influence much help in meeting the challenge he faced in 1931. Possessed with aplomb and superb negotiating skill for confrontation with foreign diplomatic adversaries, Shidehara had few political resources for gaining support in the hustings. Given the peculiar character of the Japanese political structure, such support was doubly necessary. Yet Shidehara and the Minseitō had not devised the means to sell their foreign policy to a questioning public. An apolitical career diplomat in the Foreign Ministry could not easily command broad national support for his policies. And Shidehara had not put down political roots. He was in the Minseitō Cabinet but not of the Minseitō. The American Ambassador remarked about Shidehara as Acting Prime Minister, "He is a member of the Minseitō, but he is not a party politician and has little influence in the organization beyond the influence which his character and ability command."[51] Indeed, professional diplomats in Japan generally formed such an elitist group, aloof from the public, neither conversant with nor sympathetic to social concerns. A "misty barrier" had arisen between the Foreign Office and the people, admitted one professional, using a popular pun derived from the literal meaning of Kasumigaseki where the Foreign Office was located.[52]

Ultimately the Tanaka era, sandwiched between two Shidehara phases, brought such a drastic change to Sino-Japanese relations that even Shidehara diplomacy could not adjust. Until the Mukden Incident, Shidehara sought to recapture the spirit of the first-term friendship policy; thereafter, he accommodated by donning the unbecoming garments of spokesman for those who resorted to direct action in defense of Japan's Manchurian interests. Privately, he may have agreed with their objectives, for his youthful indignation over temporary loss of a fragment of Manchuria in 1895 had called him to a diplomatic career in the beginning. Did Shidehara perhaps have some secret admiration for their methods? Is it possible that Shidehara inwardly approved of men who took action on their own responsibility? He liked to reminisce, after all, about his own youthful resort to direct action: when he was Consul in 1904 at Pusan he cut the telegraph wires before the declaration of war on Russia to help the Japanese Navy; and when he was Cable Chief at the Foreign Office in 1905 he rescinded orders to the Japanese delegation in Portsmouth on his own initiative.

If Shidehara did have some sort of secret admiration for the radical young officers, they, on the contrary, continued to regard him as their natural enemy. For the next decade he made every list of national enemies the radical officers marked for assassination. In 1936, when Stimson's book—replete with favorable references to Shidehara—went on sale at Maruzen's book store in Tokyo, it sold briskly to men in uniform. At that time someone, possibly a purchaser of the Stimson volume, chalked up on Shidehara's gate the warning, "Death to the traitor!" When servants erased the threat, the menacing words continually reappeared.

Shidehara retired from government throughout the rest of the 1930's, his career apparently ending in failure. After Japan's surrender in World War II, however, Shidehara emerged from fourteen years of political obscurity to serve as Prime Minister in the early months of the Occupation and to reestablish the Anglo-American orientation of Shidehara diplomacy. It was almost as if Japan, longing for a return to the more comfortable pre-Mukden era, had elevated Shidehara in belated recognition of the wisdom of his policies. Appropriately a diplomat, the seventy-three-year-old Shidehara took the office of the Prime Minister; his chief duties now involved dealing with a representative of a foreign power, General Douglas MacArthur. An old man, Shidehara (1872-1951) even tried his hand at party politics at the very end of his career, too late to display much skill in election campaigns and far too late to compensate for the disastrous course of events after 1931.

Notes

1 Between June 1924 and April 1927 Shidehara served as Foreign Minister in the two Cabinets of Katō Kōmei and in the first Cabinet of Wakatsuki Reijirō. In his second period as Foreign Minister, from July 1929 to December 1931, he worked in the Cabinet of Hamaguchi Osachi, in his own Cabinet while he was acting Prime Minister, and in the second Wakatsuki Cabinet.
2 Shidehara heiwa zaidan (Shidehara Peace Foundation) (ed.), *Shidehara Kijūrō* (Tokyo: Kokuritsu Kokkai Toshokan, 1955), pp. 22-24. This is the official biography, and it follows the pattern of these memorial works in providing extensive quotations from documentary materials. It is a principal source of this paper, particularly on Shidehara's early life.
3 The Shidehara ancestral home was located in Kadoma-mura, Kitaka-wauchi-gun, Osaka-fu.
4 The elder brother, Hiroshi, graduated from the College of Letters, Tokyo Imperial University, to become president of Taihoku Imperial University in Taiwan. A younger sister Setsu became the first lady medical doctor in Kobe. Shidehara heiwa zaidan, *Shidehara Kijūrō*, p. 8.
5 Shidehara Kijūrō, *Gaikō gojūnen* (Fifty Years of Diplomacy) (Tokyo: Yomiuri Shimbun Sha, 1950), pp. 37-38. Shidehara dictated these anecdotal memoirs late in life for publication serially in the *Yomiuri Shimbun.*
6 *Ibid.,* pp. 245-249.
7 *Ibid.,* pp. 38-44.

8 Ambassador George W. Guthrie to Secretary of State, Tokyo, November 6, 1915, United States Department of State Files 894.021/1 (National Archives, Washington, D.C.). Cited hereafter as DSF.

9 Shidehara, *Gaikō gojūnen*, pp. 241-244.

10 Shidehara held a startling variety of posts, and he came to know personally almost every man in the service, carefully cultivating and encouraging the ablest of these such as Tani Masayuki as his protegés. Starting as a probationary consular assistant in Jinsen (Inchon), Korea, in 1897, Shidehara held posts around the world, among them prestigious ambassadorships to the Netherlands (1914-1915) and to the United States (1919-1922). These far-flung assignments were interspersed with duties at home—Chief of the Cable Section (1903-1911) and Vice Minister of Foreign Affairs (1915-1919). Distinguished service in the latter post won for him among underlings a reputation as an effective champion of unified civil control over diplomacy as he sidetracked Prime Minister Terauchi Masatake's several schemes to increase the power of the military in diplomacy. Shidehara heiwa zaidan, *Shidehara Kijūrō*, pp. 94-117.

11 A December 1929 speech by the president of the Mitsubishi Trust Company was almost interchangeable with a Shidehara foreign policy pronouncement. "A country as deficient in natural resources as Japan buys raw materials from foreign countries at low prices and processes [them] at low cost," said Yamamuro Sobun. "To that end we must do our best to create an amicable atmosphere in international relations." Ryusaku Tsunoda *et al., Sources of Japanese Tradition* (New York: Columbia University Press, 1958), pp. 757-758.

12 Text of the platform in *ibid.,* p. 757.

13 *New York Times,* January 2, 1926.

14 Shidehara appended here a quotation from the Emperor Meiji: "Beneficence to all classes of people and friendship to all the nations of the earth." Translations of portions of this speech to the Diet were included in the despatch of Ambassador Charles MacVeagh to the Secretary of State, Tokyo, January 18, 1927, DSF 794.00/37.

15 *New York Times,* May 12, 1927.

16 This is one thesis of the most important English-language volume on East Asian diplomacy in the 1920's, the remarkable and meticulous study by Akira Iriye, *After Imperialism* (Cambridge, Massachusetts: Harvard University Press, 1965).

17 Imai Seiichi, "Shidehara gaikō ni okeru seisaku kettei," (Policy Decisions in Shidehara Diplomacy), *Gakkai tembō* (1967), p. 94.

18 Ujita Naoyoshi, *Shidehara Kijūrō* (Tokyo: Jiji Tsushin Sha, 1958), pp. 52-73. This is a volume in the Sandai Saishō Retsuden series. Kobayashi Tatsuo *et al.* (eds.), *Taiheiyō sensō e no michi* (The Road to the Pacific War) (Tokyo: Asahi Shimbun Sha, 1963), 1:17-47.

19 Shidehara rejected a Tokyo suggestion that Japan hire a paid propagandist, for he felt qualified to say what had to be said. Ironically, the American State Department which eavesdropped on these communications found Shidehara to be an upright man, so Shidehara believed later on reading the extensive work of American cryptographers in Herbert O. Yardley, *The American Black Chamber* (Indianapolis, 1931); Shidehara, *Gaikō gojūnen,* p. 68.

20 *New York Times,* August 10, 1931, p. 15.

21 Shidehara, *Gaikō gojūnen,* pp. 58-65.

22 United States Department of State, *Papers Relating to the Foreign Relations of the United States, 1921* (Washington, D.C., 1936), 2:315. Cited hereafter as *FRUS, 1921,* vol. 2.

23 Iriye, *After Imperialism,* p. 18; J. Chalmers Vinson, *The Parchment Peace* (Athens: University of Georgia Press, 1955), pp. 149-168; Shidehara, *Gaikō gojūnen,* pp. 55-58.

24 *Ibid.,* pp. 84-86.

25 *Ibid.,* pp. 72-84. Shidehara excelled in negotiating compromises on specific disputes such as the one over the American cable station on Yap Island in the Japanese mandated area. At this time whimsical fellow Japanese diplomats greeted him with exclamations of "Yappu da. Yappu da," knowing that the word had "connotations of a low-class dog."

Once Shidehara impressed Elihu Root with a stirring defense of the sanctity of treaties. The Chinese were trying to bring up the infamous Twenty-One Demands Treaty ("One dose of poison would be fatal; but China was administered twenty-one doses of poison.") In the colloquy Shidehara responded, "No country whatever may be excused for advocating that it concluded a treaty against its own wishes with the intention of breaking it someday." Still Shidehara conciliated the Chinese some by disavowing the notorious Group V of the Twenty-one Demands.

26 *Ibid.,* pp. 107-113.

27 The standard, comprehensive English-language account of Japan's response to the Northern Expedition is Iriye, *After Imperialism,* pp. 89-159.

28 Tōyama Shigeki, Imai Seiichi, and Fujiwara Akira, *Shōwa shi* (History of the Shōwa Era) (Tokyo, 1955), p. 18.

29 Shidehara made this comment in an interview with Chargé d'Affaires Norman Armour. Armour to Secretary of State, April 11, 1927, DSF 894.00/252. Elsewhere Shidehara argued that an ultimatum would be self-defeating no matter how Chiang handled it. "If [Chiang] . . . agrees to the ultimatum, swallows it whole, he will be a coward in the eyes of the Chinese people: he will be attacked for making a concession which disgraces the whole nation." Shidehara, *Gaiko gojunen,* pp. 108-113.

30 *New York Times,* March 3, 1927, p. 4.

31 In fact, Minister Yoshizawa Kenkichi made his first visit to Nanking after the fall of the Cabinet to which Shidehara belonged, but the new Cabinet of Tanaka Giichi adhered to the principles of Shidehara China policy for a time. Iriye, *After Imperialism,* pp. 153-159.

32 Shidehara believed that an abyss separated his own diplomacy from that of Tanaka. Privately, Shidehara observed that Tanaka served as Foreign Minister himself because no career man of sufficient rank for the post agreed with Tanaka's force diplomacy. From his seat in the House of Peers Shidehara asked Foreign Minister Tanaka what was so positive about the new policy? Sending soldiers seemed positive, but if they accomplished nothing, was his not really a weak policy? Tanaka replied with irrelevancies.

33 Toyama, *Shōwa shi,* pp. 54-56.

34 Foreign Minister Shidehara to Ambassador Matsudaira Tsuneo (in London), Cable September 1, 1919, in Imai, "Shidehara," p. 98. Imai's account of Shidehara's role in the London negotiations is firmly grounded in primary sources.

35 Raymond G. O'Connor, *Perilous Equilibrium: The United States and The London Naval Conference of 1930* (Lawrence: University of Kansas Press, 1962), p. 82.

36 Vice Council Chairman Hiranuma Kiichirō, Councilors Itō Miyoji and Kaneko Kentarō formed the extremist group.

37 Sadako N. Ogata, *Defiance in Manchuria: The Making of Japanese Foreign Policy, 1931-1932* (Berkeley: University of California Press, 1964), pp. 8-11.

38 "In order to deal with this situation, we should extend the application of Shidehara diplomacy. It is necessary that Japan always be in the forefront of the movement for basic revision of the unequal treaties," Shigemitsu asserted during a visit to Tokyo in April 1931. Shidehara told him quite frankly, "The present government does not have the political strength to allow consideration of this question." Imai, "Shidehara," p. 111.

39 *Ibid.*, p. 109. Imai points out that there were 30,660 small shareholders of the private half of the South Manchurian Railway stock apart from big bank and *zaibatsu* shareholders. These people were alarmed by competition of parallel lines and by the threat to their future presented by Hulutao port, a warm-water facility then building in rivalry to Japan's outlet at Dairen.

  A typical slogan among the Japanese settlers ran, "Protect the Manchurian-Mongolian rights which were bought with the blood of our forefathers in the Sino-Japanese and the Russo-Japanese Wars."

40 *Ibid.* "In this area anti-Japanese feeling has probably died down some in the last year or two," Consul-General Hayashi Kyūjirō in Mukden cabled in January 1931. Inflammatory press reports out of Mukden that same month telling of a powerful anti-Japanese movement had been fabricated by the army, charged the Consul-General Hayashi to Shidehara, Cable, Mukden, January 31, 1931.

41 Daniel B. Ramsdell, "The Nakamura Incident and the Japanese Foreign Office," *Journal of Asian Studies,* 25(November, 1965):63-67.

42 This is Imai's phrase.

43 Shidehara, *Gaikō gojūnen,* p. 172.

44 *Ibid.*, p. 180. At his country home the following year the Army Chief of Staff Prince Kanaya Hanzō apologized to Shidehara explaining that his own life would have been forfeited had he interfered with troop movements.

45 Quoted in Ogata, *Defiance in Manchuria,* p. 106.

46 The Chinese preferred to work with third parties or with the League of Nations. Just before he left office Shidehara finally agreed to the investigation of the Manchurian situation by the Lytton Commission.

47 Shidehara's joint principles were quoted in a despatch by E. Neville to Stimson, Tokyo, November 5, 1931. United States Department of State, *Papers Relating to the Foreign Relations of the United States, 1931* (Washington, D.C., 1946), 3:377. Cited hereafter as *FRUS, 1931,* vol. 3.

48 Shidehara, *Gaikō gojūnen,* p. 185.

49 Ambassador W. Cameron Forbes to Stimson, Tokyo, November 6, 1931, DSF 793.94/2490.

50 *FRUS, 1931,* 3:603.

51 Forbes to Stimson, Tokyo, November 17, 1930, DSF 894.002/152.

52 Kase Toshikazu, *Journey to the Missouri* (New Haven: Yale University Press, 1950), pp. 16-18.

Hirota Kōki

The Diplomacy of Expansionism

A DIPLOMAT by choice and training but a devoted nationalist by instinct, Hirota is today an historical figure in search of his niche. Coming to the Foreign Ministry at a time when the military was in ascendancy, he sought to develop a "diplomacy of conciliation" which would preserve Japan's special position in East Asia while avoiding hostilities with China, the United States, or the Soviet Union. Unable to fully satisfy aggressive military leaders or to resolve the mounting international crisis, Hirota was shunted out of political life in 1938. Yet although he played a less than decisive role in actual policy-making, Hirota incurred the blame—unfortunately and perhaps unjustly—for the diplomatic endeavors of the 1930's. He was the only civilian among the seven "war criminals" convicted* and hung by the International Military Tribunal, Far East.[1] In too many ways this final act blurs the real events and character of his life.

Hirota consistently fulfilled the obligation of a good diplomat to represent his nation's interests. Even though there is substantial evidence that he was more nationalistic than was prudent, he always maintained that Japan's interests could be achieved and protected best by diplomatic means. He had a deep interest in China affairs, and his activities during the 1930's centered almost exclusively on this problem. Characteristically he agreed with the nationalists that Japan had special interests in China and that Japan's geographic position and power gave her special rights there.

Hirota's career falls into four parts: Foreign Service Officer (1906-1932), Foreign Minister (1933-1936), Prime Minister (1936-1937), and

*Even here the verdict was not unanimous: four of the eleven judges voted against conviction and five against the death sentence.

227

again Foreign Minister (1937-1938). As a career Foreign Service Officer he performed admirably and won recognition in diplomatic circles. In his final post as Ambassador to the Soviet Union, Hirota made his first contribution to the developing Asian crisis: he explained the behavior of the Kwantung Army in Manchuria during 1931 and generally succeeded in calming Russian fears.

During his initial stint as Foreign Minister, no major military "incidents" occurred and Hirota successfully concluded the purchase of the Chinese Eastern Railway. He was able to control foreign policy and participate fully in all decisions largely because of internal disunity in the military, a welcome but temporary blessing. The troubles began when Hirota accepted the Prime Ministership in 1936 following the February 26 Incident. The Military Tribunal charged that he had sought, overzealously, to protect and enlarge Japan's position in China, and when diplomacy failed, he had willingly endorsed military threats and aggression.

Actually, Hirota's role and the problems he confronted were not nearly that simple. In 1936 he faced a more united army; furthermore, the navy had established a *modus vivendi* with the army for a two-pronged military strategy. Consequently Hirota's diplomatic principles for settling the China problem were cast aside. The primary diplomatic accomplishment of his Cabinet was the Anti-Comintern Pact, and even that in reality was a military achievement concluded outside regular foreign service channels. One critic has observed that Hirota as Prime Minister made no preparations for meeting emergencies at a time when every situation had become a crisis.[2]

With his second appointment as Foreign Minister, Hirota again had visions of diplomatic success limiting military excess. By now, however, the question was clearly one of conflicting interests. While Japan debated her priorities, and China was unsure of what interests it was willing to defend, diplomacy momentarily remained a possibility. The loss of Japanese lives through renewed clashes with the Chinese by mid-1937 finally removed the issue from diplomacy, and the military demanded the right to resolve conflicting interests. The Japanese Army, even if divided over tactics, decided that Hirota's principles, originally intended as points for negotiation, were to be the final ultimatum to the Chinese. It was only a short distance from there to the Pacific war.

I

Hirota was born February 14, 1878, in rural Fukuoka Prefecture, the son of an apprentice stone carver.[3] The family was very poor, both parents having been adopted by the master stone carver Hirota after the birth of Kōki (who was originally named Jotaro). Young Hirota worked hard in order to attend primary school; it is said that he was a "young Abe Lincoln" who earned money by selling pine needles, carrying lanterns at funeral processions, and copying the texts of his friends. Disciplined by these efforts to stay in school, he earned high marks and was able to skip the first year of middle school. His father felt that he had exceptional talent in calligraphy and could become a famous stone carver. Hirota's teacher discouraged this, predicting that one day he would become a great admiral or even Prime Minister. In the third year of middle school he ranked second of 109 classmates, scoring over 90 in all subjects except physical education; significantly he scored 99 in the ethics course (Shinto nationalism). By this time his father's business was prospering and Hirota could concentrate more on his studies.

Many of the attitudes that influenced his future career were formed in these early days. With his closest friend Hirata Tomoo, a tall, loud, active boy who was nearly the opposite of Hirota in character, he regularly attended a Zen temple to learn to discipline his mind. At the same time he studied the art of Judo to discipline his body. Another significant activity was the local Genyōsha meetings.[4] The philosophical teachings of the neo-Confucianist Wang Yang-ming taught here provided the basis for Hirota's ideas. He adopted Wang's saying of "Unity of Thought and Action" as his own motto. Together with Hirata he formed a group called the Chikakukai, a name derived from Wang's concept of arriving at true knowledge by observing the nature of things. The goals of the society were expressed in the question, "What can we become to help the country?"

The international events of this period (1894-1898) overwhelmingly influenced Hirota's attitudes. Japan fought the Sino-Japanese War and gained footholds in Korea, Taiwan, and the Liaotung Peninsula, plus indemnities from China. Hirota had already decided to become a military officer and had applied to a military academy; he changed his mind, however, when the Triple Intervention forced Japan's return of the Liaotung Peninsula and allowed Russia's subsequent occupation in 1898. Japan's weak diplomacy, he reasoned, was responsible for the retreat after a great battlefield sacrifice. He decided, therefore, to become a diplomat (as did his friend Hirata).

Often in financial straits, Hirota received monetary and moral support for his career ambitions from his friends in the Genyōsha. Both he and Hirata passed the examination to enter Tokyo's First Higher School, an important step on the road to Tokyo Imperial University and a governmental career. Upon arrival in Tokyo, Hirota met Tōyama Mitsuru, the founder and patriarch of the Genyōsha. This was the beginning of a long relationship.[5] Tōyama tried to discourage Hirota from becoming a diplomat; a military career was judged more suitable for a true nationalist. Hirota convinced him that he was not seeking fortune, fame, or power but an opportunity to help Japan overcome its weakness in diplomacy, as evidenced by the recent events on the Liaotung Peninsula.

In 1899 Hirota and Hirata established their own dormitory with financial assistance from Tōyama and *Genyōsha* friends in Fukuoka. This became a kind of "Fukuoka House" for students in Tokyo. The "house ideology" stressed "quality and fortitude"; members were (1) "to live together in spirit and purpose—like brothers" and (2) "to live together in the spirit of self-control and harmony." This was reminiscent of Hirota's middle school activities, with the same strong Zen and neo-Confucian underpinning. During this period, Hirota spent much of his time studying the Confucian *Analects*.

This routine continued through Hirota's years at Tokyo Imperial University, ending in 1905. There he met Tsukinari Kotaro, a man so poor that he had sent his daughter and son to work at the Fukuoka student house in return for food. Tsukinari was also a member of the *Genyōsha* and later became its president. Hirota eventually married Tsukinari's daughter, thus cementing his ties with *Genyōsha* for life.

In 1902 Tōyama introduced Hirota to Yamaza Enjiro, a senior diplomat from Fukuoka, who provided Hirota with his first opportunity to serve his country. In 1903 Yamaza sent Hirota off to Korea and Manchuria armed with some thirty letters of introduction. Traveling ostensibly as a student-tourist, Hirota was given secret instructions in Korea by agents for the Japanese Consul-General Uchida Yasunori in Peking.[6] After three months of travel he judged his two most exciting experiences to be the two days he spent in a Russian lumber camp at Yong Dong Po in Korea, where he was carefully guarded, and his visit to the Russian fortress at Port Arthur where he smuggled himself in disguised as a Japanese laborer. Hirota's report was taken directly to Yamaza who in turn passed it on to Tōyama, commenting that it was equivalent to the report of a seasoned diplomat. The document eventually reached a reporter who wrote a series of articles in *Nihon Shimbun* pondering whether or not Japan should engage in war with Russia, a question that Hirota himself had to answer in the 1930's.

Hirota took the foreign service examination in 1905 but failed. He spent the ensuing year as a subordinate clerk in the Governor-General's office in Seoul, returning in 1906 to pass the examination, this time with the highest score. Among the others successful in the examination were his boyhood friend Hirata, Yoshida Shigeru, and Mushakoji Kimitomo—the last named serving as Japan's Ambassador to Germany in 1936 when Hirota was Prime Minister.

Hirota's first diplomatic assignment was in Peking, where he researched various treaties between China and other Asian nations. This work helped to establish him as a China and Asia expert. From 1909 to 1913 he was assigned to the embassy in Great Britain under Ambassador Katō Takaaki and Counselor Yamaza. Hirota studied English and the English people, often by spending much time on a park bench, despite criticism from other staff members that this was degrading. When Katō became Foreign Minister in 1914, he asked Hirota to become his private secretary, an invitation Hirota declined.

Following service in the United States, Hirota returned to Tokyo in 1920 to the Intelligence Bureau, becoming vice-chief in December 1921. He became European-American Bureau Chief in 1923 and achieved First Rank in 1925. Later that year he helped write the Basic Treaty with Russia which was subsequently to be a concern in his role as Foreign Minister. This treaty ended Japanese occupation of Russian territory in Northern Sakhalin and granted Japan oil, coal, and fishing rights in and about the same territory. It also proclaimed the two nations' "desire and intention to live in peace and amity with each other."[7] From 1927 to 1930 Hirota was Minister to the Netherlands. He traveled to The Hague by way of the Soviet Union, in order to see Russia in its post-Revolutionary period. He claimed to have learned two lessons from Dutch diplomacy: Japan should take a "third person" role in world affairs, and a diplomat should always be calm.

After an extended rest following his return to Tokyo, Hirota was assigned as Ambassador to the Soviet Union. As he was leaving Tokyo Station for Moscow he witnessed the assassination attempt on the life of Prime Minister Hamaguchi on November 14, 1930, an event of fateful significance both for party government and democracy.

During his Soviet assignment Hirota was called upon by the Russians to explain the September 18, 1931 Manchurian Incident. He assured the Soviet Union that Japan would make no further advances and he repeated these assurances on November 18, upon receiving word from Tokyo that the army was going to stop. For the first time Hirota experienced the use of diplomacy to "cover up" militarist activities. Despite the Manchurian difficulties, however, Hirota got along well in Moscow. During his tenure new fisheries agreements were signed, and conversations were carried on regarding the possibilities of a new non-aggression and neutrality pact. Hirota felt, however, that the Basic Treaty of 1925 sufficiently protected Japan's interests. Overall he apparently impressed the Russians, because on March 9, 1934, Soviet Ambassador Yurenev in Tokyo told the American Ambassador that Hirota as Foreign Minister was an important force for peace in Japan. Still, the Russian concluded that in the last analysis the final decisions would be made by the military.[8]

Hirota returned to Tokyo in October 1932 and retired from public life at age 54, the typical retirement age for bureaucrats in Japan. This ended what can be termed the "preparatory phase" of Hirota's career. He had risen above his humble beginnings through hard work, sacrifice, and strong determination. He was influenced by the ultra-nationalistic *Genyōsha* in his early years and maintained contact with it throughout his career, especially through his father-in-law. There was also the strong Zen and neo-Confucian influence on his life. He gained early experience and insight into the "China problem" and then spent many years learning his trade in Great Britain, the United States, and the Soviet Union. In Moscow he found that diplomacy could even soften the blows of the army during the Manchurian Incident and that friendly relations could continue. He became acutely aware, moreover, of the radicalism of the young military officers and of the effect of their actions upon foreign affairs. These early experiences strongly influenced both the manner and motivation of his ensuing career as Foreign Minister and Prime Minister.

II

Hirota achieved his school-boy dreams on September 14, 1933. His appointment as Minister of Foreign Affairs reversed the situation of the 1880's and placed him in a position to use diplomacy to protect rather than cover up military gains made in China after the Manchurian Incident of September 1931. Whereas his predecessor, Count Uchida, had a reputation for a "scorched earth diplomacy," Hirota announced a "diplomacy of conciliation."[9] He judged accurately that it was a time for retrenchment, since feeling against Japan was increasing worldwide, particularly in China and the Soviet Union. Japan had already withdrawn from the League of Nations over the Manchurian issue. The Soviet Union evidenced fear of further Japanese expansion northward and concern about the future of its Chinese Eastern Railroad, and the T'ang-ku Truce of May 31, 1933, had further infringed on China's sovereignty north of the Great Wall.

American Ambassador Joseph C. Grew responded to Hirota's initial conciliatory attitude with the assertion that it had "warmth and resiliency."[10] At Grew's first meeting with the new Foreign Minister, Hirota grasped his hands warmly and spoke of the development of better relations with the United States. Grew came away from the meeting, "convinced from his manner that he meant it." Grew did note, however, a few weeks later that one of his "diplomatic colleagues" was quite convinced that in spite of his stated policy of improving relations, Hirota supported the Pan-Asiatic movement in Japan and sympathized with expansionist ideas. There is evidence that Hirota did worry about foreign opposition to an expansionist policy. Harada's notes in the Saionji-Harada *Memoirs* (October 24, 1933) indicate that Hirota was concerned about the possibility that American recognition of Russia might prompt a triple effort of those two nations, plus China, against Japan. To avoid this possibility, Hirota argued that "we must act now on Japan's relations with America, China and also Russia."[11]

Presumably Hirota accepted the Foreign Ministership only on condition that (1) Japan's diplomacy would be in accordance with the imperial edict on withdrawal from the League and (2) Japan's foreign policy would center on the Minister of Foreign Affairs.[12] Apparently Hirota was able to influence the early Five Ministers' Conferences to his point of view, i.e., Japan would seek its goal of world peace by diplomatic means and would bring national defense into harmony and balance with national power.

Hirota's initial policy declaration proposed a Japanese-led mutual aid and cooperation program among Japan, Manchukuo, and China, including programs to force the Chinese to abandon anti-Japanese policies and movements. He expressed caution and distrust toward Russia but recognized the need to avoid any collision. Toward the United States he expressed enthusiasm for achieving an understanding regarding Manchurian problems.[13] At first the military allowed Hirota sufficient latitude to begin his diplomatic offensive against the Soviet Union. The most pressing problem was that of the Chinese Eastern Railway. By 1935 Hirota had successfully concluded the purchase of the Soviet rights—thus carrying out his youthful dream of securing militarily-acquired territory on the continent by diplomatic means. His success was partially due to the reputation he had established as Ambassador to the Soviet Union. On March 14, 1935, Soviet Foreign Minister Litvinov confirmed that the successful negotiations over the Chinese Eastern Railway were due to Hirota's invaluable service.[14] Grew, too, continued to be impressed with the Foreign Minister, commenting on January 23, 1934, that Hirota was succeeding in his goal of conciliation with most countries, although he saw "no evidence of improved relations with China." He gave Hirota credit for success in "creating a better atmosphere with the United States, mainly through keeping the military quiet and exerting a calming influence on the press.[15]

On April 17, 1934, the Foreign Office spokesman, Amau Eiji, issued a public statement to the effect that Japan alone was responsible for maintaining peace in East Asia and that foreign interference, even in the form of technical or financial assistance to China, would be opposed strongly by Japan. There was an implied threat that such interference

might even necessitate discussion of problems like fixing zones of interest or even international control or division of China, which would be the greatest possible misfortune for China, and at the same time would have the most serious effects upon East Asia and, ultimately, Japan.[16]

The "Amau Declaration," as it was called, originated in an off-the-record talk with Japanese reporters which was picked up and published throughout the world as Japanese policy. Hirota did not deny the statement but simply had the official translation altered to indicate that Japan could not "remain indifferent" to threats to order in East Asia and that, because "of her geographical position," Japan had a "most vital concern" in China.[17]

This declaration was in obvious conflict with the Nine Power Pact of 1922, particularly Article One which enjoined the powers to (1) respect China's sovereignty, independence, and territorial integrity, (2) provide China full opportunity to develop a government, (3) maintain equal commercial opportunity for all nations in China, and (4) refrain from seeking special rights or privileges which would abridge the rights of other states. In Hirota's war crimes trial his defense argued that Hirota reprimanded Amau for his indiscretion and remained faithful to the provisions of the pact. Furthermore, Hirota allegedly assured both Grew and British Ambassador Francis Lindley that the Amau statement was unauthorized and unofficial, and that it was Japan who did not enjoy equality in China by virtue of the Chinese boycott of Japanese goods. Hirota took this position, according to the defense, "notwithstanding a substantial body of opinion in Japan regarding the Nine Power Treaty as a dead letter since the Chinese announced unilaterally from at least 1929 the abolition of all extraterritorial rights of all powers."[18]

Both Japanese and American observers agree that the maintenance of Japan's special position in China formed the basis of Hirota's China policy. As to military influence over this policy, one postwar analyst concluded that "there was not particularly any pressure from the military. The point can be made that one can take the expressions of Hirota as his own policy."[19] This analysis argues that Hirota's diplomacy at the time "was a mixture of a superiority complex as the leader in the Far East and an inferiority complex toward the advanced nations." This psychology, accordingly, "was subsequently exhibited in the form of a coercive policy toward China."

The Okada Cabinet of July 1934, with Hirota continuing as Foreign Minister, appeared to be a continuation of the moderate faction. Grew commented that if the United States itself had made the selections its interests could not have been better served. Hirota told Harada on August 29, 1934, that he would not "carry out straitlaced diplomacy" but preferred to resign rather than have his hands tied. He also asked to have Cabinet sessions in the Imperial presence,[20] but the other ministers were opposed.

On July 14, 1934, the foreign policy thrust of the Okada Cabinet became clear when it decided to abrogate the Washington and London naval treaties, even if the Western powers met Japanese demands.[21] This move harmonized with the Cabinet's military ambitions expressed in the pamphlet, *Basic Theory of National Defense,* which stressed the policy of an "autonomous national defense." Hirota had no argument with this course. A hint of this "pro-military" stance appeared in a letter from Grew to the American Consul in Geneva Prentiss Gilbert, wherein the former judged that Hirota was working toward friendly relations, but he also indicated that many of his colleagues "believe Hirota's moderation to be one of manner and strategy rather than substance." These observers felt that Hirota could not have retained his office "unless he was pledged to support Japan's continental adventure and unless he profoundly believed in Japan's mission to preserve the peace of East Asia." Grew considered this to be evidence of an antithetical policy, seeking friendship on the one hand and hegemony over East Asia on the other.[22]

The year 1935 began and ended with the policy of "three principles." Wang Ch'ung-hui,[23] Chiang Kai-shek's intermediary, conferred with Hirota on February 5 regarding a proposed Sino-Japanese Friendship Treaty. Wang proposed negotiations based upon the "three principles" of (1) absolute international equality, (2) abolition of unequal treaties, and (3) cessation of Japanese assistance to "local governments" in North China. He reported to Chiang Kai-shek that Hirota had agreed to these principles, and the subsequent upgrading of the Japanese mission in China to embassy status seemed to support Hirota's acceptance of international equality. This policy reversed the trends of late 1934 when the Japanese military moved south of the Great Wall line agreed upon in the T'ang-ku Truce and exerted influence over the local regimes in North China. It appeared therefore that Hirota was indeed succeeding in his desire to achieve goals by diplomacy. In a statement before a Diet committee on February 21, 1935, Hirota asserted that he still sought improvement in relations with China and awaited only a "favorable opportunity in Chinese internal affairs." His continuing anxiety to achieve his objectives in China was apparent when he said: "Perhaps, if one of these days the Cabinet collapses, I shall not have had an opportunity to deal with the Chinese question which I consider my life's work."[24]

Hirota's earlier address to the Diet on January 22, 1935, emphasized the need for better relations with the United States, Great Britain, the Soviet Union, and China. He insisted that the termination of the naval treaties (effective in 1936) did not mean Japan was going to rearm but rather that Japan had found a new disarmament formula. He also suggested that the other nations could promote the stability and peace of Asia by reducing high tariffs directed against Japan. The successful transfer of Soviet rights in the Chinese Eastern Railway, the Wang-Hirota talks, and the changed status of Japan's embassy in China *seemed* to indicate Hirota's successful introduction of the "friendly policy." Contrarily, as will be seen, it only heralded the beginning of a more militant China policy.

On March 30 the Kwantung Army issued its own China policy statement, recommending no action by the government until China carried out some "pro-Japanese" deeds, and denouncing the Chinese proposals as deceptions to gain time. Thus, Japan's China policy persisted as an admixture of forcefulness by the army and friendliness by the Foreign Ministry—at times they appeared to be two separate policies.[25] Hirota continued to insist that the army should not take the lead in international relations.

In recalling this period, then Vice Minister of Foreign Affairs Shigemitsu Mamoru wrote: "In truth the schemes of the Kwantung Army in North China bore no resemblance to the declared policy of the Government which the Army just ignored."[26] The Japanese Army acted in secret to achieve its version of China policy. Just as the military had previously taken control of Manchurian policy by action in the field, it now proceeded similarly in North China. In June 1935 regional military commanders negotiated the Ho-Umezu and Chin-Doihara "local" agreements by which all Nationalist troops were removed from Hopei and Chahar. Meanwhile, Hirota assured the Chinese that the Japanese military was not insisting on any special powers of appointment, but he thought it would be unfortunate if Chinese officials with "anti-Japanese proclivities" were appointed over Japanese Army objections. Hirota claimed, furthermore, that Japanese troops would not violate the Tangku Truce or advance beyond the Great Wall, as no change in policy was involved. Despite Hirota's disclaimers, there is evidence that by the end of May 1935 the military had resumed control of Japan's policy in China.[27]

The Chinese were intensely interested in consummating a friendship treaty based upon Wang's three principles. Hirota assured them that this was being considered but asked for more time. Discussing the matter on June 27, one staff member complained that the Foreign Ministry could not formulate a China policy unless it knew the specific intentions of the army. Shigemitsu, while acknowledging it was a valid point, replied, "Today, we must first decide the policy of the foreign ministry." The policy turned out to be one that they hoped would be acceptable to the military and would simultaneously avoid the appearance of a new Twenty-one Demands.[28]

For the next four months Hirota tried to regain the upper hand. The emerging policy was the so-called Hirota "three principles."[29] The objectives of this new policy were threefold: (1) Chinese control of anti-Japanese activities and establishment of friendly relations, (2) Chinese recognition of Manchukuo, and (3) mutual Sino-Japanese defense against communism. After three months of debate the Foreign, War, and Navy Ministries announced a final statement of policy. It was stronger than the diplomats originally intended, including in point number one the statement that China would not play off Western powers against Japan. Concerning the recognition of Manchukuo, the final statement called only for tacit recognition and cessation of anti-Manchukuo activity in North China regions sharing boundaries with Manchukuo. Finally, China was ordered to cooperate with Japan and Manchukuo in both economic and defense activities. In this fashion the military tightened the vise on diplomatic flexibility.

Thus a year that began with China's "three principles" for friendship and a fair amount of diplomatic independence ended with Hirota's "three principles" and close military-diplomatic cooperation. Although it is often stated that "dual diplomacy" existed at the top levels, this is not completely true. Hirota had early agreed to a strong policy toward China, but he always favored utilizing diplomatic means for its success. The Hirota "three principles" were a joint effort of the Inner Cabinet and were based upon the decision of December 7, 1934, to exclude the Nationalists from North China.[30] Hirota confirmed this on October 4, 1935:

In carrying out the present policy, we can capitalize on the political situation in China by playing the provincial and central governments against one another. . . . Our objective is to negotiate a Sino-Japanese understanding based on the three principles adopted by the Imperial government.[31]

Actual "dual diplomacy" appeared to be defined by field-level activities. The actions of a Colonel Takahashi and Major Sakai in May-June 1935 led to the "local" agreements in North China. By the fall of 1935, as one writer has said, "control of foreign policy had passed to the field." The "forces on the spot" insisted they knew what was best and the War Minister simply transmitted staff policy while the civil government acquiesced.[32] Thus we find Prime Minister Okada informing Harada on October 28, 1935, that he had cautioned the War Minister to refer all matters pertaining to the North China problem to the Foreign Office. Yet that same day Hirota informed Harada that the army had started an autonomy movement in North China.[33]

One of Hirota's final speeches as Foreign Minister responded to Franklin D. Roosevelt's message to Congress in which the President warned expanding nations that "trends toward aggression" and "increasing armaments" might lead "to the tragedy of war." Hirota's answer before the Diet defended his role in establishing Japan's special position as a leader in Asia:

It is to be regretted that there are abroad statesmen of repute who seem determined to impose upon others their private convictions as to how the world should be ordered, and who are apt to denounce those who oppose their dictates as if they were disturbers of peace. No one is qualified to talk world peace unless he not only knows the national aspirations and obligations of his country but also understands and appreciates the standpoints of other countries. . . . We have succeeded in building up our national strength and prestige by adding and adapting to our civilization Occidental Art and science, which we have imported during the past years. Now it is time for us, I believe, to try to introduce our arts and culture to other lands, and thus contribute toward international good understanding and to the enrichment of the world civilization and the promotion of the peace and happiness of mankind.[34]

Hirota's first Ministry ended abruptly on February 26, 1936, when revolutionary elements of the First Imperial Division moved to assassinate leading public and private leaders. He had not yet accomplished his "lifelong" goal of solving the China problem through diplomacy.

III

Hirota took office as Prime Minister on March 9, 1936. This has caused some writers, in retrospect, to wonder why Hirota had not been marked for assassination by the extreme nationalists and why he was acceptable to the control faction of the military. Relative to the first point, Hirota was a close friend and associate of Tōyama Mitsuru, founder of the *Genyōsha* and one of the most honored super-patriots. Hirota, along with Prince Konoye, had also joined moderately patriotic associations, such as the *Kokuikai* (Society for Maintenance of National Prestige) in 1932 and the *Dai Ajia Kyokai* (Greater Asia Association) in 1933. Although involved in such associations, they have been judged not ultranationalists but "professional nationalists."[35] Membership in these associations seems to have been consistent with Hirota's life-pattern and it is not likely that his participation was simply a "hedge" for future security, even though it may well have had such an effect.

As to the second point—Hirota's acceptability to the military—Prince Saionji, who as the last *Genrō** made such nominations, first selected Prince Konoye as his nominee for Prime Minister. But Konoye refused to accept the position, claiming illness. Saionji's civilian advisers suggested Hirota as an alternate because of his insistence on restraint of the military in foreign affairs. Hirota preferred to remain in his profession as a diplomat, but upon further persuasion he agreed to the appointment.[36] Hirota probably was selected as the most liberal and civilian-oriented person acceptable to the military, even though the army reluctantly and conditionally acquiesced in the choice.[37]

After 1932 the army had secured veto power over nominees; if the military were displeased with a nominee they exercised this power. By 1936 there was only one military faction—the Imperial Control group. The Imperial Way group had suddenly found its generals on the retirement lists. This was to be a blessing to Hirota only in the sense of greater personal security from the "Young Officers." In the area of foreign policy, however, Hirota's diplomatic offensive in China was in jeopardy, for while the Imperial Way generals endorsed a northern defense posture against the Soviet Union, the Control generals favored penetration south into China.[38] The navy eventually worked out a mutual noninterference agreement with the Control group, with the navy making its own plans for expansion into Southeast Asia.

*Elder Statesmen from the Meiji period (1868-1912) who were usually consulted on important policy matters.

In constructing his Cabinet, Hirota initially requested five liberals for key positions, most notably Yoshida Shigeru as Foreign Minister. The army selected General Terauchi for War Minister but refused to allow him to participate in a Cabinet of liberals. Grew called Hirota's selection of Yoshida a mistake, "precisely like waving a red flag at the bull," because Yoshida was "a pronounced liberal." Grew, who had called Hirota the best possible choice for Prime Minister for America's interests—given the need for domestic conciliation in Japan—thought that Hirota unnecessarily alienated the military in his Cabinet selections and thus found himself forced to revamp the Cabinet at the army's command. "There must have been some deep-seated purpose in the maneuver, possibly to place squarely on the army the responsibility for tampering with Hirota's foreign policy."[39] This may have been so, but it could also have been aimed at securing other concessions. For instance, the army demanded that the Cabinet contain only one seat for each of the two major parties, but Hirota insisted, and got, two seats for each.

In April 1936 Hirota appointed as Foreign Minister Arita Hachirō, a close friend and confidant who announced that his policy would be a continuation of Hirota's. In introducing his new Cabinet, Hirota pointed out that the Imperial instructions included a request "not to conduct foreign policy by force." The Emperor reportedly informed Hirota in April that:

> The viewpoint of the Foreign Ministry must be thoroughly understood and adopted by the Military. . . . The Army constantly says that we should cooperate with Great Britain and the United States. However, when it comes to actual practice, it does not seem to carry out this policy.[40]

Hirota's father noted at the official inauguration party that Hirota had been easy to raise. He never punished him—just fed him and left him to his studies. He noted, however, that if Hirota had followed his father's advice he would by now have been a great master of stone carving.[41] Considering his subsequent fate, Hirota might well have wished he had been more filial.

In Terauchi Hisaichi the military may not have picked its strongest representative for War Minister. He has been judged a "weak and simple person, also naive," but the army leaders made other hedges and gained power over treaty ratification by having Baron Hiranuma, their second choice for Prime Minister after Konoye, made president of the Privy Council four days after Hirota's inauguration. The military also set out to augment its strength by proposing in May a bill to once again require that the military ministers be active duty officers (as they had been until 1913). The rationalization behind this proposal was that the February 26 Incident made it necessary that "the Army and Navy Ministries have the duties of supervising troops belonging to the Supreme Command, of maintaining military discipline and of strengthening the unity of the Army; therefore equally they themselves must be soldiers belonging to the Supreme

Command, that is, on the active list."[42] This move would not only consolidate the military power of the Imperial Control group in the Cabinet, but it would also eliminate any future competition from the Imperial Way generals now retired. The bill passed after Terauchi assured Hirota that there was no need to fear that this "reform" would make it difficult for future Prime Minister designates to appoint the military ministers. Thus in the name of discipline the Cabinet, and Cabinet policy, came under greater military influence.

When the Hirota Cabinet took office it faced four essential foreign policy problems. The preeminent issues were (1) the concluding of new naval limitations treaties, (2) the need to compensate for the failure to establish a treaty of friendship with China based on Hirota's three principles, (3) the pressures from the West under the Nine Power Treaty commitments, and (4) the problems of Northern China, including the Soviet Union in Outer Mongolia, the development of warlord-type rule in autonomous regions, the relocation of the Chinese Communists in Shensi province, and the continued refusal of the world to recognize Manchukuo.[43]

As with any government, there was serious debate over the proper allocation of resources. A Five Minister Conference on June 30, 1936, presented the basic military plan in its "outline of National Policy." The joint army and navy plan, supplemented in August, was called "The Fundamental Principles of National Policy." It included such goals as making North China pro-Japanese and anti-Communist—in order to frustrate Soviet Far Eastern policy—and acquiring greater resources and transport facilities for defense. The ultimate plans were the product of a joint committee of the two military ministries and the Foreign Ministry—the Hirota-appointed Committee on the Current Situation—which was to "study, investigate, legislate, and report on our North China policy . . . including policies which we will permit the governments in North China to adopt."[44] The 1937 budget proposals, prepared by the Hirota Cabinet, reflected these policies with more than 50 percent of the over-extended budget allocated to the military.

The culminating event in the usurpation of foreign policy by the military came with the conclusion of the Anti-Comintern Pact in November 1936. The Ambassador to Germany, Hirota's "classmate" in the Foreign Office, Viscount Mushakoji Kimitomo was ignored in the preparations for the agreement. Rather, the negotiations began in early 1936 when Japanese general staff officers contacted the Polish and German embassies. The final agreement was prepared in Germany with Major General Ōshima Hiroshi, the Military Attaché in Berlin, and Ambassador Shiratori Toshio at Stockholm consulting with the Nazis' Colonel Eugen Ott and Joachim von Ribbentrop (the Ambassador to London). Ott, as German Military Attaché in Tokyo, returned the document to Japan.

Even Hirota was not consulted, for as one contemporary observer noted, "There is reason to believe too, that the Japanese government had little knowledge of what was going on and that the Japanese army first placed it before Premier Hirota after Colonel Ott had brought the text from Berlin."[45] Hirota, however, did seem to encourage ultimate acceptance of the tripartite agreement by authorizing on November 18, 1936, the closing of the Japanese legation in Abyssinia, a move that pleased the Italian government. The Italians, in turn, opened a consulate in Mukden, thus giving *de facto* recognition to Manchukuo.[46]

Meanwhile, relations with China were deteriorating rapidly. Anti-Japanese incidents in Ch'engtu, Pakhoi, Hankow, and Shanghai in late summer of 1936 resulted in the loss of Japanese lives and caused greater Japanese pressure on China to eradicate all anti-Japanese movements. Just as these irritants were nearly settled to Tokyo's satisfaction, the Suiyuan Incident occurred in Inner Mongolia, further inflaming the Chinese. Here Mongol irregulars, encouraged by their Kwantung Army advisers, began moving westward. Shortly thereafter the Sian Incident, with the "kidnapping" of Chiang Kai-shek by Marshal Chiang Hsueh-liang, led to a united front with Chiang and the Chinese Communists against Japan.[47] All of these incidents combined to destroy Hirota's China policy.

No one was pleased. The army made greater demands through General Terauchi for expanded control of the economy. The parties, and their *zaibatsu* supporters, bridled under these demands and questioned the direction of foreign policy. On January 21, 1937, Representative Hamada of the *Seiyūkai* party lashed out in the Diet at the War Minister for taking too much initiative in political matters and accused the Cabinet of devoting itself to fascist policies. Terauchi demanded apologies from Hamada, who suggested opening the matter to full investigation and obliging the loser to commit *harakiri*. Terauchi's demand for dissolution of the Diet* was met with a refusal from Hirota. Instead, the Cabinet fell, and a new one led by General Hayashi Senjūrō was formed.[48]

Evaluations of Hirota's Cabinet are mixed. The "war crimes" tribunal convicted and executed him for the events of this short ten month period—withdrawal from naval agreements, change of status to active military in the Cabinet, and the Anti-Comintern Pacts. His biography, however, completely ignores these controversial problems in a sympathetic account. In a more balanced evaluation Morijima Gorō praises Hirota for remaining in

---

*Terauchi and his military colleagues assumed a new election would lead to gains by the military-oriented Kokumin Dōmei Party, but the April election proved that the public, too, was unhappy with the militarist direction of the state.

office during a "difficult time" rather than seeking more power, a course which might have resulted in his being fired or assassinated. Hirota, he argues, chose to work against the military from the rear and not by a futile frontal attack. He concludes, however, that the task proved too difficult, and hence the military was not restrained from any direction.[49] It must be remembered that Hirota ended his ministry by stating: "Between the military and me there were many twists and turns before the organization of the Cabinet was completed, but there was no difference between their ideas and mine."[50] Hirota always sided with the expansionists; the only question was whether it would be by peaceful diplomatic method or by military means.[51] Perhaps Shigemitsu best summed up the problems besetting the idea of dual diplomacy in 1936: "In Japan there were now two Governments—the Supreme Command (General Staff) and the Cabinet—each exercising diplomatic functions independently. There was no coordination in the will of the country, which spoke with two voices. What could result but disaster?"[52]

IV

Hirota's final opportunity to influence foreign policy came in June 1937 when he was appointed Foreign Minister in the first Konoye Cabinet. Both Konoye and Saionji felt that Hirota could provide the desired expertise and civilian balance. Both qualities were needed because by now it was regular practice for the War, Navy, and Foreign Ministries (or their subordinate bureau chiefs) to jointly recommend policies. Meanwhile, although Tokyo's general policy direction aimed at marking time and avoiding incidents, time was running out and war was near at hand.

The Marco Polo Bridge Incident of July 7, a major military clash with Chinese forces, once again plunged Hirota into the midst of a crisis of the gravest consequences. Hirota did influence the initial policy, which was to avoid spreading the incident and to settle it at the local level. This meant that Chiang Kai-shek was expected not to interfere in the settlement—ultimately an unfulfilled expectation. The army requested the mobilization of five divisions, but meanwhile the issue seemed to be on the verge of resolution at the local level in North China. Before the matter could be settled, however, further skirmishes between Japanese and Chinese troops occurred on July 25 and July 27, forcing a change in policy from local settlement to a direct confrontation with Nanking for a "fundamental solution" of outstanding problems.[53] The new and sole basis for settlement was not new at all but was a reiteration of Hirota's three principles.[54]

There was talk of Konoye sending Hirota directly to Nanking, but Hirota felt that it would be not only a waste of time but also embarrassing because the army itself did not know what it wanted. The War Office favored further involvement in China, while the General Staff opposed enlarging the conflict. There was also fear that this turmoil in the army would lead to some military opposition to Hirota's visit.

In spite of this opposition, the Japanese government decided to transmit to the Chinese the latest joint plan for settlement, which still called publicly only for establishment of unfortified zones in North China and joint withdrawal of troops, rather than for annexation of additional territories or indemnities.[55] For this purpose Hirota sent Funazu Tatsuichirō, a businessman, to Shanghai for direct talks with Chinese officials. In his August 8 instructions to Ambassador Kawagoe, with whom Funazu would work, Hirota emphasized that Chinese-Japanese relations had reached a turning point. He authorized opening negotiations with China, hopefully with recognition of Manchukuo as a basic point. Japan, he said, "considers itself a stabilizing force in the Orient," and he felt that "the broad-minded policy of our government will probably be beyond the expectation of the Chinese themselves and is worthy of winning the respect of the whole world for the fair and disinterested attitude of our Empire."[56] Consul-General Okamoto in Shanghai also received similar instructions from Hirota asking him to cooperate with the Chinese authorities and to seek to prevent further incidents there.[57]

But it was already too late for diplomatic efforts. On August 9 a Japanese naval officer was killed in the Oyama Incident, and on August 14 the Chinese Nationalists bombed naval installations at Shanghai. China immediately had decided to defend her vital interests and honor by force. The war had begun, but Hirota chose to ignore this fact. He apparently instructed a Japanese official on August 21 to report to the Emperor that "there was still some hope of a peaceful settlement."[58] In support of these hopes Hirota dispatched his former Foreign Minister, Arita, to Shanghai in search of an opening for informal talks with any designated Chinese official. First Arita was to go to Manchuria and North China on a "tour of inspection" and to await word there from Hirota for the best time to leave for Shanghai. Neither the Japanese military nor the Chinese were cooperative and the "best time" never came. Arita returned to Tokyo in late September.[59]

Grew later reported that Hirota still felt strongly on September 1 that the war could be ended if China would only accept the equivalent of his three principles. He quoted Hirota as saying, "Chiang Kai-shek is weak and he is in a very difficult position. If China possessed a single strong statesman today our troubles could be quickly solved. If Chiang Kai-shek will accept my conditions I can stop the war immediately."[60]

Though war had begun, Hirota desired at least to soothe Western feelings. The military, however, opposed sending good will envoys to Great Britain, and President Roosevelt vetoed any emissary to the United States;

indeed, in October, FDR suggested that Japan be isolated from the world.[61] In late September Hirota did manage to send Hatoyama Ichiro to England and Germany. Both the United States and Great Britain expressed hope that there were voices of reason in Japan and offered their "good offices" to help settle the dispute, but this also was too late. The military rejected such negotiation as tantamount to entrusting Japan's fate to the enemy.

The War Ministry made it very clear in a secret document of October 11, 1937, how they felt about any unfriendly intervention.[62] In brief, the military decided that Japan would "forcibly refuse and exclude any intervention or pressure by America, or European powers, or the League of Nations in connection with the Sino-Japanese Incident but will accept peace-recommending arbitration after it has achieved the object of its military movements against China." In elaboration, the document asserted that China would not "feel contrition" if "interference and arbitration" preceded accomplishment of the goal. Japan did not reject arbitration but preferred it to be initiated by Germany and Italy, "at the request of China," because of "their special relations with us." It concluded that after negotiation among the Navy, War and Foreign Affairs Ministers this formula would "become the foundation of the diplomatic measure of the country." Even though Hirota was aware of the necessity of American and British involvement, he followed this new military advice by turning to Germany for mediation. To the former demands, Hirota added indemnity. Unknown to Hirota, apparently, the General Staff extended simultaneous peace feelers through General Ott without the new indemnity demand. Neither attempt was successful and, according to Shigemitsu, Hirota concluded that compromise was impossible; subsequently he joined in the Cabinet decision for a strong hand in China.[63]

Thus Hirota gradually moved toward the army's position and away from diplomacy. For instance, German Ambassador Herbert von Dirksen was told in mid-November that the early November peace proposals stood, but by early December Hirota said they no longer held because of the military advances toward Nanking. This change must have been principally due to the pressure from the War Ministry. Yet it was reported that Konoye sought Hirota's resignation at this time for his unwillingness to discuss problems with the army, even though he was willing to talk with the navy. Apparently Konoye tried (but failed) to use the ultranationalist Tōyama's son as a go-between with Hirota in seeking the latter's resignation.[64] Among other reasons for Hirota's inclination toward the military stance, it may be remembered that strong anti-Chinese feeling was growing in Japan, that people felt Konoye had lost control of foreign policy, and that Hirota's life was possibly in danger.[65]

Grew sensed the situation: "Hirota's position is shaky; the military and the chauvinists want Matsuoka to take his place. . . . " The American

Ambassador continued to feel that Hirota was a victim of circumstances. As late as November 16 Hirota assured Grew that his fundamental policy still included good relations with the United States. Nevertheless he suspected that America was losing its impartiality, and well he might, for Grew had several times chastised Hirota for not keeping the military in check. The greatest blow came with the bombing of the *USS Panay* after Grew had personally demanded that Hirota insure protection of the ship. On December 13, 1937, Hirota called at the embassy to inform Grew of the bombing: "I can't tell you how badly I feel." Hirota's "eyes were really filled with tears," Grew understandingly reported, but the China problem was now out of both their hands. As Grew had noted in September, "We must reluctantly face the fact that the civil government in Tokyo has very little influence with these forces where their general objectives are concerned."[66]

Hirota's policy from this point until May 1938—when Konoye formed a second Cabinet, dropping both Hirota and War Minister Sugiyama—was to support the War Ministry's "strong policy" in China (as opposed to the more conciliatory stand of the General Staff). The most obvious evidence of this final course was Hirota's January 1938 public announcement of the new China policy, which included his three principles plus the demand for indemnity. In the Diet on January 18, 1938, he categorically asserted: "We will not treat with Chiang Kai-shek." The army was not satisfied, however, and organized a new agency, the "China Organ," to deal with questions relative to the China problem. They also refused to allow this agency to be placed in the Foreign Ministry, even though Hirota did acquiesce in its establishment.[67]

A report on May 29, 1938, the date of the Cabinet reorganization, indicated that the Foreign Ministry had been "the most unpopular of all the departments of government for months past."[68] The report quoted the *Hōchi Shimbun* as contending that Japan's foreign policy was based on its relations with China and in this field "most active diplomatic work is needed." This was an unfortunate, but true, epitaph for the diplomat who considered China to be his lifelong special area of interest and expertise. As Grew noted, "Hirota had fallen because he was too weak in opposing the army while at the same time insisting that the Foreign Office has control of Japan's foreign relations in China."[69]

In summing up Hirota's second term as Foreign Minister, one is prone to agree with the analysis that there were no long range government policies. The Cabinet acted on, or after, arbitrary decisions and actions by the military. Hirota seemed to have decided to let things take their own course. He clearly expressed the nature of the problem by saying that when Prime Minister Konoye acceded to the power of "another institution," he made it very difficult to carry out diplomatic goals.[70]

V

The final march to total war in China, colonization of Southeast Asia, and war with the United States found Hirota in the shadows. He became a senior statesman by virtue of being a former Prime Minister, but he possessed only limited influence.* Arita later claimed that he unsuccessfully suggested Hirota for Foreign Minister in 1940 on the grounds that "he was against the conclusion of the Tripartite Pact between Japan, Germany, and Italy." Still Hirota remained concerned with the termination of the China Affair; the Tripartite Pact, he felt, simply diverted attention from the basic problem while causing unnecessary political and economic difficulties with Great Britain and the United States. Hirota's concerns elicited little response for, as Prime Minister Yonai reportedly said of Hirota, "state councillors . . . have no competency to participate in the decision of the government, and accordingly, are not responsible for it."[71]

In his final influential act, Hirota once again favored the military. One of the postwar charges against Hirota was that he presided over the decision to require the military ministers to be active duty general officers. In 1941, after the fall of the third Konoye Cabinet, Hirota as a senior statesman agreed with the argument that one way to control and make more prudent "the reckless actions" of some military officers was to choose the Prime Minister from among the generals on the active list. As this was also the consensus of the other senior statemen, General Tōjō formed the Cabinet that inaugurated the Pacific war.

Only once more did Hirota become active, and this was to make one final diplomatic effort—an effort no longer to avert the crisis but to end the tragedy that the crisis had brought upon Japan. Foreign Minister Tōgō, who had always considered Hirota a top Soviet expert (and had even offered him the post of Ambassador to the USSR), asked Hirota in 1945 to hold talks with Jacob Malik, the Soviet Ambassador to Japan. Now Hirota sought to employ diplomacy not to preserve military gains but to prevent military losses from becoming total disaster. On June 29, 1945, Hirota informed Tōgō that Malik had promised to forward to the Soviet government the Japanese proposals,[72] which, of course, had no effect on events. And on this final note of failure the diplomatic career of Hirota Kōki ended.

Notes

1 For an evaluation of the trial, based primarily on rejected defense documents, see Carl L. Gilbert, Jr., "The Hirota Ministries: An Appraisal.

*For a short time in 1940 he served as a state minister without portfolio in the Yonai Cabinet.

Japan's Relations with China and the U.S.S.R., 1933-1938" (unpublished Ph.D. dissertation, Georgetown University, 1967). For a Japanese evaluation see Usui Katsumi, "Hirota Kōki Ron" in *Nihon Gaikō Shi Kenkyū* (Studies in the History of Japanese Diplomacy) (Tokyo: Yuhikaku, 1966), no. 1, pp. 41-53. Cited hereafter as Usui.

2 Usui, "Hirota," p. 50.

3 The primary source of Hirota's early life: Hirota Kōki Denki Kankōkai (Hirota Kōki Biography Publication Society), *Hirota Kōki* (Tokyo: Chūō Kōron Jigyō Shuppan, 1966).

4 The *Genyōsha* was a patriotic organization formed in Fukuoka prefecture in 1881 and is said to stem from an organization formed in 1877 by close supporters of Saigō Takamori, the leader of the Satsuma Rebellion. Its name connotes its objectives, crossing the nearby Genyō (Sea of Genkai) to expand on the continent. It is considered to be a forerunner of Japanese fascism. See Robert A. Scalapino, *Democracy and the Party Movement in Prewar Japan* (Berkeley: University of California Press, 1953), p. 350.

5 Most studies of Hirota refer strongly to his early affiliation with *Genyōsha*, as well as his enrollment in *Fukuoka Uyoku Dantai* (Fukuoka Rightwing Group). See an elaboration of this in *Taiheiyō Sensō e no Michi* (The Road to the Pacific War) (Tokyo: Asahi Shimbunsha, 1963), III, p. 70.

6 These two agents later helped blow up parts of the Chinese Eastern Railway and still later were killed at Harbin. Hirota, *Hirota*, pp. 31-32.

7 For treaty text see John M. Maki, *Conflict and Tension in the Far East: Key Documents, 1894-1960* (Seattle: University of Washington Press, 1961), pp. 57-61.

8 International Military Tribunal Far East, Exhibit 324. Cited hereafter as IMTFE.

9 *Taiheiyō*, 3:305. Also reported in IMTFE, Defense Document 3241.

10 Joseph C. Grew, *Ten Years in Japan* (New York: Simon and Schuster, 1944), p. 99.

11 Quoted in IMTFE, Defense Document 3010-B.

12 Usui, "Hirota," p. 44.

13 *Ibid.*, p. 45; *Taiheiyō*, 3:71.

14 Dorothy Borg, *The United States and the Far Eastern Crisis of 1933-1938* (Cambridge, Massachusetts: Harvard University Press, 1964), p. 142; and IMTFE, Defense Exhibit 3252. For treaty text see Maki, *Conflict*, pp. 74-76.

15 Grew, *Ten Years*, p. 115.

16 Usui, "Hirota," pp. 45-46; Grew, *Ten Years*, pp. 129-130.

17 Grew, *Ten Years*, p. 129.

18 IMTFE, Defense Document 3107.

19 Usui, "Hirota," p. 46.

20 IMTFE, Exhibit 3870-A.

21 James B. Crowley, *Japan's Quest for Autonomy* (Princeton, New Jersey: Princeton University Press, 1966), p. 199.

22 Grew, *Ten Years*, pp. 136-137.

23 Wang was a judge on the Permanent Court of the International Court of Justice and was asked by Chiang Kai-shek to perform this "indirect diplomacy."

24 IMTFE, Exhibit 3249.
25 *Taiheiyō*, 3:91-92; Crowley, *Japan's Quest*, pp. 211-214; Usui, "Hirota," pp. 46-48.
26 Mamoru Shigemitsu, *Japan and Her Destiny* (New York: E.P. Dutton and Co., Inc., 1958), p. 100.
27 Borg, *United States*, pp. 144-151. See also *Taiheiyō*, 3:98.
28 Crowley, *Japan's Quest*, pp. 218-220.
29 There are numerous discussions of Hirota's Three Principles. See *Taiheiyō*, 3:127-135; Crowley, *Japan's Quest*, pp. 236-237; and Borg, *United States*, p. 158.
30 Crowley, *Japan's Quest*, pp. 211, 230-232.
31 Quoted in *ibid.*, p. 230. Also in IMTFE, Defense Document 2218. IMTFE, Exhibits 3253 and 3254 are secret telegrams to Ambassador Ariyoshi in China that give further substantiation of Hirota's closeness to the views of the military ministers as early as August 5, 1935.
32 Yale Candee Maxon, *Control of Japanese Foreign Policy: A Study of Civil Military Rivalry, 1930-1945* (Berkeley: University of California Press, 1957), p. 100.
33 Quoted in Maxon, *Control*, p. 100. See Saionji-Harada, *Memoirs* (October 30, 1935), pp. 1342-1344.
34 Grew, *Ten Years*, pp. 162-164.
35 Richard Storry, *The Double Patriots* (Boston: Houghton Mifflin Company, 1956), p. 48. See also William Henry Chamberlain, *Japan Over Asia* (Boston: Little, Brown and Co., 1938), p. 264.
36 Hirota Kōki Denki Kankōkai, *Hirota*, pp. 175-177, 188-189.
37 Maxon, *Control*, p. 110.
38 Masao Maruyama, *Thought and Behavior in Modern Japanese Politics* (New York: Oxford University Press, Expanded Edition, 1969), p. 362. Maruyama warns against a simple Imperial Way–Control dichotomy. The Control group was not a cohesive well-organized entity, as was the Imperial Way group.
39 Grew, *Ten Years*, p. 178. See also Scalapino, *Democracy*, p. 384, and Hirota Kōki Denki Kankōkai, *Hirota*, pp. 177-181.
40 Quoted in Maxon, *Control*, pp. 114-115. See also IMTFE, Sworn Deposition of Tsugita Daizaburō (Chief of Bureau of Legislation in Hirota Cabinet), Defense Document 435.
41 Hirota Kōki Denki Kankōkai, *Hirota*, p. 185.
42 IMTFE, Tsugita Deposition, Defense Document 435.
43 Crowley, *Japan's Quest*, pp. 279-280.
44 Maxon, *Control*, pp. 115-116, 242 (f.n.); Hirota Kōki Denki Kankōkai, *Hirota*, pp. 202, 214; and Crowley, *Japan's Quest*, p. 291.
45 Wilfrid Fleisher, *Volcanic Isle* (Garden City, New York: Doubleday, Doran and Co., 1941), pp. 166-172.
46 F.C. Jones, *Japan's New Order in East Asia* (London: Oxford University Press, 1954), pp. 99-100.
47 See IMTFE, Exhibit 3241, Affidavit of Kawashima Kazue. See also *Taiheiyō*, 2:214-216, 225.
48 See Hirota Kōki Denki Kankōkai, *Hirota*, pp. 243-246; Scalapino, *Democracy*, pp. 384-385; Crowley, *Japan's Quest*, pp. 308-331; and *New York Times*, January 22, 1937.

49 Usui, "Hirota," p. 49. For other evaluations see IMTFE, Exhibit 3236, and Hirota, *Hirota*, p. 247.
50 Usui, "Hirota," p. 49.
51 *New York Times*, October 22, 1936.
52 Shigemitsu, *Japan*, p. 125.
53 For this period see: IMTFE, Exhibit 3260, Desposition of Horinouchi Kensuke; Hirota Kōki Denki Kankōkai, *Hirota*, p. 261; Usui, "Hirota," p. 51; and Crowley, *Japan's Quest*, p. 322 ff.
54 Crowley, *Japan's Quest*, p. 341.
55 Hirota Kōki Denki Kankōkai, *Hirota*, p. 273; David J. Lu, *From the Marco Polo Bridge to Pearl Harbor* (Washington, D.C.: Public Affairs Press, 1961), p. 16.
56 IMTFE, Exhibits 3280, 3280A, 3280B, and 3277. Also see Borg, *United States*, p. 445.
57 IMTFE, Exhibits 2515 and 3260.
58 IMTFE, Exhibit 3273.
59 IMTFE, Exhibit 3260; and Hirota Kōki Denki Kankōkai, *Hirota*, p. 275.
60 IMTFE, Exhibit 3716-B.
61 Hirota Kōki Denki Kankōkai, *Hirota*, pp. 292, 295.
62 IMTFE, Exhibit 3268.
63 Shigemitsu, *Japan*, pp. 144-145.
64 Another report indicates the opposite of this story. It says that Toyama's son himself proposed to Konoye that since Hirota was a very important person, he should not be scarred now because he might be necessary for future leadership (Prime Minister again?). Usui, "Hirota," p. 10.
65 See Hirota, *Hirota*, pp. 320-321; Borg, *United States*, pp. 474-475; and IMTFE, Exhibit 3876.
66 Grew, *Ten Years*, pp. 211-226.
67 Shigemitsu, *Japan*, p. 146.
68 *New York Times*, May 29, 1938.
69 Grew, *Ten Years*, p. 248.
70 Usui, "Hirota," p. 51.
71 IMTFE, Exhibits 3290 and 3291.
72 Usui, "Hirota," p. 52; and Shigenori Tōgō, *The Cause of Japan* (New York: Simon and Schuster, 1956), pp. 288-289.

Manchuria

Alvin D. Coox

Shigemitsu Mamoru

The Diplomacy of Crisis

SHIGEMITSU MAMORU (1887-1957) is perhaps best remembered as the peg-legged Foreign Minister who limped aboard the *USS Missouri* on September 2, 1945, to sign the instrument of surrender "by Command and in behalf of the Emperor of Japan and the Japanese Government."[1] At that time Shigemitsu was a seasoned diplomat with 35 years of distinguished service, including the ambassadorships to China (1931-1932, 1941-1943), the Soviet Union (1936-1938), and Great Britain (1938-1941), as well as the Cabinet post of Foreign Minister (April 1943-April 1945 and August-September 1945). In the liberal postwar clime, he again became Foreign Minister (1954-1956) after the Allied Occupation ended.[2]

These later activities are remarkable since Shigemitsu was arrested by the Occupation authorities as a suspected "war criminal," was jailed in Sugamo with Tōjō and others, was convicted in 1948 by the International Military Tribunal for the Far East, and was sentenced to seven years imprisonment. Such a term, however, represented the lightest sentence imposed on any of the twenty-five surviving Class A defendants. Although no individual went free, Shigemitsu was exonerated of three counts, most particularly Count 1, Over-all Conspiracy, on which twenty-three of the twenty-five defendants were condemned.[3] Indeed, reliable evidence indicates that Shigemitsu's name had been removed by the American prosecution from the original list of war criminals but was restored after the Soviet judge arrived in Tokyo.[4]

What exacerbated Russian antagonism in the case of Shigemitsu? The answer is to be found mainly in Shigemitsu's tour as Ambassador in Moscow, especially during 1938 when the two powers came to the brink of all-out war.

251

Such exploration also sheds light on the interworkings of the Japanese Foreign Ministry, the military services, and Japan's important embassy in Moscow. In this sense the actions of Shigemitsu may serve as a case history for examination of Japanese crisis diplomacy.

I

Shigemitsu Mamoru was born July 29, 1887, in Oita prefecture on Kyūshū. On reaching his teens, he determined to become a diplomat, but he had no particular counselor and only knew that training in German law, which was reputedly best in those days, was indispensable. After completing high school in Kumamoto and studying with a German professor, he was accepted by Tokyo Imperial University. There he continued his study of German law and worked with German professors until he graduated in July 1911. He promptly passed the diplomatic and consular examinations and was quite logically posted to the Japanese embassy in Germany soon thereafter. After a pleasurable forty-day voyage, he began his service in Berlin as a diplomatic probationer and served in that position from April 1912 until the outbreak of World War I in August 1914. He was then transferred to London.[5]

Service in England, Shigemitsu later said, "opened [my] eyes." Having looked at Europe through German eyes, he had equated Europe with Germany. Now he realized the narrowness of his viewpoint and decided to explore the background of Anglo-Saxon democracy and its immense influence on the world. So he immediately began studying with a British tutor to improve his skills in speaking and writing. Shigemitsu's sympathy for British-style institutions, his establishment of life-long friendships with prominent Britons, and his antipathy to militarists of any nationality stemmed from this period.[6]

In the spring of 1918 Shigemitsu was assigned as Consul in Portland, Oregon. He arrived in June after a leisurely tour through France, Italy, and the United States, and with characteristic seriousness of purpose he began studying America as thoroughly as he had studied Germany and England. As a result he made friends in influential circles and prevailed upon Christian Scientist acquaintances to get the *Monitor* to soften its editorial policies toward Japan.[7]

When the armistice was signed in November 1918, orders came for Shigemitsu to join Baron Makino's delegation at Versailles. At the Paris Peace Conference he associated with other rising stars such as Matsuoka Yōsuke, Yoshida Shigeru, Arita Hachirō, Lieutenant Colonel Hata Shunroku, and Commander Nomura Kichisaburō. After the conference he took a long trip through Central and Eastern Europe before heading for Tokyo via the United States. When he finally reached Japan in the summer of 1920, he had been away for nine years.[8]

For the next five years Shigemitsu served at Foreign Ministry headquarters in such varying capacities as counselor, treaty bureau section chief, and consultant on the Marshall Islands and the Washington Conference. During this time he managed to visit the South Sea islands, Taiwan, Hong Kong, Canton, Shanghai, Peking, Manchuria, and Korea.

With Germany temporarily in the shadows, China loomed increasingly important for Japan and Shigemitsu. Posted to Peking as First Secretary in 1925, he began years of dedicated but dangerous service centering on the improvement of Sino-Japanese relations, with clear respect for China's sovereignty. The result was many lasting personal friendships with Chinese officials and diplomats. Except for a brief stint of six months in 1928 as Counselor of Embassy in Berlin, he remained in China until 1933, as Consul-General (and Chargé d'Affaires) in Shanghai after 1929, and as Minister from 1931.

During these critical years, Shigemitsu dealt effectively with such Chinese statesmen as Chiang Kai-shek, C.T. Wang, and T.V. Soong and collided with such Japanese military leaders as Generals Shirakawa and Tashiro. He faced a particularly severe test at the time of the explosive Shanghai Incident of 1932 when, after defeating the tenacious Chinese 19th Route Army, Japanese ground forces set out in full pursuit. Fearing not only escalation in China but major difficulties with the League of Nations, which was then considering the affair, Shigemitsu conferred with the Japanese Navy on March 3 about the advisability of an immediate ceasefire. The navy commanders posed no objection but could not, of course, speak for the Japanese Army. Since time was of the essence, Shigemitsu dared to issue a public announcement of a truce before securing army approval.

On his way to see Army Commander Shirakawa and Chief of Staff Tashiro, Shigemitsu was joined by Matsuoka, who had been sent to Shanghai by the *Gaimushō* (Japanese Foreign Office) to assist. The two veteran diplomats reasoned for hours with their military counterparts but encountered stony silence. Matsuoka made one of his "famous speeches" (in Shigemitsu's words), but the generals remained hostile. When lunch was served, Shirakawa and Tashiro pushed their plates away and kept silent, while the army headquarters bustled with activity. After five hours of talks, Shigemitsu was at last able to persuade the loyal warrior Shirakawa by bringing up the delicate subject of the Emperor's profound anxiety about the Shanghai crisis. To the diplomat's intense relief, the army commander agreed to issue an immediate ceasefire order and his deputy concurred. Shigemitsu sincerely complimented Shirakawa for his statesmanlike decision. A full-scale Sino-Japanese truce was eventually hammered out on April 28. Ironically, the next day at the ceremony in Shanghai celebrating the accord, a Korean fanatic hurled a bomb into the Japanese reviewing stand, and Shigemitsu, China's constant friend, was badly injured. Still, he refused to allow the outrage to becloud the tenuous truce; a week later, he signed the final agreement from his hospital bed.[9]

Tributes to Shigemitsu's popularity and esteem were many. The British Minister worried about him at the hospital like a grieving brother. Prime Minister Inukai and Foreign Minister Yoshizawa sent personal greetings and gifts. But most poignant was the fact that every time Yoshizawa was received in audience at the Imperial Palace, the Emperor asked after Shigemitsu's wellbeing. When he learned of this, Shigemitsu wept.[10]

After the amputation of his leg, the indomitable Shigemitsu returned to duty in May 1933 as Vice Minister for Foreign Affairs under Uchida and then Hirota. During this time he encountered mounting military hostility, particularly because of his benign attitude toward Nationalist China and Great Britain. Following the February 26 Mutiny in Tokyo in 1936, the new Premier Hirota attempted to appoint Shigemitsu as Ambassador to China, a move welcomed warmly in that country. When the objections of the Japanese military frustrated this excellent appointment, Foreign Minister Arita asked Shigemitsu whether he would like to be Ambassador to Germany or Russia. Shigemitsu chose the USSR. Typically, he explained that he was interested in studying the true situation prevailing in Russia since the Bolshevik Revolution. The army was again displeased with his appointment to a major diplomatic post. Shigemitsu, in turn, feared that the military activists were seeking to "emasculate" the embassy's functions in Russia as effectively as they had in China.[11] But Arita arranged the appointment in August 1936. Shigemitsu arrived in the Soviet capital on November 25 after a thorough preparatory trip through Korea, Manchuria, and the USSR via the Trans-Siberian Railway. The day of his arrival in Moscow could not have been more poorly timed; the Nazis and the Japanese had just concluded the Anti-Comintern Pact.[12] Moreover, within a year and a half of Shigemitsu's appearance in Moscow, Japan and the USSR were at each other's throats on a Far Eastern battlefield.

II

Shigemitsu seemed destined to exercise his greatest influence in crisis situations. His Shanghai experience revealed the fundamental difference in approach between his belief in conciliatory diplomacy which aimed at "cooling down" local incidents and the Japanese Army's tendency toward diplomacy by ultimatum, in which it often seized local affrays as an opportunity to expand its own influence and power. After the Shanghai episode neither Shigemitsu nor the army quite trusted each other again. To the diplomat, the army seemed to care little for the long-run political risks involved in its reckless adventures; to army officers, Shigemitsu appeared unable to understand that they wanted "diplomacy" only to maximize their gains or extract them from uncomfortable positions without penalty. In the Changkufeng Incident of 1938 this mutual distrust complicated Japan's position and revealed the weakness in her dependency on crisis diplomacy.

Soviet-Japanese tensions mounted after the Japanese Army overran Manchuria and set up the puppet empire of Manchukuo, for now the Japanese troops of the Kwantung Army defended the 2,500 miles of frontier which stretched between Manchukuo and the Soviet Union. The historical seesaw originally meant little to the border residents whose interest centered upon survival and not patriotic loyalties. But with the buildup of Manchukuo and the Soviet Far East under the Five Year Plans, both sides began to pay attention to the problem of the frontier. Pillboxes, barbed wire entanglements, observation posts, and armed patrols appeared along the huge frontier zone. Matters usually devolved upon *force majeure,* since the few or ruined old markers along the land boundaries were not usually supplemented by ditches or fences. Affrays erupted constantly, including kidnappings, raids, and violations of air space by reconnaissance planes. Such incidents, most often occurring on the eastern Manchurian borders, always contained the seeds of a general war.[13] The Japanese kept detailed records of the numbers of clashes: 1936–152; 1937–113; 1938–166. Of the 431 disputes alleged to have taken place on all the frontiers between 1936 and 1938, only forty-seven were listed as "half-solved" and two as "fully solved."[14] Of course, the USSR maintained its own running account; thus, in 1938, 124 Japanese violations of the Soviet border were cited.[15]

Early in July 1938, the most dangerous Russo-Japanese border controversy to date erupted close to the juncture of the frontiers of northeast Korea, southeast Manchuria, and the Soviet Maritime Province near Posyet Bay. The focus of the boundary dispute was Changkufeng [Chōkohō], an obscure hillock lying just west of Lake Khasan in the disputed Manchurian appendix. A relatively small Soviet ground buildup atop Changkufeng in early July provoked a sharp clash of patrols on July 29. Crossing the Tumen River a Japanese reinforced battalion attacked and cleared both Changkufeng and Shachaofeng [Shasohō] of Russian garrisons by dawn on July 31. The Japanese infantrymen clung doggedly to their positions, without air support or tanks, until the end of the incident on August 11, although the Russians counter-attacked repeatedly and fiercely by land and air.[16] Throughout the fighting equally stubborn diplomats carried on a struggle of their own.

At the outset of the controversy, pourparlers were initiated in vain by the Manchukuoan-Japanese side through the Soviet consular authorities at Harbin.[17] By July 14 the focus of diplomatic attention had shifted to Moscow, when Foreign Minister Ugaki directed the Japanese embassy to "demand the urgent withdrawal of Soviet troops which had illegally occupied

Manchukuoan territory" at Changkufeng. In the temporary absence of Shigemitsu, Chargé d'Affaires Nishi Haruhiko opened the exchanges, which centered largely on the cartographic problem; they proved inconclusive. Sensing the potential gravity of the affair, Ugaki sent new instructions to Nishi on July 17 and at the same time telegraphed Shigemitsu to cut short his journey.[18]

Shigemitsu, the indefatigable tourist, was on a trip in northern Europe at the time.[19] He had just arrived at Stockholm when Tokyo sent the urgent wire instructing him to conduct the negotiations with the Russians. To return to Moscow from Stockholm, he could proceed via Finland or Germany, either of which trips would require several days. A new Swedish air route, however, had just been opened to Moscow; the first plane was due to depart on July 18. Shigemitsu managed to get aboard, reaching Moscow on the evening of July 18. He found rigorous instructions awaiting him from Ugaki: unless the Russian "intruders" got out promptly, "any kind of development could be expected."[20]

On July 20 Shigemitsu opened what proved to be extremely difficult negotiations with the Soviet Foreign Affairs Commissar, Maxim Litvinov. Shigemitsu apparently earned the enduring resentment of Soviet authorities by his remarks about the map Litvinov presented purporting to "prove" Russian boundary claims.[21] According to the official Japanese release, Shigemitsu argued that the map itself was known only to the Russian government. Shigemitsu himself subsequently explained his position:

> Litvinov was vindicating a border line as determined by the Hunchun agreement [of 1886].... The Russian text showed a boundary running through the crest of Changkufeng, so the Soviet army's actions were supposedly quite valid—mere border defense operations. Litvinov was going to show me the map in the Russian language text attached to the Hunchun protocol. But I declined to look at it. "The point of today's negotiations," I said, "centers on the fact that the Soviet forces suddenly moved into a place which the Japanese-Manchukuoan side believed to be inside Manchurian territory, and [the Russians] are constructing works, etc. Both armies face the danger of an armed clash. The immediate objective should be to relax the unfortunate tension along the border. To avoid trouble, the most practical method would be for the Soviet forces, which had pushed forward, to withdraw to their original points; only then would there be thorough joint commission investigations of the dangerous border matter." Both sides could submit materials at such a time, but it was useless to study the line just now, when priority efforts should be made to avert a clash.[22]

Litvinov's diary records the commissar's famous reply:

> I must say that I am greatly surprised at hearing you, an old and experienced diplomat, speaking so slightingly about official maps and calling them "some maps." You must know that these maps are the only means of establishing frontiers. It surprises me that you want to blame the map, declaring that it was not published. I do not know whether it was published

or not. Even if it was not published, it did not, from this fact, cease to exist. It is especially strange to hear such a statement from the representative of Japan, which has by no means published all of her treaties . . . and has not a few secret agreements; but, because of this, these agreements do not lose their force in the mutual relations between the parties. . . . This agreement exists. What can you present against this argument? Without presenting any other document, the Japanese side brings in an unfounded demand of evacuation of Soviet troops from Soviet territory. It is like this: In the meantime you go out, and we leave later.[23]

After this failure to achieve a meeting of minds, Shigemitsu did not see Litvinov until August 4. Since Tokyo authorities optimistically thought that a peaceable solution to the Changkufeng affair was in sight, Ugaki informed Shigemitsu on July 27 that the government was going to maintain "attentive silence" for awhile.[24] Local Japanese Army forces, however, took matters into their own hands and on July 30-31 occupied the disputed territory.[25]

Ugaki instructed Shigemitsu to see Litvinov immediately, but Shigemitsu adhered to his earlier position and sought no interview with Litvinov regarding latest developments. The position of both sides, judged the Ambassador, was clearly expressed in the interview on July 20.[26]

At the outset of August, the Soviet Air Force went into action at the front and the Russian ground forces commenced major counteroffensives. Premier Konoye and his colleagues were worried and determined to break the diplomatic impasse. Konoye told the Emperor on August 2 that he intended to leave matters to diplomacy and to suspend military operations as soon as possible—an approach with which the high command *now* concurred in full. The Changkufeng dispute would be accorded priority, preceding an overall settlement and the creation of joint commissions to redefine the borders.[27]

The Japanese General Staff and War Ministry officials were particularly anxious about a ceasefire, the dimensions of a buffer zone, and the requirement for *Gaimushō* negotiation with the USSR. Taking prompt action to implement the government's decisions, the Japanese Foreign Ministry examined the necessary "countermeasures" in close coordination with the armed forces. Finally, on August 3, instructions were wired to Shigemitsu.

Since the situation at the front is extremely critical, we have recognized the necessity to propose emergency suspension of combat action now. The Soviet chargé d'affaires is being called, but urgency is dictated; so we would like you to contact the foreign commissariat, on an urgent basis, and propose quick suspension of fighting action. If the Soviet government concurs, we are prepared to discuss concrete steps.[28]

These "concrete steps" meant a pullback of Soviet forces to a line running through the heights east of Lake Khasan and of Japanese troops to a line extending through the high ground west of Changkufeng and west of Shachaofeng—the setup as of July 30.

Foreign Minister Ugaki told Premier Konoye on August 2 that "we are having trouble because we haven't received any cables from Shigemitsu."[29] Although Shigemitsu had been receiving repeated wires from the worried *Gaimushō*, he reported to Tokyo that "the Soviet Government is displaying a very passive outlook. The attitude of the foreign affairs commissariat shows that they are treating the incident as trifling. Public opinion in the USSR is extremely calm and quiet. I therefore hope matters will be handled coolly in Japan."[30]

In spite of the mounting flow of telegrams from Tokyo, Shigemitsu had deliberately not renewed conversations with the Russians in the hope that they would come around to his view. But when the Soviets responded with a heavy air and ground counterassault upon the contested hilltop, Shigemitsu was forced to request an appointment with Litvinov. The roles changed, the commissar now refused to see the Japanese envoy.[31] Joseph Grew, the U.S. ambassador to Japan, attributed Litvinov's evasion to Soviet indecision. Officials and other informed Japanese grew more apprehensive; the decision for war or peace seemed now to rest with Moscow.[32]

III

Shigemitsu finally got to see Litvinov again on August 4, at which time he sought to carry out the *Gaimushō* instructions for a cease-fire.[33] Shigemitsu now believed that the situation had become critical. Japan would have to decide whether to treat the Changkufeng Incident as a problem more serious than a mere border affair, entailing large-scale military operations, or whether to handle it as one of a series of frontier difficulties. The Japanese forces had already sustained severe losses from the Russians' massive counterassaults; circumstances had taken a decided turn for the worse. When Shigemitsu conferred with Litvinov on August 4, his objective was to avert a major collision: "My insistence followed the previous line of approach that Japanese troops would withdraw from the site of the clash, but at the same time the Soviet forces should pull back too. After that, the boundary could be fixed by a bilateral commission, and the clash solved. I repeated this plan persistently."[34]

Although examination of the transcripts of this conversation between Litvinov and Shigemitsu reveals no particular rapprochement, the Japanese government (according to *Gaimushō* records) surmised that the Soviet side was disposed to cease fighting if the conditions were satisfactory. Given the go-ahead by government leaders on August 5, the Japanese Foreign Ministry labored on new directives for Shigemitsu.[35] The work was all the more important because, by August 6, high Tokyo circles had formed the opinion that the Russians were stalling: "They proffer such excuses as Litvinov's absence, but they are expending every effort to retake Changkufeng in the meantime."

The instructions for Shigemitsu drafted on August 6 were based on decisions reached at a three ministers' conference between the military and foreign ministers, who had been guided by the policy laid down by the Cabinet. The gist of the cable to Shigemitsu evidences a substantial retreat:

(1) Settlement of the Changkufeng Incident is to be based upon the Hunchun agreement, as the USSR proposed.
(2) Although Changkufeng may be given up by the Japanese if necessary, it is desirable that there be an immediate ceasefire and confinement of the affair within the limits of a sheerly local dispute between the Japanese and the Russians.[36]

Prompt negotiation with Litvinov along these lines was urged on the Ambassador.

The "urgent" instructions wired to Shigemitsu on August 6 contained concrete conditions for him to introduce during conference with the Foreign Commissar.[37] He was to propose two alternatives: mutual withdrawal (if the Soviets had not advanced west of the lake) or a unilateral Japanese pullback, neither side to enter the mid-zone until the dispute had been settled. Following a ceasefire, the Japanese would be willing to enter into discussions concerning boundaries; there was no objection to the use of the Hunchun accord as the basis for deliberation. Demarcation should be accomplished by joint investigation on the spot, in consultation with documents of both Manchukuo and the USSR. The interested parties were those two countries; the Japanese side would merely attend.

Shigemitsu conferred again with Litvinov on August 7, but he felt that no progress was made. "Litvinov insisted that a clash could be averted only if the Japanese forces pulled out," Shigemitsu noted. Litvinov also asserted that "Soviet troops would never cross the border which they claimed as their own." Complaining of a new incident near Grodekovo, the Commissar used strong language:

... it appears essential to declare that the Soviet government does not intend in the future to permit the unpunished, periodic killing and wounding of its border guards, nor the even-temporary occupation of Soviet territory by Japanese forces; and that it fully intends ... in similar instances, to use the most severe measures—including the use of artillery and aviation. Let the Japanese government oblige the Kwantung and Korea Armies to respect the existing frontier. It is time to put an end to the endless "incidents" and clashes on the frontier.[38]

The *New York Times* correspondent in Moscow judged that Litvinov's stance represented "little less than an ultimatum: 'Either you call off your dogs or we will let loose our planes.'"[39] Japanese papers noted that the parleys were "on the right track" but that Russian provocations had not ceased and that Russian contentions were inconsistent.[40]

By August 8 Baron Harada had grown extremely concerned about reports of furious ground fighting in the Changkufeng area, major Soviet air attacks, and considerable Japanese casualties. According to Ugaki,

Telegrams from Shigemitsu are not arriving with regularity yet. At the front, the local personnel seem to be very excited. When I discussed matters with the navy minister [Yonai], he too was quite worried and said that at tomorrow's cabinet meeting he would again venture to suggest sending instructions [to Shigemitsu]. From what wires we do have from Shigemitsu, he seems to be wanting a ceasefire at the present stage; but although the Soviets had requested withdrawal of our forces, we did not accept right away. Under these circumstances, Shigemitsu is apparently attempting certain "tactics" designed to effect a ceasefire. To the minister of navy, however, it seems that *Shigemitsu has a fear of the [Japanese] Army; or, if not, that he just does not comprehend the characteristics of this [Changkufeng] incident; i.e., he does not grasp the fundamentals of his instructions.* His method of drawing out the negotiations by utilizing "tactics" is not desirable.[41]

Navy Vice Minister Yamamoto claimed that the new draft of instructions for Shigemitsu was still not clear enough. "We should wire directions which are specific and easy to comprehend," Yamamoto remarked to Harada. "I'm afraid the ambassador may not understand the situation well unless his instructions are stronger and more direct." Ugaki assured Harada, however, that the necessary steps would be taken promptly. "It may become clearer in a few days," the Foreign Minister added, "whether the Soviets are really serious about a ceasefire or whether they are doing this in order to check Japan during the China Incident, before Hankow is taken."[42]

Gaimushō records reveal the contents of the instructions finally dispatched to Shigemitsu on August 9.[43] The conversation with Litvinov on August 7 had suggested that the Russians were inclined to conclude a truce on the basis of certain more specific conditions. Consequently, a third Japanese proposal (Point A) was being added to the plans transmitted on August 6. It was now acceptable to separate the troops of both parties by some fixed distance behind the borders, possibly one kilometer each. By "borders" the Soviets meant the so-called Hunchun treaty line that connected the peaks south of Shachaofeng to Changkufeng. Point B reiterated the proposal of August 6 with respect to border demarcation and documentation. Point C concerned the border commission but now stipulated that the Manchukuoan and Soviet sides should consist of two members each. Of the preceding points, A was the main objective. Suitable modifications concerning B and C, if necessary, were left to the Ambassador's discretion.

A number of high-level Japanese officials were still of the opinion that the instructions to Shigemitsu ought to be made more precise. Accordingly, on the afternoon of August 10, the Foreign Ministry wired yet another set of directions. This proposal did not differ in substance from the plan sent the day before but it was couched in terms that would apparently facilitate Soviet acceptance. The Japanese forces were to withdraw to the line existing on July 29, as the Soviets had insisted. In addition, neither side was to allow its troops to enter a buffer zone (to be set at a fixed distance—perhaps one kilometer—on either side of the Hunchun boundary claimed by the USSR) until demarcation had been accomplished by the proposed border commission.[44] Yamamoto told Harada that the instructions sent to Shigemitsu by the Foreign Minister called for settling the Changkufeng affair promptly.[45]

On the basis of the latest *Gaimushō* proposals of August 10, Shigemitsu conferred once more with Litvinov. The basis for the agreement, submitted by the Ambassador that same day, was to be the map appended to the Hunchun border protocol and the *status quo ante* July 29. If either side happened to have troops across the agreed-upon boundary at the time of the accord, they must be withdrawn on a mutual basis and must not again approach the line. Demarcation procedures would only follow the cessation of fighting, since the present confrontation was so dangerous.

The Foreign Commissar agreed that Shigemitsu's precis of the Soviet position was generally accurate, but he noted several exceptions. He had only said that the Hunchun line must be recognized and crossed neither by men nor gunfire, but he had not said Russian troops would withdraw from that boundary. A retreat by Japanese forces would be welcome—it was their affair. Litvinov also noted that redemarcation and not demarcation was involved. In reply, Shigemitsu reiterated that the situation was fraught with danger due to the proximity of opposing forces. Did the USSR object to a withdrawal by both parties to a suggested distance of one kilometer on either side of the Soviet-claimed Hunchun boundary, in order to restore tranquility and lay the groundwork for subsequent determination of the borders? Litvinov objected to any withdrawal by Russian forces. The area under discussion was Soviet territory, and Russian soldiers were entitled to remain wherever they wanted. The USSR had never attacked Manchukuoan soil, nor did it intend to; the presence of Soviet troops should therefore present no difficulties in settling the border problem.

Of course, Soviet troops could be stationed in Soviet territory, answered Shigemitsu—and so could Japanese troops in Japanese territory. It was expedient, however, to relax the confrontation; otherwise demarcation would be impossible. A practical solution, he repeated, might be to remove the opposing forces beyond rifle range and then to proceed with other concrete matters concerning settlement on the spot. The Japanese side earnestly desired a peaceful solution to the whole unfortunate incident. Representatives of both armies at the front could attend to details.

Litvinov restated his own stand. Japanese troops might pull back from the line of occupation claimed to be Manchukuoan territory, thus creating a buffer zone to be respected by each side, but Russian soldiers would never withdraw from their own territory at the demand of a foreign country. Litvinov did agree, however, to a cessation of hostilities. "What would you say," asked the Commissar suddenly, "to issuing an order to cease all hostile operations as from noon (Maritime Province time) on August 11?" It would also be necessary to agree upon the border demarcation commission at the same time as a truce accord.

To implement any ceasefire, replied Shigemitsu, representatives of both sides ought to confer on the scene. No, said Litvinov, an agreement could be reached between himself and the Ambassador; it was not necessary to trouble local representatives. Shigemitsu stuck to his point; it seemed practical and necessary in order to avert misunderstandings and unexpected developments. Litvinov gave in. As for the frontier commission, the Commissar proposed appointing a mutually acceptable neutral umpire in addition to the two representatives from each side. Shigemitsu asked that Litvinov withdraw this particular proposal; discussion of an entirely new question would only serve to complicate the whole problem and delay the central negotiations for a ceasefire.

Litvinov then returned to the matter of the authentic maps to be used by a commission. The Ambassador made no objection to the use of such materials but pointed out the need to investigate other items in the possession of the Japanese and Manchukuoan side. He said that various past treaties certainly would be the most useful items, but he thought the border commission ought also to investigate such practical matters as border markers and monoliths. Litvinov was not adamant. All materials not incompatible with international pacts might be considered but, where they conflicted with treaties, the latter should be decisive.

On the subject of the truce itself, Litvinov wanted the decision made as soon as possible, if it were to be announced next noon. "I said to Shigemitsu that I wished to know what he thought regarding the cessation of hostilities. We can adopt the first proposal; that is, the proposal on the cessation of hostilities, and then continue to study other questions." The Ambassador replied that the Japanese side would be able to reply within two hours, after further study of the proposed ceasefire agreement. On the other points of discussion, however, Shigemitsu stated that he was in no position to give an immediate reply, pending consultation with Tokyo.[46] When Shigemitsu returned to his embassy after 9:30 P.M. on August 10, he was carrying the draft of a provisional truce agreement.

(1) At noon (Maritime Province time) on August 11, the forces of both sides shall cease fire.

(2) Japanese troops are to pull back one km. west of the present line; that is, from the line of occupation retroactive to midnight . . . on August 10 (before the time of the ceasefire). Soviet troops shall retain their present positions (i.e., the retroactive line).
(3) The preceding agreement shall be carried out by representatives of both armies on the spot. Once the fighting has terminated, these military representatives may convene immediately, to agree on necessary conditions (exchange of corpses, prisoners, etc.).[47]

Early word of the final agreement conveying the new stance of the Soviet Foreign Office reached the Tokyo papers via special cable from New York on August 10. Shigemitsu's first official telegram, however, had been extremely brief, and details were not yet known to the *Gaimushō*—only the following text: "Soviet side gradually yielded to our contentions, and we achieved concrete agreement concerning ceasefire. Said plan to be confirmed officially by midnight of 10th."[48]

The night, however, was not over. About 11 P.M. a phone call came from Litvinov's office requesting to see First Secretary Miyakawa in behalf of the Ambassador. Miyakawa set out promptly. Several dozen anxious minutes went by at the embassy, Shigemitsu remembered. Finally Miyakawa returned, rushing excitedly into the Ambassador's study where the staff had been waiting with concern.

"The Japanese troops need not withdraw!" he yelled, gesticulating wildly. It was a really dramatic scene. Litvinov, it seems, had advised Miyakawa that, on the basis of orders from the Kremlin, it would not be necessary for the Japanese side to pull back unilaterally. I therefore reported this news immediately to Tokyo: that both sides would cease fire in the shape of the present *status quo*.

As soon as the elated Japanese called to confirm the agreement, Litvinov asked Shigemitsu to come to the Foreign Office. The Ambassador arrived around midnight. Litvinov showed him a draft of the written accord prepared beforehand.

(1) Japanese and Soviet forces shall cease all military activities on August 11 at 12 noon, local time. Instructions to that effect are to be issued immediately by the governments of the Soviet Union and Japan.
(2) Japanese as well as Soviet troops shall remain on those lines which they occupied at midnight, local time, on August 10.
(3) For redemarcation of the portion of the frontier in dispute, there shall be created a mixed commission of two representatives from the Soviet Union and two representatives from the Japanese-Manchurian side with an umpire selected by agreement of both parties from among the citizens of a third state.
(4) The commission for redemarcation shall work on the basis of agreements and maps bearing the signatures of plenipotentiary representatives of Russia and China.

Litvinov asked whether Shigemitsu had any objections. The Ambassador replied that he could accept the first two paragraphs in full, but he reiterated his earlier stand regarding the composition of the envisaged boundary commission. He agreed that the Manchukuoan delegation consist of one commissioner from Manchukuo and one from Japan (a compromise from the earlier desire that Japan be represented only by an observer); he could not assent to inclusion of a neutral member. In reply, the Foreign Commissar pointed out that the most effective guarantee of agreement on redemarcation would be the presence on the commission of an "unbiased, disinterested umpire," but since the Ambassador had objections, he would not insist at this time. Litvinov and Shigemitsu also disagreed about the documentation to be used by the frontier committee. Shigemitsu repeated that the Japanese-Manchukuoan side desired to introduce other basic materials which till now had not been submitted to the USSR and "concerning which it therefore had no knowledge." The Ambassador assured Litvinov, however, that he would lodge inquiries with Tokyo as to the nature of these documents and he promised "amicably to answer at the earliest possible moment."

The net result of the conversation was that the USSR and Japan agreed upon a mutual cessation of military operations as of noon on August 11, with neither side to pull back from lines held as of the preceding midnight. Practical details as to implementation would be left to the respective military representatives on the spot. Regarding border demarcation (or redemarcation, as the Russians still insisted), there definitely was to be a joint commission, but Litvinov and Shigemitsu agreed privately to defer final decision as to the precise composition. The public releases stressed only the agreement on the ceasefire itself.[49]

At the time it was difficult to judge whether the Japanese or the Russians were more eager to consummate the ceasefire at Changkufeng by August 10. Shigemitsu had pressed his interview at Tokyo's urging, but Litvinov had responded with alacrity, in accordance with Kremlin guidance.[50] Even today, few historians know that the USSR took an unexpected step to appease the Japanese or at least to save face for them, even after Shigemitsu had pleaded for and won a ceasefire. The Soviet releases stressed that there had been an exchange of opinions on August 10, after which Litvinov had made a number of proposals in the name of the Soviet government. In other words, the world was told that specific overtures for a ceasefire had originated with the Russian authorities.

The Japanese Ambassador, in fact, had been surprised at Litvinov's proposal of what seemed to have already been suggested by the Japanese. Shigemitsu himself has asked the inevitable question: "Despite the Japanese side's assent to a unilateral withdrawal of forces to a distance of one kilometer, why did Litvinov later modify this as being 'unnecessary'?" One reason for this, Shigemitsu later reminisced, was that he had been misled by information "to the effect [that] the Japanese Army had retaken Chang-kufeng and was fighting on the eastern skirt at present. This information differed from the facts in reality, yet not only I, who was in charge of negotiations, but also the army attaché, were merely advised that our troops had recaptured [the hill], so far as the fighting on the scene was concerned." He continued, "The real story was not conveyed to us. So it was our impression then that the combat at Changkufeng had developed rather favorably for the Japanese side and that our soldiers had indeed succeeded. . . . " In truth, he later thought,

> The Soviet forces had already driven off the Japanese troops by August 10 and had recovered the crest of Changkufeng, thus reaching the line which they had, all along, been putting forth as their border. This indicated that the Soviet Army had already achieved its mission of defending the state frontier; so they may have wanted to make clear that they had no intention of advancing farther and that it was also no longer necessary for the Japanese to withdraw.[51]

In general, high-level Japanese reaction to the ceasefire with the Russians was one of cautious relief. Nevertheless, there was considerable displeasure in certain quarters with Shigemitsu's "tactics" and with the delays in reporting. Horinouchi voiced some of these sentiments to Harada, while Admiral Yonai commented that Shigemitsu seemed to fear the army or else did not fully comprehend his instructions. When Harada visited Saionji on August 12, the old prince was highly explicit in discussing problems: "Well, it's fine that the dispute at Changkufeng has been settled but, on the basis of having examined the messages between the *Gaimushō* and Shigemitsu, I must say that the diplomatic negotiations were an utter mess. I suppose it must have been difficult [for Shigemitsu? Ugaki?] —being so confined by the army, etc. Still, as I say, things were nothing but a mess."[52] There were also misgivings about the *Gaimushō* leadership. Harada was sufficiently troubled to explore the possibility of securing consultant assistance for the "amateur" Foreign Minister Ugaki.[53]

Coupled with Yonai's guess that Shigemitsu feared the army, there is Harada's citation of Horinouchi, who said the *Gaimushō* was "flabbergasted" by the "military sounding" telegram transmitted by the Ambassador on August 10. At the postwar Tokyo trials, however, when the prosecution sought to press Ugaki on this particular point, the former Foreign Minister denied knowledge of every contention which the prosecutor was obviously extracting from the Harada journal.[54] Ugaki, on the contrary, praised Shigemitsu's diplomacy at various times before and after the war. In his diary entry for August 11, 1938, Ugaki attributed the success in obtaining a ceasefire to the performance both of the Japanese Army in the field and of the Ambassador in Moscow.[55] In a postwar deposition, Ugaki insisted that contact between the *Gaimushō* and Shigemitsu was excellent throughout the crisis: "I was kept constantly informed by . . . telegrams and knew that my instructions were being carried out." Ugaki called Shigemitsu's handling of negotiations "skillful and expert"; the Ambassador had prevented the border confrontation from escalating into general war. The Foreign Minister therefore had sent Shigemitsu a cable of commendation and appreciation. Ugaki "heard from no one in Russia or anywhere else that the Soviet Union did not desire [Shigemitsu] as ambassador, nor that that country was dissatisfied with his work."[56]

Nishi Haruhiko, the Counselor of Embassy at Moscow during Shigemitsu's tour of duty, maintained that the Ambassador was "rather rough" in his dealings on occasion. "But," adds Nishi, "he was extremely loyal and obedient to the instructions of the home government—so much so that even I sometimes had to raise objections to those instructions." Ota Saburō, Third Secretary at the embassy, told the press publicly on August 5, 1938, that Shigemitsu was "very happy and energetic" in his post. It was even said that every time the Ambassador saw Litvinov, "they would get into a fight." According to Matsuoka, Shigemitsu was designated Ambassador in the first place because he was "a type who can endure boiling water in the bathtub."[57]

As for the Japanese Army's evaluation of Shigemitsu's performance, Nishi tells us that the Ambassador received a most unusual telegram of appreciation from the Kwantung Army at the time of the settlement of the Changkufeng Incident. "It was rare indeed for a diplomat to be thanked by the Japanese military for anything," he noted. At the general staff level, however, a most knowledgeable army officer, Operations Section Chief Inada, did not feel that the diplomatic proceedings at Moscow had gone too well, from the Japanese point of view. "This was due to the ambassador's ignorance of the real situation," said Colonel Inada, "by which I mean that he was not kept well-informed."[58]

Shigemitsu would have been the first to agree; he termed the negotiations "very unpleasant and severe" and decried the lack of essential and accurate information about the front-line situation at Changkufeng. "From the beginning to end," he recalled, "I adhered to the same view; namely, that the clash should be stopped and tranquility restored by separating the opposing forces, ceasing the combat, and only then determining the uncertain boundaries, but fairly. There was no other method of concluding the negotiations and ending the dispute, I was convinced, than by our steadfastly maintaining a position of justice and reason throughout." He did not believe that any other policy would achieve the desired objectives: "There was no other real way except to adopt the method I did, in order to consummate the negotiations with the USSR (a truly unique country), while I had the tough Japanese Army on the other hand."

Shigemitsu came to believe that the main reason the army endorsed his handling of the Changkufeng affair was that it had, at the same time, mounted a general offensive against Hankow. Consequently, the Japanese military were greatly relieved by the successful negotiations with the USSR. Ultimately, Shigemitsu wrote, "I felt keenly, however, that it was necessary to change our routine ways, by intensively restudying Japanese policies vis-à-vis the Soviet Union, as viewed through the problem of Changkufeng. I was therefore thinking that I'd like to return to Japan [from Moscow], when there was a chance, to submit my recommendations. But, unexpectedly, the government sent a wire transferring me to London."[59]

Shigemitsu called his own assignment to London "a promotion, in a way," while the Japanese press welcomed the appointment as a reward for his good work in Moscow. Ugaki agreed. The fact that Shigemitsu was so promptly transferred to the Ambassadorship in London (in late September 1938, after the Changkufeng Incident had been settled) did represent a promotion, according to the Foreign Minister, because Anglo-Japanese relations were at a delicate stage and required expert handling.[60]

IV

Shigemitsu Mamoru, an experienced, tough-minded, and patriotic diplomat, had successfully concluded negotiations in behalf of Japan in the summer of 1938 at Moscow. His stern and stubborn tactics were not popular with the Russian authorities. About the time of the Changkufeng settlement, the Soviet press printed cartoons caricaturing the Ambassador as he limped up the stairs to the foreign commissariat. Shortly after the incident, *Pravda* published an insulting article suggesting that Shigemitsu go home. The ambassador claimed *Pravda* was playing up to the Japanese military who had thwarted his original assignment to the post in China.

Thus, when the Changkufeng Incident erupted. Shigemitsu bore the brunt of the Russian "counteroffensive" stemming from accumulated grievances. Nishi privately thought it might be best if the Ambassador did leave the USSR after the Changkufeng dispute was settled, despite Shigemitsu's great patience and staying power.[61]

If Shigemitsu's outlook and tactics were displeasing to his Soviet hosts, there can be little doubt that he developed warm rapport at more congenial but equally difficult posts in China and Britain. For example, when Shigemitsu was in prison after World War II, Lord Hankey rose in the House of Lords, "under inescapable impulse of personal conscience and public duty," to call attention to the plight of "an old and true friend" of England. Hankey spoke movingly of Shigemitsu's "love of peace, his patriotism, his vision to see that Japan's higher interests lay in peace and friendship especially with this country and America, his courage to press his views on his government, even when they were unpopular, and the aura of integrity and goodness that surrounded the man." Hankey stressed that his opinions were based upon long and repeated conversations with Shigemitsu, sometimes in the presence of other officials "whose estimate of Shigemitsu was as high as my own." Churchill called Shigemitsu "a man most friendly to peace between our countries." He "was generally regarded as a man of high character," said R.A. Butler, Parliamentary Under Secretary of State in 1940. Lord Sempill added that Shigemitsu "was essentially a man of peace and one quite incapable, in my judgement, of any action, open or underhand, that would lead to war." According to an article in the *London Times* on June 20, 1941, "Mr. Shigemitsu has won personal respect everywhere in London."[62]

The British tributes were shared by American officials who knew Shigemitsu well. "I can recall no instance during my fifteen years in the embassy at Tokyo," wrote Eugene H. Dooman, "that any commentary was made by the embassy to the Department of State on Mr. Shigemitsu that was not complimentary and favorable to him." Diplomats acquainted with Shigemitsu in Moscow agreed with his approach and personal qualities. Loy Henderson called him "a man of personal integrity and idealism, a view that was shared by most members of the American embassy at Moscow." Ambassador Joseph Davies said Shigemitsu was "definitely a liberal, progressive and altruistic humanitarian in his approach to international relations." As Lord Hankey had noted, sixteen eminent British and American citizens spontaneously volunteered to send statements in Shigemitsu's behalf to the international military tribunal for the Far East. "All these men knew Shigemitsu well; and it is impossible that, without some such qualities as ascribed to him, so remarkable a collection of tributes from the countries of his former enemies could have been written."[63]

In Japan itself, Shigemitsu had the reputation for being methodical, deliberate, self-assured, and orthodox in his diplomacy. His passionate devotion to the Throne was well-known.[64] But not every homeland associate was an admirer. The harshest critics went so far as to term him a cold and petty bureaucrat of limited lights, even a tool of the army.[65] Ugaki's postwar testimonials smack of excessive protestation. Regarding the diplomacy of 1938, Shigemitsu himself spoke of misunderstandings and blamed part of the difficulty upon lack of information. Certainly communication problems caused by the great distance between Moscow and Tokyo played some part. More importantly, arbitrary Japanese military action by the units in North Korea did not facilitate the Ambassador's dealing with the Russians.

Japanese Army field forces, typically anti-communist, Anglophobic, anti-American, and pro-German, were known for seeking to outfox the more conservative and better-balanced central military and civilian authorities and to drag them along by *faits accomplis*. In the 1930's they flagrantly undertook unilateral action without securing prior Imperial Sanction.

However patriotic or idealistic the local forces may have been, their fault was to equate national interest with policies of imperialism and to decide problems on a blinkered and individual military basis. The British diplomat Sir Robert Craigie once noted that most Japanese line officers sprang from peasant stock and received only rudimentary general education. "Indeed their ignorance and narrowness of outlook on all subjects other than strictly military ones, combined with their inclination to poke their fingers into every political pie, [was] one of the tragedies of modern Japan."[66] Such were the realities which explain Shigemitsu's critical allusions to the "tough" Japanese Army.

Shigemitsu achieved his objective of a ceasefire and de-escalation in 1938 as a result of Soviet preoccupation with Spain and Czechoslovakia and because of Japanese concern with the "final" Hankow campaign. That he was dubbed a war criminal by the Soviet prosecution after the war represents a supreme irony, for on Count 35 (conspiracy to wage aggressive war at Changkufeng) Shigemitsu won the rare distinction of an acquittal by the international military tribunal. The year after the Changkufeng affair, Shigemitsu was already in London when the fire-eating Kwantung Army, which learned nothing and forgot nothing, dared to cross swords with the Russians in the disastrous border war at Nomonhan on the Mongolian frontier. Yet, long before, Shigemitsu had warned that an aggressive border policy against the USSR would be counterproductive.[67] It is not surprising that he engendered an equal and undying resentment from the Soviet authorities and the Japanese military.

Notes

1 For an emotional Japanese account of Shigemitsu's "travel to grief," see Toshikazu Kase, *Journey to the Missouri* (New Haven: Yale University Press, 1950), pp. 4-10, 13-14. The official American version is found in *Reports of General MacArthur* (Washington: Government Printing Office, 1966), 1:454-458.

2 The author gratefully acknowledges the assistance rendered him by the Rockefeller Foundation and by the San Diego State University Foundation in obtaining materials for this essay.

3 Solis Horwitz, "The Tokyo Trials," *International Conciliation* (November, 1950), pp. 582, 584.

4 Author's interviews in Tokyo with Ben B. Blakeney and George A. Furness. Also see Lord Hankey, *Politics, Trials and Errors* (Oxford: Pen-in-Hand, 1950), p. 142; Sasagawa Ryō'ichi, *Sugamo no hyōjō* (The Look of Sugamo) (Osaka: Bunkajin Shobō, 1949), pp. 170-173.

5 Shigemitsu Mamoru, *Gaikō kaisōroku* (Diplomatic Memoirs) (Tokyo: Mainichi Shimbunsha, 1953), pp. 3-6, 21-23.

6 *Ibid.*, pp. 24-27.

7 *Ibid.*, pp. 32-37.

8 *Ibid.*, pp. 38-47.

9 *Ibid.*, pp. 48-140, *passim.*
10 *Ibid.*, pp. 164-165.
11 *Ibid.*, p. 204.
12 *Ibid.*, pp. 140 ff., 166-170, 204-207.
13 Akamatsu Yūsuke, *Shōwa jūnen no kokusai jōsei* (The International Scene in 1935) (Tokyo: Nihon Kokusai Kyōkai, 1936), pp. 20-21; *Shōwa jū'ichinen no kokusai jōsei* (1936) (Tokyo: Nihon Kokusai Kyōkai, 1937), p. 8; *Manshūkuoku gensei* (The Present State of Affairs in Manchukuo) (Hsinking: Manshūkoku Tsūshinsha, 1939), p. 11.
14 Gaimushō Ō-A kyoku dai ikka kirokuhan (Records Subsection, 1st Section, Euro-Asiatic Bureau, Foreign Ministry), *Shōwa jūsannendo shitsumu hōkoku* (Official Report, 1938) (Tokyo, December 1938), Document SP 312 (microfilm copy), p. 77. Cited hereafter as Gaimushō, SP 312; *Chūō Kōron,* August 1938, pp. 123-124; International Military Tribunal for the Far East, *Transcript,* June 3, 1947, p. 23,480 (excerpt from Gaimushō records for 1941). Cited hereafter as IMTFE.
15 The citation from Soviet frontier guard records for 1932-1945 (dated February 20, 1946) will be found in IMTFE, *Transcript,* June 2, 1947, p. 23,414. Also see *Ibid.,* February 17, 1948, pp. 39,827-828.
16 The author presented preliminary findings from his field researches in a paper, "Japanese Handling of the Changkufeng Incident, 1938: The Question of Escalation," read before the inaugural meeting of Asian Studies on the Pacific Coast, San Francisco State College, June 17, 1966. Also see Hata Ikuhiko, Usui Katsumi, and Hirai Tomoyoshi, *Ni-Chū sensō* (The Sino-Japanese Conflict), Part 2, vol. 4 of *Taiheiyō sensō e no michi* (The Road to the Pacific War) (Tokyo: Asahi Shimbunsha, 1963), pp. 82 ff.
17 Gaimushō, SP 312, p. 53. Gaimushō Tō-A kyoku dai sanka (3rd Section, East Asia Bureau, Foreign Ministry), *Chōkohō jiken to Manshūkoku* (The Changkufeng Incident and Manchukuo) (Tokyo, September 1938), Document SP 235 (microfilm copy), pp. 8-9. Cited hereafter as Gaimushō, SP 235; United States Department of State, *Papers Relating to the Foreign Relations of the United States, 1938, The Far East* (Washington, D.C., 1954), 3:456. Cited hereafter as *FRUS, 1938,* vol. 3. Also author's interview in Tokyo with Katakura Tadashi.
18 Gaimushō, SP 312, pp. 52-54; Akamatsu Yūsuke, *Shōwa jūsannen no kokusai jōsei* (The International Scene in 1938) (Tokyo: Nihon Kokusai Kyōkai, 1939), pp. 345-346; *FRUS, 1938,* 3:455-456. Also interviews in Tokyo with Nishi Haruhiko, and his *Watakushi no gaikō hakusho* (A Diplomat's White Book) (Tokyo: Bungei Shunjū Shinsha, 1963), p. 169.
19 Shigemitsu, *Gaikō kaisōroku,* pp. 215-216. Walter Duranty, in Moscow, claimed Shigemitsu had been on a Scandinavian holiday; *New York Times,* July 22, 1938, p. 1.
20 Shigemitsu Mamoru, *Shōwa no dōran* (The Showa Era: Years of Upheaval) (Tokyo: Chūō Kōronsha, 1952), 1:202.
21 Nishi says he had already detected something odd on the black-and-white photocopy of a tsarist-Ching map shown him by Stomonyakov: the boundary was *drawn* in vermilion. At least that was the color it looked by artificial light in Moscow. Ten years later, when Nishi saw the same or a similar photo-map at the Tokyo trials, the color of the marking was yellow. Shigemitsu also felt that the *ex post facto* nature of the markings

on the Soviet-served photo-maps produced at the Tokyo trials constituted a weak or painful feature of the USSR's case. Shigemitsu Mamoru, *Sugamo nikki* (Sugamo Diary) (Tokyo: Bungei Shunjūsha, 1953), pp. 54-55, entry for October 15, 1946.

22 Shigemitsu, *Gaikō kaisōroku*, p. 217; *Shōwa no dōran*, 1:203. Also see IMTFE, *Transcript*, June 10, 1947, pp. 22,894-896.

23 Litvinov Diary, July 20, 1938, Pros. Doc. 2241, Exhibit 754, IMTFE, *Transcript*, October 15, 1946, pp. 7,759-763; Def. Doc. 1540, Exhibit 2633, *Ibid.*, May 22, 1947, pp. 22,803-818; Tass statement, July 21, 1938, *Mirovoe Khoziaistvo*, 1938, nos. 7-8, p. 195, in Jane Degras (ed.), *Soviet Documents on Foreign Policy, 1917-1941* (London: Oxford University Press, 1953), 3:294-295; *New York Times*, June 22, 1938, p. 7; *FRUS, 1938*, 3:456.

24 Gaimushō, SP 312, pp. 54-55; *FRUS, 1938*, 3:457.

25 Gaimushō, SP 312, p. 56; *Tōkyō Asahi*, July 31, 1938 (a.m. edition), p. 3; *FRUS, 1938*, 3:459, 462; *New York Times*, August 2, 1938, p. 1.

26 Harada Kumao, *Saionji Kō to seikyoku* (Prince Saionji and the Political Situation) (Tokyo: Iwanami Shoten, 1950-1952), 7:58-59, information from Matsudaira; *FRUS, 1938*, 3:464.

27 See *Kido nikki* (The Kido Diary) (Tokyo: Heiwa Shobō, 1947), no. 99, p. 48; War Ministry Secret Wire 134 (Manchukuo Affairs), from Vice Minister of War Tōjō to Korea Army Chief of Staff Kitano, August 1, 1938, *Chōkohō jiken no keii* (Particulars of the Changkufeng Incident), Chōsengun shireibu (Korea Army Headquarters), August 30, 1938 (microfilm copy), p. 45, Attachment B.

28 Gaimushō, SP 312, p. 56; *Tōkyō Asahi*, August 4, 1938 (p.m. edition), p. 1.

29 Harada, *Saionji Kō*, 7:60. For Ugaki's later denials, see IMTFE, *Transcript*, June 10, 1947, pp. 23,898, 23,900.

30 Harada, *Saionji Kō*, 7:58-59; information from Matsudaira, August 3, 1938.

31 *Ibid.*, 7:62.

32 *FRUS, 1938*, 3:465-466.

33 Based upon Litvinov Diary, August 4, 1938, Def. Doc. 1522, Exhibit 2635, IMTFE, *Transcript*, May 22, 1947, pp. 22,825-36; Tass communiqué, *Pravda*, August 5, 1938; *FRUS, 1938*, 3:467-469; *New York Times*, August 7, 1938, pp. 1, 29. Also see Gaimushō communiqué, August 6, 1938, Def. Doc. 1652 (Blakeney Collection); Gaimushō jōhōbu (Information Bureau, Foreign Ministry), *Chōkohō jiken: Gaikoku shimbun ronchōshū* (The Changkufeng Incident: Foreign Press Comments) (Tokyo, September, 1938), Document SP 233 (microfilm copy), pp. 112-115. Cited hereafter as Gaimushō, SP 233; Gaimushō, SP 312, p. 57; Nakamura Bin, *Man-So kokkyō funsō shi* (A History of Manchukuoan-Soviet Border Disputes) (Tokyo: Kaizōsha, 1939), p. 264; Akamatsu, *Shōwa jūsannen*, p. 347; *Tōkyō Asahi*, August 6, 1938 (p.m. edition), p. 1; *Ibid.*, August 7, 1938 (p.m. edition), p. 1; *New York Times*, August 7, 1938, p. 29.

34 Shigemitsu, *Shōwa no dōran*, p. 203; *Gaikō kaisōroku*, p. 218.

35 Gaimushō, SP 312, pp. 57-58.

36 Harada, *Saionji Kō*, 7:68-69.

37 Gaimushō, SP 312, pp. 57-58; *FRUS, 1938*, 3:472.

38 Shigemitsu, *Gaikō Kaisōroku*, p. 218.
39 *New York Times*, August 8, 1938, p. 4.
40 *Tōkyō Asahi*, August 8, 1938 (a.m. edition), p. 3.
41 Harada, *Saionji Kō*, 7:70-71, italics added.
42 *Ibid.*, 7:71-72.
43 Gaimushō, SP 312, p. 59.
44 *Ibid.*
45 Harada, *Saionji Kō*, 7:74.
46 Based upon Gaimushō communiqué, August 12, 1938, Def. Doc. 1654
     (Blakeney Collection); Gaimushō, SP 233, pp. 117-121, supplement;
     Gaimushō, SP 312, p. 60; Nakamura, *Man-So*, pp. 265-266; "Chōkohō
     jiken no keika" (Details of the Changkufeng Incident), *Shōkōdan hō*
     (Officer Group Report), Kōbe Regimental District, November, 1938, no.
     217, pp. 25-28; *Tōkyō Asahi*, August 12, 1938 (p.m. edition), p. 1; *Ibid.*,
     August 13, 1938 (a.m. edition), p. 3; Litvinov Diary, August 10, 1938,
     Def. Docs. 1670 A-D, Exhibits 2716, 2716 A-C, IMTFE, *Transcript*, June
     10, 1947, pp. 23,905-910, 23,918.
47 Gaimushō, SP 312, p. 60; Harada, *Saionji Kō*, 7:75.
48 *Tōkyō Asahi*, August 12, 1938 (p.m. edition), p. 1.
49 Based upon Shigemitsu, *Gaikō kaisōroku*, p. 219; *Shōwa no dōran*, p.
     204; Nakamura, *Man-So*, p. 267; Gaimushō communiqué, August 12,
     1938, Def. Doc. 1654 (Blakeney Collection); Gaimushō, SP 233, p. 121;
     Gaimushō, SP 312, p. 60; Akamatsu, *Shōwa jūsannen*, p. 348; *Tōkyō
     Asahi*, August 12, 1938 (a.m. edition), p. 2; *Ibid.*, (p.m. edition), p. 1;
     New York Times, August 13, 1938, pp. 1, 28. Also see Tass communiqué,
     August 11, 1938, in *FRUS, 1938*, 3:478; IMTFE, *Transcript*, May 22,
     1947, p. 22,875, Pros. Doc. 623, Exhibit 273; Litvinov Diary, August 10,
     1938, Def. Doc. 1670-D, Exhibit 2716-C; *Ibid.*, June 10, 1947, pp.
     23,910-911; Robert M. Slusser and Jan F. Triska *et al.*, *A Calendar of
     Soviet Treaties, 1917-1957* (Stanford, 1959), p. 122, citing *Mirovoe
     Khoziaistvo i mirovaia politika*, 1938, no. 9, p. 211, and Degras, *Soviet
     Documents*, 3:298-299; *New York Times*, August 11, 1938, p. 1.
50 Def. Doc. 1552 (Furness Collection); *FRUS, 1938*, 3:480. Walter
     Duranty, in Moscow, noted that news of the Litvinov-Shigemitsu
     agreement came only four hours after a Red Army communiqué
     indicating that the situation at Changkufeng was growing more dangerous;
     New York Times, August 11, 1938, p. 1.
51 Shigemitsu, *Gaikō kaisōroku*, pp. 219, 220; *Shōwa no dōran*, p. 204. Also
     see Nishi Haruhiko, *Kaisō no Nihon gaikō* (Recollections of Japanese
     Diplomacy) (Tokyo: Iwanami Shoten, 1965), p. 84.
52 Harada, *Saionji Kō*, 7:75-76.
53 *Ibid.*, 7:63-64, 69-71.
54 IMTFE, *Transcript*, June 10, 1947, pp. 23,898-901.
55 *Ugaki nikki* (The Ugaki Diary) (Tokyo: Asahi Shimbunsha, 1949), p. 320.
56 Based upon Ugaki Kazushige (Kazunari) affidavit, May 28, 1947, Def.
     Doc. 1685 (Blakeney Collection); also found as Exhibit 2715, IMTFE,
     Transcript, June 9, 1947, pp. 23,868-72.
57 Interview in Tokyo with Nishi Haruhiko; *Tōkyō Asahi*, August 6, 1938
     (a.m. edition), p. 11; Nishi, *Kaisō*, p. 86.
58 Nishi, *Kaisō*, p. 84; interview in Tokyo with Inada Masazumi.

59 Shigemitsu, *Gaikō kaisōroku*, pp. 220-221; *Shōwa no dōran*, p. 204, brackets added.
60 Shigemitsu, *Gaikō kaisōroku*, p. 224. Also see footnote 56, above.
61 Nishi, *Kaisō*, pp. 84-86.
62 Hankey, *Politics, Trials and Errors*, pp. 80-84; and author's interviews in Tokyo with George A. Furness.
63 Hankey, *Politics, Trials and Errors*, pp. 83-84.
64 For a recent evaluation, see Hayashi Masayoshi, *Himerareta Shōwa shi* (Hidden History of Showa) (Tokyo: Kashima Kenkyūsho, 1965), p. 316. Also see Matsumoto Shun'ichi, *Mosukuwa ni kakeru niji: Ni-So kokkō kaifuku hiroku* (Rainbow to Moscow: Hidden Record of the Reestablishment of Japanese-Soviet Relations) (Tokyo: Asahi Shimbunsha, 1966), pp. 105-118; Major-General F.S.G. Piggott, "Editor's Note" to Mamoru Shigemitsu, *Japan and Her Destiny: My Struggle for Peace*, trans. Oswald White (London: Hutchinson, 1958), p. 15. Also see Shigemitsu's own poignant remarks dating from his diplomatic service in China, in *Gaikō kaisōroku*, p. 164.
65 Kiyozawa Kiyoshi, *Ankoku nikki* (Dark Diary), in *Shōwa sensō bungaku zenshū* (Showa War Literature Series) (Tokyo: Shūeisha, 1965), 14:111, 118, 123.
66 See Alvin D. Coox, *Year of the Tiger* (Tokyo and Philadelphia: Orient/West, 1964), pp. 46-48; and Shigemitsu, *Gaikō kaisōroku*, p. 204.
67 *Gaikō kaisōroku*, p. 218.

Barbara Teters

Matsuoka Yōsuke

The Diplomacy of Bluff and Gesture

THE SHIFTING SANDS of Japanese politics in July 1940 brought to the Foreign Office a man who talked so much and revealed so little that in consequence of his very volubility almost nothing of real substance was known about him. Indeed, for that very reason Matsuoka Yōsuke is even today an enigma, the source of endless questions for which his own recorded words supply a multitude of possible and contradictory answers.[1] His behavior as Foreign Minister ceases to defy understanding only if one accepts the intuitive judgment of those Japanese contemporaries who believed that the Matsuoka who died insane in June 1946 was, in fact, already insane when he presided over the *Gaimushō* from July 1940 to July 1941.

There were a few political figures in the summer of 1940, such as Kido Kōichi, Hirota Kōki, and Arita Hachirō, who recognized that Matsuoka would be a "problem foreign minister," as Kido put it, rather than a solver of problems.[2] Many men of greatly divergent views, however, deemed him the best choice possible, given the critical and complex nature of the time. Moderates such as Shigemitsu were optimistic about the prospects for a solution to the China Incident with a Foreign Minister who was known to have deplored the affair from its start and who was understood to favor a generous settlement with the Chinese. Some reassured themselves that although Matsuoka publicly committed himself to an alliance with the Axis and to a totalitarian future, he was nonetheless at heart pro-American and pro-Western. Some, including the new Prime Minister, Prince Konoye, thought the incoming Foreign Minister, with his "nerve, vigor, skillful eloquence, and unlimited ingenuity," might be the one man able to master the army.[3] The army, on the other hand, noted the all-important fact that

Matsuoka had for years identified himself as a supporter of a military alliance with the Axis; it was further reassured by Matsuoka's leadership of the movement to dissolve political parties and was confident that any wayward tendencies could be controlled.

They were all mistaken in their various ways. When Matsuoka was forced from office in July 1941, it was because the very groups who had found him acceptable, if not welcome, one year before had discovered on closer acquaintance that what had seemed to be assets were indeed liabilities. They were in fact symptoms, some speculated, of the presence of a disordered mind.

I

Matsuoka once remarked that "the Western Powers had taught the Japanese the game of poker but . . . after acquiring most of the chips they pronounced the game immoral and took up contract bridge."[4] What was called "international" law was in fact the "family" or "house" law of the great Western powers. The failure of the League of Nations, as Matsuoka himself had seen when he defended Japan's case at Geneva in 1932-1933, revealed the unworkability of a single world order based on the assumption of the sovereign equality of all states. That system and that principle disguised the tyranny of the "haves," that is, the Western democracies, over the "have-nots." Germany's triumphs in the early months of the European war signalled the approaching destruction of the British Empire; with it would come the passing of the traditional world order, unlamented by the new Japanese Foreign Minister.

The "new order" envisaged by Matsuoka would consist neither of one world nor a multiplicity of sovereign states, legally equal but in fact at the mercy of the strongest and most unscrupulous. Instead, four regions or blocs, economic, political, and geographic units, each seeking its *lebensraum* to the south, would be guided and controlled by the Great Powers who were their natural and acknowledged leaders. Believing as he did that the disintegration of the empires of the Western democracies would bring the collapse of their power, Matsuoka anticipated a Western European and African bloc dominated by Germany. The Soviet Union and its satellites comprised a second bloc that was already in existence, like the American bloc in North and South America. Japan's natural role was hegemony in East Asia and the Western Pacific, including Oceania and perhaps extending as far as India in the West. As Matsuoka once described the scheme, "the world should be reorganized and re-formed in a more rational way as crystals are formed according to the law of nature."[5]

Ardent nationalist though he was, the Japanese Foreign Minister had little appreciation or sympathy for the nationalist aspirations of other Asian peoples; he had no conception of nationalism as a universal and over-riding force, nor did he foresee the disruptive power of nationalism and communism in combination. The "have-nots" of his world view were not the colonial peoples of Asia, Africa, and the Western Hemisphere, but rather the existing states which were out of power in the contemporary world order. Thus Matsuoka's "new order" was not new at all. It was merely the traditional system reorganized, with Japan and Germany sharing what had previously belonged to the Western European democracies, Russia contained between them, the United States isolated in the Western Hemisphere, and the colonial peoples as they had been before, albeit under different masters.

Japan's role in the postwar world was thus to provide political, economic, and social leadership to the peoples of Eastern Asia and the Western Pacific and also to give to the world at large the spiritual leadership that the hypocritical and decadent Western democracies had failed to provide. Always willing to expound at length on this theme, variously labeled "Japanism," "moral communism," and "Hakkō Ichiu" ("the whole world under one roof"), Matsuoka never explained exactly what he had in mind, but he always reiterated, "Japan can achieve this task. She has it in her."[6] Only a renewed and reordered Japan, however, stripped of the debilitating, materialistic accretions of recent years, could perform that mission. Thus Matsuoka explained his establishment in 1933 of the League to Dissolve Political Parties and his espousal of the Shōwa Restoration.[7]

Lacking in material resources, burdened as well as blessed by an exploding population, bogged down in the morass of the China problem, Japan counted for nothing in world affairs; she was subject to constant abuse and misuse by the world's great powers and was incapable of achieving her mission. Throughout his career, Matsuoka feared Japan's isolation above all else. If one relationship were weakened or destroyed, another must be created to take its place. In the early part of the century, Japan had allied herself with the Western democracies and had loyally supported them during World War I, only to be betrayed, first at Versailles and then at Washington where the cherished Anglo-Japanese alliance disintegrated. So it was that Japan had found herself friendless and defeated at Geneva where Matsuoka and his countrymen conceived of his role as that of "a Horatius defending his people against the onslaughts of the world."[8]

Disillusioned by the performance of the democracies, fearful of isolation, and inordinately ambitious, Matsuoka thus came to the *Gaimushō* committed to the Tripartite Pact. Indeed, his known predisposition toward an alliance with the Axis was one of the reasons his appointment as Foreign Minister had been acceptable to the army. There is no doubt that Matsuoka expected to be master of Japan's foreign policy as no Foreign Minister before him had been. Proud, supremely confident, aggressively self-assertive, still smarting from his defeat in the struggle with the Kwantung Army for control of Manchukuo's economic development, Matsuoka meant it when he said as he took office that he was resolved that he, not the army, would guide Japan's foreign policy. At the same time he was ambitious enough to have recognized that in his lifetime the Prime Ministership would be beyond the reach of any aspirant who did not enjoy the army's active support. By adopting policies desired by the army, and utilizing them for his own rather than the army's purposes, he hoped to remain master in the *Gaimushō* and ultimately to become Prime Minister.[9]

One of the new Foreign Minister's nicknames was "I, me, my," and he was known to boast of the label.[10] His frank and hearty manner and well-known loquacity masked a strong tendency toward deviousness and a marked preference for keeping his left hand from knowing what his right was doing even when this led to the frustration of his own design. The Matsuoka so often described as "blunt," "direct," "American" in his manner and ways was in fact addicted to the greatest secrecy, the most roundabout approaches, the most convoluted route to any objective, immediate or distant; as a consequence of his very strong visionary streak, his goals were often distant indeed.

Although the new Foreign Minister had been a career member of the Foreign Service, he scorned professional diplomats and their methods. He had little taste or talent for accommodation or negotiations, preferring rather the use of bluff and gesture. Always sure of the superiority of his own techniques, of his own insight into the behavior of other peoples, particularly Americans, of his own understanding of history and Japan's place in it, Matsuoka made little use of his professional staff. Almost on arrival in the *Gaimushō,* he set in motion a purge of more than forty career officers, who had "gone Western," replacing them with amateurs. His Vice-Minister, Ōhashi Chūichi, later recognizing that this program of dismissals had been a serious error, remarked, "A rice-cake dealer is a rice-cake dealer", but as he conducted the affairs of his office in the strictest secrecy, Matsuoka never felt the loss of the professionals.[11] Seventeen years as a career officer in his country's diplomatic service had left him with a profound contempt for professional diplomacy, a feeling vividly revealed in a comment he once made to Ambassador Grew: "even I know how to be correct as a Foreign Minister if I want to be but . . . such an attitude on my part will not be conducive to better understanding between us."[12]

II

Matsuoka's native village, Murozumi in Chōshū, before the Restoration had often been the rendezvous of such famous patriots as Sakamoto Ryūma and Takasugi Shinsaku, and all Chōshū children were brought up on the legend of

Chōshū's great Yoshida Shōin. Matsuoka's own family had given heavily to Chōshū causes in the years before 1868. By 1880, however, when Matsuoka was born, both village and family were rich only in memories of past glories and prosperity. Murozumi, once a flourishing seaport, had become almost a ghost town as trading patterns changed during the early years of the Meiji era. The family fortune, based on the shipping, banking, and warehousing activities of the firm known as Imago, had been greatly depleted as a result of the family's large contributions to Chōshū before the Restoration and vanished altogether with Murozumi's decline in importance as a commercial center.[13]

The Foreign Minister before Matsuoka, Komura Jutarō, had been to school in the United States, as a government scholar dispatched to Harvard, where one of his classmates was Theodore Roosevelt. Matsuoka Yōsuke crossed the Pacific at thirteen to make his own way, first washing dishes, doing yard work, selling coffee door-to-door, and later, contributing to newspapers, working for a contractor, serving as defense counsel for the indigent, and performing as substitute minister in his adopted Methodist Church. All these were part-time jobs (*arubaito*) while he worked his way through school—junior high school in Portland, high school in Oakland, and law studies at the University of Oregon in Eugene. He graduated at the age of twenty with a bachelor of law degree, second in his graduating class although his classmates remembered him as well for his gift of gab and his skill at poker. During these years too, "Frank" Matsuoka acquired a foster-family who became part of the legend of Matsuoka Yōsuke, pro-American at heart.[14]

The ten years Matsuoka spent in the United States coincided with a remarkable decade in the history of both the United States and Japan. While American nationalism, self-confidence, and expansiveness reached new heights, Japan came near its Meiji goal, recognition as a great modern power. It must have been a thrilling experience for Japanese far from home to read and hear of Japan's victory over China in 1895, and Matsuoka's pride in the news may have been all the greater for having heard it while serving as "houseboy" in an American household. Almost at once, however, the same newspapers which had brought the exhilarating word of triumph carried the story of national humiliation as Germany, France, and Russia intervened to require retrocession of the Liaotung Peninsula to China. Each succeeding year brought new European encroachments in East Asia and increased anger and apprehension among Japanese.

Matsuoka's stay in the United States also coincided with the first serious friction to develop between the United States and Japan. America's pursuit of its Manifest Destiny led to the annexation of Hawaii and the conquest of the Philippines, and thus to direct confrontation with Japan. By the 1890's anti-Japanese attitudes had developed on the West Coast, and

Matsuoka, living in Oregon and California in this decade, could hardly have escaped exposure to these antagonisms. Moreover, it is probable that like most of his countrymen who went abroad he often suffered the indignity of being taken for a Chinese, all the more galling after 1895 when the Sino-Japanese war had displayed China's backwardness in contrast to Japan's progress.

When he returned to Japan in 1902 at the age of twenty-two, Matsuoka carried home with him a heightened awareness of himself as Japanese, an almost classic fusion of love and hate for the country in which he had spent his youth, and an illusion, one shared with many of his countrymen and indeed with many American acquaintances as well. This was the fancy that ten years in America had given him an insight into the American character possessed by few, if any, other Japanese. He also brought with him a facility in English; indeed, American English is said to have become the language of his thought at the time. This command of the American tongue was accompanied by the directness, even bluntness of manner, which is often associated with Americans. These superficial characteristics, which caused him to be known as "the delegate from Oregon" when he served in the Diet in the early 1930's, marked Matsuoka all the rest of his life as being different from other Japanese. They contributed to his compatriots' conviction that this un-Japanese Japanese must possess the key to the understanding of the American character. They also led the Americans with whom he dealt to expect too much of him when it came to understanding themselves and their country, expectations Matsuoka himself shared fully. Disappointed in their hopes for him, Americans were later inclined to regard Matsuoka as an "ingrate," while Matsuoka himself never forgot that he had worked long and hard for the fluent English, the law degree, the knowledge of the West, and the American manner he brought home in 1902.

The American chapter in the life of Foreign Minister Matsuoka was thus the cause of numerous misunderstandings, countless frictions, and exaggerated and unrealistic expectations on the part of Japanese, Americans, and Matsuoka himself. This delusion of an insight he did not in fact possess helped to shape the enormous and fatal bluff which was an essential element in "Matsuoka diplomacy."

After a few months' study at Meiji University in Tokyo, Matsuoka placed first in a field of one hundred and thirty applicants in the 1904 Foreign Service examinations and began his seventeen-year career as a diplomat. It was a remarkable achievement for a graduate of the University of Oregon to enter a service traditionally dominated by graduates of Tokyo Imperial University. Despite this brilliant beginning, however, Matsuoka was never at home in the service. The most significant associations of Matsuoka's lifetime were established during his career as a diplomat, but on the whole, they were relationships linking him to the army, the Chōshū faction, the Seiyūkai, and the *zaibatsu*, particularly Mitsui, and not to the Foreign Office.

Matsuoka's close connection with General Minami Jirō began when he was assigned as Foreign Affairs Section Chief in the Office of the Kwantung Governor-General. At that time he came to know and admire Count Gotō Shimpei, the South Manchurian Railway Company's (SMRC) first president, who was simultaneously adviser to the Kwantung Governor-General from November 1906. In later years Matsuoka often said, "I am a disciple of Gotō's." During the same assignment, when the Governor-General was the Chōshū general Ōshima Yoshimasa, Matsuoka also came under the benevolent eye of the great Chōshū *genrō* Yamagata, who recalled with gratitude the pre-Restoration contributions of Matsuoka's family to the Chōshū cause. When Matsuoka married in November 1912, the go-between was Yamagata's associate General Tanaka Giichi, then Chief of the Bureau of Military Affairs and later Prime Minister. While stationed in Shanghai, the young Matsuoka became intimately associated with Yamamoto Jōtarō, then Mitsui's branch manager in that city. This relationship lasted all Yamamoto's life; to Matsuoka, he was always *"oyaji,"* a kind of honorary uncle through whom he made many other friendships among the Mitsui men and the politicians of the Seiyūkai.[15]

For a young man who not long before had been making his own way on America's West Coast, Matsuoka had not done badly in achieving powerful connections with the head of the Chōshū faction, the Mitsui house, and the army, but still he remained an outsider in the Foreign Service. His route into the service had been unusual, his manner was unconventional, and his views of Japan's foreign policy did not accord with the orthodox line in the *Gaimushō* during those years.

There was great animosity between Matsuoka and Shidehara Kijūrō, eight years Matsuoka's senior in the diplomatic service. Shidehara, unlike Matsuoka, had come to the Foreign Office via Tokyo Imperial University and had been aided in his rise by powerful family connections. Just as Matsuoka's entire diplomatic career was spent in China and Manchuria (except for brief assignments to Russia and the United States), Shidehara's assignments were all to Europe and America, with the exception of some time in Korea. To Matsuoka, Shidehara and "Shidehara diplomacy" typified the disservice done to Japan's national interests by the "orthodox" diplomats who dominated the Foreign Office during most of the century's first three decades.

An incident which occurred during World War I revealed the difference between "Shidehara diplomacy" and "Matsuoka diplomacy." In 1917 Matsuoka was acting as private secretary to both Prime Minister Terauchi and Foreign Minister Motono Ichirō. In that capacity he consulted with his old friend Tanaka Giichi, then Vice-Chief of the General Staff, to urge unilateral intervention in Siberia by Japanese troops as a basis for a massive expansion of Japan's power in Northeastern Asia. Shidehara and Makino Shinken, however, prevailed in the end with their arguments in favor of deferring to President Wilson's insistence on multilateral action. As late as 1941, Matsuoka still recalled with bitterness Shidehara's role in the lost opportunity.[16]

Matsuoka left Kasumigaseki for the SMRC in June 1921. The company's new president, Hayakawa Senkichiro, had been a member of the special committee for Siberian economic aid established largely through the efforts of Matsuoka, who had seen it as a means of checking the continental economic advances of the United States and furthering those of Japan. Yamamoto Jōtarō also encouraged him to leave the Foreign Office. An important factor in the decision was no doubt the fact that the Foreign Service was now dominated by the Shidehara faction; Shidehara himself was at this time Ambassador to the United States and would soon participate in the Washington Conference.

As a director of the SMRC, Matsuoka once again had an opportunity to observe at close hand the consequences of Japanese policies in Northeastern Asia. When his old rival Shidehara became Foreign Minister in June 1924, Matsuoka bitterly protested his policy of non-intervention in Manchuria's civil strife; he held the Foreign Minister responsible for not acting vigorously and effectively to strengthen Japan's Manchurian lifeline.

Matsuoka left the Mantetsu (SMRC) for a time in 1926, and when Tanaka Giichi took office as Prime Minister, Matsuoka returned to the SMRC in April 1927 as vice-president, with Yamamoto Jōtarō as president. The Mantetsu and its leaders were intended to be the vanguard for the Tanaka continental policy: resistance to the unification of China, opposition to the Nationalists' "rights' recovery" movement, and protection and enhancement of Japan's special position in Manchuria and Mongolia. This program was interrupted, however, by the fall of the Tanaka Cabinet as a result of the murder of the Manchurian warlord Chang Tso-lin, and Matsuoka and Yamamoto together left the SMRC and returned to Japan to engage in national politics as members of the Seiyūkai. Shidehara once again returned to power in the *Gaimushō*.

Matsuoka spent a good deal of time in 1929 as spokesman for Japan's interests in Manchuria and Mongolia. As he then stated the problem, it was a matter of Japan's right to live. For example, in a pamphlet entitled "Economic Cooperation of Japan and China in Mongolia," published in the summer of 1929, Matsuoka wrote: "If the individual man is inalienably endowed with the right to life, liberty and the pursuit of happiness, it follows that the individual nation's right to exist is no less sacred. If this be admitted, it follows that each nation should make its surplus resources available for the needs of others."[17] A few weeks later Matsuoka again presented Japan's case when he appeared as one of Japan's delegates before the Kyoto Conference of the Institute of Pacific Relations. A *New York Times* correspondent described his speech as "the dialectical rout of Dr. Hu Shih by Yōsuke Matsuoka . . . whose directness of manner and mastery of the facts surprised the foreign delegates into loud cheering."[18]

No doubt these public and effective expositions of the justice of Japan's cause on the continent aided in Matsuoka's election to the Diet in 1930. As a member of the Seiyūkai and a veteran of long experience in Northeastern Asia, he used the Diet again and again as a forum to express the classic *lebensraum* argument: "We feel suffocated as we observe internal and external situations. What we are seeking is that which is minimal for living beings. In other words, we are seeking to live. We are seeking room that will let us breathe."[19]

III

When he became president of the SMRC in 1935, Matsuoka, referring to Japan's actions in North China, said, "The arrow has already left the bow."[20] He might well have been referring to the determination of his own course in 1932-1933.

Matsuoka's qualities were uniquely suited to the needs of the Japanese government, which recognized that its case had been ineptly and ineffectually presented in Geneva by the three diplomats who had represented Japan there after the outbreak of the Manchurian Incident. Effective diplomacy at the League of Nations required above all else fluency, if not eloquence, in either English or French. Matsuoka's eloquence had not yet become unbridled verbosity; his English was easy, even colloquial. He was a Seiyūkai member of the Diet, an advocate of a "positive" continental policy, a veteran of many years on the continent, first as a member of the Foreign Service, then as a director and vice-president of the Mantetsu. He had been a diplomat for almost twenty years but had never been tainted with the orthodox diplomacy blamed by many powerful Japanese in 1932 for much of Japan's trouble. He was thought to be singularly qualified to understand Americans in particular, and Westerners in general. Retired from the Mantetsu, he had never been linked in any way to the September 1931 incident which precipitated the Manchurian crisis.

On the whole no one faulted Matsuoka's defense of Japan, which was probably the best that could have been made, given his country's case. Using essentially the same arguments advanced by his predecessors, Matsuoka spoke with unusual vigor and eloquence, for the most part with tact and taste, and in easy and effective English. Generally, he was perceptive in his choice of arguments most likely to be palatable, if not attractive, to the particular audience he was addressing. He now minimized, for example, the *lebensraum* argument he had been developing over the years, emphasizing instead others more likely to appeal to the "have" nations who mattered at Geneva: the menace of anarchy and communism, peace and order as prerequisites for profit-making, and the contrast between China's modern history and that of Japan.

Taken in the context of this highly competent performance, Matsuoka's January 1933 interview with Lady Drummond-Hay was all the more remarkable. "Japan's mission," he declared, "is to lead the world spiritually and intellectually. Japan can offer spirituality to America and the entire Western world. Japan, I am convinced, will be the cradle of a new Messiah."[21] It was an odd and prophetic lapse of judgment in a Geneva performance otherwise almost unflawed.

After leading Japan's departure from the League Assembly on February 24, 1933, Matsuoka travelled briefly in Europe, including a visit to the new Nazi Germany; although the Foreign Office had "misgivings," he also made a propaganda tour of the United States. It was a hardworking trip. Once again in the country where he had acquired his direct manner, Matsuoka employed it now in speech after speech. Frederick Moore, an American lobbyist for Japan, later recalled that his own chief task during the American tour was that of "constantly trying to restrain him [Matsuoka]," struggling always to persuade him to maintain a greater degree of discretion and moderation.[22]

There were probably no beneficial effects of this tour, nor was there any immediate harm to Japanese-American relations. The consequences in the long run, however, were unfortunate. This was Matsuoka's last glimpse of what he himself called his "second country," and he carried home with him a vivid impression of Americans so thoroughly absorbed in a state of domestic crisis that it was inconceivable that they would consent to expenditure of men and treasure in some far distant part of the world. Katō Matsuo, who was with Matsuoka throughout the American journey, wrote, "That was the last time he saw America, but the idea that America should stay out of the Pacific and could be talked into staying out or influenced by threats to remain aloof never left him."[23]

Matsuoka returned home to Japan at the end of April 1933 to a hero's welcome, another experience which left an indelible impression. Tokyo at once buzzed with rumors regarding his personal ambitions, but early in May he suddenly dropped from sight. The six months that followed may have been his forty days in the wilderness. He later said that it was then, in solitary reflection while fishing, that he realized Japan's future lay with Germany.[24]

On December 10, 1933, Matsuoka reappeared in public to announce his withdrawal from the Seiyūkai, his resignation from the Diet, and his establishment of a movement to bring about the dissolution of all political parties, the Seitō Kaishō Remmei. Many observers, Ambassador Grew among them, believed that these actions meant that Matsuoka had concluded that support of party government no longer promised a future to an ambitious man.[25] "To wait for political parties to improve," Matsuoka declared, "is like waiting for pigs to fly. . . . "[26] Nonetheless, Matsuoka's League to Dissolve the Parties was apparently not a very serious venture. Tsukui Tatsuo, a prominent right-wing and national socialist figure of the 1930's who himself participated in the League, recalls that "Matsuoka himself didn't seem to know what to do with the movement," and when Matsuoka returned to the SMRC as its president in the fall of 1935, the Seitō Kaishō Remmei quietly faded away.[27] In the meantime, however, it had no doubt helped to prepare the way for the dissolution of the parties and the establishment of the Taisei Yokusan Kai (Imperial Rule Association) in 1940. The Association had offered Matsuoka a modest platform during 1934 and most of 1935, and, more important, it validated his credentials in 1935 for the presidency of the Mantetsu and again for the Foreign Ministership in the summer of 1940.

Matsuoka was in many ways an appropriate choice for the leadership of the SMRC which in 1935 was still the main vehicle for Japan's economic thrust on the continent. He had been identified with the "continental faction" in Japanese foreign policy throughout almost all of the twentieth century. He had been associated with the Mantetsu in one capacity or another for many years. He had attracted the favorable attention of the military by his eloquent defense of Japan's interests at Geneva and again when he left the Seiyūkai and called for the dissolution of all parties.

The American embassy in Tokyo reported to Washington that Japanese business interests were much less pleased with the appointment. Having seen glimpses of Matsuoka's visionary qualities, they feared that "backed by the Kwantung Army, with equally or perhaps more visionary ideas, [he] may plunge the finances of 'Manchukuo' and the South Manchurian Railway into such difficulties that Japanese backers of enterprises in Manchuria will be faced with ruin. . . . " Furthermore, they had a tendency to fear any appointment approved by the Kwantung Army for it had traditionally been hostile to the *zaibatsu.*[28]

Japanese businessmen need not have worried about an alliance between the Kwantung Army and the Mantetsu with Matsuoka as president. When the first Konoye Cabinet took office, the SMRC president became a member of the Cabinet Advisory Council. By the fall of 1937 there was speculation that Matsuoka might replace Hirota as Foreign Minister in the Konoye Cabinet, and Matsuoka himself once remarked that he had thrice refused office in the first Konoye government. The reason may well have been that he was deeply involved in the final crisis the Mantetsu was then experiencing. Although the public knew Matsuoka as a member of a group called the "Niki Sansuke" (including Tōjō Hideki, Hoshino Naoki, Ayukawa Gisuke, Kishi Nobusuke, and Matsuoka), which was thought to control the economy of the state of Manchukuo, the united front "Niki Sansuke" presented to the world covered a serious disagreement in which Matsuoka as president of the SMRC set himself and his company against the Kwantung Army and lost.

Matsuoka saw the Mantetsu as having "carried the light of civilization into Manchukuo" for thirty years and he saw no reason why it should not continue to bear the burden and reap the glory for the country's development.[29] The Kwantung Army, however, greatly distrusted the Japanese government which, of course, controlled the SMRC. In the words of Ayukawa Gisuke, whose Nissan group eventually replaced the Mantetsu as the instrument of Manchuria's economic development, "This group of men who controlled the Kwantung Army in the beginning was dissatisfied with both army policy and governmental policy and they hoped and desired to establish in Manchuria what they had been unable to do in Japan." The Mantetsu, moreover, had earned enemies as a result of its high-salaried bureaucracy and had caused alarm in many circles by extending its operations far beyond its ability to raise capital.

The Kwantung Army, however, could not bring itself to rely on the zaibatsu which had been too intimately associated with the "soft" foreign policy of the past, too often susceptible to corruption, and too closely identified with the West. The China Incident in July 1937 finally convinced the Kwantung Army that the development of the army's "model state" would be far beyond the resources of the Mantetsu, the Japanese government, or the state of Manchukuo itself. It therefore adopted Ayukawa's proposal for the creation of a new organization based on his Nippon Sangyo K.K., a "new zaibatsu" group which would unify under its control all forms of economic development in Manchuria. This group was intended to absorb the SMRC's non-railroad enterprises and to invite the participation of foreign capital. In November 1937 the army compelled the SMRC to turn over its various administrative rights to the state of Manchukuo. In 1938 all of the SMRC's enterprises outside of the railroad industry were transferred to the Manchuria Heavy Industry Development Company, in other words to Ayukawa's Nissan interests.[30]

Matsuoka was furious yet helpless, unable to prevail even though it was his nephew, Kishi Nobusuke, who conducted the negotiations. When he left the SMRC in 1939, Matsuoka was replaced as president by Omura Takuichi, formerly chief of the communications supervisory section of the Kwantung Army. Thus the Kwantung Army compelled Matsuoka, who had been closely identified with the Mantetsu for over thirty years, originally as disciple of its first president, Count Gotō Shimpei, then as a director, vice-president, and finally president, to preside over the SMRC's liquidation as the instrument of Manchuria's progress. Matsuoka lamented in departing, "If they [the army] would just let a businessman run the country, I would put it on a paying basis in ten years."[31] A few months later, Foreign Minister Matsuoka sat in the second Konoye Cabinet with the Kwantung Army's General Tōjō Hideki as Minister of War.

IV

There is a proverb often quoted in Japan to the effect that the man who pursues two rabbits catches neither. Prince Konoye came to the Prime Ministership in the summer of 1940 committed to disparate and seemingly incompatible objectives: alliance with the Axis, avoidance of war with the United States and England, resolution of the China Incident which had begun during his first government, and mastery of the army. He found in Matsuoka a Foreign Minister quite capable of embracing the same divergent goals and ingenious enough to integrate them into a plan of action. Konoye's objectives became steps by which Japan would solve its obvious problems of population and resources, achieve hegemony in East Asia, and play a significant role in a peaceful and reordered world. In the end, as in the proverb, Matsuoka achieved none of his objectives.

The first step in the design and the one upon which all the others depended was the Tripartite Alliance, which Matsuoka had selected in 1933 as the route most likely to lead him to power. Now in office in 1940, he justified it as the most appropriate means to the nation's ends and expected its success to bring him ultimately to the Prime Ministership. The Tripartite Pact was based on the expectation that Germany would be victorious in the European War and on the conviction that such a victory was in Japan's interests. Matsuoka was not altogether blind to the possibility of a limitless German appetite once she had triumphed in Europe and the British Empire. "If we are careless," he said, "Germany will cross Siberia or will approach the Far East by sea, and our country will probably be overwhelmed by its power."[32] Still, in July 1940 when Matsuoka became Foreign Minister, there seemed little reason to doubt that Germany would indeed prevail, perhaps soon, and it was in Japan's interests to attempt to ensure that outcome and to utilize it for Japan's purposes. The dangers from a victorious Germany might well be prevented if Japan's leaders.showed sufficient foresight, while a victory for the democracies could not possibly be to Japan's benefit. Only if Germany won could Japan hope to inherit the estates of Britain, France, and the Netherlands in the East.

The alliance was also intended to deter America from intervening in the European war or in the Pacific, and to facilitate a settlement with the USSR.

Japan would thus be free to advance peacefully in the south toward a solution to its population and resource problems and toward establishment of the East Asia and Western Pacific blocs. Deprived by the alliance of both German and Russian support, Chiang Kai-shek would accept a reasonable settlement, after which Japan's troops could be withdrawn from the mainland and the army at last be mastered. Under these circumstances, there would no longer be any obstacle to an adjustment of Japanese-American relations, and Japan and the United States could join together in mediating the European conflict, thus bringing to mankind the blessings of a peaceful world order based on Japanese, German, Russian and American hegemony, and guided in some vaguely mystic fashion by Japan's spiritual leadership.[33]

As a plan of action the alliance design was extraordinarily elaborate and grossly ambitious. Held together by a lengthy chain of "ifs," the scheme was based largely on Matsuoka's magnificent confidence in his own capacity to understand and manipulate not only Japan's numerous, headstrong, and irresponsible factions but also the great powers of Europe and America whom he in fact understood hardly at all. The grandeur of the scope and the magnitude of omissions in all this were appropriate to what we know of the complex and unstable personality of Matsuoka himself.

By the New Year, failure was apparent even to Matsuoka.[34] The Tripartite Pact, the keystone of the design, had brought America closer to war, rather than deterred her. Germany was increasingly restless with the performance of the new Pacific ally whose reliance on verbal threats and gesture was no substitute for an attack on Singapore.

Count Gotō's dream of a Eurasia led by Germany, Russia, and Japan, the outer pair controlling between them the strong but wayward third, had been translated by Matsuoka's vision into a quadruple alliance which would emerge from the Tripartite Pact. The project had come to naught, thanks to Balkan problems of which Matsuoka was only dimly aware. Moreover, the bilateral negotiations between Russia and Japan that had once seemed very near successful conclusion had collapsed, perhaps in part because the able and experienced Tōgō Shigenori was purged at a critical point in the discussions and replaced by General Tatekawa, another "rice-cake dealer" in the world of diplomacy.[35]

Matsuoka had come to the *Gaimushō* boasting that if the army did not interfere, he would bring about a diplomatic settlement of the China Incident before the end of October.[36] On New Year's Day the prospect of peace in China seemed more remote than ever. Germany's good offices had brought no results, nor had the secret discussions between Matsuoka's agents and Kuomintang representatives in Hongkong. Worse yet, in order to increase the pressure on Chiang Kai-shek, Matsuoka had opened negotiations with Wang Ching-wei, not fully anticipating that pressure would build up in Japan and force him to sign a treaty with Wang on November 30 in Nanking. The agreement with Wang made the Kuomintang more adamant than ever.[37]

By the early spring of 1941, Matsuoka had also recognized that there was no prospect of gaining peaceful access to the resources of the Netherlands East Indies.[38] Only the negotiations with France had proceeded satisfactorily, offering some faint hope that Japan might increase military pressure on China from the south to induce Chiang Kai-shek to think again about negotiating before Japan's troops were withdrawn from the mainland.

The French accord was Matsuoka's only success in his first months in office, and even that could not be attributed to the Tripartite Pact but rather to the fact that Matsuoka was dealing with a France that had lost both the will and the capacity to resist. The grand alliance from which he had promised and expected so much, which had brought him to the *Gaimushō* and which he had expected to carry him even higher, had produced none of the consequences he had anticipated. The basic assumptions underlying the policy were proven invalid, thus revealing the inadequacies of Matsuoka himself. Unable to let go of the vision that was his pot of gold at the end of the rainbow, unable to relinquish his own ambition, Matsuoka deteriorated rapidly in physical and mental health.

The loquacity for which he was famous grew excessive. The increasing bellicosity of his speeches and statements and his growing reliance on the efficacy of "gesture diplomacy" or diplomatic bluster manifested the emptiness of his policy. Lapses of judgment were frequent as the winter passed into spring, and Matsuoka pursued his personal ambition with an openness which was self-defeating in his political culture. Compelled to improvise by his inability to acknowledge the collapse of his scheme, he followed an erratic and disastrous course during the spring and early summer of 1941.

Seen in retrospect, Matsuoka's famous trip to Europe—March 12 to April 22—reveals the bankruptcy of his policy. The Germans considered that the journey, if undertaken in time, might sway votes in the United States Congress where a decision on the Lend-Lease Bill was pending (it was to take place on March 11, 1941). The Nazis, growing increasingly restless with Japan's performance as an ally, also expected to use the occasion to insist on a Japanese attack on Singapore. Matsuoka himself claimed publicly that the trip was an exercise in personal diplomacy designed to cement relations with the Axis.

The journey evoked little enthusiasm in Tokyo. The professionals in the Foreign Office were apprehensive. Matsuoka's increasing garrulity was alarming, and they prevailed on the ultranationalist leader, Tōyama Mitsuru, whom Matsuoka greatly admired, to caution the Foreign Minister to watch his tongue while abroad. The Cabinet and the army, no doubt for somewhat different reasons, feared a commitment to attack Singapore. They obtained Matsuoka's word that he would commit Japan to nothing, and the army sent along Colonel Nagai Yatsuji to see that the promise was kept. Others were apprehensive lest the journey still further exacerbate American-Japanese relations.[39]

Although the Indochinese-Siamese conflict and its Japanese-imposed settlement delayed his departure until after the passage of the Lend-Lease Act, Matsuoka himself still saw the trip as an escalation of the bluff designed to dissuade America from more active intervention in the war. Konoye and Ōhashi persuaded him with difficulty to relinquish his plan of leading to Europe a large and, he hoped, imposing delegation of Diet members and other dignitaries.[40] It was generally understood at the time, however, that the primary purpose of the European trip was to negotiate a non-aggression or at least neutrality treaty with the USSR.[41] Indeed, many observers in both Axis countries and the West speculated that the visit to Europe was a manifestation of growing Japanese disenchantment with the Axis alliance.[42] Matsuoka's confidant and counselor, Saitō Yoshie, claims that the Foreign Minister went to Berlin prepared to determine once and for all whether the pact was going to lead to a rapprochement with Russia. If not, he proposed to abandon the partnership and proceed on his own for a settlement in Moscow; he was even in the process of constructing in his mind a new scheme of alliances, this time with Soviet Russia and the Western democracies.[43]

Tōyama's warning to the Foreign Minister to be guarded in his speech abroad did little good. There was much malicious speculation in advance as to what would happen in Berlin when the two famous egotists met, but in the end it was Matsuoka who bored and irritated Hitler and upset the schedule with his rambling, vague, and protracted discourse on "Hakkō Ichiu," while in Moscow he took up fifty-eight minutes of an hour with Stalin in an exposition of what he called "moral communism," in effect, another and no less hazy version of "Hakkō Ichiu."[44]

Later evidence reveals that Matsuoka in fact made no commitments to Hitler regarding Singapore. He indicated that he himself favored action but he left the Germans with distinct doubts as to his capacity to produce results in view of what they now realized was a most complex political situation in Tokyo. Matsuoka himself insisted on his return that he had made no promises for his country. Hearing no supporting testimony, Konoye and others concluded that it was impossible to be sure, and the disturbing uncertainty increased the growing tension between the Cabinet and the army on the one hand and the Foreign Minister on the other.[45]

Matsuoka's primary objective in Berlin had been to ascertain whether the alliance was going to be useful in reaching a settlement with Russia.

Although Hitler had given express orders that the Japanese leader was not to be told about Operation Barbarossa, the evidence suggests that he was given ample warning that something of the sort was brewing.[46] Nevertheless, Matsuoka proceeded at once to Moscow and signed a treaty with Russia, an action inexplicable in the light of what he had learned in Berlin, unless we accept Saitō Yoshie's testimony that the Foreign Minister went to Europe determined to secure a settlement with the USSR even if doing so meant abandoning the alliance.

While in Moscow Matsuoka took a step in highly personal and secret diplomacy—he sent a message to President Roosevelt through Ambassador Steinhardt in which he proposed to open negotiations.[47] Returning home with the Russian treaty as the *omiyage* (souvenir) he had promised on his departure and optimistic about the results of his overtures to the Americans, the ebullient Matsuoka was greeted with the triumphal reception so necessary to his well-being. Almost at once, however, he was deeply shaken by the news that in his absence and without his knowledge, the Prime Minister had begun negotiations with the United States.[48]

Piqued by the commencement of actions in which he had played no part and alarmed as to what those actions might mean in terms of his own political ambitions, exposed now without a foreign policy and perhaps anxious as to the consequences of what he had done in Moscow, Matsuoka proceeded to delay and obstruct the American talks. Simultaneously, he abandoned circumspection and began to display in a most un-Japanese way his ambition to replace Prime Minister Konoye, whom he now treated with a frank contempt. It was even rumored that he saw himself as Japan's Führer. In a notorious speech to a "welcome home" rally staged by the Imperial Rule Assistance Association at Hibiya, he "showed off" in German, boasted of his European conquests, raved about the miracles he had seen wrought by fascism, and as he rambled on, engaged in some frank and most indiscreet criticism of his fellow Cabinet members. Distribution of 200,000 copies of the speech was banned by order of Home Minister Hiranuma who had been one of Matsuoka's targets at Hibiya.[49]

Matsuoka's Cabinet colleagues were infuriated by the public criticism and alarmed by his manifest ambition. United for the moment in their desire to pursue negotiations with the United States, they were exasperated by his obstruction. Moderates and extremists alike were unnerved by the doubt as to the nature of Japan's commitments regarding Singapore. As the weeks wore on, there were repeated warnings from Europe that a Russo-German break was imminent, and apprehension grew regarding Japan's dilemma if Hitler attacked the Soviet Union. Over and over again Matsuoka denied the accumulating evidence. Even when Ambassador Oshima cabled that Hitler himself had told him at Berchtesgaden that Germany would attack the USSR, Matsuoka continued to insist that the chances were sixty to forty that the partnership would continue.[50]

When the attack began on June 22, some Japanese were furious that their country's hands were tied by treaty at a time when the Soviet Maritime Province might otherwise be acquired with relative ease. Others, including the Cabinet and armed forces, committed now to military action in Southeast Asia and still pursuing the negotiations with the United States, were appalled at the prospect of a two-front war. The government therefore adopted a temporizing position that it hoped to maintain indefinitely, unless of course it became obvious that Germany would march through Russia unchallenged, in which case some might argue that it would be useful to be a party to the peace treaty.

Matsuoka himself urgently and insistently demanded that Japan go to war against Russia, the country with whom he had just completed a neutrality treaty. He and Saitō Yoshie both claimed that he took this position with the conviction that there was no danger that his advice would be taken; his hope was that the prospect of the long-sought Russian war would divert the army from the projected military advance into Southeast Asia.[51]

Always fearful of isolation in world politics, Matsuoka had adopted alliance with Germany in 1933 as the *leitmotiv* of his rise to power. If briefly in the spring of 1941 he considered abandoning the Tripartite Pact, the intention had been in the context of a fantasy in which Japan was allied with the USSR and the democracies. When he was faced with the reality of the German attack on the Soviet Union at a time when it was apparent that control of relations with the United States had slipped from his grasp, Matsuoka realized that he could not be the architect of a Tokyo-Moscow-Washington axis. If, however, Germany triumphed effortlessly over the USSR, Matsuoka might be the man who secured for Japan the whole of Eastern Siberia, which would otherwise fall to a rampant Germany brought by victory to the very shores of the Sea of Japan. He might also claim credit for a great alliance of all the capitalist nations against the dreaded menace of world communism.

Naked to his enemies without the Tripartite Pact, Matsuoka therefore reverted to his original position, asserting that it was a matter of honor for Japan to fulfill her obligations to Germany. This was the stand he had taken in 1936 when supporting the army's campaign for an anti-Comintern pact: "This alliance cannot be close enough; it must mean going together through thick and thin and it must be based on complete loyalty and mutual self-sacrifice, as these find expression in Japanese *shinjū* [the double suicide of lovers]."[52]

V

It is not clear whether Matsuoka really expected an easy German conquest in the East or whether he anticipated a long, cruel, and uncertain Russo-German war and was in fact prepared to join a lover in suicide. The nation was not. The prevailing mood of the country in the summer of 1941 favored facing the future alone, relying on Japan's own strengths and pursuing Japan's own goals, unencumbered by alliances that had once again proved to be treacherous.[53] Moreover, the events of Matsuoka's year in office had revealed that he was not in fact able to manipulate the Americans and that he did not understand European politics, although he had pursued a plan based entirely on assumptions regarding the United States and European power relationships. He had come to office in 1940 because the moderates, the army, the ultranationalists, and the Konoye circle found him acceptable, each group for reasons which by the summer of 1941 had proved to be invalid.

The deterioration of Matsuoka's personality during the year had not gone unnoticed. The distinctive personal characteristics he brought to the Foreign Ministry—the volubility, the ambition, the secretiveness, the visionary and unrealistic quality, the extraordinary confidence in his own ability—had all become increasingly apparent during the year, and there was speculation that he was now in fact insane. Informed of the gossip, the aged Prince Saionji, watching events with a growing despair, wryly observed that if the Foreign Minister were indeed insane, then one might hope for his return to sanity.[54]

The Konoye Cabinet and the army were therefore unanimous that there was every reason for letting the Foreign Minister go. The only question was the form his departure should take since he had so manipulated negotiations with the United States that his dismissal might be interpreted as submission to American pressure. That consideration became the dominant one, and the Konoye Cabinet resigned on July 16 *en masse*. The following day, the third Konoye government was constituted with almost the same membership as the second, the significant exception being the absence of Matsuoka. The fiction was successful, and Matsuoka departed from office without public outcry. Perhaps still anticipating an easy German victory in Russia, Matsuoka left the *Gaimushō* expecting to return shortly to the Prime Ministership which in his unrealistic way he continued to see as the very pinnacle of power.

Notes

1 That Matsuoka remains today a mystery is due in part to the fact that, as Ambassador Grew once remarked, the Foreign Minister talked so much and so loosely that an abundance of contradictions was inevitable. There has as yet been no full biography of Matsuoka. He died during the Tokyo

war crimes trials, and we therefore do not know what evidence he would have produced in his own defense. He himself left only a very brief statement (released in June 1946) which in the circumstances of its writing (defeat, arrest and trial, and approaching death) is subject to considerable skepticism. In most Japanese and English-language accounts of the events preceding Pearl Harbor, he shares with Tōjō Hideki the responsibility for the tragedy of war.

Probably the accounts most sympathetic to him are, in English, David Lu's *From the Marco Polo Bridge to Pearl Harbor* (Washington, D.C.: Public Affairs Press, 1961) and in Japanese, Saitō Yoshie, *Azamukareta Rekishi–Matsuoka to Sangoku Dōmei no Rimen* (Tokyo: Yomiuri Press, 1955) and Ōhashi Chūichi, *Taiheiyō Sensō Yurai Ki* (Tokyo: Yōshobō, 1952) (Saitō Yoshie was Matsuoka's confidant and held the title of Counselor in the Foreign Office while Matsuoka was Foreign Minister. Ōhashi Chūichi was Matsuoka's Vice-Minister). Highly critical testimony is found in Kido Kōichi's *Kido Nikki* (Tokyo: Heiwa Shobō, 1947) and Prince Konoye's memoirs, written between October 1941 and March 1942. The latter can be read in English in *Hearings before the Joint Committee on the Investigation of the Pearl Harbor Attack,* 79th Congress, 2d Session, part 20, pp. 3,985-4,029. Cited hereafter as Konoye Memoirs. A portion of Kido's diary in English translation is kept at the University of California in Berkeley.

2 Kido, *Kido Nikki,* p. 66; International Military Tribunal for the Far East, "Interrogations," Hirota, March 23, 1946. Cited hereafter as IMTFE; Hashimoto Tetsuma, *Untold Story of Japanese-American Negotiations* (Tokyo: Shiunsō Press, 1946), p. 41; Ishii Itarō, *Gaikōkan no Isshō* (Tokyo: Yomiuri Shimbunsha, 1950), p. 352.

3 Yabe Teiji, *Konoye Fumimaro* (Tokyo: Kōbundō, 1952), 2:117-122. Yabe has also published a short study of Konoye under the title *Konoye Fumimaro,* vol. 8 in the Jiji Press series, *Sandai Saishō Retsuden* (Tokyo, 1958).

4 Frederick Moore, *With Japan's Leaders* (New York: Charles Scribner's Sons, 1942), pp. 38-39.

5 *New York Times,* December 19, 1940, 11:1; February 25, 1941, 1:5; Saito, p. 72.

6 *New York Times,* January 8, 1933, VIII, 4:1.

7 United States Department of State, *Papers Relating to the Foreign Relations of the United States, 1935* (Washington, D.C.: Government Printing Office, 1953), 3:330-333. Cited hereafter as *FRUS, 1935,* vol. 3.

8 United States Department of State, *Papers Relating to the Foreign Relations of the United States, 1933* (Washington, D.C.: Government Printing Office, 1949), 3:713-715. Cited hereafter as *FRUS, 1933,* vol. 3.

9 Saitō, *Azamukareta,* pp. 6-7; Ōhashi, *Taiheiyō,* p. 22; Joseph Grew, *Ten Years in Japan* (New York: Simon and Schuster, 1944), p. 345.

10 IMTFE, "Proceedings," Stahmer, p. 24, 406.

11 Ōhashi, *Taiheiyō,* p. 32; Ishii, *Gaikōkan,* pp. 353-354; Yabe, *Konoye,* II, pp. 192-195; Sir Robert Craigie, *Behind the Japanese Mask* (London: Hutchinson, 1946), p. 107; IMTFE, "Proceedings," Kido, pp. 30,904-05; "Proceedings," Kadowaki Suemitsu, pp. 35, 517-19; "Proceedings," Tōgō Shigenori, pp. 35,640-42; Grew, *Ten Years,* p. 461; Moore, *With Japan's,* pp. 117-119.

12 Grew, *Ten Years*, p. 389.
13 Miwa Kimitada, "Futatsu no Bunka to Hitotsu no Sokoku—Matsuoka Yōsuke no Higeki," *Seiyō Bunka Narabi ni Tōsei Bunka Kōryū no Kenkyū*, 14(4[winter, 1965]):64-67.
14 *Ibid.*, pp. 65-66.
15 Hayashi Shigeru (ed.), *Jimbutsu—Nihon no Rekishi*, vol. 14 in *Sensō no Jidai* (Tokyo: Yomiuri Shimbunsha, 1966), pp. 184-186.
16 *Ibid.*, pp. 186-192.
17 C.W. Young, *Japan's Special Position in Manchuria* (Baltimore: Johns Hopkins Press, 1931), pp. 310-313.
18 *New York Times*, November 6, 1929, 14:5.
19 Ogata Sadako, *Defiance in Manchuria; The Making of Japanese Foreign Policy, 1931-1932* (Berkeley: University of California Press, 1934), p. 35.
20 *FRUS, 1935*, 3:330-333.
21 *New York Times*, January 8, 1933, VIII, 4:1.
22 Moore, *With Japan's*, p. 134.
23 Katō Masuo, *The Lost War* (New York: Alfred Knopf, 1946), p. 119.
24 *New York Times*, March 27, 1941, 3:1, 4, 5.
25 *FRUS, 1933*, 3:713-715.
26 *Ibid.*
27 Tsukui Tatsuo, *Watakushi no Shōwashi* (Tokyo: Tōkyō Shōgensha, 1958), p. 118-119.
28 *FRUS, 1935*, 3:330-333.
29 Dan Kurzman, *Kishi and Japan* (New York: Ivan Obolensky, 1960), pp. 131-132.
30 IMTFE, "Interrogations," Aikawa Yoshisuke, January 30, 1946; IMTFE, "Interrogations," Hoshino Naoki, February 4, 1946; "Manchuria's New Economic Policy," *Pacific Affairs* (September 1938), p. 329; F.C. Jones, *Manchuria Since 1931* (New York: Oxford Press, 1949), p. 34; Kurzman, *Kishi*, pp. 22, 130-139.
31 *Current Biography, 1941* (New York: H.W. Wilson, 1941), pp. 563-565.
32 Saitō, *Azamukareta*, pp. 76-77.
33 Ōhashi, *Taiheiyō*, pp. 67-71; IMTFE, "Interrogations," Admiral Nomura, February 14, 1946; IMTFE "Interrogations," Suma Yakichirō, April 16, 1946; Saito, *Azamukareta*, pp. 47-109. Miwa Kimitada has presented a descriptive rather than critical review of Saitō's book under the title, "The Case for Matsuoka," *Monumenta Nipponica*, 16(3-4):182-186.
34 Katō Matsuo, *Lost War*, p. 21; *New York Times*, February 5, 1941, 5:4; IMTFE "Interrogations," Katō Matsuo, February 6, 1946.
35 United States Department of State, *Papers Relating to the Foreign Relations of the United States, 1941* (Washington, D.C.: Government Printing Office, 1956), 4:925. Cited hereafter as *FRUS, 1941*, vol. 4.
36 Ōhashi, *Taiheiyō*, pp. 45-46.
37 Ōhashi, *Taiheiyō*, pp. 45-49; Saitō, *Azamukareta*, pp. 82-83.
38 Ōhashi, *Taiheiyō*, pp. 23-26; Hubertus J. Van Mook, *The Netherlands Indies and Japan: Battle on Paper* (New York: W.W. Norton, 1944).
39 Otto D. Tolischus, *Tokyo Record* (New York: Reynal and Hitchcock, 1943), pp. 56-57, 92; IMTFE, "Proceedings," Nagai Yatsuji, p. 24,580; IMTFE, "Proceedings," Kido, p. 30,920; IMTFE, "Interrogations," Katō Masuo, July 2, 1946; Kido, *Kido Nikki*, pp. 71-72; Ōhashi, *Taiheiyō*, pp. 16-17.
40 Ōhashi, *Taiheiyō*, pp. 79-81.

41 Craigie, *Behind*, p. 115; *FRUS, 1941,* 4:915-918, 921-923, 961-965.

42 *FRUS, 1941,* 4:917-920; IMTFE, "Proceedings," Kido, p. 30,922; *New York Times,* March 26, 1941, 4:1; Ernst von Weiszäcker, *Memoirs of Ernst von Weiszäcker* (London: Victor Gollancz, 1951), p. 261.

43 Saitō, *Azamukareta,* pp. 192-194, 206-209.

44 Grew, *Ten Years,* pp. 378, 381; *FRUS, 1941,* 4:929; IMTFE, "Interrogations," Eugen Ott, February 27, 1946.

45 Konoye Memoirs, p. 3,991.

46 IMTFE, "Interrogations," Eugene Ott, February 26, 1946; March 19, 1946; March 25, 1946; Weiszäcker, *Memoirs,* pp. 249-250.

47 Grew, *Ten Years,* pp. 382-384; *FRUS, 1941,* 4:936-937.

48 Konoye Memoirs, p. 3,987; Yabe, *Konoye,* 2:260-262; Tolischus, *Tokyo,* pp. 105-106.

49 United States Department of State, *Papers Relating to the Foreign Relations of the United States, 1941* (Washington, D.C.: Government Printing Office, 1946), 5:976; Ōhashi, *Taiheiyō,* pp. 17-18, 21-22; Tolischus, *Tokyo,* pp. 114-115, 118, 134-136; Grew, *Ten Years,* pp. 385, 393-394; Kido, *Kido Nikki,* p. 75; Hashimoto, *Untold,* p. 84; *New York Times,* May 1, 1941, 7:2; Craigie, *Behind,* p. 115. Saitō, *Azamukareta,* pp. 183-187.

50 Kido Diary, California microfilm, document no. 1632 W (51), p. 1.

51 Saitō, *Azamukareta,* pp. 180-181; Ōhashi, *Taiheiyō,* pp. 151-161.

52 John Huizenga, "Yōsuke Matsuoka and the Japanese-German Alliance," in *The Diplomats, 1919-1939,* eds. Gordon A. Craig and Felix Gilbert (Princeton: Princeton University Press, 1953), p. 619; Saitō, *Azamukareta,* pp. 211-213, 220-221.

53 Tolischus, *Tokyo,* pp. 124, 138-139; Grew, *Ten Years,* pp. 402, 413.

54 Hashimoto, *Untold,* pp. 86-87; Konoye Memoirs, p. 3,990; Harada Kumao, *Saionji kō to Seikyoku* (Tokyo: Iwanami, 1950-1952), 8:360.

Hilary Conroy

Nomura Kichisaburō

The Diplomacy of Drama and Desperation

ADMIRAL NOMURA'S last-minute, tension-filled negotiations, conducted between the Konoye government and the Roosevelt administration, represent one of the most significant diplomatic episodes of the present century.[1] Considering the magnitude of the Pacific war that followed and the immensity of the international complications that ensued during the post-1945 years, Nomura's failure may be perhaps the most dramatic and tragic of all time. Indeed, had the Hull-Nomura negotiations of 1941 met with success and settlement instead of failure and infamy, not only would the Pacific war have been averted, but the subsequent strife-ridden course of Chinese, Korean, and Vietnamese history might also have been markedly altered.

The immediate post-Pearl Harbor view of Nomura's diplomacy was that it had been treacherous in the extreme, a mere mask for the military schemes and preparations of the Japanese government. Post-war scholarship has altered this view and has produced instead the image of Nomura as a well-meaning but bumbling diplomat who sincerely wanted to avert war, but whose "communication" ability was inadequate for the task, both in terms of his relations with his American opposite, Cordell Hull, and with his own government. Hull's postwar reflections in his *Memoirs* contain the much quoted comment that Nomura "spoke a certain—sometimes an uncertain—amount of English." In Hull's assessment, "His outstanding characteristic was solemnity, but he was much given to a mirthless chuckle and to bowing. I credit Nomura with having been honestly sincere in trying to avoid war between his country and mine."

297

Hull also added,

> Nomura himself was a serious difficulty. He was not a professional diplomat, and his assistants who should have given him adequate technical help were not equal to their task. I believe he was serious and honest, but he made blunders and embarrassed his government. . . . I was never sure that Nomura understood my points, even when I had Joseph Ballantine repeat them in Japanese. He and his assistants did not keep a full record of our conversations as they should have. . . . At times we were not sure that Nomura understood some of his own Government's points since he seemed so vague in explaining them.[2]

Professor Butow concludes that the inadequacies of Nomura's reporting produced the "fundamental misconception" whereby Tokyo thought her Ambassador's proposals were Hull's, resulting in a communication breakdown that greatly contributed to wrecking the negotiations. Professor Hosoya likewise believes that though Nomura might have been a "good negotiator" he was a "bad communicator."[3]

There is ample evidence for such judgments. Indeed, Nomura's correspondence provides an intriguing, perverse model of ambiguity as to who was proposing what. The more this problem is pondered, however, the larger looms another and perhaps more significant question: was this ambiguity merely the result of ineptitude or stupidity, or was it purposefully used to expand opportunities for averting hostilities. In Washington the Roosevelt administration did not want war; and in Tokyo, at least until General Tōjō assumed the Premiership in October 1941, many influential elements of the Japanese government, including Premier Konoye and the Emperor, were anxious to avoid a military confrontation with the United States.[4] At the same time, neither side would accept "peace at any price," an idea that was as much anathema to political leaders then as now. Given the complicated international diplomatic setting and the highly charged internal politics (both in Tokyo and Washington) of 1941, could it be that Nomura's ambiguity was a desperate, consciously employed diplomatic maneuver?

I

Born in 1877 in Wakayama prefecture Nomura Kichisaburō was adopted into the Nomura family at an early age (his original family name was Masuda). His schooling led him to the Imperial Naval Academy where he graduated in 1898. All cadets there studied English, a factor to note since Nomura's English, or lack of it, was subsequently an "obstacle" in the famous "conversations" with Cordell Hull. In 1915 he was stationed for a time at the Japanese embassy in Washington D.C. where he became acquainted with then Assistant Secretary of the Navy, Franklin D. Roosevelt. The two exchanged correspondence periodically thereafter. Also about this time in Washington, Nomura became acquainted with Matsuoka Yōsuke, a rising young man from Yamaguchi prefecture (formerly Chōshū) who had visited America as a youth, gone to school in Oregon for a time, and who in 1915-1916 was an assistant secretary at Japan's Washington embassy. (Their paths were to cross later, but Matsuoka, it should be noted in passing, had excellent connections in the army hierarchy. Baron General Tanaka Giichi supervised his marriage, and it is said he was favored in his youth by the Military *Genrō,* Yamagata, and by Field Marshal Terauchi Masatake.)

Nomura in contrast pursued his career in the navy, became a full admiral in 1933 and subsequently occupied various posts, including secretary to the Navy Minister, Naval Attaché at the Japanese embassy in London, Deputy Chief of the Naval General Staff, and Commandant of the Yokosuka Naval Base. He served briefly as Foreign Minister in the Abe Cabinet from September 25, 1939, to January 16, 1940. He was known among naval factions as a follower of Admiral Katō Tomosaburō, Japan's chief delegate tò the Washington Conference of 1921-1922 and an advocate of cooperation with Britain and the United States, in opposition to the hard-line faction of Admiral Katō Kanji.

Admiral Nomura served for a time as director of the Peers' School in Tokyo which prompted the son of another admiral to say that Nomura did not appear to be a real military man—he was rather "more of a professor type." His education and experience at any rate were quite broad and international. As to his competency in English, Nomura's daughter-in-law, who speaks English fluently and who nursed the aged admiral during his last illness until his death at age eighty-six (May 8, 1964), asserts that he had a very large vocabulary and knew English well, though he spoke with a rather peculiar "Wakayama accent." But then Nomura said that Hull had a strange accent! (Biographer Julius W. Pratt says that Hull had a "soft southern accent and a slight defect in his speech which transformed r's into w's." This, combined with his gift for profanity, led President Roosevelt to inquire on occasion, "Was this one of Cordell's Chwist days?")[5]

Admiral Nomura kept a diary of the Washington negotiations in both English and Japanese. This was the basis for his memoir *Beikoku ni Tsukaishite* (Mission to the United States), which he compiled at the end of the war and published in Tokyo in July 1946. According to the Nomura family, the manuscript of the diary was seized by American Occupation authorities, but historians have been unable to locate it among the International Military Tribunal seized documents. Obviously, because of the circumstances at the time of its issuance, the compilation should be used with care. It consists of 203 pages of Japanese text plus 241 pages of documents in English. The Japanese text includes an account of the circumstances of

Nomura's appointment as Ambassador; resumés of his meetings with Roosevelt, Hull, and other American officials and descriptions of the general course of the negotiations in Washington; a statement that he had no advance knowledge of the attack on Hawaii; a number of telegrams between Nomura and high government officials in Tokyo; and sundry notes on his repatriation, the Roosevelt family and American navy men he had known. The documents in English consist of various versions of the "draft proposals" which were discussed in Washington.

The main point to be noted here is that considering the rather bewildering array of suggested alterations, oral explanations, annexes, and supplements which were involved, Admiral Nomura's documents tally remarkably well with Hull's recollections, though certain points of emphasis are different. Nonetheless, it is a carefully kept record, no less so than Hull's, though much shorter and more laconically written. While Hull's memoirs have been widely used, this compilation of Nomura's has largely gathered dust on the shelves of used book stalls in Tokyo.[6]

Nomura's first opportunity to arrest the deterioration in Japan's relations with the United States came in September 1939. Already retired from active duty with the navy and serving as president of the Peers' School in Tokyo, Nomura accepted Premier General Abe Nobuyuki's summons to become Foreign Minister. Abe's Cabinet was a shaky compromise between Axis- and Western-oriented elements, with Abe promising to devote his full energy to solving the China conflict, while depending on Nomura to improve relations with the United States. These had reached a low ebb in July, when in retaliation for Japanese intransigeance on the military adventure in China, the United States served notice of abrogation six months hence (January 26, 1940) of her commercial treaty with Japan, thus endangering the flow of important raw materials to Japan.

Nomura's principal activity as Foreign Minister was to seek an agreement with the United States to maintain trade, if not by treaty then by a *modus vivendi*. Unfortunately he could not, or would not, arrange some major concession on the China question to achieve this détente. In any event Nomura's opportunities as Foreign Minister ended with the fall of the Abe Cabinet in January 1940. According to his Foreign Office section chief, Nishi Haruhiko, Nomura had accomplished "nothing much because his time was so short."[7]

Again retired from public affairs, Nomura was asked on August 24, 1940, by his old acquaintance Matsuoka Yōsuke, now Foreign Minister in the second Konoye Cabinet, to come to Tokyo to discuss the Ambassadorship to the United States. Nomura was wary. He immediately consulted the Navy Minister, Admiral Yoshida Zengo, and then two other navy leaders, Admiral Oikawa Koshiro, soon to become Navy Minister, and Admiral Toyoda Teijirō. He explained to them that it would be an impossible task, "like chasing two rabbits in different directions," to pursue peace with the United States and an Axis power orientation at the same time. Only after receiving assurances that the navy understood his dilemma and would back him in his American effort did he agree to discuss the appointment seriously with Matsuoka. He then sought similar assurances from Matsuoka, sent a memorandum to Premier Konoye warning that a war with the United States could come to "no good end," and finally accepted the post on November 9, after eliciting a statement from Prince Fushimi, Chief of the General Staff, "that he agreed with me."[8]

Perhaps Nomura might better have spent his time analyzing the course of events than in seeking affirmations of support. While he was making up his mind, Matsuoka negotiated the Tripartite Pact (September 7-27), claiming all the while that it was not directed against the United States, and on September 23 Japanese troops entered northern Indo-China "by agreement" with the French Governor-General.[9] These events obviously increased the difficulty of the Washington assignment; yet, Nomura still believed there was a good chance for his efforts to succeed. It was his understanding, he states in his memoirs, that "the various leaders in Japan wanted to avoid war," and he took them at their word. Ever optimistic, like his American counterpart in Japan, even up to December 7, 1941, he thought that the worst that could happen would be a break in diplomatic relations.[10]

Nomura left Tokyo for Washington on January 23, 1941; he arrived in Honolulu on January 30, in San Francisco on February 6, and in Washington on February 11. His reception at each of these cities was cordial, even friendly, including interviews with Admiral Kimmel in Honolulu and General DeWitt in San Francisco. He was so pleased with the East Coast press notices that he saved the clippings: "Affable and cordial" (*New York Times*), "a man of keen intelligence and of decided amiability" (*Baltimore Evening Sun*).[11] President Roosevelt received him on February 14, and Nomura left their interview in good spirits:

> President Roosevelt said, "I am a friend of Japan and you of America, so there can be frank discussions. As for Japanese-American relations, they have deteriorated though more than 200 notes have gone out to Japan from our State Department. Like the *Maine* of old there is now the *Panay* ship incident and if the Secretary of State and I don't restrain public opinion the situation might become truly dangerous. It seems as though Japan is almost committed to a national policy of southward expansion into the area of French Indo China and Thailand . . . and due to the Tripartite alliance we fear that Japan will not be independent in her course but forced on by Germany and Italy."
>
> I said I believe deeply that there must be no such thing as a fight between Japan and America and I am convinced that the day is coming when our two countries will cooperate to maintain peace in the world. The President expressed the same sentiments and then he talked of things he had told his wife about me. It was indeed an openhearted [*uchitoketa*] discussion.[12]

II

Nomura felt that his mission was off to a good start. He had further reason to think so because of certain unofficial negotiations which had commenced. These were the Drought-Walsh, Ikawa-Iwakuro talks which began in Tokyo in November 1940. James E. Walsh and James M. Drought, two Maryknoll Catholic priests anxious to improve the prospects for peace, sought and received the assistance of New York financier Lewis L. Strauss in making contact with highly placed persons in Japan. Strauss' introduction led them to Ikawa Tadao, a banker who was also a personal friend of Premier Konoye, and the talks began. Later Colonel Iwakuro Hideo, who was close to General Mutō, Chief of the Military Affairs Bureau, if not to Tōjō, was brought into the discussions.

Several draft proposals were drawn up by these four in the ensuing months as Ambassador Nomura was making his way to Washington and settling in there. First, there was a proposal by Drought in Tokyo that was highly favorable to Japan, since it practically accepted the Japanese position in China and admitted the predominance of her position in Southeast Asia. Ikawa sent this draft directly to Konoye. The priests then returned to the United States, where another draft was prepared, one less favorable to Japan. While recognizing a "Japanese Monroe Doctrine" in East Asia, the agreement would require Japan to settle the China affair by negotiation with Chiang Kai-shek, cease military pressure in Southeast Asia, and reorient her foreign policy away from Germany toward the United States.

Through the intercession of Postmaster General Frank C. Walker, the most highly placed Catholic layman in the Roosevelt administration, this second draft proposal was presented to the President and Secretary Hull in Washington on January 23, 1941. Five days later, after consulting Walker again, Drought and Walsh cabled Ikawa that things looked "exceedingly hopeful." Ikawa reported to Konoye and Mutō, and shortly thereafter he, and then Iwakuro, were sent to the United States, where the four got down to the serious work of drawing up a "preliminary draft of agreement in principle" between the United States and Japan. Iwakuro, with the latest word from Tokyo, was probably the principal author of the final version.

Meanwhile Ambassador Nomura waited. He had been informed of the negotiations by Ikawa, but he also discovered that Foreign Minister Matsuoka resented these private conversations even though, or perhaps because, they were arranged through Konoye. Matsuoka was unreceptive to Drought's suggestions in Tokyo, and Vice-Minister Ōhashi tried to block Ikawa's journey to the United States, until it became clear that the Premier wanted him to go. When Nomura, perhaps innocently, sought to clarify Ikawa's status with the Foreign Office, Matsuoka implied that Ikawa was not to be trusted.[13] Matsuoka also sent Nomura on February 14 a long telegram of instructions entitled "Enlightening the Government and People of the United States." He emphasized that it would be a "ridiculous mistake" for Americans to assume that some Japanese were "secretly opposed to the Tripartite Pact." Nomura did not comment on this nor did he mention it to Hull. The next month, however, when he learned that Matsuoka was planning a diplomatic mission to Moscow and Berlin, he warned the Foreign Minister that "viewed from the United States" the trip would seem "disadvantageous."[14]

While Matsuoka was away, far from mistrusting Ikawa, Nomura gave positive assistance to the "private" drafting sessions which were being carried on in New York. Hull, who had authorized Postmaster General Walker to participate in the sessions on a purely private basis, also sent his Japanese language specialist Joseph Ballantine to visit the principals in New York on March 24.[15]

There followed a double drama in which Nomura and Hull, though seeking the common goal of reorienting Japan away from the Axis and toward rapprochement with the United States, became enmeshed in such misunderstandings that at a critical stage in July, when the opportunity for progress was maximal, Hull refused even to talk to Nomura. In the literal sense, as Butow points out, the fault lay in Nomura's ambiguity. His vagueness led Tokyo to believe that the "draft proposal" that he had submitted from Washington was an American proposal or a joint proposal or at least something in which the Americans concurred, when in fact Hull had got him to say that it was to be a Japanese proposal.[16]

Hull complained later that Nomura was not a professional diplomat. After years of political experience, Hull certainly was quite capable of out-maneuvering Nomura. He was unwilling, however, to give Nomura room for "unprofessional" conduct, namely attempting to unseat his Foreign Minister. Previous studies have not dealt with this issue so dramatically, for Nomura never admitted, even to himself, that he was attempting so insubordinate an act. It is interesting to note that the newly issued version of Premier Konoye's fragmentary and somewhat mysterious memoirs does emphasize the reality of a "confrontation" (*tairitsu*) between Ambassador Nomura and Foreign Minister Matsuoka.[17]

Bearing this developing "confrontation" in mind let us review certain heretofore neglected aspects of the draft proposal negotiations. Hull recalled in his *Memoirs*: "The informal conversations conducted by Walsh, Drought and Postmaster General Walker with Japanese representatives, including Nomura, reached a head on April 9. On that day I received from them a draft proposal on which the participants had agreed. During the next few days I went over this carefully with experts on Far Eastern affairs in the State Department."[18]

This "draft proposal," running to something over 2,000 words, contained seven sections: (1) The concepts of the United States and Japan respecting international relations and the character of nations; (2) The attitude of both governments toward the European war; (3) China affairs; (4) Naval, aerial, and mercantile marine relations in the Pacific; (5) Commerce between both nations and their financial cooperation; (6) Economic activity of both nations in the Southwestern Pacific area; and (7) Conference. It accepted the "independence of China" and the "resumption of the Open Door," but the "withdrawal of Japanese troops from Chinese territory" would be only "in accordance with an agreement to be reached between China and Japan" and required the "coalescence of the governments of Chiang Kai-shek and Wang Ching-wei," the recognition of Manchukuo, and "joint defense against communistic activities."[19] It maintained that Japan's Axis Alliance was "defensive," promised that Japanese activities in the southwestern Pacific area would be carried on "by peaceful means, without resort to arms," and promised a joint guarantee of the independence of the Philippines, in return for which the United States would resume trade with Japan. In addition Japan "requested" the "friendly and diplomatic assistance of the United States for the removal of Hong Kong and Singapore as doorways to further encroachment by the British in the Far East." Finally the proposal "suggested" that a conference between President Roosevelt and Premier Konoye should be held at Honolulu for "the drafting of instruments to effectuate the understanding."[20]

Father Drought also advised Secretary Hull via Mr. Ballantine that before presenting the proposals officially,

the Japanese would want some intimation that the Japanese proposals would be substantially acceptable to this government. He explained that following such intimation the Cabinet would act on the proposals and instruct Nomura to present them and that it was desired to act on this matter prior to Matsuoka's reaching Tokyo, as it was feared that otherwise Matsuoka upon his return would create difficulties. Father Drought added that the Japanese Army and Navy were behind the proposals and that the only difficulties so far encountered were from the Japanese Foreign Office. If prompt action should be taken Matsuoka would be confronted with an accomplished fact and he would either have to go along or resign.[21]

While Hull was pondering this recommendation, his advisor on political relations, Far Eastern specialist Stanley K. Hornbeck, was criticizing the proposal—which he referred to as the "John Doe draft"—on a paragraph by paragraph basis. Hornbeck pointed out that since 1894 Japan "has achieved one diplomatic victory after another by processes of diplomacy backed by threats, implied threats, or inferred threats of force." He argued that "at any time throughout this period of forty years, a conviction on the part of

Japan's leaders that the United States would fight" would have been effective.[22] The Chief of the State Department's Division of Far Eastern Affairs, Maxwell M. Hamilton, drew up a proposed statement insisting that Nomura himself make the proposal in order to bring it to the discussion stage; this effectively postponed discussion of any specific features.[23]

Whether because of these warnings or his own predilections on the subject, Hull met Nomura in an essentially negative frame of mind on April 14 and 16. "Our disappointment was keen. . . . Numerous questions at once rose to our minds. To what extent and when would Japan evacuate her troops from China? How would she interpret and apply the Open Door? What did the coalescence of the Chiang Kai-shek and the puppet Nanking regime mean?"[24]

While Nomura showed eagerness, even anxiety, to begin negotiations on the basis of the draft proposal, Hull emphasized that conversations were impossible until the Japanese government officially submitted the proposal to him. Even then the Japanese government would have to give

a definite assurance in advance . . . to abandon its present policy of military conquest by force and the taking of title to all property and territories seized, together with the use of force as an instrument of policy; and to adopt the principles which this Government has been proclaiming and practicing as embodying the foundation on which all relations between nations should properly rest.

Hull then handed Nomura

the following four points on a blank [sic] sheet of paper: (1) respect for the territorial integrity and the sovereignty of each and all nations; (2) support of the principle of non-interference in the internal affairs of other countries; (3) support of the principle of equality, including equality of commercial opportunity; (4) non-disturbance of the *status quo* in the Pacific except as the *status quo* may be altered by peaceful means.

As for the draft proposal itself Hull said that Nomura was "at the fullest liberty" to submit the document to his government, "but of course this does not imply any commitment whatever on the part of this Government with respect to the provisions of the document, in case it should be approved by your Government." Pressed to say whether he would approve its contents "to a fairly full extent," Hull replied that "there would be ready approval of several items, while others would have to be modified or eliminated and this Government would offer some independent proposals."[25]

As Butow says, "Hull had patiently built up his position like a mason carefully laying one stone upon another." Nomura, however, merely cabled the draft proposal to Tokyo, recommending full acceptance and implying that Hull had "on the whole no objections."[26]

III

What defense is there for Nomura? One technical point stands in his favor. Regarding the Four Points and his statement of principles Hull had said, "You can answer the questions or submit them to your Government for its answer through you, as you prefer." The record shows that Nomura did give an immediate "answer" of sorts, mentioning such matters as Latin America, immigration, and Manchukuo in connection with the meaning of the Four Points.[27] His main defense however for withholding Hull's firm statements was that optimistic reports would give Konoye and other waverers in the Japanese Cabinet a crucial push toward breaking Matsuoka's hold on foreign policy and bringing about a retreat from his Axis orientation. The transmission of Hull's principles at that point would certainly have cooled enthusiasm for an American rapprochement, whereas Nomura's optimistic tone produced a decidedly favorable reaction. Before Matsuoka returned from Europe, all major factions in the Cabinet, navy, army, and civilian, had approved the proposal, but they decided to hold the news for Matsuoka. Konoye went to the airport to inform him on his return from Germany (April 22).

Matsuoka however did not want to hear Konoye's news. Playing the hero for his "diplomatic triumphs" in Berlin and Moscow he allowed himself to be separated from the Premier by the airport crowd, missed his invitation to ride to Tokyo in the Premier's car, and made his way first to the Imperial Palace for a personal report directly to the Emperor on his European successes. Then pleading illness he retired to think about the American situation.[28]

Matsuoka emerged in a fighting mood. Branding the draft proposal as 70 percent "evil intent" he sought to derail it with a message to Nomura to forget all this and merely seek a non-aggression pact with the United States. Matsuoka then sent his own two "preconditions" for negotiations: (1) that the United States guarantee not to enter the European war and (2) that she persuade Chiang Kai-shek to open peace negotiations. Nomura sidetracked these demands. He told Hull that many things Matsuoka said were "wrong" and, utilizing Hull's hint that if they were "wrong" perhaps he should not present them, he merely pocketed them.[29] The Foreign Minister then revised the draft proposal so as to eliminate restrictions on the Tripartite Pact, substituted mention of "Konoye's three principles" for the specifications on a China settlement, and deleted the Konoye-Roosevelt Honolulu conference "suggestion." Nomura presented this but added "Oral Explanations" (carefully written down) which restated previous assurances. He now asked that the "conversations" become "negotiations."[30]

Meanwhile in Tokyo Matsuoka treated Ambassador Grew to a stormy session on May 14. He made remarks that "were bellicose both in tone and substance," contrasting Hitler's "patience and generosity" with American "indecence" (later corrected to "indiscretion"). Grew gave Hull a full account, and Hull in turn told Nomura about Matsuoka's "offensive" language. Nomura responded that "Matsuoka was out for his own interests politically" and "laughed at the idea of Matsuoka controlling the situation so as to defeat any further conversations." He reassured Hull on May 28 that "under the Japanese constitutional system other ministers in addition to the Foreign Minister are consulted in matters relating to foreign policy."[31]

Reacting to Hull's disclosure, Nomura contributed to the developing "confrontation" with Matsuoka by informing the latter that Hull had told him of the attempt to "intimidate" Grew. Matsuoka was "furious" with his Ambassador; he complained about him openly, claiming that the rapprochement proposals were "merely Nomura's," and he accused Nomura directly (May 24) of having told Hull that everyone in the Japanese government except the Foreign Minister was in favor of them. Nomura responded that he had simply told Hull that "Japanese policy would be decided by the whole Cabinet, not just by the Foreign Minister."[32]

The "confrontation" thus ignited exploded as a result of Hull's "Oral Statement," the text of which he handed to Nomura along with an American revision of the "draft proposal" on June 21. It began: "The Secretary of State appreciates the earnest efforts which have been made by the Japanese Ambassador and his associates to bring about a better understanding between our two countries and to establish peace in the Pacific." He had found, however, that

> some Japanese leaders in influential positions are definitely committed to a course which calls for support of Nazi Germany and its policies of conquest. . . . The tenor of recent public statements gratuitously made by spokesmen of the Japanese government emphasizing Japan's commitments and intentions under the Tripartite Alliance cannot be ignored. So long as such leaders maintain this attitude in their official positions and apparently seek to influence public opinion in Japan in the direction indicated, is it not illusory to expect that the adoption of a proposal such as the one under consideration offers a basis for achieving substantial results along the desired lines?[33]

Hull indicated to Nomura that this "Oral Statement" and an accompanying note regarding the China situation might "be omitted or modified" if they "contained points which the Ambassador found difficult to recommend to his Government for approval."[34] Not only did Nomura transmit the "Oral Statement," but he followed it up with a special personal telegram to Matsuoka which came as close to directly accusing him of trying to sabotage the American negotiations as the language of diplomacy permits. He said,

> I have heard a rumor that unbelievable information has come here from Ambassador Grew. That is there exists an inside report saying the Foreign Minister considers Ambassador Nomura's diplomatic actions to exceed his

powers and that the Foreign Minister will torpedo whatever agreement is reached. Both the State Department and the White House, fearing failure of the agreement therefrom and concerned about the great question of responsibility, are anxious to know the true intentions of the Japanese government, and so the Secretary of State referred to this in his Oral Statement of June 21.[35]

Nomura continued to press Matsuoka for assurances with subsequent telegrams on June 29, July 3, and July 8. In the July 8 message he said: "Although it has been a long time since I asked for instructions, I have not yet received a reply to my request. As is clear from the Oral Statement of June 21, they have suspicions about our true intentions. . . . The delay in o r reply added to other conditions has underlined their suspicions and makes them lose hope for a settlement." He then warned Matsuoka: "A certain Cabinet member indicated unofficially to a member of our staff at this Embassy that he is worried that the situation inside the United States will become more and more disadvantageous if the negotiations are not continued immediately."[36]

Matsuoka responded by instructing Nomura to send one of his staff members to Tokyo for consultation, to which the Ambassador immediately replied that such would make it "meaningless for me to stay here" and that he would come himself.[37] Matsuoka's answer was almost a scream: "Regardless of what you think, absolutely no, it cannot be allowed that you should depart your place of appointment because of public reaction."[38]

But Nomura had already gone over (or around) the Foreign Minister's head. On July 10 he addressed a long complaining telegram to the Navy Minister and the Chief of Staff, which he sent via the Japanese Naval Attaché, not through embassy channels. He emphasized that he had "taken this position [the Ambassadorship] not because it was offered by the Foreign Minister but at the urging of the Navy," after having "talked to everyone at the time of the appointment and ascertained that they wanted to avoid a clash with the United States." There had been "a lessening of anti-Japanese criticisms in America" at the beginning of his negotiations, but since the outbreak of the German-Russian war the argument that "Japan and the Axis are inseparable" was growing stronger. If things went on like this, "eventually Japan must face England, America, Russia, China, and the Netherlands Indies, all as enemies." Japan was "at a crossroads," and he wished to explain his feelings.[39]

Meanwhile in Tokyo, Matsuoka took his case to the Premier and the military chiefs at the highest decision making level, the Liaison Conference. He spoke as follows:

First of all, Hull's statement is outrageous. Never has such a thing occurred since Japan opened diplomatic relations with other countries.

Nomura and I are good friends, but it is inexcusable for him to transmit such an outrageous statement. I was truly amazed that he would listen without protest to a demand that Japan, a great world power, change her Cabinet. . . .

Second, we cannot dissolve the Tripartite Pact. Third, acceptance of the American proposal would threaten the establishment of a Greater East Asia Co—Prosperity Sphere, and this would be a very grave matter. . . .

This proposal came on June 22, not two weeks ago; yet Nomura has already pressed me for an answer four or five times. . . . Furthermore Hull speaks of the Ambassador and his associates; so I have demanded that Nomura explain who 'his associates' are. It is improper to have a lot of people involved in it.[40]

The Liaison Conference was unmoved. Later that day, Konoye met secretly with the Army, Navy and Home Minister to discuss the problem of Matsuoka. The Foreign Minister had the floor for the last time at the Liaison meeting of July 12. He said: "So long as I am Foreign Minister I cannot accept it. I am willing to consider anything else, but I cannot accept the 'Oral Statement'. . . . I propose here and now that we reject the 'Statement', and that we discontinue negotiations with the United States."[41]

The diary of Marquis Kido, Lord Keeper of the Privy Seal, tells more of the story, under the entry for July 15, 1941.

Mr. Matsudaira came from Tokyo at 8:00 A.M. to report on his meeting with Premier Konoye. Foreign Minister Matsuoka's attitude toward the agreement between the United States and Japan is uncompromising. Until yesterday the Premier was not without hope that he could with a minor amendment obtain the Foreign Minister's assent to a plan prepared by the Army and Navy Bureau Chiefs. Though he expressed no objection to the Military Chief's compromise of yesterday, the Foreign Minister insisted on instructing Ambassador Nomura first to file a protest against the Oral Statement of Secretary Hull as a national insult, and only after that might we send a compromise proposal. Regarding this the Premier was of the opinion that our compromise should be sent at the same time as any protest lest the American negotiations end in failure. Mr. Saitō (of the Foreign Office) was in favor of the Foreign Minister's idea, but the Premier contradicted Saitō and sent him to the Foreign Minister to insist that he accept the Premier's opinion.

This was the situation up to 10:50 A.M. yesterday. At 1:30 Premier Konoye telephoned me to say that he had waited long enough for the Foreign Minister's answer, had instructed (American) Bureau Chief Terasaki to investigate the circumstances, and was coming to (the Emperor's villa at) Hayama to work out remedial measures that afternoon. With regard to this I was to make previous arrangements with the chief secretary for the resignation en bloc of the Cabinet. At this time, when popular tension concerning the situation was such that even the high schools were closed throughout the country lest an unexpected disturbance arise, the resignation of the Cabinet for some obscure reason should be avoided. Hence we wished to try first of all to obtain the resignation of the Foreign Minister, but if this failed, we resolved to have the Emperor issue an imperial command to

Premier Konoye to form a new cabinet. I reported the above to the Emperor between 1:35 and 2:00 P.M. and went to talk with Premier Konoye from 3:00 to 4:20. . . . I thought it would be advisable to urge the Foreign Minister to resign and avoid the fall of the Cabinet, but the Premier disagreed with me, saying that in that event Matsuoka's party would certainly make propaganda that the United States had compelled us to change our Cabinet, and there was no other way than resignation of the Cabinet en bloc.[42]

Meanwhile Matsuoka fired off a blunt rejection of Hull's statement to Nomura, disregarding the wishes of his Cabinet colleagues while pointedly informing the German Ambassador of the fact. When other officials in the foreign office learned of this they tried to soften it by sending a hastily prepared counter proposal, without Matsuoka's permission. Nomura simply did not deliver either of these documents to Hull.

On July 16 Premier Konoye submitted the resignation of the entire Cabinet. Two days later he received an Imperial mandate to organize a new Cabinet without Matsuoka, who was replaced by Admiral Toyoda Teijirō. The admiral, it will be recalled, was one of the three senior naval officers from whom Nomura had obtained assurances of support at the inception of his mission to the United States. The stage was set for reducing the Tripartite Pact to a dead letter.[43]

IV

It is against this background that Nomura's diplomacy and his concept of his role as Ambassador should be explained and assessed. Clearly he did not see himself as a mere transmitter of documents and statements between his own Foreign Office and the American State Department. Perhaps his prior experience as Foreign Minister or his naval commands accustomed him to think in terms of policy execution, if not policy making. He told Matsuoka in one telegram that in the navy he had "always been permitted more or less freedom of decision" under his instructions.[44]

Nomura always maintained that he had accepted the Ambassadorship on condition that rapprochement with the United States receive the top foreign policy priority. He had clearly indicated that this was the one "rabbit" he was going to pursue. The corollary to this endeavor was clear: if the other "rabbit," the Tripartite Pact, got in the way, that had to go. Hence Nomura's estrangement from Matsuoka, who personified the Axis orientation, was policy, not a personal matter; when a confrontation could no longer be avoided the Ambassador did not flinch from igniting the tinders that led to the ouster of the Foreign Minister.

It was no small victory for Nomura that his "ambiguous" handling of the draft proposal played an important role in substituting a like-minded admiral, Toyoda, for the fiery Matsuoka. In addition, immediately after

Nomura received the news of Toyoda's appointment, he sent the new Foreign Minister a lengthy despatch which, had it come from the other direction, would surely be categorized as a "general policy guideline." Nomura made very clear what he thought of Hitler's Germany.

Our country has a very different national policy from one in which a popped up revolutionary tries a great adventure, dictatorially using the whole people and nation. Our country should always follow the highly respected Imperial way of morality and justice. The use of our armed forces should be to defeat evil and show the right, avoiding even the slightest hint of selfish aggression.

Then, after a discourse on the European war situation casting doubt on the likelihood of a German victory, he concluded by saying:

Of course, we must honor treaties, but from our position of isolation in the Far East and the basis of our imperial uniqueness, we should put Japan first, and without relying on undependable foreign countries manage tactfully within the limits of our own national strength. That is the safest thing. . . . It would be very bad to face a united front of Allies after the European war.[45]

Nomura's handling of the various versions of the draft proposal is another interesting point. Any one of the versions was acceptable to him, whether Drought's, Walsh's, Ikawa's, Iwakuro's or another revision. He did not care whether it was regarded as a Japanese, American, or joint proposal. His main concern was to move Japanese foreign policy off the Axis track.

As for the China question, which loomed so large in the minds of Roosevelt, Hull, and especially Hornbeck, Normura saw no reason why a resolution of the problem was not possible along one of the lines developed in the draft proposal conversations. It is clear that Nomura along with the "pro-American" members of the Japanese Cabinet conceived of the suppression of communism in China as a legitimate, necessary, and valorous project; Japan's proper role in Eastern Asia was thus based on a "Monroe Doctrine" of the Teddy Roosevelt variety.

Nomura's views of these matters were quite pointedly expressed in an article he published in December 1937 in *Gaikō jihō*, the Japanese equivalent of *Foreign Affairs*. As the China Incident escalated into widespread warfare, he sought to explain "to friends in the United States" just what the issues were. The Japanese troops were in China, he said, because Japan was worried about communism there. "If China turns red, not only Japan but other countries will be in danger." Japan was making "sacrifices" to prevent this disaster; the United States especially should appreciate her position. "Just as the President's 'good neighbor' policy toward South America is being developed, so Japan, in order to safeguard the peace in East Asia requires cooperation with China." The bombings and military action were unfortunate but necessary, he argued, because of Chinese attacks, but they were not directed at non-combatants or foreigners in China.[46]

It is no small irony that many Americans of the Vietnam generation have found the "domino theory" and "justified bombing" arguments compelling. By 1941, however, Nomura and some of his peers in Tokyo, like their American counterparts of 1968, were exceedingly weary of the war on the Asian mainland, and were seeking a face-saving way out. Hence there is good reason to read the China aspects of the draft proposal as a move toward de-escalation. But while willing to abandon the grandiose *weltpolitik* of Matsuoka, army leaders insisted on carrying through their previously planned occupation of Southern Indochina before considering such de-escalation. Nomura warned in vain that further movement of armed forces southward might leave no room for negotiations.[47]

The decision on Indochina was made on July 2, and unfortunately, Hull knew of it, for the Japanese code had been broken. Therefore, instead of responding optimistically to the change of Cabinet, the Secretary avoided talks on the draft proposal, waited for the Indochina story to unfold, and when it became clear that the occupation would proceed, informed Nomura that the talks were suspended. On July 26 President Roosevelt issued an executive order, freezing Japanese assets in the United States.

This was prudent "wait and see" diplomacy by Hull, but thereafter the negotiations went downhill all the way to Pearl Harbor because the Secretary never ceased "waiting." Despite frantic efforts to retrieve the situation by promoting a last ditch meeting between Roosevelt and Konoye, Nomura's diplomacy was consigned to the scrap heap of lost causes. Yet the question remains: if Hull had taken advantage of Matsuoka's fall to initial any one of the versions of the draft proposal so that Nomura could have taken an "agreement" back to Tokyo, might the balance have tilted the other way?

Much later in his *Memoirs* Hull admitted that "we could easily have had an agreement with the Konoye government at any time by signing the dotted line. But," he continued, "we should have negated principles on which we had built our foreign policy and without which the world could not live at peace."[48]

V

Just how much peacemaking potential did Nomura's diplomatic efforts possess? The historian's general view of the processes of international relations will set the framework for any estimate. It is interesting in this regard that competing volumes on the background of the Pacific war in the two great historical series produced in Japan take opposite stands on this view of processes. While Hayashi Shigeru's volume in the *Chūō Kōron* series gives careful attention to details of the diplomacy of Matsuoka and Nomura, Ienaga Saburo's equivalent volume in the Iwanami series does not. Considering such details unimportant, Ienaga argues that the Pacific war was the product of larger forces, a logical consequence of Japanese aggression in China and the general military-ideological complex behind it; an individual diplomat like Nomura was merely a weak reed against the tide.[49]

If we argue without much regard to individuals that the Japanese drive for *lebensraum* came into direct confrontation with a deep rooted segment of American national interest, the Open Door in China, thus producing the Pacific war, then this essay and other efforts to unravel the diplomacy of that era must be judged vain endeavors. But postwar history mockingly informs us that Japan has learned to live without her *lebensraum* and America without her Open Door. Furthermore, it is becoming increasingly clear that the old idea of warlike nations versus peace-loving nations is giving way to war-minded versus peace-minded elements *within each nation*.

Notes

1 This should be characterized as an interim report because an excellent initial study has already been made by Professor Butow, and more definitive studies than this short essay may be/are in process by Professors Butow, Hosoya Chihiro, and others. It is the present author's purpose not to attempt a full scale analysis of the diplomatic efforts that preceded Pearl Harbor and failed to avert it, but merely to outline a profile of Nomura's effort, focusing on certain features which have been, and are likely to continue to be, missed. See Robert J.C. Butow, "The Hull-Nomura Conversations: A Fundamental Misconception," *American Historical Review*, 65(July, 1960):822-826. A preliminary version of this essay appeared in the *Proceedings of the American Philosophical Society*, 114(June, 1970):205-216.

2 Cordell Hull, *Memoirs* (New York: Macmillan, 1948), 2:987, 1030-31.

3 Butow, "Hull-Nomura Conversations," pp. 830-831, 833; Hosoya Chihiro, "Miscalculations in Deterrence Policy: Japan-U.S. Relations, 1939-1941," *Hitotsubashi Journal of Law and Politics*, 6(April, 1968):29-47; "Japan's Decision for War in 1941," *Peace Research in Japan*, 1(1967):41-51. International Military Tribunal for the Far East, reels WT 72-5 contain microfilms of documents on the Nomura negotiations. Cited hereafter as IMTFE.

4 For an opposite view, see Charles A. Beard, *President Roosevelt and the Coming of the War* (New Haven: Yale University Press, 1948). While Beard's "folly," as this volume is sometimes called, might be profitably restudied, especially his warnings against presidential misuse of war powers, the evidence for his chapter on "Maneuvering Japanese into Firing the First Shot" has been sympathetically reconsidered by William Neumann but discounted. See William L. Neumann, *America Encounters Japan* (Baltimore: Johns Hopkins University Press, 1963), pp. 276-277.

5 Julius W. Pratt, "Cordell Hull, 1933-1944," in S.F. Bemis and R.H. Ferrell (eds.), *The American Secretaries of State and Their Diplomacy* (New York: Cooper Square Publishers, 1964) 12:5. Details on Admiral Nomura from interviews in Japan in the summer of 1968 with Mr. and Mrs. Nomura Tadashi, son and daughter-in-law of the admiral, Mr. Masaki Masaru, son of Admiral K. Masaki, Dr. Tsunoda Jun of Japan's National Diet Library, Professor Hosoya Chihiro of Hitotsubashi University, and by letter from Captain George F. Hodge, USN, Ret., to the author, dated May 31, 1968. The author is indebted to Mr. Ushioda Sukemichi for providing a setting for some of these interviews and to his sons, Sukekatsu and Suketaka, for their assistance. Photostats of three letters from Franklin D. Roosevelt to Admiral Nomura are reproduced in the preface to Admiral Nomura's memoir of his mission to the United States.

     Regarding Matsuoka, see Hayashi Shigeru, *Taiheiyō Sensō* (Tokyo: Chūōkōronsha, 1967), pp. 186-187.

6 Nomura Kichisaburō, *Beikoku ni tsukaishite* (Mission to the United States) (Tokyo: Iwanami Shoten, 1946). Cited hereafter as Nomura, *Beikoku ni.* The author found a copy, literally gathering dust in a second hand book stall in the Kanda district of Tokyo in the summer of 1968, price 200 yen (about 80 cents).

7 David J. Lu, *From the Marco Polo Bridge to Pearl Harbor* (Washington, D.C.: Public Affairs Press, 1961), pp. 59-66. The question of Nomura's personal attitude on the China question will be discussed subsequently in this paper. Mr. N. Hagihara interviewed the now aged Nishi on behalf of the author in July 1968; Dr. Tsunoda Jun also emphasized this point in an interview with the author on August 5, 1968 at the Diet Library, Tokyo. He knew Nomura at the time and talked with him at the Foreign Ministry.

8 Nomura, *Beikoku ni,* pp. 12-17; Tsunoda Jun, *Nihon no taibei kaisen* (The Beginning of Japan's War Against the United States) in Kokusai Seiji Gakkai (ed.), *Taiheiyō sensō e no michi* (Tokyo: Asahi Shimbunsha, 1963), 7:129-131.

9 See John Huizenga, "Yosuke Matsuoka and the Japanese-German Alliance," in Gordon A. Craig and Felix Gilbert (eds.), *The Diplomats, 1919-1939* (New York: Atheneum, 1967), 2:615-648.

10 Nomura, *Beikoku ni,* foreword.

11 *Ibid.,* pp. 26-29.

12 *Ibid.,* pp. 36-37.

13 John H. Boyle, "The Drought-Walsh Mission to Japan," *Pacific Historical Review,* 34(May, 1965), 141-161; Lu, *From the Marco Polo Bridge,* pp. 159-162; Butow, "Hull-Nomura Conversations," pp. 824-826; R.J.C. Butow, *Tojo and the Coming of the War* (Princeton: Princeton University Press, 1961), pp. 229-230; Tsunoda, *Nihon no,* pp. 133-153. To what extent Iwakuro changed earlier drafts is not clear. Boyle says "scrapped," but a memo from Postmaster General Walker to Secretary Hull (April 4, 1941) says that Iwakuro "gave his consent to every substantial point"; United States Department of State, *Papers Relating to the Foreign Relations of the United States, 1941* (Washington, D.C.: Government Printing Office, 1956), 4:119. Cited hereafter as *FRUS, 1941,* vol. 4.

14 Matsuoka to Nomura, telegram, February 14, 1941, IMTFE Exhibit 1045; Nomura, *Beikoku ni,* pp. 46-47.

15 *FRUS, 1941,* 4:113-117.
16 Butow, "Hull-Nomura Conversations," pp. 830-831.
17 Kyodo Tsushinsha (ed.), *Konoye Nikki* (Konoye Diary) (Tokyo: Kyōdō Tsushinsha, 1968), pp. 206-214.
18 Hull, *Memoirs,* 2:991.
19 Defined by Iwakuro to mean in the five northern provinces of China. See Boyle, "Drought-Walsh Mission," p. 160.
20 Nomura, *Beikoku ni,* appendix, pp. 2-9; Nobutaka Ike, *Japan's Decision for War: Records of the 1941 Policy Conferences* (Stanford: Stanford University Press, 1967), appendix A; United States Department of State, *Papers Relating to the Foreign Relations of the United States, Japan, 1931-1941* (Washington, D.C.: Government Printing Office, 1943), 2:398-402. Cited hereafter as *FRUS, Japan, 1931-1941,* vol. 2.
21 *FRUS, 1941,* 4:127.
22 *Ibid.,* 4:147-148; Boyle, "Drought-Walsh Mission," p. 160; *FRUS 1941,* 4:123-126, 130-131, 135-138, 142-146, 149-150. Also on May 23 Hornbeck presented a scathing analysis of "why these Japanese are engaging us in conversations," *FRUS, 1941,* 4:212-215.
23 *FRUS, 1941,* 4:146-147.
24 Hull, *Memoirs,* 2:991-992.
25 *FRUS, Japan, 1931-1941,* 2:407-409.
26 Butow, "Hull-Nomura Conversations," pp. 829-831; Nomura's telegram explaining and recommending the draft proposal is reproduced in Tsunoda, *Nihon no,* pp. 153-154.
27 *FRUS, Japan, 1931-1941,* 2:408-409.
28 Kido Diary, April 18, 30, 22, 1941. The Diary of Kido Kōichi, Lord Keeper of the Privy Seal, has been partially translated as IMTFE, IPS, Doc. no. 1632. The original Japanese version has been published by Tokyo University, Shuppankai, 1966. Tsunoda, *Nihon no,* pp. 173-175.
29 *FRUS, Japan, 1931-1941,* 2:412-415.
30 *Ibid.,* 2:420-425; Nomura, *Beikoku ni,* pp. 53-55, and appendix, pp. 10-20 (here dated May 11).
31 *FRUS, Japan, 1931-1941,* 2:145-148, 426, 440; Waldo H. Heinrichs, *American Ambassador: Joseph C. Grew and the Development of the United States Diplomatic Tradition* (Boston: Little, Brown and Co., 1966), pp. 331-332.
32 *FRUS, 1941,* 4:204-206; Kyōdō, *Konoye Nikki,* pp. 209-210; Nomura to Matsuoka, May 24, 1941, in Nomura, *Beikoku ni,* pp. 180-181.
33 *FRUS, Japan, 1931-1941,* 2:485-492; Nomura, *Beikoku ni,* pp. 65-66 and appendix, pp. 57-66.
34 *FRUS, Japan, 1931-1941,* 2:492-494.
35 Nomura to Matsuoka, personal, June 25, 1941, in Nomura, *Beikoku ni,* p. 181.
36 *Ibid.,* Nomura to Foreign Minister, July 8, 1941, and July 3, 1941, pp. 181-182.
37 *Ibid.,* Nomura telegram, no addressee stated, July 10, 1941, pp. 182-183.
38 *Ibid.,* July 11, 1941, afternoon, p. 183.
39 *Ibid.,* Nomura to Navy Minister and Chief of Staff, July 10, 1941, pp. 184-186.
40 38th Liaison Conference, July 10, 1941, Ike, *Japan's Decision,* pp. 93-98.
41 *Ibid.,* 39th Liaison Conference, July 12, 1941, pp. 98-100.

42 Kido Diary, July 15, 1941. This translation (hopefully) improves upon the translation contained in IMTFE, IPS, Doc. 1632.

43 Ike, *Japan's Decision*, pp. 103-104.

44 Nomura to Matsuoka, July 14, 1941, in Nomura, *Beikoku ni,* p. 183.

45 *Ibid.*, Nomura to Toyoda, July 19, 1941, pp. 187-189.

46 Nomura Kichisaburō, "Beikoku no yūjin ni atau," (To Friends in the United States), *Gaikō jihō,* 84(December, 1937):233-236. The word "friends" might be singular, hence "friend" (perhaps President Roosevelt?).

47 Nomura to Matsuoka, July 3, 1941, in Nomura, *Beikoku ni,* p. 181.

48 Hull, *Memoirs,* 2:1037.

49 Earlier studies display a similar cleavage, with the Kokusai Seiji Gakkai's *Taiheiyō sensō e no michi* (The Road to the Pacific War) (Tokyo, 1962-1963), 7 vols., being in the first category and Rekishigaku Kenkyukai's *Taiheiyō sensō shi* (History of the Pacific War) (Tokyo, 1953), 3 vols., being in the second.

Professor Butow, in his article entitled "Backdoor Diplomacy in the Pacific: The Proposal for a Konoye-Roosevelt Meeting in 1941" (*Journal of American History,* 39(1 [June, 1972]):48-72) assigns a large measure of responsibility for the failure of President Roosevelt to respond to Premier Konoye's proposal for a summit meeting in the Pacific in late August, 1941, to the confusion caused earlier by Messrs. Drought, Walsh, etc. ("the John Doe Associates") in their dealings with Nomura. As he puts it, "The fundamental misconception that had been planted in April had become a tangled, impenetrable growth by August." *Ibid.*, p. 59. Of course, this provided an excellent rationale, or even reason, for Hull and FDR to discount Nomura's efforts, but if they had taken a somewhat more positive attitude might this not have helped those efforts become more meaningful?

REFERENCE
MATTER

United States Officials

Secretaries of State

Robert Lansing	June 24, 1915	February 13, 1920
Bainbridge Colby	March 23, 1920	March 4, 1921
Charles Evans Hughes	March 5, 1921	March 4, 1925
Frank B. Kellogg	March 4, 1925	March 28, 1929
Henry L. Stimson	March 28, 1929	March 4, 1933
Cordell Hull	March 4, 1933	November 21, 1944

Chiefs, Division of Far Eastern Affairs

John V.A. MacMurray	August 20, 1919	November 18, 1924
Nelson Trusler Johnson	July 1, 1925	August 14, 1927
John K. Caldwell (acting)	August 15, 1927	February 14, 1928
Stanley K. Hornbeck	February 15, 1928	August 15, 1937
Maxwell Hamilton	August 16, 1937	June 4, 1943

Ambassadors to Japan

Charles B. Warren	June 29, 1921	March 1, 1923
Cyrus E. Woods	May 3, 1923	July 1924
Edgar A. Bancroft	September 23, 1924	July 28, 1925
Charles MacVeagh	September 24, 1925	December 9, 1929
William R. Castle, Jr.	December 11, 1929	June 30, 1930
W. Cameron Forbes	June 17, 1930	March 22, 1932
Joseph C. Grew	February 19, 1932	December 7, 1941

Ministers to China

Paul S. Reinsch	August 15, 1913	September 1, 1919
Charles R. Crane	March 22, 1920	March 4, 1921
Jacob G. Schurman	June 2, 1921	March 16, 1925
John V.A. MacMurray	April 9, 1925	November 22, 1929

Minister and Ambassador to China

Nelson Trusler Johnson	December 16, 1929	February 10, 1941

Chinese Officials

Peking (North) Government

1 President	Hsü Shih-ch'ang	October 1918-June 1922
Premier	Ch'ien Neng-hsün	October 1918-August 1920
	Chin Yun-p'eng	August 1920-December 1921
	Liang Shih-yi	December 1921-January 1922
Foreign Minister	Lu Cheng-hsiang	1917-December 1920*
	W.W. Yen (Yen Hui-ch'ing)	
2 President	Li Yuan-hung	June 1922-June 1923
Premier	W.W. Yen	June 1922-January 1923
	Chang Shao-tseng	January 1923-June 1923
	Li Ken-yuan	June 1923-January 1924 (?)
3 President	Ts'ao Kun	January 1924-November 1924
Premier	Sun Pao-chi	January 1924-July 1924
	Wellington Koo	July 1924-October 1924
	W.W. Yen	October 1924
	Huang Fu	October 1924-November 1924
4 Chief Executive	Tuan Ch'i-jui	November 1924-June 1926**
Foreign Minister	Tang Shao-yi (appointed but not accepted)	
	Shen Jui-lin (acting)	
5 Premier	W.W. Yen	May 1926-June 1926
Finance Minister	Wellington Koo (?)	May 1926-

*Lu was Foreign Minister under both Ch'ien and Chin.
**Tuan actually retired in April 1926. Feng Yü-hsiang's military coup.

6 Premier	Tu Hsi-k'uei	
	(acting)	June 1926-October 1926
Finance Minister	Wellington Koo	-October 1926
7 Premier	Wellington Koo	
	(acting)	October 1926-January 1927
	(confirmed)	January 1927-June 1927
Foreign Minister	Wellington Koo	October 1926-June 1927
8 (Military Government)		
Generalissimo	Marshal	
	Chang Tso-lin	June 1927-June 1928
Premier	P'an Fu	June 1927-June 1928
Foreign Minister	Wang Yin-t'ai	June 1927-June 1928

Canton (South) Government

1 President	Sun Yat-sen	April 1921-March 1925
	(ousted by General	
	Chen Chiung-ming)	June 1922-February 1923
Foreign Minister	Wu Ting-fang	April 1921-June 1922
2 Chairman	Wang Ching-wei	July 1925-March 1926
3 Acting Chairman	Tang Yen-k'ai	March 1926-April 1927
Foreign Minister	Eugene Chen	May 1926-July 1927

Wu-han Government

| Chairman | Wang Ching-wei | April 1927-September 1927 |

Nanking Government

1 Chairman	Hu Han-min	April 1927-August 1927
	Chiang Kai-shek	October 1928-December 1931
2 Premier	Tan Yen-k'-ai	October 1928-September 1930
3 Foreign Minister	Huang Fu	February 1928-May 1928
	Chengting Wang	June 1928-November 1931

Nanking Government

1 President	Lin Sen	December 1931-1943
2 Premier	Sun K'o	December 1931-January 1932
	Wang Ching-wei	January 1932-November 1935
3 Foreign Minister	Eugene Chen	December 1931-January 1932
	Lo Wen-kan	January 1932-1933
	Wang Ching-wei	1933-November 1935

4 Premier	Chiang Kai-shek	November 1935-1938
5 Foreign Minister	Chang Ch'ün	November 1935-March 1937
	Wang Ch'ung-hui	March 1937-April 1941

Chungking Government

1 Chairman	Lin Sen	1931-1943
2 President of Executive Yuan	H.H. Kung (Kung Hsiang-hsi)	1939-December 1939
		December 1939-Fall 1943 (surrogate)
3 Foreign Minister	Wang Ch'ung hui	March 1937-April 1941
	(Quo) Kuo T'ai-chi	April 1941-December 1941
	T.V. Soong	December 1941-July 1945

Reformed Nationalist (Nanking) Government

| 1 Premier | Wang Ching-wei | 1940-1944 |
| 2 Foreign Minister | Chu Min-i | 1940-1945 |

Japanese Officials

Prime Ministers

Hara Takashi	September 29, 1918	November 5, 1921
Takahashi Korekiyo, Viscount	November 13, 1921	June 6, 1922
Katō Tomosaburō	June 12, 1922	August 26, 1923
Yamamoto Gonnohyōe, Count	September 2, 1923	December 29, 1923
Kiyoura Keigo, Viscount	January 7, 1924	June 6, 1924
Katō Takaaki	June 11, 1924	January 28, 1926
Wakatsuki Reijirō, Baron	January 30, 1926	April 17, 1927
Tanaka Giichi	April 20, 1927	July 1, 1929
Hamaguchi Osachi	July 2, 1929	April 13, 1931
Wakatsuki Reijirō, Baron	April 14, 1931	December 12, 1931
Inukai Ki	December 13, 1931	May 25, 1932
Saitō Makoto, Viscount	May 26, 1932	July 3, 1934
Okada Keisuke	July 8, 1934	February 26, 1936
Hirota Kōki	March 9, 1936	January 23, 1937
Hayashi Senjurō	February 2, 1937	May 31, 1937
Konoye Fumimaro, Prince	June 4, 1937	January 4, 1939
Hiranuma Kiichirō, Baron	January 5, 1939	August 28, 1939
Abe Nobuyuki	August 30, 1939	January 14, 1940
Yonai Mitsumasa	January 16, 1940	July 16, 1940
Konoye Fumimaro, Prince	July 22, 1940	October 16, 1941
Tōjō Hideki	October 18, 1941	July 18, 1944

Foreign Ministers

Uchida Yasuya, Count	September 29, 1918	September 1, 1923
Yamamoto Gonnohyōe, Count	September 2, 1923	September 18, 1923
Hikokichi Isuin	September 19, 1923	January 6, 1924
Matsui Keishiro	January 7, 1924	June 10, 1924
Shidehara Kijūrō, Baron	June 11, 1924	April 19, 1927
Tanaka Giichi (also Premier)	April 20, 1927	July 1, 1929
Shidehara Kijūrō, Baron	July 2, 1929	December 11, 1931
Inukai Ki (also Premier)	December 13, 1931	January 14, 1932
Yoshizawa Kenkichi	January 14, 1932	May 16, 1932
Saitō Makoto, Viscount (also Premier)	May 26, 1932	July 6, 1932
Uchida Yasuya, Count	July 6, 1932	September 14, 1933
Hirota Kōki	September 14, 1933	April 2, 1936
Arita Hachirō	April 2, 1936	January 23, 1937
Satō Naotake	March 3, 1937	May 31, 1937
Hirota Kōki	June 4, 1937	May 26, 1938
Ugaki Kazushige	May 26, 1938	September 30, 1938
Arita Hachirō	October 29, 1938	August 28, 1939
Nomura Kichisaburō	September 25, 1939	January 14, 1940
Arita Hachirō	January 16, 1940	July 16, 1940
Matsuoka Yōsuke	July 22, 1940	July 16, 1941
Toyoda Teijirō	July 18, 1941	October 16, 1941
Tōgō Shigenori	October 18, 1941	September 1942

Ambassadors to United States

Shidehara Kijūrō	1919	1923
Uehara Masanao	1923	1925
Matsudaira Tsuneo	1925	1928
Debuchi Katsuji	October 24, 1928	February 13, 1934
Saitō Hiroshi	February 13, 1934	December 22, 1938
Horinouchi Kensuke	December 22, 1938	October 20, 1940
Nomura Kichisaburō	February 14, 1941	December 7, 1941

Index

Date Due